Irish Migrants in the Canadas:
A New Approach

MCGILL-QUEEN'S STUDIES IN ETHNIC HISTORY
Donald Harman Akenson, Editor

1

Irish Migrants in the Canadas

A New Approach

BRUCE S. ELLIOTT

McGill-Queen's University Press
Kingston and Montreal

The Institute of Irish Studies
The Queen's University of Belfast

© McGill-Queen's University Press 1988
ISBN 0-7735-0607-1 (cloth)
ISBN 0-7735-0703-5 (paper)

Legal deposit first quarter 1988
Bibliothèque nationale du Québec

Reprinted 1988
First paperback edition 1988

Printed in Canada

Printed on acid-free paper

Published in the United Kingdom by
The Institute of Irish Studies
The Queen's University of Belfast
8 Fitzwilliam Street
Belfast, Northern Ireland
ISBN 0-85389-297-0

Canadian Cataloguing in Publication Data

Elliott, Bruce S.
    Irish migrants in the Canadas
    (McGill-Queen's studies in ethnic history; 1)
    Co-published by the Institute of Irish Studies,
    Queen's University of Belfast.
    Includes bibliographical references and index.
    ISBN 0-7735-0607-1
    1. Irish – Canada – History – 19th century. 2. Land
    settlement – Canada. 3. Canada – Emigration and immi-
    gration. 4. Ireland – Emigration and immigration.
    5. Protestants – Ireland – Tipperary (County).
    6. Protestants – Canada – History. I. Queen's
    University of Belfast. Institute of Irish Studies.
    II. Title. III. Series.
    FC106.16E44 1988   971'.0049162   c87-095061-4
    F1035.16E44 1988

To Gail Haskett Clothier
1938–1986

Contents

Maps

Tables

Foreword

North America in the nineteenth century was constantly influenced by immigrants. This was even more true of Canada than of the United States, for the initial settlement of most of the English-speaking portions of British North America took place later than occurred in the United States. Not surprisingly, any good university research library has several hundred feet of shelves filled with books, monographs, and journals that describe and analyse the process of migration from the Old World to the New.

What is surprising is that almost all of the historical literature, both as pertains to Canada and to the United States, is devoted to discussing emigration from the Old World and immigration into the New as an abstract process or an aggregate phenomenon. That is, there are sophisticated statistical studies of the nineteenth-century data on the migration flow, and there are innumerable general descriptions of the general background of the immigrants in their homeland and accompanying assertions of how these affect them in their new homelands. But studies that deal with actual migrants and which trace the lives of a significant number of real people – not aggregated census numbers – from one side of the ocean through their successive residences and careers on the other, are very rare. The most notable exception is Jon Gjerde's *From Peasants to Farmers: The Migration from Balestrand, Norway, to the Upper Middle West* (Cambridge 1985).

Of course, there are numerous biographies of individual migrants and even more numerous pieces of family history put together by filially pious genealogists, but these are too unsystematic, too tiny a subset, to permit their being the basis of meaningful conclusions about migrants in general. One notes with admiration the many local studies of nineteenth-century ethnic communities, but almost invariably these start with the group's arrival on this side of the Atlantic and do not document with adequate precision the origin of the various individuals in the given community in the Old World. Thus, observations about the nature of migration and about the process of cultural transfer cannot be drawn with the confidence that one would like.

That is why Bruce Elliott's study is such a breakthrough. He traces with precision the life paths of hundreds of individual migrants, pinpointing their place of origin in the Old World and tracing with equal precision their life course in the New. This is done with a significant number of individuals drawn from a similar background, so that one can generalize about the migration process as it occurred in this group. Most important, one can draw these generalizations not from frequently misleading aggregate statistics, but from observations of the lives of specific individuals. Elliott's methods, if widely adopted, have the potential to do for nineteenth-century migration history what the development of prosopography did for classical studies.

Because historians for the most part have been dismissive of the activities of genealogists – who has not been inconvenienced in some archive or research library by enthusiasts tracing their family histories? – there is likely to be resistance among historians to undergoing an apprenticeship in the techniques of genealogical research. Also, scholars in search of a topic that will pay off quickly are apt to be put off by the sheer amount of hard slogging that is required in such research. However, that Elliott could trace 775 families should be taken not only as a monument to his own scholarly devotion (which certainly it is), but also as an indication that nineteenth-century migration studies indeed can be done without taking the shortcuts that have become virtually habitual in the field.

The people whom Elliott studies, the Irish, were the largest non-French ethnic group in nineteenth-century Canada. Among the Irish, Protestants were in a roughly 2:1 ratio to Catholics. Thus, in dealing with a group of Irish Protestants, Elliott is not studying an exotic species, but one of the major groups defining the cultural complexity of this country during the last century. One hopes that this book will be read as much by historians of the United States as by those of Canada, for the Irish in the United States are one of the most important of nineteenth-century immigrant groups and one of the least understood. Despite the existence of hundreds of studies of the Irish in North America, there is not a single book that traces at a satisfactory level of accuracy and analytical sophistication the paths of a significant number of migrants to, and through, the United States or Canada. In that context, Bruce Elliott's work serves as a useful model.

Donald Harman Akenson, FRSC
Queen's University, Kingston

Acknowledgments

A microstudy of 775 families soon assumes major proportions, and inevitably one's debts to others increase proportionally. I am grateful to the Ontario Ministry of Colleges and Universities, the Social Sciences and Humanities Research Council of Canada, and Carleton University for the awards which supported me during the research and writing of this study, to Professors Fernand Ouellet, S.F. Wise, and B. Carman Bickerton who wrote in support of my applications, and to the Advisory Research Committee of Queen's University for material assistance during revision of the manuscript. The book has been published with the help of a grant from the Canadian Federation for the Humanities, using funds provided by the Social Sciences and Humanities Research Council of Canada.

This study has benefited from the comments and interest of academics and fellow students. Among the former I must note Donald Akenson, Marilyn Barber, John Clarke, David Fitzpatrick, Robert and Peter Goheen, Keith Johnson, and especially S.R. Mealing, my critical yet tolerant thesis supervisor at Carleton University, and among my fellow students Joe Goski, Jim Kennedy, Glenn Lockwood, Mary Lu MacDonald, Christina Thiele, and John D. Blackwell (who alone of the six can claim Tipperary ancestry). Catharine Anne Wilson provided an especially useful critique of the manuscript. I am grateful also to Dan Brock, whose MA thesis on the Richard Talbot emigration is the starting point for any study of the Tipperary Protestants in the Canadas, for generously sharing his early settler files and for giving me access to his own material and to the files of London Branch, Ontario Genealogical Society, then in his keeping. Jemima Thompson of Port Coquitlam, BC, first directed me to Dan's thesis.

Those familiar with the "Leicester School" of English local history will notice some of its influences in these pages. The exploration of settlement patterns and of contrasting communities, and the estate typology, among other things, owe something to my time at Leicester. Carleton University, the

University of Ottawa, Algonquin College, the Ottawa, London, and Kingston branches of the Ontario Genealogical Society, the Carleton Place Historical Society, the Historical Society of Ottawa, the Ontario Historical Society, and the Canadian Historical Association all provided forums in which I presented earlier drafts of several sections of this work. The assistance of the archivists and librarians of the various repositories listed in the note on sources was essential to the success of this project.

The co-ordinating efforts of the Ontario Genealogical Society enabled me to tap into an indispensable network of 180 correspondents, listed in the note on sources. Special thanks are due to Lois Long of Nepean and Gail Clothier and Laurena Storey of London, Ontario. All three shared a wide range of genealogical information on a regular basis and put me in contact with other people of Tipperary background. Gail and Bill Clothier and the Storey family provided me with places to stay during research trips to London, as did Bruce and Twyla Atchison. Providing accommodation when I was researching in the other London were Margaret Horton of Berkhamsted, Herts. and, for especially lengthy periods, Sally Jollans Butler, formerly of Stoke Newington but now of Onehunga, Auckland. I have also to thank Sally for obtaining New Zealand death certificates for me since moving to the South Pacific. I am grateful to John D. Blackwell for providing me with accommodation in Kingston, and in Toronto I was housed by Colm J. Brannigan and, on numerous occasions, by J. Brian Gilchrist. At the production stage, I am grateful to Ross Hough for redrafting many of the maps, and to my copy-editor, Rosemary Shipton.

My greatest debt is to my own family, who have no connection with North Tipperary, but who have inevitably come to know more about the place than anyone else who has no particular interest in it. They will, nonetheless, be happy to have the documentation of these Irishmen off the living-room floor, and out of three other rooms of the house it now largely occupies.

For favours both great and small I must also record my appreciation to the following: Charles Addington, London; Mona Aitken, London; Gladys Arnold, Ripley; Rev. and Mrs S.C.D. Atkinson, Cloughjordan; Mr and Mrs Shaker Balasa, Ottawa; Albert Bannister, London Township Clerk; Hon. Richard A. Bell, Nepean; Rev. Robert W. Birtch, St Marys; the late Mrs W.A. Bonell, Nepean; Archdeacon W.H. Bradley, Ottawa; Bill Britnell, Mississauga; Howard M. Brown, Ottawa; Dean Francis R. Burke, Killaloe, Co. Clare; Michael Byrne, Tullamore, Co. Offaly; Elizabeth Cahill, Montreal; Mrs J.G. Clahane, Dublin; Mrs J.E. Coderre, Ottawa; Lt-Col. Kenneth Collins, Ottawa; Rev. Joseph Condell, St Cronan's, Roscrea; George Cunningham, Roscrea; Felicity Devlin, National Museum of Ireland, Dublin; Patrick M.O. Evans, Tenaga, PQ; Raymond L. Fazakas, Hamilton; Rosemary ffolliott, Fethard, Co. Tipperary; Dr Denise Foulkes, Gortlandroe, Nenagh; John Francis, Ottawa; Professor David Gagan, McMaster University, Hamilton; Muriel Gingras, Goulbourn Township Historical Society; Glenna Good, Merrickville Blockhouse Museum; the late Elizabeth M. Gordon, Ottawa; Danny and Mary Grace, Ardcroney, Nenagh; Timothy Graham, Ottawa; Adam and Edith Guest, Garraun, Cloughjordan; George Hancocks, Agincourt; Marjory Harper, Aberdeen, Scotland; Carolyn Heald, Kingston; Professor Susan Houston, York University, Downsview; Rev. Colin Johnson, Sutton, Ontario; Canon F.StG.H. Johnston, Templemore; Judith Ann Keen, Nepean; Marion Keffer, Toronto; Joan Kennedy, Kilkeary, Nenagh; Patricia Kennedy, Ottawa; Rev. J.R. King, Kincardine; Shirley Lancaster, Thornhill; Marion Logan, Mountshannon, Co. Clare; Rev. C. Glenn Lucas, Toronto; Fr Thomas V. MacNamara, Inniscaltra; Tom McGrath, Dublin; Joan McKay, Ottawa; Marianne McLean, Ottawa; Byron McLeod, London; John McMahon, London; E. Marjorie Moodie, Stittsville; Norma Morrison, Ottawa; Donal and Nancy Murphy, Tyone, Nenagh; Dr George A. Neville, Ottawa; Michael Newton, Ottawa; Dr William Nolan, Dublin; Breda O'Brien, Dublin; Michael and Helen O'Brien, Tuamgraney, Co. Clare; Paddy O'Brien, Ashley Park, Ardcroney, Nenagh; the late J.E. O'Meara, Etobicoke; Cis and Seumas O'Rourke, Roscrea; Edward Phelps, London; Tom Power, Dublin; Professor George Rawlyk, Queen's University, Kingston; Professor James Reaney, London; Mr and Mrs D. Roche, Storehouse Point, Mountshannon; Mervin Quast, Ottawa; Dorothy A. Relyea, Ottawa; Gerry Ryan, Dublin; Mr and Mrs Albert Shortt, Garrane, Cloughjordan; Ann Simmons, Irish Architectural Archive, Dublin; Marjorie Simmons, Kingston; Jessie Sloan, Edmonton; Cindy Southgate, Ottawa; Shirley Spragge, Kingston; Canon Eric Stanley, St Mary's, Nenagh; Harry and Myra Stanley, Streamstown, Roscrea; Rosamond Sterling, Castletown, Coolbawn; Elizabeth S. Stuart, Osgoode; Georgie Tupper, Kars; Hugh W.L. and the Hon. Grania Weir, Whitegate, Co. Clare; Dr Kevin Whelan, National Library of Ireland, Dublin; Dr Randy Widdis, Queen's University, Kingston; and Donald R. Wilson, Fonthill.

Illustration 1

The landscape of North Tipperary. Looking northeast towards the Devilsbit Mountain from near Borrisoleigh, 1970. The hills that ringed the Ormond plain were home to the poor and the dispossessed, and the ancient agricultural practices there strongly contrasted the commercial agriculture of the Ormond plain that was home to most of the region's Protestant population. Cambridge University Collection, BDL-54;

Illustration 2
Aerial view of Shinrone, County Offaly, 1963, a village typical of the late seventeenth-century English foundations in the region. The Protestant population persisted: Shinrone in 1828 was termed "a perfect hot-bed of rampant Orangeism." T.L. Cooke, *The Early History of the Town of Birr, or Parsonstown* (Dublin 1875), 193. Note the infilling at the head of the marketplace. Cambridge University Collection, AIG-6; copyright reserved.

Illustration 3
Castle Otway in the 1850s, drawing by J.J. Barralet, from an Incumbered Estates
Rental. Such houses incorporate in their walls much of the history of Tipperary.
A mid-eighteenth-century Georgian house attached to an older defensive tower
house, largely rebuilt and landscaped in the nineteenth century, complete with deer
park, Castle Otway was the main residence of a family of stern landlords of
Cromwellian ancestry who favoured Protestant tenants. It was burned during the
Civil War in 1922. Courtesy of the National Library of Ireland, 1666 TB.

Illustration 4
The original St John's Anglican Church, Arva, London Township. Staunch sup-
porters of the established Church of Ireland at home, most of the Tipperary Protestant
emigrants supported the United Church of England and Ireland in Canada. The first
Anglican service in London Township was held in 1822 in the barn of William
Geary, son-in-law of the rector of Templeharry, King's County. The frame church
was built the following year. It was extensively rennovated by carpenter John
Haskett in 1845 and was replaced by the present brick building in 1875. In the
churchyard lie the remains of many of the earliest members of the township's
Tipperary community. University of Western Ontario, Regional Collection.

Illustration 5
Captain George Thew Burke (1776–1854). As superintendent of the Richmond
military settlement, Burke located some of Richard Talbot's Tipperary settlers in
Goulbourn and Nepean townships in 1818. Burke, a native of Tipperary himself, had
known some of the emigrants in Ireland. A member of an old Catholic gentry
family, he was nonetheless required as an army officer to be a Protestant. However,
most of his family remained Catholic, and the Anglican minister of Bytown
officiated at Burke's interment in the Roman Catholic cemetery at Richmond. Public
Archives of Canada, c-54471, Mrs Collis Lewis Collection.

Illustration 6

Lt-Col. James Hodgins (1782–1867) and his wife Jane Napier Hodgins (1790–1880). As resident agent in Biddulph Township for the Canada Land Company, Hodgins encouraged many of his fellow Tipperary emigrants to settle there. Violent, intemperate, and quarrelsome, Hodgins nonetheless won for himself a favoured position in the new land. In return for leading gangs of Tipperary bully boys at the elections in favour of Canada Company candidates, he was rewarded with land and the posts of magistrate and lieutenant-colonel of militia. University of Western Ontario, Regional Collection, Spencer Armitage-Stanley Papers.

Illustration 7
Francis Abbott (c1787–1870) from Cloonawillan, Aglishcloghane parish. Frank
emigrated in 1821 to Montreal, where he joined a small cluster of friends from
Tipperary for a few years, working as a sawyer to build up capital to commence a
farm. He moved to Nepean in the Ottawa Valley around 1828. Never an extensive
landowner, he used his influence in the Orange Order to secure apprenticeships for
his sons as printers with local Orange newspapers. Mrs Dorothy Munro, Richmond,
Ontario.

Illustration 8

Rice Lewis's hardware store in King Street, Toronto, 1851. Lewis was a member of a Nenagh mercantile family, several of whose members moved their business interests to England. Rice emigrated to Toronto in the 1840s and left a personal estate valued at $100,000 at his death in 1871. Even such merchants were not immune to Old World ties; in the 1860s one of Rice's daughters married a New York man whose family had known the Lewises in Ireland. The Lewises were of Welsh ancestry but were long resident in Tipperary. An earlier Reic Lewes was recorded in the hearth money rolls of the 1660s living in Kilcoleman in the parish of Youghal-arra, near the Cromwellian Colonel Symon Finch. Public Archives of Canada, C-128058. Robert W.S. MacKay, *The Canada Directory* (Montreal 1851), 447.

Illustration 9

The six sons of Frederick William Richardson of March Township near Ottawa, posing left to right, with their wives, in order of birth. The group photograph is symbolic, for the Richardsons became successful farmers in Canada by helping one another work their 900 acres, ploughing the profits back into the land. Their father retained ownership until shortly before his death at the age of eighty-four, when he conveyed title to all six sons and to his two eldest grandsons of the farms they occupied. These co-operative efforts, combined with the early fruits of small-scale timbering and careful management, laid the foundations for the Richardson family's leadership in the local community in the early twentieth century. Left to right: William, Ferdinand, Gardiner, Richard, Thomas, and Samuel Haskett with their wives Elizabeth Clarke, Mary Ann Bradley, Mary Jane McEldowney, Mary Ann Alexander, Margaret Ann Armstrong, and Adelaide Bradley. Lois (Richardson) Bidgood, South March, Ontario.

Illustration 10
Victoria Terrace, residence of the late James Hodgins (1809–1876), a successful emigrant farmer from Modreeny parish, in Huntley Township near Ottawa, 1879. Hodgins was given 100 acres by his father upon coming of age in 1831. Partly through timber dealings he built up his holdings to 893 acres, despite a bankruptcy in 1844. He in turn provided five of his six sons with land and educated the other son to become a lawyer in Ottawa. Advertising family success was the major reason for having cuts such as this one included in the county atlases of the late 1870s. H. Belden & Co., *Illustrated Historical Atlas of the County of Carleton, Ont.* (Toronto 1879), 43.

Irish Migrants in the Canadas

CHAPTER ONE

Introduction

This study of international and internal migration is based upon tracing, over several generations, the genealogies, movements, land-holding strategies, and economic lives of some 775 immigrating Protestant families who came to the Canadas, largely between 1818 and 1855, from a region of Ireland measuring thirty by forty miles. It is only through this type of study, linking Irish and Canadian experiences, that we can begin to answer certain important questions about the nature of immigration and settlement and about the economic and societal consequences on both sides of the Atlantic of the massive nineteenth-century displacement of Irish population. Sources for the study of Irish emigration to Canada consist of runs of aggregate statistical material, supplemented by a few collections of qualitative and nominal information. The latter are particularly rich for atypical assisted movements such as those of the government-sponsored Peter Robinson emigrants of the 1820s. Even the statistical material is problematic, however, and we are almost totally lacking passenger lists for the pre-1855 period when Irish emigration to Canada was most intensive.[1]

Cecil Houston and William Smyth recently attempted to study Irish immigration indirectly through the use of a "better source," the Canadian census. Houston and Smyth, and Donald Akenson in a similar article, manipulated aggregate ethnicity and religion data from the printed census abstracts to describe the characteristics of Ontario's Irish immigrants in the broadest terms. Their studies have shown that two-thirds of the Irish in Upper Canada were Protestants throughout the nineteenth century and that, contrary to stereotype, the Irish, both Protestants and, to a slightly lesser degree, Roman Catholics, were as rural a people as the rest of the Canadian population.[2]

Unfortunately the aggregate approach, however useful, cannot help us to answer a number of more specific, important questions. In the absence of nominal lists of passengers and of immigrants we cannot begin even to link records of immigration with those of settlement. As a consequence we must find other ways to discover the geographical and social origins of immigrants, the directions and volumes of migration corridors, the settlement patterns in the new land, and the direction, nature, and volume of subsequent internal migration. The only way of doing this is to study the migrants individually to determine their social and regional origins, their economic circumstances at home, their dates of departure and subsequent migrational histories, their process of settlement in Canada and their lives there, and then to move beyond to try to understand the key decisions of the life course in terms of the people's own aims and strategies. The technique amounts to family reconstitution and individual biography pursued on a wide scale.

Most family reconstitution projects have been undertaken within strictly delimited municipal boundaries, and the authors of such studies have consequently been criticized for basing their demographic profiles of society on the possibly atypical experiences of non-migrants. Discussion of migrants has been limited to determining mobility rates (generally found to have been high)[3] and to tracing the broad demographic characteristics of those who left a particular place. We learn nothing about the experiences of the migrants before they arrived in the subject community nor about their destinations or ultimate fates following their departures from it.

Even when one does undertake the laborious task of tracking the destinations of those who left a particular municipality, the results of the investigation will not always provide evidence of the processes involved, for political boundaries often cut apart and render unrecognizable the areas from which the migrants are drawn or in which they settle.[4] Chain migration, in which one emigrant is followed by another, who is followed by others in turn, draws upon kin groups, the members of which need not necessarily have lived close together before the move.[5] For this reason, the most sensible way to commence a study of internal migration using family reconstitution techniques is to begin with immigration.

An investigation such as the present one requires the linkage of records on both sides of the Atlantic to build up the individual cases and eventually a profile of the immigrants generally. We can have no idea even of the make-up of the immigrating family until the genealogy has been completed using records dating from many years both before and after the move in which the investigator is interested. This wide-ranging approach to family reconstitution may be new to Canadian academics,[6] but its necessity is a commonplace to genealogists, who confront the individual implications of high rates of population mobility every day in their research.

Linkage on such a massive scale does necessitate some regional limitation, and in this study I have traced the movements around Ontario and Quebec of people coming from a common overseas place of origin, North Tipperary,

Ireland, delimiting the region of origin in terms of social rather than political boundaries, but remaining cognizant of movement to other parts of the world. Understanding the migrants in such a context also requires a detailed examination of the communities at both ends of the migration corridors investigated. The present study is therefore, to some degree, also an exercise in Irish and Canadian local history.

A study focusing on actual Irish men and women and linking their experiences at home and abroad can at least attempt to avoid the mythologies about the Irish that have grown up on both sides of the ocean. The biased and erroneous perceptions that prevail at home and abroad are not unrelated. To a major degree it is the folksy image North Americans have of Irish society which lies behind their tendency to view the Irish emigrant as ill-equipped for pioneer life – as a failure, a belligerent rebel, and a fundamentally emotional and irrational soul.[7] The Atlantic islands and the rocky, scenic west still largely define Ireland to the academic no less than to the tourist, but North Tipperary was very different from the regions studied by the Victorian reformers and romantics and by twentieth-century anthropologists. Such studies have focused upon marginal communities tied to the sea more than to the land, isolated by poor communications, where the Gaelic language survives, or did till recently, where the population was Roman Catholic, where estates were large and the landlords seldom seen, and where the farms were miserably small and dependent upon potato culture.[8] By contrast, North Tipperary in the early nineteenth century was an area of commercial agriculture and improving communications, with both large and small farms aggregated into the small estates of a numerous, resident, but economically precarious minor gentry. North Tipperary was economically more backward than the southern parts of the county, but this was as true in the sixteenth century as it was in the nineteenth. The mountains hemming in the district may have facilitated the survival of partnership farming and primitive agricultural methods in the hills themselves, but the strong demesne agriculture of the Ormond plain is merely one of many elements that gave evidence of a strong market orientation. Culturally, too, North Tipperary was not a traditional society. The Irish language was dead in the region by 1820.[9] Faction fighting in the region was viewed as barbarous both by Dublin Castle and by O'Connell's Association, but it has not been proved that faction fighting was a traditional form of violence. It has recently been suggested, indeed, that such struggles may have been led by members of an emerging middle class.[10] Neither were the agrarian disturbances for which the area became infamous in the second quarter of the nineteenth century traditional in the region. They reflected the people's conservative, defensive attachment to the *status quo,* but that *status quo* was of the nineteenth century. The disturbances themselves were a reaction against the economic consequences of the nineteenth-century conjuncture of North Tipperary's distinctive social and tenurial structure with an atypically high continuing rate of population growth.

Akenson has argued that the Irish emigrant adjusted well to North American rural life. He had typically been the manager of a small-scale commercial farm at home and the skills necessary to succeed in pioneer agriculture were certainly not beyond his abilities and have in any case been vastly exaggerated.[11] Akenson has shown that in one Ontario township on the St Lawrence River the Protestant Irish were not only successful farmers but possessed a sense of group identity and an aggressive assertiveness that enabled them to assume cultural and political dominance in their adopted region. What is perhaps more surprising is his demonstration that the small Catholic community there was apparently even more prosperous than the Protestants.[12] However, the aims of the Irish as farmers and the means by which they succeeded, as opposed to the statistical evidence that their farms were more developed than those of their Canadian-born neighbours,[13] remain unexplored, and we are not told how or why the members of the small Catholic community succeeded so well, merely that they did. Culturally, too, the Irish of Leeds and Lansdowne remain anonymous followers of the Orange politician Ogle Gowan. We are not told where they came from or why, we are given only broad suggestions of when they arrived, and we learn little about their individual as opposed to their collective objectives.

Success can be measured in many ways. Objective measures of relative economic success mean little in areas like those settled in greatest numbers by the Tipperary emigrants, where the Irish were among the earliest inhabitants and where they constituted a majority of the population. The cultivation of a large acreage in itself is evidence neither of success nor of rationality. One Canadian social historian has argued that the expansion of acreage was a counterproductive squandering of valuable resources.[14] We must judge the success of the Irish in terms of their own aims and ambitions.

The Irish of this study were rational men and women who crossed the Atlantic after weighing carefully the advantages and disadvantages of remaining where they were. Immediate economic difficulties provided a reason to move but were not paramount in their deliberations. Betterment of self was less important to them than was providing a secure start in life for the rising generation.[15] Migration in this sense was a strategy of heirship and, as such, it was sometimes merely one of a number of options.[16] The family played another role in migration, too. If the prospect of economic distress stimulated the decision to migrate, the location of distant kin, more than soil capability, nearness of markets, and transportation routes, influenced the choice of destination. Even those who emigrated as victims in the Famine years of the 1840s made their way to relatives who had gone to Canada before them. The family, like class, is not so much a structure to be quantified as a functional socio-economic unit which must be understood.

There are several reasons for limiting this study to Protestants. Some of them are practical. Though sources for the study of Protestants in Tipperary leave much to be desired, materials concerning the Roman Catholic population are in a much worse state. Despite the destruction of some Church of Ireland parish registers in the bombardment of the Four Courts in 1922, many of those surviving for North Tipperary date from early in the nineteenth century and several date back to the eighteenth. Catholic registers were not in the Four Courts during the Civil War, but they generally begin very late. Few date from before the late 1820s, and many start only in the 1830s or 1840s; only one antedates 1800.[17] The paucity of register information is more serious in the case of Catholics than it is for Protestants because of the lack of alternative sources with which to identify emigrating families. The index to diocesan marriage licence bonds identifies many Protestant emigrants with the region, but Catholics were married by licence only when marrying across religious lines. The Catholic population was nearly twelve times as numerous as the Protestant in North Tipperary, and Catholic families bearing the more common surnames numbered in the hundreds. It is impossible to identify an emigrating John Ryan with any of dozens of that name in tithe and valuation records without further information.

In addition, the large county of Tipperary was divided among several socio-economic regions, any one of which can be meant by a Canadian reference to "Tipperary," the most accurate statement of origin one usually finds. It is therefore difficult to delineate regional patterns of migration of the Catholic population, but easier to do so for the Protestants, who were far fewer in numbers, left better records behind them, and lived mostly in two areas in the northernmost baronies of the county. The Tipperary Catholics remained a distinct people. Some emigrating Protestant families were of ultimate Catholic descent and a few were of "mixed" religion, but of the 775 families followed in this study the numbers of mixed families can be counted on the fingers of two hands. There was very little intermarriage between the two groups in Canada. Because family was the major mechanism of chain migration, the process may be studied adequately by confining detailed research to Protestant and mixed families. Identified origins of the residents of the Tipperary Catholic communities in Biddulph and Nepean suggest that these two settlements drew upon the same northern baronies as did the adjacent Protestant colonies, and certainly their presence there was due to earlier Protestant emigration. Therefore, brief accounts of the major North Tipperary Catholic colonies are included in chapter 6.[18]

This study begins in Ireland by examining the geography, economy, and society of the North Tipperary region, probing the origins and spread of the

Protestant population there, examining the social and economic conditions that disposed them to look favourably upon emigration, and pinpointing the stimuli that initiated the flow of people to the Canadas. After examining the course and character of Protestant emigration from Tipperary, the focus switches to Canada, where a general consideration of Irish settlement patterns is followed by an examination of the origins and growth of the two largest Tipperary colonies in the context of the settlement history of the regions in which they were located. Internal migration, pointing up the continuance of chain migration as a major mechanism of population movement, emphasizes the continuing importance of the family in Canada, and the work closes by viewing migration as one of several strategies adopted by families in the pursuit of their desire to provide for the rising generation.

One of the most articulate members of a North Tipperary emigrant family summed up her own story in words that have a wider application: "In Canada we are developing a pattern of life and I know something about one block of that pattern. I know it for I helped to make it, and I can say that now without any pretense of modesty, or danger of arrogance, for I know that we who make the patterns are not important, but the pattern is."[19] Often these patterns change, or are obscured by the passage of time. It is then the historian's task to recreate the patterns by tracing the individual lives and histories of those who made them. The writer of those words, author and pioneer feminist Nellie McClung, is herself the best argument against urging the primacy of patterns over the importance of the individual. But the historical individual assumes meaning as he or she exemplifies or departs from the pattern, and the pattern becomes reality, rather than an analytical abstraction, only when it can be proved to reflect the collective tendencies of individuals.

CHAPTER TWO

The Protestants of
North Tipperary

THE NORTH TIPPERARY
SOCIAL REGION

The North Tipperary of this study is not an artificial unit that serves political, administrative, or data-collecting functions but means little on the ground. The area to which I refer for ease of reference as North Tipperary constitutes a geographical entity even though for most of recent history it has not been organized as a single political unit. Separated from surrounding areas by major topographical features, the various administrative zones that in different eras have subdivided this section of the Shannon Valley have historically as well as geographically had more in common with one another than with the political entities that lay beyond the region's natural boundaries of hill and bog. The term North Tipperary as used here is therefore a form of shorthand, sometimes used by the emigrants who are the focus of this study, by which the Offaly panhandle and the border parishes are meant as well as the northern part of the administrative county of Tipperary.

At the time of the Cromwellian invasion in the 1640s North Tipperary had a scattered population and was essentially pastoral, while the southeastern baronies of the county were dotted with small farming villages and numerous corn mills.[1] Well into the nineteenth century North Tipperary remained more economically backward and less densely populated than the more fertile lands of the Suir Valley immediately to the south. It was these very circumstances, however, that facilitated the clearance of new cultivated lands from the wood and bog by new English settlers in the late seventeenth century. The descendants of these colonists, numbering some ten thousand in 1820,[2] formed the only appreciable concentration of Protestant population in County Tipperary apart from clusters in the towns and administrative centres of the southern part of the county.

As in most of Ireland, the people of Tipperary have depended for a living upon agriculture. The county comprises several distinct farming regions distinguished by differing soils and economies, set apart by low, rugged hills of thin soil resting on slate and sandstone. Much of the southern and central

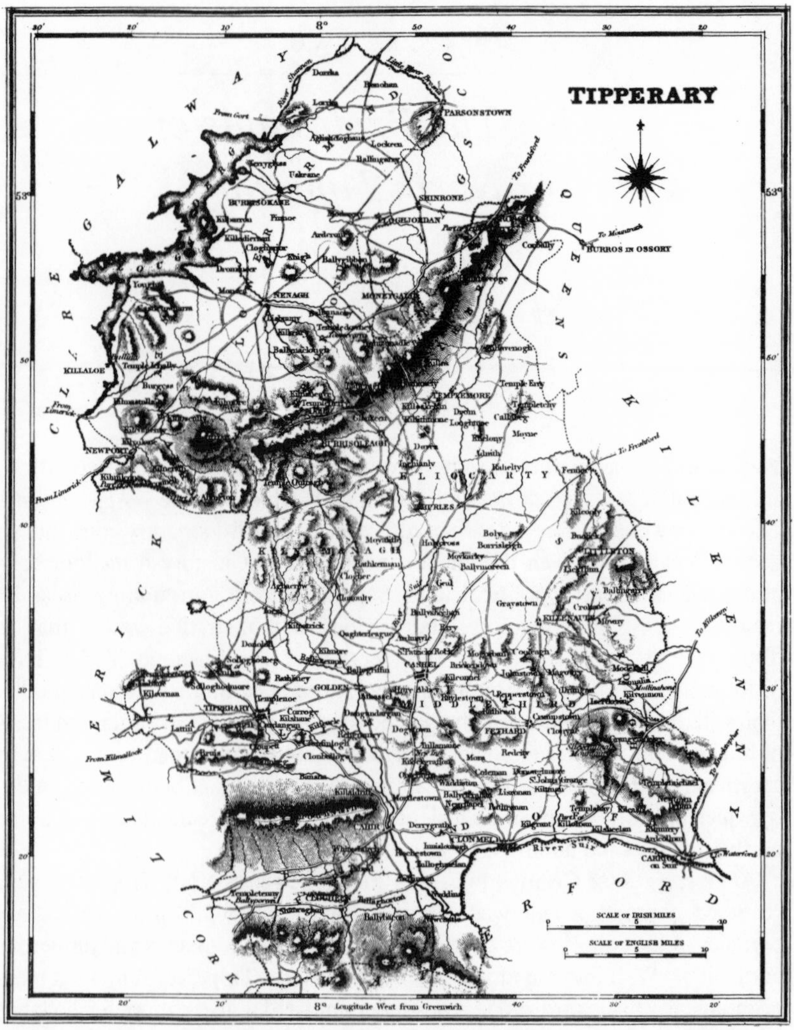

MAP 1   County Tipperary was an administrative unit, but not a social region. We are concerned with the area north of the mountain range, including the panhandle of King's County that sticks southwest into Tipperary, between Cloughjordan and Roscrea.
Source: *Lewis's Atlas*, 1837.

portion of the county consists of "lime-rich drift-covered lowlands drained by the river Suir,"[3] a region "exuberantly fertile." To the west, on the borders of Limerick, lie the heavy grasslands of the Golden Vale. The northern third of the county, to the north of the Keeper range, comprises the Shannon plain of North Tipperary with which this study is concerned. In the early nineteenth century the low mountain ranges that mark its southern limit were wild tracts of territory forming barriers more formidable than their height, measuring in the hundreds of feet, would suggest.[4] The lowland of North Tipperary is for the most part flat, though it becomes gently rolling as it descends to the northwest towards the Shannon. As in the Ottawa Valley to which many of its residents emigrated in the nineteenth century, the line of low, rocky hills that marks its perimeter is always visible on the horizon.

The vale of North Tipperary so defined measures roughly twenty miles wide by thirty miles long, commencing some ten miles east of the City of Limerick and lying between the River Shannon and the gentle northeastward sweep of the Keeper, Silvermine, Devilsbit, and Slieve Bloom mountains. These heights form a single range of hills forty miles in length, declining from slate mountains in the west into low sandstone hills to the east. These natural features roughly enclose the baronies of Upper and Lower Ormond in Tipperary and the western panhandle of King's County, now known as County Offaly. To the northeast, beyond Birr, the plain of occupied land deteriorates to a maze of small pieces of arable and pasture scattered in patches amongst extensive bogland that becomes ever more dominant and emerges in central Offaly as Ireland's vast Bog of Allen. On the northwestern boundary of Tipperary the Shannon widens to form Lough Derg, on the northern shore of which lies the village of Mountshannon. Isolated by mountains from the rest of County Galway,[5] the social links of Mountshannon's people were across the river with Tipperary. The same comment largely applies to other border parishes such as Ogonnelloe and Killaloe, in Clare, and Stradbally (Castle Connell) in County Limerick. As a social region, North Tipperary may be said to dip south through passes in the mountains as far as the estate market town of Templemore, but beyond that area the historical associations and migratory and surname patterns of the people were quite distinct.[6]

Historically, as well as geographically, economically, and socially, North Tipperary may be viewed as a distinct region. The area defined above as North Tipperary corresponds almost exactly with the eastern portion of the Church of Ireland diocese of Killaloe,[7] which perpetuates the ancient boundaries of the medieval diocese of that name. In Ireland, as in England, the diocesan boundaries derive from civil boundaries existing at the time of diocesan organization, in Ireland the twelfth century.[8] The diocese of Killaloe, centred upon the cathedral town of that name on the Shannon between Clare and Tipperary, approximated the ancient boundaries of the principality of

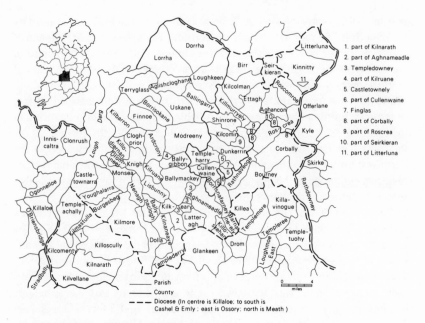

1. part of Kilnarath
2. part of Aghnameadle
3. Templedowney
4. part of Kilruane
5. Castletownely
6. part of Cullenwaine
7. Finglas
8. part of Corbally
9. part of Roscrea
10. part of Seirkieran
11. part of Litterluna

MAP 2   North Tipperary parishes and dioceses.
Source: Adapted from LDS Irish Probates Register.

Thomond, and comprised all of County Clare, the parishes of Inniscaltra and Clonrush (the Mountshannon area of Galway), the Ely O'Carroll territory in what is now the Offaly panhandle, and the North Tipperary baronies of Ikerrin, Upper and Lower Ormond, and the western half of Clanwilliam. The County Limerick portion of Thomond, except the Union of Stradbally (Castle Connell), was separated from Killaloe and attached to Limerick probably as a result of forfeitures following the Desmond rebellion. For a short period in the late twelfth century the portion of the diocese east of the Shannon became a separate see centred upon Roscrea, where the remains of some of the structures associated with this period may yet be seen, but the new diocese was soon after reunited with Killaloe.[9] More recent administrative divisions perpetuate later events in the civil history of the region, from the incursion or infiltration of Irish clans up to the eve of the Cromwellian invasion in the 1640s, but the socio-economic region of North Tipperary corresponds closely with eastern Thomond, a principality bounded here by natural geographical barriers.

It has been noted by a number of authors that the tenurial and social relics of ancient Irish culture lingered in North Tipperary long after they were extinct in most of the country outside the far west. To a very large degree this was due to the expulsion from the region of the twelfth-century Anglo-Norman invaders following a rebellion in the thirteenth century by the O'Kennedys, the dominant family in what were to become the Ormond baronies. The more prosperous southern baronies of the county underwent manorialization in the medieval period, but the north retained its Gaelic traditions and system of common ownership until the Cromwellian conquest of the mid-seventeenth century.[10] The Anglo-Norman Butlers recovered their great castle at Nenagh and took control of the manor of that name in the 1530s and were recognized as overlords by the O'Kennedys and their followers, but the shiring of the Ormonds as a part of the Butlers' County Palatine of Tipperary actually aided the retention of the O'Kennedys' independence and the survival of Irish laws and institutions in the region. Hostile clans and English officials alike hesitated to interfere with a jurisdiction exempt from royal government and in the hands of the Butler family, now the powerful earls of Ormond.[11] James I pursued a policy of extinguishing the old clan-like tenures in Ireland. Though the policy of surrender and regrant was successful at the level of the great lords, the old tenures survived among the lesser Irish of the Ormonds and the Cromwellian inquisitions showed the land still held in undivided fractions by members of a family, quite unlike the Norman individual freeholds in the southern part of the county.[12] Some features continued into the nineteenth century. Ingeborg Leister found evidence of numerous *clachans*, small open-field farming hamlets, on the 1840 Ordnance Survey maps of Tipperary, all north of the Devilsbit-Keeper Hill range.[13] In the mountainous baronies of both Kilnamanagh and Owney and Arra that fringe the region to the south and west, partnership farming was still practised in half the townlands in 1850.[14]

North Tipperary, defined as a geographical rather than as a political entity, therefore constituted a social, economic, and cultural region distinct from surrounding areas. "On the edge of the more commercialized farming regions" in the nineteenth century,[15] it displayed in its landholding and settlement patterns numerous traces of the Celtic past, and historically it had been quite distinct from the Norman southern part of the county. Its geographical situation in the Shannon Valley, ringed by wild stretches of mountain and bog, preserved its essential unity as a region despite its political dismemberment into parts of several counties in recent centuries.

PROTESTANT SETTLEMENT IN NORTH TIPPERARY

The Protestant population of the North Tipperary region was of predominantly English descent, but the pattern of Protestant settlement that may be mapped using the parliamentary religious returns of 1831[16] reflects the cumulative effects of population movements, conversions from Catholicism, village foundations, and the encouragement of Protestant colonies in previous centuries as well as the earliest influx of English immigrants. Protestants

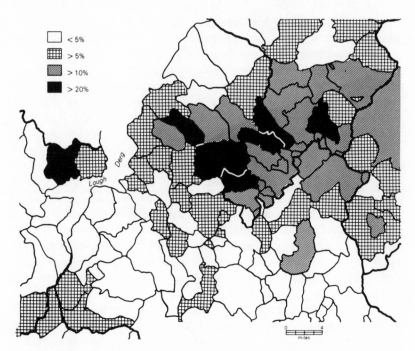

MAP 3   Percentage of Protestants, 1831, by parish. Protestants accounted for 8.5 per cent of the population of the region, but they were most concentrated in the vicinity of Borrisokane and Cloughjordan, and in the parishes of the King's County panhandle to the east.
Source: HC (1835) XXXIII.

numbered some 17,000 of a total population of some 200,000 in 1831, or 8.5 per cent.[17] Though they nowhere became a majority of the population as they did in parts of northern Ireland, in some parishes they nevertheless constituted a quarter of the population, and the collection of statistics at the parish level conceals the clustering of people into Protestant colonies in areas smaller than a parish, as on the Dunalley estate in the eastern half of Modreeny parish. Map 3 reveals that the Protestant population occupied the lowland areas, particularly in the eastern part of the region – in the Borrisokane-Modreeny area of Lower Ormond and the adjacent parishes of Clonlisk barony in the King's County panhandle. These parishes formed the heartland of English settlement.

The King's County panhandle came under limited English plantation in the early seventeenth century, but the Ormond baronies of County Tipperary that form the central part of the region came under secure English control at the time of the Cromwellian invasion in the 1640s, and extensive English settlement there awaited the Restoration and royal confirmation of the

Cromwellian confiscation of Irish lands. Protestant colonization continued through the eighteenth and even into the early nineteenth centuries, especially in parishes on the fringes of the region. The Protestant concentrations at Mountshannon and Templemore both represent late eighteenth-century foundations established by landlords desirous of encouraging a Protestant tenantry. However, after the seventeenth century such Protestant colonies were formed by internal movements of population rather than by further immigration from England.

Infiltration of English settlement up the River Shannon from Limerick may to some extent have predated the Cromwellian incursions. Certainly John Strangman had purchased land in Castletownarra parish from the O'Briens before 1640, and the earl of Cork had bought property there and in neighbouring Youghalarra and Kilmastulla parishes.[18] There was also a small colony of miners on the slopes of the mountains southwest of Nenagh, at the Silvermines in Kilmore parish, but some of the miners were killed and most of the remainder fled to Limerick at the outbreak of the 1641 Rebellion.[19] Nonetheless, most of the English population at mid-century must have been Cromwellian. The greatest concentration of English in the Cromwellian poll-tax and hearth money returns lived on the lower Shannonside lands at the foot of the Arra Mountains between Killaloe and Newport, extending northeastward through the vale between the Arra Mountains and the Keeper Hill range to Nenagh. The Shannon parishes of Dromineer, Monsea, Kilbarron, and Lorrha also were home to important concentrations of Protestant settlers.[20]

This predominance was not to last. In the nineteenth century the Protestant population of the Castletownarra area was miniscule, and by 1850 almost non-existent. The town of Newport, to the south, was home to 115 Protestant families in 1766, nearly as many as lived in the important administrative centre of Cashel in the southern part of the county, but in contrast to the situation in most of the region the numbers there were no larger in 1831. Kilbarron and Lorrha lost most of their Protestant populations much earlier than this, probably to the new town of Borrisokane, founded on better soil inland in the second half of the seventeenth century.[21]

By 1660 there was also a scattering of English settlers throughout Ballybritt and Clonlisk baronies of King's County and in the adjoining Tipperary parishes. They were fairly numerous in the Lower Ormond border parishes of Ballingarry, Uskane, and especially Modreeny, and in the lowlands of Upper Ormond, notably on the Cole (later the Cole Bowen) estate in Ballymackey, and in Lisbonny and Aghnameadle, as well as in the mountainous Borriso-leigh neighbourhood to the south and in the garrison town of Roscrea.

This distribution suggests that there may have been some movement into the area from an earlier English plantation in southwestern Offaly. Plans for the plantation of central Ireland had been advanced in the sixteenth century in the same period that such policies were pursued with success in Ulster and America. The Ely O'Carroll territory (the baronies of Ballybritt and Clonlisk in the King's panhandle) was severed from Tipperary and attached to Offaly by order-in-council in 1606 for plantation purposes.[22] An English colony was planted in the 1620s at Birr, thereafter known also as Parsonstown for the family name of the proprietorial family who later held title as earls of Rosse.[23] The Parsons family actively promoted their town of Birr and in 1660 the parish had the largest English population in the region.[24]

The exempt jurisdiction of the Butler earls of Ormond had preserved the Tipperary part of the region from the grasp of Elizabethan land sharks, but following the abolition of the Palatine jurisdiction by James I in 1621 after a quarrel with the earl, proposals were also advanced to plant the Ormond baronies in order to secure the Shannon against the men of Connaught. Strafford held inquisitions in North Tipperary in the 1630s and had the area surveyed in 1639, but plans to advance the Ormond plantation were cut short by the outbreak of hosilities between the king and parliament at home and by the 1641 Rebellion in Ireland.[25]

Persistent oral traditions assert that Tipperary's Protestants are descended from Cromwell's soldiers, but this can be true in only a few instances.[26] Though the English government met its financial obligations to the army in Ireland and to the merchant adventurers who financed it by issuing debentures redeemable for confiscated lands, and allocated most of the North Tipperary region seized from the native Irish to satisfy the claims of the military, including the baronies of Upper and Lower Ormond, Owney and Arra, and Clonlisk,[27] very few of the common soldiers settled in the country. Their debentures were worth little and lack of capital would have prevented the men from developing their lands even if they had redeemed them for small acreages surrounded by hostile, dispossessed Irish. The vast majority instead sold out to their officers, often for paltry sums, and returned to England.[28]

A number of senior officers invested heavily in debentures and secured grants to large territories in the conquered country.[29] Some of these colonels and a number of lesser officers settled upon their new estates in North Tipperary and became the ancestors of such landed gentry of later centuries as the Sadleirs, Pritties, Poes, Gasons, Abbotts, Andrewses, Cambies, Tolers, Breretons, Wallers, and Atkinsons.[30] The titles of many were confirmed after the Restoration, for the new king had not the power to expel them, but there was some shuffling of lands which may have contributed to the shift eastward of the focal point of Protestant settlement. Col. James Hutchinson, for example, left his earlier location in Youghalarra for Knockballymeagher near Roscrea.[31] However, half the lands in the Ormond baronies were allocated under the new monarch to "land sharks, nepotists, and Court favourites."[32]

This left the door open to speculation in Irish lands and the acquisition of estates by those arriving in the late seventeenth and early eighteenth centuries.

Some of these later gentry families acquired their Tipperary estates by marriage, as exemplified by the Heads of Derry Castle on Lough Derg, who descend from a Waterford wool buyer who married the heiress of Captain Samuel Wade, a Cromwellian grantee.[33] Others with capital immigrated from England after the 1688 Revolution and acquired property. George Stoney of Kettlewell, Yorkshire, mortgaged a maternal estate and emigrated to Ireland in this period and is reported to have settled at Knockshegowna in Ballingarry. The next generation leased the later family seat at Greyfort in Borrisokane from the Saunders family, who had acquired part of the Stopford grant.[34] Trafficking in lands by non-residents continued, a major example of speculation being the purchase of the town and lordship of Roscrea in 1727 by John Damer, an Englishman whose uncle had begun a family tradition in the 1660s by investing in Irish military debentures. The Damers were always non-resident, but the property descended through a female line to the earls of Portarlington in the Queen's County, who let it out on long-term lease but held the fee until 1858.[35]

The Cromwellian officers and their assignees formed the new landlord class, but the gentry made up only a small proportion of the later Protestant population. It was nevertheless this landlord class that provided the initial stimulus to general English settlement and founded much of the later village network to house their English tenantry.

Only a minority of Tipperary's later Protestant population descended from settlers who actually arrived in the Cromwellian era. Some sixty of the just over two hundred non-Irish surnames borne by nineteenth-century Protestant emigrants to Canada are to be found in the hearth money rolls of the 1660s, a defective transcript of which provides our only long list of seventeenth-century inhabitants. Cromwellian officers account for a half dozen of these sixty, and many of the remaining surnames are so common (Brown, Cox, Taylor, etc.) that the existence of any genealogical link with later residents of the same name in the same region – often in distant parishes – is not at all certain. However, some twenty names are sufficiently distinctive or sufficiently uncommon in the region to suggest that the individuals recorded are the ancestors of the later bearers of these names. Examples include Abbott, Acres (found in the hearth money returns at Ballingarry and Borrisokane as Akers and Eggers), Alloway (Attaway in the returns), Blackwell, Boate, Farmer, Goulding, Harding, Hardy, Rivington (variously Revington, Remmington, and Riddington in seventeenth- through nineteenth-century sources), Sharpley, Sheppard, Smallman (the probable interpretation of the transcription Swallman and Swatman entered at Corbally; Smallman occurs later at Roscrea), Stanley, and Watkins.[36] Some of these individuals may have been soldiers who remained in Tipperary without exchanging their debentures,[37] but it is more likely that such names represent early English immigrants, perhaps tradesmen or retainers and employees of the new gentry.

The ancestors of the majority of the emigrants studied here, and of the Protestant population of North Tipperary generally, below the ranks of the gentry, came into the region after the 1660s and settled in new villages and on new farms that they cleared in underpopulated areas. North Tipperary before the confiscations was a backward rural area, and Lower Ormond in particular had a notably high proportion of woodland, scrub, and bog with few nucleated settlements.[38] The Civil Survey conducted in 1654 reflects the devastation of the Cromwellian wars in its references to small numbers of houses and cabins, vast areas lying waste, and numerous ruined castles.[39]

Apart from ports and monastic settlements, almost all towns and villages in Ireland date from the seventeenth and eighteenth centuries, and North Tipperary is no exception to this generalization.[40] The Civil Survey records a few insignificant villages of a half-dozen or so cabins clustered around ruined castles or old monastic foundations, but most were so small as to dispel any pretensions to an urban character. There were few enough villages, but the only towns were the old monastic centres of Birr, by this time part of the King's County and under English plantation, and Nenagh and Roscrea, all small by English standards and bearing marks of the recent war. Nenagh may have shrunk to little more than a hamlet by the early seventeenth century. In the Civil Survey it boasted a "large stronge castle wth sixty cottages & thatcht houses," but they were "lately built & the castle lately repayred by Collonell Abbott,"[41] the Cromwellian governor.[42] At Roscrea were "a large castle & a bawne in repayre many thatcht houses and cabbins a ruined Abby a corne mill upon a brooke [and] a markett weekely on Thursday a Fayre twice a yeare."[43]

Most of the villages existing in the early nineteenth century were built by the new landlords. Among the oldest and most important are Borrisokane and Cloughjordan. There is no trace of either in the Civil Survey. Both came into being in the late seventeenth century as a result of a deliberate policy of plantation by the Cromwellian grantees. All of Borrisokane parish apart from Tombrickane was granted to Captain James Stopford, along with lands in Modreeny.[44] Stopford laid out the village, a long tapering street, adjacent to the ancient parish church, and a "pretty English settlement" was reported there in 1691.[45]

Captain John Harrison redeemed his debentures around Cloughjordan. At that time there was no centre of population on his estate, for the terriers to the Down Survey note only "several cabbins, disperst in ye said parish" of Modreeny.[46] Either John (d. 1697)[47] or his son James (d. 1727)[48] built the street village of Cloughjordan and populated it with "disbanded soldiers," according to one account,[49] or more likely by importing tenants from England.[50] The village of Cloughjordan, which received a market grant in 1706,[51] and the farmland nearby, which became the centres of Protestant population on the estate, were the most sparsely settled parts of Modreeny parish before Harrison arrived. The Down Survey map depicts Harrison's 919 plantation acre[52] grant of Garrane and Cloughjordan[53] as two very large units with high proportions of bog and woodland.[54] The later townlands that were created there and became the homes of the Protestant population bear names like Burnwood, Newtown, Islandwood, Stoneyacre, and Oxpark, names that testify to their origins in the clearance of marginal scrubwood and bog by English settlers.

The establishment of the new English on sparsely populated marginal land has been noted elsewhere as typical of North Tipperary in general[55] and underlines the fact that wholesale removal of the Irish population at the time of the Cromwellian confiscations proved impractical. One historian has noted, however, that Tipperary landowners transplanted to Connaught were accompanied by unusually large numbers of retainers. Though most of the Irish population stayed behind, the landowners who remained were transformed into tenants.[56] In the second quarter of the eighteenth century the Harrison estate passed to the Prittie family of Kilboy by reason of the marriage of James's daughter in 1702 to Henry Prittie, grandson of Col. Henry Prittie, a Cromwellian grantee who resided in Kilmore parish south of Nenagh. The fifth Henry Prittie was elevated to the peerage as the first Baron Dunalley in 1800. This major Protestant colony was thus in the nineteenth century part of the Dunalley estate, which in 1876 totalled 18,000 acres.[57]

Though the continuing high concentration of Protestants on the Dunalley estate at Cloughjordan and also at Borrisokane suggests that large numbers of the people descended from English settlers imported by the new gentry, others were later migrants from surrounding counties. The process was ongoing, and continued far beyond the end of the seventeenth century. The Quaker Boakes moved to Cloughjordan from settlements of Friends in Queen's County early in the eighteenth century,[58] the Hoppers moved to Roscrea in a step-wise migration from mid-King's County in the late eighteenth century,[59] and the Kingsmills and Howards came to Templemore from the east later still. One later emigrant, William Geary, was himself an immigrant, a native of England who had gone to Ireland to promote agricultural equipment and married locally.[60] Geary was, however, exceptional. Though some Canadian families of Tipperary descent have heard oral traditions that suggest that their families lived in Ireland only a short time, most of these accounts minimize the time spent there by telescoping unknown generations.[61] The ramification of surnames suggests that most families had been in central Ireland, if not in North Tipperary itself, since at least the early eighteenth century.

Most of the surnames of the Protestant population were English, though a few such as Colbert are problematical. A few interestingly are Welsh – Evans, Jones, Lewis, Morgan, Owens, and Powell certainly, and possibly Edwards, Roberts, and Williams. Most of these Welsh names occur in the seventeenth-century hearth tax rolls, but how they came to Tipperary is uncertain. A number of the Powell families of North Tipperary must descend

from a Limerick family of the name, for many use the forename Caleb, and
Lenihan records Caleb as a name that ran in the family of Robert Powell, an
officer who settled there in 1649.[62] The only name that is surely Scottish is
McLeod, and a Caesar McLeod, the name borne by an emigrant of a later
generation, is found at Borrisokane in 1776.[63] Scottish settlement in Ireland
was confined almost entirely to the North, where Prebyterianism serves as a
reasonable surrogate for Scottish origins. A very few North Tipperary
Protestants bear the names of Palatine families who migrated east from
County Limerick in the eighteenth century. The Shouldices of Glankeen and
Switzers of Templederry bear names of Palatine Germans settled at Rathkeale
around 1709. The Sparlings of Killaloe migrated eastwards more recently,[64]
while those at Rathnaveoge were possibly an English family.[65] Palatine
names are much more common further south in the Kilcooly region of
Tipperary, where a deliberate policy of recruitment attracted such families in
the 1770s.[66]

Several dozen emigrant Protestants also bore the names of Irish Catholic
families long resident in the North Tipperary region, though often single
families account for the appearance of these names in the list.[67] Such families
descend from ancestors who conformed to the Church of Ireland for secular
reasons during the penal time or converted as a result of intermarriage in the
late eighteenth century when religious tolerance was widespread and before
the 1798 Rebellion and deteriorating economic conditions again sharpened
social cleavages.[68]

The Reformation had technically followed the same course in Ireland as in
England, but despite the loss of church buildings and lands the people of
Ireland did not, of course, become Protestants. The monasteries were
dissolved and churches seized but the church lands were granted to Irish
families, and many of the new clergy and even the first Protestant bishop of
Killaloe were native Irish whose reformation was not based upon strong
conviction. Serious attempts to eradicate Roman Catholicism were not made
until the enactment of the Penal Laws in the reign of Anne.[69] Secular reasons
for conversion were greatly reduced as legal disabilities against Roman
Catholics were eased in the late eighteenth century; the later emigrant,
Captain George T. Burke, however, a member of a family of Roman Catholic
gentry that managed to retain some of its ancestral lands near Borrisoleigh,
though holding under Protestant head landlords,[70] converted to Anglicanism
in order to secure a commission in the British Army.[71] Intermarriage became
less common following the upheavals of the 1798 Rebellion. Nevertheless, a
few of the emigrating families were of "mixed" religion in Ireland, and
remained so in Canada, some members adhering to the Protestant faith and
others being Roman Catholic. For example, Jane Giles of Bourney, wife of
Michael Ryan, a Roman Catholic who settled near Belleville, was initially
Protestant,[72] and other mixed families included the Searsons of Killea,

Oakleys of Carney, Armitages and Baskervilles (these last from Youghalarra, an area with a tiny Protestant population), and the Somervilles of Ballymacegan and Birr. In the case of the John Morgan and William Derham families the Catholic parties to the marriages seem to have converted to Protestantism before emigrating, and a single Irish baptism in both cases provides the only evidence of Catholicism.[73] Nonetheless, both saw a child marry a Catholic in Canada.

The Protestant population of North Tipperary was therefore not of uniform background, though the majority descended from families of English origin who arrived in the region in the post-Cromwellian period. The Cromwellian confiscations were crucial, however, for the new tenurial framework and the new English gentry were the stimuli that brought about the firm establishment of a Protestant population in Tipperary. Though many of the new arrivals cleared lands that were underused or left waste by the existing population, the privileged status of the English settlers, both in law and in the eyes of the landlords, remained a cause of bitter discontent for the Roman Catholic majority.

ENCOURAGEMENT AND SPREAD OF THE PROTESTANT POPULATION

Though some early concentrations of Protestant population have persisted from the seventeenth century to the present day as at Birr, Cloughjordan, and Borrisokane, others originated more recently. Establishment of Protestant colonies on estates continued through the eighteenth century and even into the nineteenth. In some cases this involved town or village foundation, in others merely a determined effort to establish dependable Protestant tenants as freeholders on large farms. By the eighteenth century such colonies were founded by attracting settlers from the growing populations of existing estates or by drawing Protestants from neighbouring counties rather than by the direct importation of settlers from England. Thus the spread of the Protestant population to other estates in the region was in part due to the desire of the gentry to develop a Protestant tenantry in the eighteenth century.

It would be a mistake, however, to attribute population movement solely to incentives offered by landlords. The existence as well as the foundation of a village or market town inevitably drew shopkeepers, tradesmen, and labourers, and in rural parishes the lack of a village did nothing to obviate the need for such ubiquitous craftsmen as blacksmiths, weavers, and shoemakers.

While the destruction of records makes it impossible to trace each family back to its first appearance in North Tipperary and so to assess the relative importance of each of the factors above in fostering the growth and spread of the Protestant population, it is certain that in many instances the bearers of a common surname must also share a common ancestor.[74] This conclusion is supported by the manner in which many surnames localized within the region in the early nineteenth century. It is likewise apparent that a sense of kinship solidarity persisted, fostered by personal inclination as well as by the growing necessity of family assistance in providing for the rising generation; the nineteenth century was economically insecure, particularly for a privileged but threatened minority being gradually overwhelmed by a burgeoning Catholic population. This sense of kinship is suggested by the widespread custom of burying in an ancestral parish for generations after a family had left its former residence[75] and by the general use of customary naming patterns. We shall see family solidarity in action when we come to consider the mechanisms of emigration and we shall observe that many of the cultural byproducts of such a sense of family persisted amongst the descendants of the emigrants in Canada into the late nineteenth century. It remains for us to examine in greater detail the manner in which the granting of freehold tenure and the foundation of villages and towns facilited the growth and spread of the Protestant population.

Protestant Freeholders

In the eighteenth century the Protestant population benefited both from the anti-Catholic legislation of the reign of Anne and from the desire of landlords to lease out their estates to improving tenants. The Cromwellian and Williamite settlements of the seventeenth century had taken most of the land in the country out of Catholic hands, and the penal laws of the early eighteenth were designed, amongst other purposes, to perpetuate this situation. Other laws crippled Irish trade in the interest of promoting English manufactures, and the Irish economy reverted to a dependence upon agriculture. Landlords sought a secure income by leasing their estates on generous terms and in large acreages to dependable Protestants whom they encouraged to improve the land.[76] Leases for a term of lives or in perpetuity for a fixed rent became increasingly common in the early eighteenth century, as the lump-sum payment or fine paid by the lessee on taking up a lease helped meet the immediate cash needs for which the more profligate of the Anglo-Irish gentry became legendary.[77] After the land was enclosed[78] and as the economy improved, especially with the easing of restrictions on the export of Irish agricultural produce, now needed to feed industrializing England, the gentry became content with a regular income easily obtained and let their estates to large Protestant farmers. It was believed that security of tenure at a fixed rent would encourage farmers to improve their lands at their own expense. In many cases the lessees sublet all or part of their tenancies; as demand for land by a growing population drove up rents, these "middlemen" became the recipients of increasing incomes that stood in stark contrast to the fixed sums

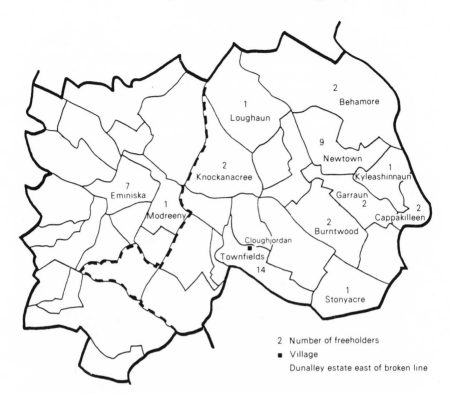

MAP 4   Modreeny parish freeholders, 1776. Protestant farmers on the Dunalley estate held their lands on leases for the term of three lives. Secure tenure was intended to foster agricultural improvement – and to boost a tenantry of loyal Protestant voters.
Sources: freeholders list, NLI, ms 787; extent of Dunalley estate, PRO, Dublin, TAB 27 N/14 (1826/7).

they in turn were required by the terms of their leases to pay the head landlords.

It is no coincidence that many of the progenitors of the nineteenth-century Protestant emigrants are first traceable in surviving estate and Deeds Registry records of the mid-eighteenth century, for many of them became the recipients of long-term leases at that time. The old Harrison estate in Modreeny parish, for example, was let out to Protestant tenants by the Pritties, the non-resident owners who lived to the west at Kilboy.[79] The 1776 freeholders list enumerates some three dozen such tenants there, bearing names that were to become familiar in nineteenth-century Tipperary communities in Canada: Anglesey, Carter, Coates, Guest, Hodgins, Lewis, Mooney, Ralph, Rimington, Shoebottom, Tydd, and Williams.[80]

There had been a significant Protestant population in Modreeny since the

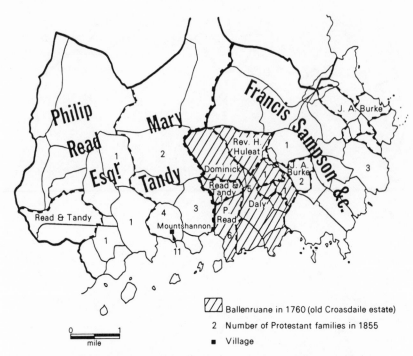

MAP 5   Estates and Protestant settlement in the Mountshannon area. Two approaches to promoting a Protestant tenantry: the Croasdailes gave leases to substantial freeholding farmers in the 1740s, while the Tandys later in the century encouraged labourers to locate in the village of Mountshannon. By the 1820s the freehold farms were much subdivided, and the labourers were impoverished. Sources: os 6–inch map, 1840; PRO, Dublin, reel 4, Inniscaltra parish register, "List of Protestants in the Union of Mt Shannon at Christmas 1855"; Primary Valuation; NLI, D.23185–23215, Croasdaile deeds.

mid-seventeenth century. In other cases, Protestant populations were attracted to estates hitherto occupied solely by Catholic Irish as the result of deliberate attempts by landlords to foster a Protestant tenantry. Such recruitment was responsible for Protestant settlement in some of the areas on the borders of the North Tipperary region: on the Croasdaile estate in the parish of Clonrush on the Galway side of Lough Derg, and on the Otway estate in the southern mountains.

By the late seventeenth century the western portion of the parish of Clonrush, known as Ballenruane, had come into the hands of the Croasdaile family of Cloghstoken, County Galway. In 1742 Henry Croasdaile of Woodford, a few miles to the north of Ballenruane, secured title to that property by paying the debts of his uncle. He moved to Ballenruane soon after and began actively to develop the estate, operating iron works there and leasing large portions of the estate for lives to farmers who, by reason of holding very large farms of close to one hundred Irish acres, were sometimes termed "gentlemen." By 1760, subdivisions of Ballenruane were held by John Long (Ballynagough), William Burke (Cartron), Henry Watson, Thomas Burke, and Mr Benn (parts of Geenenny), George Clarke, Henry Watson again, and Edmond Burke (parts of Clonolia).[81] While the Burkes were probably Roman Catholic gentlemen of the family that still held Tintrim in the eastern part of the parish in the nineteenth century, the remaining lessees were Protestants. It appears that Croasdaile brought these families in from County Clare, to the west, for Clarke's lease of 1746 describes him as of Ballyheige, County Clare, farmer,[82] and Long's in 1745 was witnessed by Thomas Long, a farmer of Killaloe in Clare. Clarke's lease connects with County Clare another family that soon appeared in Ballenruane, the Pages, described as also of Ballyheige.[83] Thus the Croasdaile estate in Clonrush was planted with a small but socially and economically dominant class of Protestant freeholders.

Another documented example of landlords planting Protestant tenants on their lands as freeholders in the mid-eighteenth century comes from the Castle Otway estate in the mountains southwest of Moneygall. This property formed the grant of the Cromwellian Captain John Otway, a native of Westmoreland, England.[84] In 1759 and 1760 Thomas Otway (1731–1786) granted freeholds to the ancestors of the Canadian Shouldice and Sifton families.[85] Although not all of Otway's original leases survive, a rent roll of 1806 indicates that ten leases for three lives and two for two lives were then in effect (see Table 1). Tenancies at will and life leases were fairly evenly divided between Protestant and Roman Catholic tenants, though the latter made up by far the greater proportion of the population in the surrounding parishes. Typically, eleven of the twelve leases for lives appear to have been held by Protestants.

TABLE 1

Tenures by Religious Denomination, Otway Estate, 1806

Tenure	Probable Religion		Remarks
	Protestant	RC	
Tenants at will	17	18	
Life lessees	18	22	
31 years		2	from 1784 and 1787
3 lives (2 for 2 lives)	11	1	
99 years		1	from 1723
Lives renewable	4		Otways, Going, Higinson
Total	50	44	

Source: NLI, ms 13,000(8), Rental of the Estates of Henry Otway Esqr in Ireland, 1st May 1806

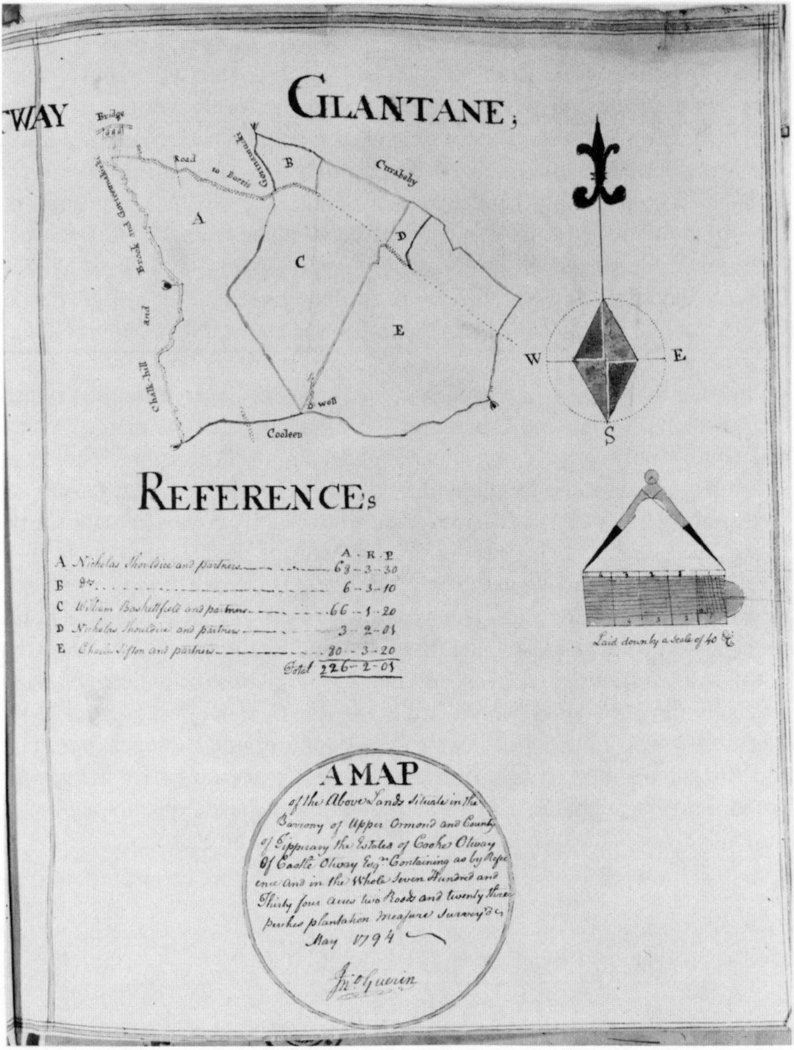

MAP 6   Glantane, part of the Otway estate, 1794. The Shouldice and Sifton families both secured leases from the Otways in the 1740s and remained neighbours until Nicholas Shouldice and Charles Sifton emigrated to Canada in 1818 and 1819. Nicholas settled in the Ottawa Valley, but Charles followed his sons to London; a descendant became Laurier's immigration minister.
Source: Courtesy of the National Library of Ireland, Otway estate maps, 21.F.129.

Thomas Otway, the member of the family responsible for granting most of the long-term leases, was a severe landlord. If those reponsible for theft of property from the demesne were not discovered, he charged his cottiers as a group the full value of the items stolen, and he set escalating scales of fines for refusing to work on a holy day other than Sunday and for minor infractions such as neglecting to tip a cart on end after unyoking the animals. The punishment for a fifth offence of the last type was demolition of the cottier's house.[86]

It is no surprise that an intolerant landlord like Thomas Otway attempted to build up a tenantry of substantial Protestant farmers. The Shouldice, Sifton, Wright, and Lee families that are known to have been on the estate by 1764[87] had by 1806 been joined by other Protestant families named Ackland, Ardill, Armitage, Baskerville, Brereton, Carter, Dagg, Harrington, Hodgins, Kent, Mills, Mooney, Morgan, Oakley, Oldfield, Searson, Short, Tucker, Wall, Wallace, and Watson. All were probably recruited from older Protestant colonies on the plain to the north, for at least half of these names were also to be found on the Dunalley estate at Modreeny and most were in evidence somewhere else in North Tipperary. Promotional activity continued into the nineteenth century. The minister at Templederry, the parish in which the Otways' residence of Castle Otway was located, reported in 1820 that the fifty Protestant families there, an estimated 4 per cent of the population, represented an increase in the last few years "in consequence of encouragement from the landlords to settle here."[88]

Village and Town Foundations

The foundation of villages and market towns revived in the late eighteenth century under the auspices of landlords anxious to upgrade their estates and enlarge their rent rolls. The date of establishment of a village may often be guessed at by examining the physical layout. Louis Cullen has pointed out that a triangular green, such as that which may still be traced in maps of the oldest part of Birr, is "the hallmark of early seventeenth-century settlement." The other villages in the North Tipperary region, which date from after this period, do not display this feature, which is common in Leix and Offaly to the east. North Tipperary market centres established in the late seventeenth century consist of lines of houses clustered on either side of a long, gradually widening street, as at Borrisokane, Cloughjordan, and Shinrone.[89] The second spate of town-building, in the second half of the eighteenth century,[90] coincided with the prosperous period following the termination of the Seven Years' War in 1763 and again following the revolution in America. Centres established at this time tend to display the Georgian love of symmetry by the incorporation into their plans of stylish squares, as in the newer additions to Birr, or the laying-out of regular rectangular marketplaces and the provision of scenic vistas as at Templemore. Where an attempt to increase the Protestant population was an integral part of the town-building scheme, such an effort may represent a reaction by the landlord to the relaxation of the penal laws against Roman Catholics in this period. This was certainly the case in some rural settlement schemes of the era.[91]

The foundation of a village in conjunction with the establishment of a Protestant population is best exemplified by the village of Mountshannon on the Galway side of Lough Derg. While the Protestants of the parish of Clonrush to the east were "generally farmers," descendants of the freeholders established there by Croasdaile in the 1740s, the Protestant population of Mountshannon's Inniscaltra parish in the early nineteenth century consisted of "a few farmers; others Carpenters & Shoemakers; most, weavers & labourers, very poor."[92] The establishment in Inniscaltra of a village inhabited largely by Protestant labourers provides the explanation for the contrast. The parochial union of Inniscaltra, Clonrush, and Moynoe which came to centre upon the parish church at Mountshannon thus provides evidence of two distinct responses by landlords to their desire to develop a Protestant tenantry.

It is claimed locally that Messrs Reade and Tandy, London bankers, acquired Inniscaltra parish about two hundred years ago through the bankruptcy of William Woods, the former owner.[93] However, Philip Reade, Esq., claimed in 1836 that the owner of the fee "above a century past, leased in perpetuity to two persons; one of whom has resided this last year; the other does not, but resides in Ireland," the former being Reade and the latter Mrs Tandy.[94] In any case, the parish comprised two estates, with the Reades living at Woodpark in the western part of the parish and the Tandys possessing the eastern half and in the mid-nineteenth century living there (see Map 5). Though the Reades were resident, they did nothing to encourage Protestant tenants and their estate remained populated with Roman Catholics. The Tandys, however, redeveloped the Daly village of Mountshannon into a classic estate village of large stone houses lining the roadway, with a new Protestant church on the north side of the street, a handsome market hall on the south, and eventually the Tandy residence at the eastern end. The Tandys populated their village with Protestant labourers and tradesmen.[95] In 1831 there were 516 Protestants in the parish, mostly in the village, to the Roman Catholics' 1682.[96]

The most important town foundation in the region in this period is the market town of Templemore in the parish of that name, which in its present form appears to have been established by the Carden family only in the 1780s. The 1766 census of religions shows only ten Protestant and seventy "papist" families in the parish, with at least seven of the ten Protestant families headed by gentry or clergy.[97] That something dramatic occurred thereafter is indicated by the fact that the population rose nearly thirteen-fold by 1831, the Protestant population alone by over seven-fold.[98] The town is in the townland

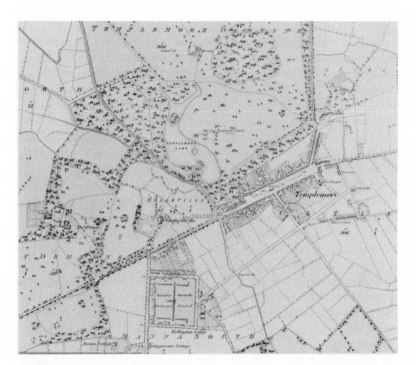

MAP 7   Templemore town and park, 1840. The landscape of landed society: the
planned town of Templemore stands at the edge of the Carden family's demesne,
complete with parkland and artificial lake. To the southwest is the Infantry Barracks.
A strong military presence was demanded by the gentry to overawe the disgruntled Catholic population.
Source: os 6–inch 1840, Tipperary sheet 29, NMC C-104740.

of Kiltillane but lies at the edge of the Carden family's Templemore demesne.
The laying out of the demesne and the creation of Templemore Lake probably
date from the same period as the establishment of the town, for the ruins of the
old church lie deep within the park while the new church is contemporaneous
with the town foundation. The appearance of the town is dramatic and its
landlord origins are unmistakable, for it consists of substantial houses built
around a huge rectangular marketplace. The naming of the road at the western
end of the marketplace for King George is typical of eighteenth-century
foundations, and Church Street to the northeast is aligned specifically to
provide a vista of the tower of the new Protestant church consecrated in
1794.[99]

The establishment of Templemore provided more employment opportunities for Roman Catholics than it did for Protestants, if the population figures
are any guide. Nevertheless, the town soon gained a respectable population of
Protestant tradesmen to add to the small number of gentlemen that had been

the denomination's main representatives in the parish a generation before. The parochial registers[100] yield the names of twenty-three tradesmen who settled in the town between 1791 and 1803. Their occupations indicate that Templemore was a typical rural service centre with a small weaving sector noticeable after 1799. The register reveals the presence of four shop-keepers, two shoemakers, two whitesmiths, a butcher, mason, tailor, saddler, cooper, and woolcomber, and seven weavers, one of them a stuff-weaver and another a weaver of carpets. A local story states that Sir John Carden brought thirty weavers who were Orange Protestants from the North in the late eighteenth century and built houses for them in New Row, but that the experiment failed after fifteen or twenty years and the weavers returned to the North or emigrated to America.[101] This story could not be documented, but most of the names of weavers listed in the parish register before occupations ceased to be given in 1803 are names familiar in the North Tipperary region, and a number of Templemore weavers later emigrated to Canada.

The destruction of contemporaneous records from other parishes makes it impossible to trace the origins of most of the migrants into Templemore but certainly a substantial number did come from within the region. Two families, the Guests and Whites, came from the neighbouring rural parish of Killea, the Hardys probably from Nenagh, the Dolmages no doubt from the Palatine colony at Kilcooly to the south, the Evanses, Prowds, and Dudleys from the King's County panhandle, the Talbots from Roscrea in the same area, and Henry Sides probably from Queen's County to the east. There are some traces of chain migration into Templemore in this period. William Evans arrived in 1797, married a Guest who had moved in from Killea, and settled down as parish clerk. Two years later George Evans of Moystown, King's County, arrived and married another Guest. William Dolmage, who appeared in 1802, was followed by John in 1803, and a large interrelated contingent of Talbots, Fitzgeralds, and Howards, many of them weavers, arrived beginning around 1801. Thus a parish which had contained an insignificant number of Protestant inhabitants in the mid-eighteenth century secured the beginnings of a large Protestant concentration by gradual migration from surrounding parts of the region. This core grew increasingly until maps and valuation records of the 1840s showed a densely populated town with many people living in rows of houses erected by early tenants in lanes off the central marketplace,[102] and a population in 1841 of 3685.[103] Twelve per cent of the population in 1831 was Protestant, a large proportion for the region.

Landlord promotion of town-building is documented also at Dunkerrin in 1767 and at Kinnitty some fifty years later. The Rolleston family drafted a prospectus of its village of Dunkerrin, which was in the heartland of local Protestant settlements in the King's County panhandle. However, nothing came of Mr Rolleston's vows "forthwith to build several Houses in the Town and to Expend a Good deal of Money he is now borrowing in such building and for the Encouragement of Manufactorers in his said Town." Dunkerrin remained a hamlet.[104] A modest but more successful attempt at village promotion occurred further north at Kinnitty in the early nineteenth century. The Rev. Mr Maude noted in 1820 that the Protestant population there "must have increased within a few years, as Kinnitty is a new place, & the bulk of the protestants reside there."[105]

Thus Protestant colonization continued into the early nineteenth century, frequently at the expense of the local Roman Catholic population as landlords indicated a preference for Protestant tenants or employees. Additional Protestant "colonies" developed in the North Tipperary area in parishes at a distance from those established by the new gentry in the late seventeenth century, sometimes as communities of privileged freeholding farmers, and sometimes as populations of tradesmen or labourers residing in newly established towns and villages. In the eighteenth and nineteenth centuries, however, these colonies were the product of internal migration, largely from within the region, rather than of immigration from England.

THE SHIFTING PROTESTANT-CATHOLIC BALANCE

While Louis Cullen has recently written that Ireland's rate of population increase was unusual only prior to 1750, and that after that date the continued increase was more or less in line with general European levels,[106] Ireland was different from England in that this rise in population was neither caused nor accompanied by industrialization. Ireland remained a rural country, with the exception of the Belfast region in the hitherto backward north. Though it now appears that demographic adjustments by the residents of the island slowed this rate of increase in the twenty-five years before the Famine of the 1840s, this accommodation was made less effectively in the impoverished western counties. Tipperary, which in many ways occupied a transitional position in terms of economic and social trends, was the most easterly of the counties whose population continued to grow most quickly up to the eve of the Famine. This population expansion in a purely agricultural area increased the demand for land and contributed to social disruptions and disturbances in the county, particularly in the second quarter of the nineteenth century. These circumstances encouraged early emigration by those financially able to undertake it, the tradesmen and middling farmers of whom Protestants in North Tipperary made up a large proportion. In addition, differential growth rates of the Protestant and Roman Catholic populations of North Tipperary made the Protestants a declining minority increasingly at odds with a disgruntled and assertive Catholic majority. This feeling of insecurity also inclined many of the Protestant inhabitants towards emigration.

TABLE 2

Barony Populations, 1793 and 1841

Barony	Houses 1793	Inhabited Houses 1841	Increase
Lower Ormond	3640	8137	×2.2
Upper Ormond	1807	4279	×2.4
Owney and Arra	2073	4941	×2.4

Sources: 1793 figures compiled from lists of inhabitants, no longer extant, required under the Militia Act to be posted on church doors before balloting. E.H.
Sheehan, Nenagh and Its Neighbourhood (Nenagh 1976), 82. 1841 figures from
census.

Regional statistical material is sketchy, but figures copied from a 1793
muster return indicate the numbers of houses in the three North Tipperary
baronies at that date, and these figures may be compared with statistics from
the censuses of 1821 and 1841, the last before the Famine (see Table 2).

The growth rate before 1821 appears to be in accord with the general trend
in Ireland as a whole. According to Connell, the island's population rose from
about 4,048,000 in 1781 to 6,802,000 in 1821,[107] a growth of 68 per cent or
×1.7. Between 1793 and 1821 the number of houses in Lower Ormond grew
from 3640 to 5965, a growth of 64 per cent or ×1.6.

We need not concern ourselves here with the reason for the general
population increase, as it is likely that in the eighteenth century the trend was
European and not one specific to Tipperary or indeed to Ireland. Recent
studies of Irish population growth have suggested, however, that in the first
two decades of the nineteenth century "Irish population may have been
increasing at a rate unparalleled in Western Europe at that time," but that the
residents of the island made demographic adjustments in the face of a
deteriorating economy which substantially reduced the growth rate in the
1820s and especially the 1830s.[108] The national pattern disguises significant
regional variations in growth, however. O Gráda's recalculation of county
growth rates based upon census age structures indicates that while the rate of
population growth declined everywhere between 1821 and 1841, the decline
was least significant in the west. Significantly for purposes of the present
study, Tipperary and Clare were the only two counties that consistently
ranked amongst those with the most rapidly growing populations in both the
1800–21 and 1821–41 periods.[109]

There is also evidence to suggest that the Protestant and Roman Catholic
populations may not have been increasing at the same rate. Had the 1766
religious census survived in its entirety, we would have had a basis for
comparing the numbers and distribution of the Protestant and Roman Catholic
populations at that date with those recorded in a parliamentary return of the
1830s.[110] As it stands, the 1766 returns exist for a few southern parishes of the

TABLE 3

Protestant and Catholic Population by Parish, 1766 and 1831

Parish	Year	Protestant no.	%	RC no.	%	Total	Increase Prot.	RC	Total
Nenagh Union*	1766	563	15	3176	85	3739			
	1831	813	6	12894	94	13707	×1.4	×4.1	×3.7
Ballingarry &	1766	c184	26	c511	74	c695			
Uskane	1831	480	13	3146	87	3626	×2.6	×6.2	×5.2
Newport Union**	1766	574	12	4052	88	4626			
	1831	428	5	8457	95	8885	×0.8	×2.1	×1.9
Templemore	1766	83	20	329	80	412			
	1831	634	12	4583	88	5218	×7.6	×13.9	×12.7
Killea	1766	64	7	817	93	881			
	1831	61	4	1430	96	1491	×0.9	×1.8	×1.7
Glankeen	1766	c95	5	c1720	95	c1815			
	1831	118	2	6467	97	6585	×1.2	×3.8	×3.6
Kilfithmone,									
Barnane, &	1766	c35	15	c230	85	c265			
Killoskehan	1831	75	4	1474	96	2049	×2.1	×6.4	×7.7

Sources: PRO, Dublin, 1766 Religious Returns; 1831: HC (1835) XXXIII.
* Nenagh, Killodiernan, Knigh, and Monsea.
** Kilnerath, Kilcomenty, and Kilvellane.

study area that were in the diocese of Cashel,[111] and a transcript survives for the parishes of Ballingarry and Uskane in Lower Ormond.[112] As well, Tenison Groves copied the statistical breakdowns for Nenagh parochial union from the parish register before it was destroyed in the Record Office fire in 1922.[113] The Ballingarry and Uskane returns give the names of heads of families but not the size of the families, while the Nenagh table provides only statistics but does give the numbers both of families and of individuals, as do some of the Cashel returns. A comparison of the 1766 and 1831 figures reveals some important demographic trends (see Table 3).

The figures display considerable variations in the rates of population increase. The extraordinary thirteen-fold increase at Templemore is readily explained by the establishment of the market town in that hitherto rural parish in the 1780s. The population of the rural part of the parish approximately tripled between 1766 and 1831, which is in line with the trend in some other parishes. In Nenagh Union, which included the region's most important market town, the population rose by 3.7 times. In the rural parishes of Ballingarry and Uskane, on the Ormond plain north of Cloughjordan, the increase was of the order of 5.2 times. At Glankeen in the southern mountains the increase was 3.6 times, similar to that in Nenagh. It is probable that, as in Templemore, landlord activity would prove to be the cause of some of the variable rates of growth, had the relevant documentation survived.

Quite apart from confirming that North Tipperary shared in the general Irish pattern of substantial population growth, Table 3 depicts quite clearly the differential rate of growth between the Protestant and Roman Catholic populations. In Nenagh Union the Protestant population grew by 250 while the Catholic population increased by 9718; the Protestant population did not quite grow by half while the Catholic population more than quadrupled. The difference was also notable in some of the farming areas, particularly in Ballingarry and Uskane where the general rate of increase was greater. Here the Protestants more than doubled but the Catholic population multiplied sixfold. Even the flood of Protestants into the new town at Templemore, which saw the Protestant population there take a sevenfold increase, from 83 to 634, was much exceeded by a fourteen-fold Catholic influx which raised the Irish Catholic population from 329 to 4583.

In all cases the proportion of Protestants in the population fell dramatically, from 15 to 6 per cent in Nenagh, and from 26 to 13 per cent in Ballingarry. In some cases the Protestant population fell in absolute as well as in relative terms. The decline at Killea is perhaps explained by migration into Templemore, but the sizeable Protestant population around Newport substantially declined as well. Protestant emigration, mostly in the nineteenth century, was responsible for some of the decrease. In a few instances this is documented by religious statistics for 1820 that appear reliable.[114] The Church of Ireland rector at Borrisokane reported 681 Protestants in 1820, and noted that the Protestant population had declined during the last ten years as a consequence of the departure of sixteen families for America. Several of these, at least, went to Upper Canada in 1818. The Protestant population had declined by a further 42 to 639 by 1831, with emigration from that parish in particular being encouraged by Protestant fears following a riot and ensuing trial in 1829. However, it is also possible that the Catholic population was outbreeding the Protestant, though if this is so it is somewhat surprising that the average household size in 1766 was generally larger for Protestants than for Roman Catholics. The difference in size cannot be completely attributed to servants, for a large proportion of these were Roman Catholic. Better economic circumstances probably account for the larger household size in Protestant families; the correlation of household size and comparative wealth is one often commented upon.[115] The returns certainly reveal that some of the gentry had surrounded themselves with a large entourage.

From the mid-eighteenth century to the Famine of the late 1840s the general population was increasing rapidly in an agricultural country where land available for colonization was fast running out and where industrial employment was lacking. Despite demographic adjustments in the quarter-century preceding the Famine that reduced the growth rate in the island generally, the damage had been done. In the west and notably in County Tipperary this adjustment seems scarcely to have occurred, and population growth continued relatively unabated. Tipperary was in other ways unlike the more westerly counties that it resembled demographically. Its economy was more commercialized and its population less impoverished, though the high rate of population growth became a major contributory cause of serious economic problems and social disturbances in the northern part of the county in the 1830s and 1840s. From a socio-cultural viewpoint, it is significant also that the Protestant proportion of the population declined between 1766 and 1831. Whether this circumstance was a consequence of differential fertility or whether it merely reflected the earlier adoption by Protestants of the option of emigration, the more rapid growth of the Roman Catholic population can only have increased the concern of Protestants who already felt threatened by the new political assertiveness of the Catholic population, aroused in the 1820s by Daniel O'Connell's popular agitation for the right of Roman Catholics to sit in parliament.

CHAPTER THREE

Tensions in an Agricultural Economy

A major part of the explanation for both the emigration of Protestant small farmers and tradesmen from North Tipperary and the spread of endemic violence amongst the Catholic labouring poor of the region lies in the deterioration of the economic condition of both groups in the early nineteenth century. North Tipperary was less developed than the southern part of the county, which combined greater natural fertility of the soil with better access to the major internal markets for produce. It was, nonetheless, an integral part of the commercial economy, and descriptions of agriculture in the early years of the century paint pictures of prosperity and progress. However, the continuing high rate of population growth, which was surpassed only in some counties of the far west, most adversely affected the poor, and the agricultural prosperity reflected in newspaper accounts of the 1840s was not experienced by the increasing proportion of the population that consisted of impoverished smallholders and labourers. The economic situation in North Tipperary was made worse by the peculiar social structure of the area. The resident gentry in the most fertile part of the region were gentlemen of moderate means and small estates who were themselves adversely affected by the economic troubles of the early nineteenth century. The uncertainty of rents forced many of them to seek economic survival by enlarging their demesne farms and converting tillage to more profitable pastoral uses. These practices drove tenants and labourers from the lands that could best support them and were major contributory causes of the distress of the common people.

Nor was there any significant internal outlet for the burgeoning population. The need for agricultural labour was already oversupplied by the second quarter of the century, and relief could not be found in the towns and villages, which were merely rural service centres dependent upon the prosperity of the agricultural sector. There was virtually no manufacturing in the region, and what extractive industries existed had never been of great significance and were in any case declining by this time. The government attempted unsuccessfully to stimulate local manufactures in the late 1820s and did manage to improve communications significantly. Transportation developments facilitated marketing of the products of commercial agriculture but did little to alleviate the worsening plight of the smallholders and labourers who eked out a bare subsistence from low wages and patches of potato ground.

The small and middling farmers were quite literally caught in the middle of an increasingly polarizing society. Realizing that they faced an uncertain economic future in Ireland and that in the absence of alternative sources of employment their children would depend upon subdivision of parental land for a livelihood, many seized the opportunity to sell out their interests and emigrate to Canada. Emigration from the region at first drew mostly upon this class of people, in large part Protestants. Most of the labourers did not have the means to choose this option, and the polarization of North Tipperary society between the gentry and large commercial farmers on the one hand and the smallholders and labourers on the other was further emphasized by the withering away of the class of middling farmers through subdivision and emigration. The endemic disturbances for which North Tipperary became infamous in the second quarter of the nineteenth century were largely the result of this polarization and were a further cause of emigration by the small farmers.

AGRICULTURE IN NORTH TIPPERARY

Descriptions of agriculture in the North Tipperary region in the eighteenth and early nineteenth centuries emphasized the improving efforts of the prosperous farmers, many of whom were members of the landed gentry. This focus was perhaps inherent in the nature of such studies, which were written by men such as Arthur Young and Charles Coote who were concerned with ameliorating agricultural practices. On the eve of the Famine of the 1840s, agricultural practices were still improving and in some small respects enlightened techniques had attracted the attention of the small farmers for the first time within the past several years. But the focus of attention in the 1840s was upon the problems of the labourer and the small farmer, who seemed to sink ever lower no matter what the state of the commercial economy. There were areas of Ireland where the misery of the common people was far worse, but it was in North Tipperary that local responses to economic problems were causing the most severe social disturbances. In 1812 Wakefield wrote enthusiastically of the tillage lands of North Tipperary, King's, and Queen's. He stated that agricultural practices were good in comparison with other districts, that a systematic course of cropping was followed, and that the land was well maintained. He found turnips, that mainstay of agricultural promoters, "universally growing" either side of the county boundary west of

Roscrea, and pronounced this locality one of the few areas of ideal turnip-land in Ireland.[1] In 1846 the *Parliamentary Gazetteer* made no mention of agricultural improvements in the area and singled out Tipperary as a county in which "the ruinous system of con-acre is extensively prevalent";[2] rents were said to be among the highest in Ireland, certainly the highest outside the hinterland of Dublin.[3]

The *Gazetteer's* concise if over-generalized characterizations of agriculture in each county on the eve of the Famine provide a convenient method of putting the situation in Tipperary in context. The counties may be categorized into four general classes. Much of the eastern coastal region and the county of Fermanagh in western Ulster may be termed, using the *Gazetteer's* terminology, "improving" counties. Here the estates were of varying sizes, but farms were generally small, husbandry was improving, much grain was grown, and rents were correspondingly high. Counties Meath, Longford, and Limerick were singled out as counties in which grazing was especially significant. Husbandry there was poor, though grains were grown, and rents were generally high because of the prosperous pastoral sector. The far west, from Cork to Mayo, and including also Donegal, comprised a generally impoverished, backward region in which estates were often vast but farms were small and miserable and often held in partnership. Husbandry was very bad, potatoes were the universal crop, and rents were low in this depressed region. Much of central Ireland ranged between these two extremes with conditions being generally better in the southeastern part of the central region, in Leinster, than in the Connaught and west-Ulster counties to the north. In central Ireland estates were large and farms small, as in the west, and husbandry was backward, but grain was grown as well as potatoes and higher rents reflected the greater productivity of the land. Tipperary was part of this central region that was neither markedly improving nor beyond hope, but the compilers of the *Gazetteer* chose to mention Tipperary as a county in which the "miserable con-acre system" prevailed.[4] As we have seen, Tipperary was the most eastern county to experience a disastrously high rate of population growth through the first half of the century, and the dependence of the people on potato ground was a consequence of this circumstance.

As J.H. Johnson has pointed out, the agricultural regions of Ireland do not neatly categorize into a commercial, maritime economy in the east and an impoverished subsistence economy in the west when one looks beyond county boundaries. No region was "identical throughout its own area,"[5] and peculiar local circumstances are frequently the major factors that explain peculiar local situations.

The roots of nineteenth-century agrarian society in Tipperary may be traced to the Cromwellian confiscations. From the late seventeenth century the new Cromwellian gentry developed large, compact farm units and extensive landlord demesnes in the county. Much of the native population was pushed down the social ladder into the position of labourers. Through the greater part of the eighteenth century the gentry expanded the area under pasturage in the northern part of the county by converting tillage land.[6] Cattle-rearing was practised by the gentry and by the larger farmers. Most of the latter were Protestant tenants who benefited from landlords' willingness to let farms on long-term or perpetual leases at a nominal but secure rental. An example of such a pastoral enterprise is provided by the 1749 probate inventory of William Newstead, son of a Cromwellian ensign, who lived at Derrynaslin in the parish of Ardcrony. £155 of his total valuation of £192 was accounted for by cattle and sheep, consisting of 44 bullocks, 3 milch cows, 2 shippens, 2 heifers, 4 yearlings, 2 horses, 140 ewes, 35 hoggits, 2 rams, and 85 lambs.[7]

When the English agricultural writer Arthur Young visited North Tipperary in the 1770s, pasturage was extensive in the lowland parts of the region. In the King's County, tillage was "very inconsiderable ... not one acre in fifteen is tilled."[8] Nonetheless, the area in tillage had doubled in the past twenty years, and tillage was also increasing in the Ormonds. Young attributed this circumstance to bounties offered on the shipment of flour to Dublin, which had occasioned the building of mills in the area. Rising grain crops in turn boosted whisky production in the neighbourhood.[9] Sheep were also raised for breeding in Lower Ormond.[10] In the mountains of Owney and Arra there was "no regular system of cattle" outside the gentlemen's demesnes, but even there the influence of the pastoral economy was felt, for the main crop was oats and "the rule is to take as long as the land will yield, and then leave it to recover itself by weeds."[11]

In 1801 when Charles Coote wrote a detailed description of King's County, the operators of large farms in the lowland areas were mostly concerned with the raising of sheep. The smaller farms on higher, drier lands were devoted to the production of wheat, oats, barley, and potatoes, but the emphasis of the large farmers was still upon grazing.[12] In Clonlisk Barony, Coote estimated, some 1500 cattle were fattened. Some were "slaughtered for home use, the country being much inhabited by gentry and wealthy farmers," and the rest were exported live. By contrast, 15,000 sheep were raised for export via Dublin and Limerick, and many of the sheep-raisers had farms in adjoining Tipperary to which they sometimes moved their animals.[13] Dairying had been extensively practised in Clonlisk, but the gentry had lately begun instead to grow grain on a larger scale than was required for home consumption, prompted by high prices for wheat during the Napoleonic Wars. The wheat was sold in Nenagh and Roscrea or to Doolan's mills at Killoge, but the major crops remained oats and barley, which fed two large local distilleries at Kilcommin.[14]

High prices during the Napoleonic Wars continued to be an incentive both to conversion to tillage and to early marriage, owing to rising rural prosperity. Continuing population growth also accelerated the subdivision of holdings.

TABLE 4

Number of Ratepayers by Acreage, Clonlisk
Barony, 1836

Persons Paying County Rates for	no.	%
less than 1 acre	122	10
less than 5 acres	359	28
5–10 acres	257	20
10–20 acres	226	18
20–50 acres	207	16
50–80 acres	54	4
80–100 acres	14	1
over 100 acres	25	2
Total	1264	99

Source: HC (1836) XXXIII, Appendix F, 92.

The change was apparent by 1801, though the rising population did not yet pose a problem. Young had considered a farm of 300 or 400 acres small, but by Coote's time a generation later the size had considerably declined: "Farms were formerly very large in this district; it was not uncommon for one person to hold one thousand or fifteen hundred acres, but their size is now very considerably curtailed, and may be rated from ten to four hundred acres; large farms may have, in the mean, about two hundred and fifty, and small plots about twenty."[15] In Clonlisk barony, Mr Lloyd of Gloster told Coote of 3000 acres of pasture formerly held by four farmers that by 1801 had been subdivided into "one hundred distinct plots, and all under tillage."[16] In Ballybritt barony, near Birr, the farms measured from ten to 100 acres, "except some few extensive graziers."[17]

Depressed conditions following the end of the wars in 1815 were the downfall of many of the small farmers. It was reported in Clonlisk barony in 1836 that "a good many small dispossessed tenantry may be found among the labourers. Many small farmers were ruined in the hard times, about a dozen years ago. Their condition must have been more comfortable as holders of land than as laborers, for the possession of land always adds, more or less, to a family's comforts."[18] Most of the land was in tillage by this time, following a course of alternating wheat and potato crops without fallow, supported only by the fortuitous abundance of lime and limestone gravel in the neighbourhood. Subdivision continued. A witness to a parliamentary commission in the 1830s reported that the size of farms in Clonlisk had decreased owing to "tenants giving portions of their farms to some members of their families who could not get ground elsewhere," and another reported that "it is almost impossible to prevent tenants subdividing their farms among the members of their family who get married."[19] The number of smallholdings in the barony was considerable, as Table 4 indicates. In every parish, however, large grazing farms still existed, "held by one or two large farmers or gentlemen."[20]

Evidence of subdivision of earlier farms is apparent in Protestant as well as Catholic communities. The tithe applotment book of Modreeny parish provides evidence that the Protestant townlands in the Newtown area had formerly consisted of large farms, often coterminous with the townlands themselves. By the 1820s these had been subdivided into farms of twenty to fifty English acres, with a multiplicity of smallholdings, and the residents lived for the most part in small hamlets of two, three, or four dwellings grouped around the original homestead. In the case of the Guest properties in Garraun and Newtown (Guest), five and three people of this name, respectively, held proportionally related acreages in 1826–7, suggesting subdivision of larger units. In both instances the homesteads formed clusters. The entire townland of Kyleashinnaun, where the residents lived in close proximity in an elongated hamlet or cluster of farmsteads, was held in parcels of about nineteen acres, though one holding was twice as large as the other six. Divided among three surnames, this pattern of land-holding probably also represents the breakup of a larger unit, in this case a partnership, with perhaps some later subdivision among heirs. The same comment applies to the ten-acre parcels in Burnwood (Little), where there were two hamlets.[21]

Similarly, in the Mountshannon area the large farms in Clonrush parish that had been leased by the Croasdailes to the farmers they brought in from Clare were divided in succeeding generations. John Long's holding of 91 acres and half of Ballenruane Mountain, let to the family in 1745, was in 1830 held by his sons and grandsons: George 39 acres, Michael 14, Ben and Ben Jr each 10, and John 12, with each also holding a share of the mountain grazing.[22] George Clarke's 97–acre holding in Clonolia in the same year was held by seven descendants. The Bourchiers, Hollands, and other Protestant families in the vicinity had also multiplied in their townlands. Some holdings could not be further divided without reducing their occupants to poverty. The families continued to occupy pews in Mountshannon Church by extended family, with sittings allocated to "Messrs Geo & Benj Long & all the Longs of Ballynagough," "all the Clerk family of Cloonolia," "The Bourchiers, John Bouchier of Clonam[erin] & Tom Henry & Jas. Bourchier & all the Bouchiers."[23] Population pressures were even greater in the vicinity of Mountshannon village, where the bulk of the Protestant population were poor labourers amd weavers. The local clergyman stated in 1823 that "the population of the part of the Country they inhabit is redundant beyond conception, and the soil barren and unable to support a large number."[24]

In Ireland generally, the form of tenure granted by the landlords became more restrictive as the population grew. As demand for land drove up rents, the gentry relet directly to the occupying tenants for shorter terms at rents reflecting current market prices, bypassing the "middlemen" who had held much of the region on long-term lease in the eighteenth century. Coote noted in 1801 that the current term in King's County was generally twenty-one years or one life, whereas thirty-one years or three lives had been "the more general and more ancient term."[25] Although leasing was still generally practised in Clonlisk in 1836, tenancy at will was reported to be much more common than previously,[26] and by 1844 annual tenancy and tenancy at will were by far the most common form of tenure.[27] On the Otway estate in 1806, half of the lessees for two or three lives, most of whom held leases of long standing, paid less than ten shillings per acre, while all tenants at will and life lessees paid more than that amount, most paying better than double that sum (see Table 5).

Though tenants at will could be ejected at any time, most remained on the rent rolls for many years, some for over half a century. The later Otways, however, were not averse to ejecting tenants in the interest of estate improvement. The 1824 rental carries an annotation stating that the thirteen tenants on Lissenhall Bog held leases, the counterparts of which were in England, and "there can be no Ejectmts. till the Leases can be g[ot?]." Ejectment of these tenants was at least being contemplated at that time.[28]

Within the region the situation was not everywhere the same. Some landlords were wealthy while others were deep in debt. Some took a keen interest in the improvement of their estates; other appointed agents to collect the rents and seldom visited the locality. The effects of the actions taken by landlords were felt beyond the borders of their own lands, for estates were not independent economic units isolated from the surrounding parishes. Some gentlemen chose solutions to the economic problems they faced that resulted in improved conditions on their own estates but increasing misery on other estates nearby.

SOCIAL STRUCTURE AND AGRARIAN CONDITIONS

The socio-economic relationship with the greatest potential for societal disruption was that between the gentry, who owned the land and derived their income from rents and improved demesne farming, and the impoverished tenantry, many of them labourers, who made up the vast majority of the population. The potential for conflict between these classes was heightened by the fact that much of the fertile lowland area of North Tipperary was home to large numbers of minor gentry holding small estates, measuring only hundreds of acres. Some of these families had lived there since Cromwellian times and had divided their estates among branches of the family or had sublet portions to other gentlemen.[29]

Such small landowners were particularly vulnerable to economic turbulence. Replies to the Devon Commission in 1844 indicate that many of their

TABLE 5

Acreable Rent on Otway Estate, 1806, by Tenure

Acreable Rent	Tenure			
	At Will	Life Lease	2–3 Lives	Longer
0 to 5/-			3	2
5/- to 10/-			4	1
10/- to £1	8	5	2	1
£1 to £1.10	13	18	1	
£1.10 to £2	5	6		
Over £2	4	3	2	
Total 30	32	12	4	

Source: NLI, ms 13,000(8), Rental of the Estates of Henry Otway Esqr in Ireland, 1st May 1806.

Note: Exact sums included in lower category; rents not calculable excluded.

estates were in receivership.[30] Desperate for cash, many gentlemen enlarged their demesne lands in the decade before the Famine and turned from tillage to more profitable pastoral pursuits. Speaking of this region, an observor from County Cork noted in 1844 that "the gentry in the county of Tipperary hold a great deal of land in their own hands, more than any other part that I know of."[31] In addition, many gentlemen found, as the farmers had, that subdividing and giving farms to their children was "the cheapest and readiest way of providing for them."[32] Thus the existence in North Tipperary of a numerous class of resident gentlemen of only moderate means was fundamentally important, for the economic troubles of this class brought them into direct competition with the peasantry for scarce resources, most notably the land itself. In the early 1840s the number of ejectments in Tipperary proportional to population was greater than in any other county but Kerry.[33]

The clearance of tenants from certain estates, either by ejectment for non-payment of rent or by compensating them to quit, lies behind the apparent contradictions in much of the mid-nineteenth literary and statistical evidence on the region. The clearance of one estate led to the settlement of ejected tenants in other places. Thus some parishes experienced the high rates of population growth that characterized the region generally while the populations of other parishes declined. It also explains why some witnesses to parliamentary commissions of inquiry reported subdivision of farms proceeding apace while others insisted that lands were being consolidated. Most witnesses were intimately familiar with conditions prevailing only within a small circle of parishes.

The very different conditions found in various parishes and on various estates, and between upland and lowland parts of the region, call to mind the distinction made by Victorian investigators between "open" and "close" parishes in the agricultural districts of England. The terms open and close referred both to the degree of control exercised by the landlords over all aspects of life on their estates and also to the ease of access to them. In its most extreme formulation, this typology rests on the premise that the preferences of landowners determined the character and social structure of a community. The underlying assumption was that landlords who monopolized estates were determined to keep out the poor because of their fear of increasing rates, and also to exclude or minimize the proliferation of elements that, for economic, esthetic, or ideological reasons, they found undesirable, such as charities, schools, cottages, rural crafts and industries, alehouses, and Nonconformist chapels. However, the need for labour implied that such close parishes of necessity existed in a symbiotic relationship with nearby open parishes with a loose landownership structure. The land in open parishes was owned by non-resident proprietors or smallholders concerned only for the income they could derive from letting miserable accommodation to the multitudes of labourers who daily walked to work on the estates where their labour was required but where they were not permitted to live. Some formulations of the argument have simplified the dichotomy so that resident owners are assumed to have been responsible for close parishes and non-residents for open ones, but the fact of residency, in England and in Tipperary, is not in itself a sufficient explanation. One must look beyond these labels to understand the motivations underlying landlords' actions.[34]

One cannot draw an exact parallel between the English and Irish situations, for until late in the period under consideration poor rates did not exist in Ireland, illicit distillation was at times an uncontrollable problem, and the subversive potential of Protestant nonconformity seemed insignificant when held up against the dangers to the ascendancy posed by the Roman Catholicism of the majority of the population. Nonetheless, the basic premise of the open/close dichotomy held in North Tipperary as much as in Northamptonshire, for in a highly rural society the control of land is the key to social control, should the owner choose to exercise it. Close estates dotted the fertile Ormond plain while the poor huddled in open areas nearby and in greater numbers in the mountains and the towns, two other forms of open settlement.

Agricultural improvement was evident in the early to mid-nineteenth century on the estates of many resident gentlemen who held large acreages in demesne or let them out to large farmers. Such estates were neither overcrowded nor impoverished, but far from being a solution to the problem of rural distress in North Tipperary the existence of such islands of progress only served to emphasize the progressive deterioration of conditions in neighbouring areas, a trend which the activity of improving landlords accelerated. This phenomenon was most obvious on the fertile Ormond plain between Borrisokane and Nenagh. Despite the continuing high rate of population growth in North Tipperary generally, the population actually declined in three of the parishes there. A large proportion of the lands of Ardcrony, Finnoe, and Cloughprior, as well as of the western half of Modreeny, was held in demesne by minor gentry.[35] The whole of Finnoe parish was mostly pasture land.[36] The socio-economic consequences of this circumstance did not go unremarked by contemporary observers. One local gentleman, William Henry Head of Modreeny House, attributed the social disturbances of the early 1840s to the peculiar pressures to which the labouring class was subjected by the presence of a numerous minor gentry:

Generally speaking, it is considered that the greater the number of resident landed proprietors in a district, the greater is the probability of its prosperity. Now, it may certainly appear paradoxical, but it has occurred to me to think that in some parts of the country the contrary may be the case, and that this is to be accounted for by considering how such resident landed proprietors are circumstanced in relation to the lower orders. In those parts to which I refer, they will be found, I think, to consist in a great degree of a great number of very small proprietors, among whom I include myself. The district is dotted over with small landowners in the upper classes, who are generally anxious for the possession of land. This tends to bring them into collision with the lower orders, and there is a struggle between them for the land itself.

Mr Head's description of the consequences of this social structure is highly reminiscent of English descriptions of the creation of open parishes by the closing of others:

[Question:] Has the desire to possess land led to the dispossessing of many of the small holders? – [Answer] I think it has; a great deal of land, I should say, has been got up from the small occupiers within the last few years, and been thrown into the larger farms. The peasantry seem to be huddled together, as it were, on particular spots, in numbers far too great to be supported by the land they occupy ... In a country not so occupied by small landowners, of course the proprietors, especially of extensive ones, do not interfere in the manner I have described with the land, and therefore I think the estates of absentees are often better circumstanced and their tenants more comfortable, than where there are a great number of small resident proprietors.[37]

Head also stated that the labour required by the grazing farms established by the gentry was obtained from surrounding areas: "Many of them belong to the class of small farmers, more are only lodgers, and take what is called quarter ground every year to supply them with potatoes. I do not think that the cottier system of labourers seems to prevail much. It is more usual to get your labourers from the estates of other people ... the latter class (whom I may term mercenaries) are much to be preferred as workmen to the cottier tenants."[38]

The appropriation by gentry proprietors of this large territory of fertile land between Borrisokane and Nenagh for grazing no doubt was the cause of the appropriation of much of the adjoining Commons of Carney in Finnoe and Cloughprior parishes by squatters. In 1836 the parish priest of Kilbarron Union reported that the 150 acres of the "Commons of Kearney" had been "much more extensive 50 years ago, but [was] now appropriated by landholders, to their own use." George Atkinson, JP, reported that the public common in Cloughprior was "now occupied by people having settled on it."[39]

The existence of open areas like the Commons of Carney adjacent to close areas of demesne land was also parallelled in the other parishes of the Ormond plain. Clearance for demesne grazing occurred also at Lorrha,[40] but not all landlords ejected tenants to expand pastoral farming. Some of the larger landowners attempted to throw farms together under improving tenants to ameliorate tillage agriculture, as at Birr, where attempts were made to increase farms to thirty or forty acres,[41] at Johnstown Park,[42] and on the estate of Mr Saurin.[43] Lord Ossory also attempted to consolidate large farms for his tenants, while Mr Carden of Barnane, a relative of the owner of Templemore, turned people out of mountain land for plantation purposes and to enlarge the park around his new house.[44]

An excellent illustration of the symbiotic relationship that existed between close and open estates was to be found southeast of Ardcrony. The parish of Ballymackey was dominated by the demesne lands of a numerous minor gentry and by the lands of large farmers leasing from them, while the parish of Ballygibbon immediately to the north was the residence of numerous impoverished labourers. Significantly, the population of Ballymackey increased by less than 7 per cent between 1821 and 1841 while that of Ballygibbon rose by nearly 75 per cent. In absolute terms, the increase in Ballygibbon (565) was three times that in Ballymackey (198), which in 1821 had four times the population of the smaller parish.[45] The Poe, Freeman, and Toler estates in Ballymackey had long before been sublet to resident minor gentry or set to middlemen who leased in turn to large farmers. Several townlands at the extremities of the Cole Bowen estate in the central part of the parish were in 1850 still let partly to middlemen and occupied by small farmers and labourers.[46] However, they were not so divided as they had been in 1825, and witnesses to the Devon Commission reported in 1844 that Henry Cole Bowen had enlarged his farms, notably in the 1830s by ejecting some undertenants from Clash when a middleman's lease fell in. The local population resisted, and two murders occurred on the estate in this period.[47] There were thus few labourers on most of the estates in Ballymackey and many demesnes were completely without them. In the eastern part of Ballygibbon parish, however, a multitude of labourers, many with small-holdings, crowded onto the boggy lands of Fitzgerald of Glenahilty and especially in Kylenaheskeragh. Fitzgerald had come into ownership since

MAP 8   Ballygibbon and Ballymackey, 1840. Open and close parishes in North Tipperary: the extensive demesne farms of Ballymackey parish were worked by labourers who lived in the eastern townlands of Ballygibbon. The genteel landscape of the former parish, with its wide open spaces, contrasted with the crowding of the poor into the latter.
Source: os 6–inch maps, 1840.

1824 and was non-resident. His neglect of the estate is apparent, for the valuators were unable even to learn his full name. Twenty-seven other labouring families occupied houses, often without land, to the north in Bantis townland, holding from partners who were middlemen under Lord Norbury.[48] The number of labourers was probably greater before the Famine of the late 1840s devastated the labouring class.

Though estate population patterns are often concealed by the collection of

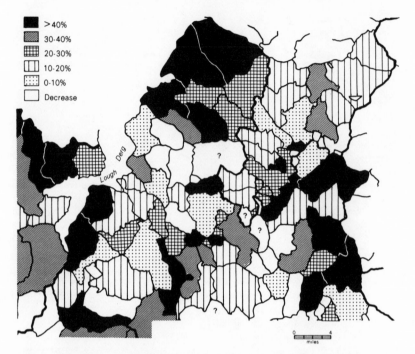

MAP 9   Percentage of population increase, 1821–41, by parish. Population rises in
an inverse proportion to the quality of the land. The population in pastoral parishes
of the Ormond plain actually declined in this period as the numerous minor
gentry converted from tillage to stockraising in an attempt to stave off bankruptcy.
The dispossessed gathered in the mountain parishes that ringed the commercial
farming district.
Source: HC (1824) XXII; HC (1852–3) XCI.

figures at the parish level, other examples of symbiotic relationships between
neighbouring estates are noted in the evidence gathered by parliamentary
commissions. The estate at Templemore of Sir Henry Carden, a "most
attentive" resident landlord, was "in the highest state of cultivation and
improvement" in 1844 whereas the adjoining absentee estate of Lord
Portarlington at Borrisoleigh was reported to be "in a state of complete ruin
and tottering down." Carden's estate was "not over-peopled" and had been
consistently well-managed by the owner's family, but the cheering prospect
of the Carden estate must have been at least partly responsible for conditions
on the neighbouring lands, where the non-resident landlord was less diligent
and did not attempt to maintain a prosperous estate by keeping his tenants in
terror of him as Carden did.[49]
    The area that perhaps most closely resembled Mr Head's neighbourhood
near Borrisokane, however, was Clonlisk barony in the King's panhandle east

of Cloughjordan. This part of the plain, too, was a bewildering network of small estates and was home to a numerous resident gentry. Here, however, the land was "principally in tillage, and much cut up into small holdings, and very populous." The gentry managed more or less to arrest further subdivision in Clonlisk by the 1840s, but were not able to increase their own demesnes: "the gentry holding the large farms are not disposed much to break them up, and as rent is very often very badly paid, they continue to hold them themselves."[50]

The mountain areas that ringed the Ormond plain of North Tipperary may, like certain parts of the lowland areas, be characterized as open territories. It has become a commonplace of Irish rural history that "population densities generally increased in an inverse relationship to the quality of the land."[51] Because mountain land had little potential for commercial agriculture, landlords often exercised little control in such areas. Their neglect allowed those without the capital to locate elsewhere to colonize marginal lands and permitted partnership farming and subdivision of holdings to continue. The agglomeration of large farms in the lowland areas of North Tipperary of course led to the accumulation of population in the hill and bogland areas.[52] The pattern becomes readily apparent when one maps population growth between 1821 and 1841 on a parish basis.[53] The greatest increases in population occurred in a ring of upland parishes surrounding the Ormond baronies and the King's panhandle, from Mountshannon south through Killaloe and Newport, east along the range of hills north of Templemore to Roscrea, and northward east of Birr and across the flatter land of Lorrha and Dorrha to County Galway again. The absence of landlord control in upland parishes was reflected in this uncontrolled population growth, and it was mainly these heavily populated areas that contributed to Tipperary's continuously high aggregate rate of increase.

The old Irish system of farming in partnership survived in the mountainous parishes of the region, which in some ways resembled the western counties of Ireland more than the commercial agricultural region of the Ormond plain. In the hills of Ikerrin barony, south of Roscrea, partnership farming was still practised in a fifth of the townlands when the Primary Valuation was made in 1850. To the west in Kilnamanagh and in the Arra mountains this proportion rose to half.[54] In the 1770s Arthur Young had considered the farms in Arra to be "small, none above 300 or 400 acres: many are taken in partnership, three, four, or five families to 100 acres. They divide the land among themselves, each man taking according to his capital."[55] Two generations later the mountain farms were smaller but the landlord system was still "only a thin veneer overlying a system of landholding which one suspects has changed least in character from the mid-seventeenth century."[56]

In another sense, too, the hills of Duharrow, the Keeper, and the Slieve Bloom mountains resembled the "open parishes" of Victorian England, for these wild territories were a refuge for outlaws. As open parishes were

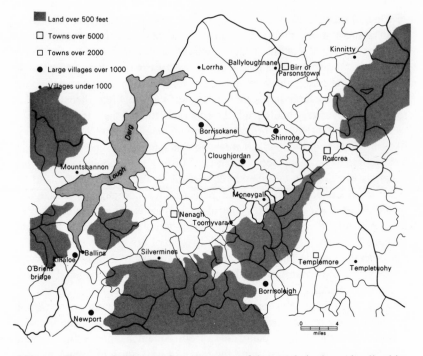

MAP 10   Towns and villages, 1821. A quarter of the people in the region lived in towns and villages, but these places were service centres dependent upon the agricultural sector for their prosperity; there was no industry here.
Source: 1821 census.

frequently havens for bandits and highwaymen, so the disaffected, the dispossessed, and the criminal found refuge in the hills of Tipperary, and neighbourhoods like Borrisoleigh were traditional centres of unrest. It has also been suggested that the system of partnership farming contributed to disorder in another way. Because agricultural partnerships were most often based upon the co-operation of relatives, they may have contributed to the prevalence in the district of faction fighting, a semi-ritualized, feud-like combination of territorialism, grievance resolution, and recreational violence that frequently pitted kin-based gangs of country people against one another in violent affrays at fairs and other public gatherings.[57]

Towns and villages constituted a final type of open community. A resident of Nenagh echoed observers of English open parishes when he commented in 1844: "Most of the labourers reside in the towns and villages, as being turned off small farms they heretofore held. And the great misfortune to all in this town is on account of the poor rate. The towns are obliged to support them, which makes this place pay seven times as much as other electoral divisions … I have known three or four families to live in a cabin or house, without an upper apartment, not more than sixteen feet square (that is quite common in Nenagh), in a most wretched and shocking state."[58] Population figures indicate a high rate of increase in Borrisokane. The moderate increase in Birr is probably attributable to the retention of ownership and control by the earl of Rosse, whose ancestors had founded the town more than two centuries before. A Canadian visitor in 1862 described Moneygall and Toomevara as "miserable and poverty-stricken villages ... where many an outrage and faction fight took place,"[59] and it is difficult to imagine how circumstances in the latter place could possibly have been better before the wholesale evictions of the Famine years that live in popular memory as the "Sack of Toomevara."[60]

NON-AGRICULTURAL EMPLOYMENT

Emigration became a particularly attractive option to the Protestants of North Tipperary because, as was the case in most of southern Ireland, there were very few jobs available outside the ailing agricultural and service sectors. The towns provided little outlet for the redundant population for there were almost no manufactures and no organized cottage industry, and the resource extraction industries which did exist in the mountain ranges that fringed the region provided little economic opportunity for local residents.

Town and Village in an Agricultural Society

The nature of life even in the towns and larger villages was intimately interwoven with the rural society of which these communities were a part. As a consequence there was no sharp rural/urban cleavage in this thoroughly agricultural region, and the absence of industry prevented the towns from being anything more than a gathering place for what contemporary investigators termed the redundant population.

As noted before, the village network of the nineteenth century was largely the creation of the landlords of the late seventeenth and eighteenth centuries. About three-quarters of the residents of the region in 1821 lived in the countryside rather than in towns and villages. The number of villages in the region did not greatly exceed the number of towns, and none of these centres was what we would consider an urban place. The nearest city, Limerick, was beyond the region to the west and the vast majority of the region's residents can have had little cause to go there. What evidence exists suggests that even emigrants were as likely to travel to Cork or Dublin as to Limerick to embark for the new world.[61] Only the three major market towns, Nenagh, Birr, and Roscrea, had populations exceeding 5000 in 1821, together comprising 15 per cent of the population, and the next largest centre was the Cardens'

Templemore, with just under 3000 people. The six smaller "towns" were really large villages with populations around 1000: Cloughjordan, Shinrone, Borrisokane, Newport, the cathedral town of Killaloe, and Borrisoleigh.[62] Only eight villages were noted in the census, each inhabited by between 200 and 500 residents, with most at the lower end of the scale. The census listed seven hamlets also, all with fewer than thirty families or 150 inhabitants.

Even the three market towns were low-level central places. Birr (Parsonstown) had no trade more exotic than that of silversmith, and the only hint of manufacturing in 1823, apart from the processing of food, is provided by the six woollen manufacturers listed at Roscrea; only one factory is mentioned there, Henry Buckley's at Hillsborough.[63] Because these towns and villages existed as service centres for the rural area, and secondarily as administrative centres, their residents were dependent upon the prosperity of the agricultural sector for their own well-being. Failures in agriculture sent shock waves through the entire economy and adversely affected everyone in the region.

Probably a majority of the inhabitants of the villages and towns were familiar with agricultural pursuits and many of the more common trades carried on in the towns also had numerous practitioners in the countryside. We have already seen that large numbers of town residents were impoverished agricultural labourers who sought what work they could obtain in the surrounding countryside. In addition, the villages had large areas of garden ground nearby that were used by their inhabitants, such as the Town Parks of Cloughjordan, the plots in Shesheraghmore outside Borrisokane, and the "Burris lands" at Borrisoleigh. Plots of garden ground outside the three market towns were held by only a minority of the population, but there were hundreds of small gardens large enough to be titheable attached to houses within the towns.[64] While tradesmen in the towns often held a smallholding outside it or a garden adjoining their houses, many smallholders in the countryside also worked at a trade. Of seventy-nine farmers in Seirkieran parish in 1821, twenty-one also practised a trade or profession while eight worked out as labourers. Viewed another way, twenty-five of the thirty-nine tradesmen in the parish worked land. Four held only one Irish acre, but the remainder were termed farmers, fifteen holding two to five acres and six from six to twenty.[65] Tradesmen and shopkeepers moved from village to town to countryside and back again as economic opportunities and disasters dictated, and most were never far from the land.

The significant divisions in North Tipperary society were not between urban and rural dwellers but between the gentry and large farmers and the labouring poor. Gentry life, as in most agricultural societies, centred partly around social life and administrative duties in the towns, but equally around their large houses on their rural estates. Many also spent a significant amount of their time in Dublin, and many members of the "county community" were married in the metropolis.

The dispossessed rural poor came into the towns because they had nowhere else to go. Lacking the capital to emigrate, and compensated poorly by their landlords or not at all, they swelled the growing numbers of underemployed labourers. The shopkeepers and craftsmen of both town and countryside were, like the small farmers, caught in the middle. Dependent upon the declining prosperity of the agricultural sector, many of this order, too, sold out their businesses and departed for Canada.

Extractive Industries

The extractive industries were of little significance and offered little employment. The silver and lead mines at Silvermines south of Nenagh were diminishing by the nineteenth century after being worked for several hundred years,[66] and the slate quarries near Killaloe, while thriving in this period, offered limited employment and did not offer any potential for the development of secondary industry or manufacturing the way the mining industry might have done had it been more prosperous.[67] Iron-making had been practised in the Mountshannon area, on the northern shores of Lough Derg, in the seventeenth and eighteenth centuries, but none of the works survived into the nineteenth. They closed down when clearance of the local woodland ended the supply of charcoal used in smelting.[68] In all these industries, too, the seventeenth- and eighteenth-century owners of the mines and works tended to employ foreign workers who were skilled in the tasks at hand rather than to train local people. Some of these immigrant workers were English or Welsh, others were continental Europeans. It is possible that some of the Protestant population of North Tipperary descend from them, but many of these skilled workmen did not become permanent settlers in the region. By the nineteenth century the employees were largely drawn from the Roman Catholic population, and any privileged status granted to such workers was clearly a thing of the past. These small extraction industries did little, however, to fill the growing need for steady employment. Similarly, weavers existed in numbers large enough to be noticeable, but what little large-scale cloth production had been carried on in the region was extinct by the early nineteenth century and weavers then served a purely local market.

Weaving and Cloth Production

The textile industry was of solely domestic importance in Tipperary in the nineteenth century. Cloth production was never carried on extensively in the northern baronies of the county, though in the eighteenth century it had been of some importance at Clonmel in South Tipperary[69] and at Mountmellick and Maryborough in the Queen's County, to the east. Statutes passed in England in the reign of William III had forbidden the export of Irish woollens and reduced the textile industry then existing to production for domestic consumption.[70] Later attempts to promote weaving in the south of Ireland generally failed,[71] as we have seen was largely the case at Templemore. In the eighteenth century sheep-raising was a major activity of the larger farmers, but most of the sheep were raised for breeding rather than wool[72] and were shipped to Dublin and Limerick.[73]

Coote noted in 1801 that there were then no cloth manufacturers in Clonlisk barony, though he felt that the region had numerous sites where factories could be developed. There were only a few serge weavers in the neighbourhood, and some women spun worsted and sold it to manufacturers in Roscrea, of which there were still six in 1823.[74] Coote admitted that "the want of a market is indeed a principal obstacle, for, since premiums have been discontinued at Maryborough in the Queen's County, the county, though never but in a small degree engaged in manufacture, has evidently felt the loss."[75] He also mentioned cloth and serge factories in Birr and "an inconsiderable serge factory" at Leap,[76] and some clothworkers were also employed in the towns and villages in the Tipperary baronies. Ledwich in 1814 lamented the state of the cloth industry in Borris-in-Ossory, on the eastern limits of the study area. He noted that the village "and indeed the whole parish were filled with combers, spinners and weavers" who were forced to become farmers and labourers after passage of the Williamite statutes a century before. In 1814 there were "ten combers, forty-eight spinners, ten stuff-weavers, [and] twelve linen weavers" in the village, but their products were mostly consumed within the parish, a testimony to the large domestic work force needed to clothe even a population that dressed very simply. The spinning efforts of girls produced a surplus of woollen yarn, for which there was often no market.[77]

Some Protestant families made modest fortunes in the woollen industry in the eighteenth century. The progenitor of the Samuel Haskett family that invested in small freeholds and later emigrated to London, Upper Canada, was a comber in Borrisokane.[78] The only emigrant known to have been heavily interested in the cloth industry was also one of the first to leave Ireland. Edward Talbot, an elderly clothier in Roscrea, moved to Templemore around 1800 and emigrated to the United States around 1808, no doubt motivated by the near-extinction of the business at home. His grandsons established extensive woollen mills in Massachusetts, but relatives who remained in Templemore lived as poor weavers until prompted to join friends in Canada by the collapse of trade after the Napoleonic Wars.[79] Emigrant Arthur Hopper's brother-in-law, George Hayes, was a stuff and woollen manufacturer in Castle Street, Roscrea, but though Hayes considered sending some of his family out to join Hopper, none ever emigrated.[80] Francis Hardy was a dyer and presser in Templemore, but in 1830 he disposed of his freehold house in the town for £160 stg[81] and emigrated. Hardy farmed in Canada,[82] but his son Robert, a dyer in Ireland, set up a weaving business on the Richmond Road in Nepean, and afterwards in New Edinburgh. He also worked briefly as a carder in Hull before becoming agent and book-keeper to Nicholas Sparks of Bytown in the late 1840s.[83] A small number of other Protestant emigrants are known to have been weavers in the old country, but weaving was only a locally oriented industry in North Tipperary, not the large-scale, export-oriented cottage industry it was in Ulster. The depressed state of the industry at home was a major cause of the emigration of practitioners of this trade.

ATTEMPTS AT ECONOMIC IMPROVEMENT

By the late 1820s agrarian disturbances were becoming more frequent in the northern baronies of County Tipperary, and the area was fast gaining a reputation for the kind of violent "outrages" that were to become endemic there by the 1840s. The economic backwardness of the area when compared with the more fertile Golden Vale of southern Tipperary was well known to local observers, and this as well as the wildness of the hills south of Nenagh, a refuge for brigands and malcontents of every description, were felt by those knowledgeable of the area to be major contributory causes of the disturbances there, in combination with the generally adverse economic climate and the potentially explosive demographic imbalances.

In 1828 the lord lieutenant, the marquis of Anglesey, put forward a plan for reviving and stimulating the economy of the area. The experiment would have required extensive funding by the British government, which had fundamental reservations about usurping the role of the free market. To its credit the government did complete the extensive roadworks that were part of the plan, though this was done mostly at the expense of the ratepayers of the county. While it is idle to speculate upon what effect Anglesey's suggestions would have had had they been entirely implemented, the proposed remedies illuminate the economic difficulties of the region and indicate that neither the constabulary nor Dublin Castle were entirely insensitive to the needs of the country.

The basis of Anglesey's proposal was to stimulate the improvement of Ireland through the sponsorship of factories. While the south of Ireland in particular was underendowed with natural resources there were areas that were rich in coal,[84] and while one observer pointed out in the 1820s that most waterfalls were occupied by flour mills in such corn-growing counties as Tipperary and Kilkenny,[85] it was still hoped that water power would offer possibilities for industrial development. The major difficulty standing in the way of Irish industrialization was the indisposition of Irish and English capital to invest in a country perceived to be in a state of perpetual disturbance.

Anglesey's proposal to Prime Minister Sir Robert Peel was that encouragement of manufactures and construction of roads as public works be pursued in tandem in the economically stagnant and socially disturbed North Tipperary region. As Anglesey noted to Peel, "you see I wish to take the Bull by the Horns."[86]

Anglesey's choice of area may have been determined by his desire to set an example in a notorious region, but it was undoubtedly confirmed by a perceptive analysis of the state of North Tipperary by Samson Carter, the chief constable of police responsible for the area. Carter explained in a memorandum that the disturbances there were aggressive defensive measures "purely of a Local Nature," adopted as a result of the heavy arrears incurred by farmers since the postwar collapse of agricultural prices and due also to the redundancy of population which had driven up rents and made unemployment a serious problem.

Carter stated that the only way to ameliorate conditions in Tipperary was to improve the economy. He commented on the agricultural situation directly, suggesting that if lands could be sublet at a standard rate, rather than allowing tenancies to be bid to unrealistic levels because of the scarcity of land, farmers would not be forced to resort to extralegal proceedings to defend their interests. He appears to have been uncertain how this could be accomplished, though he suggested that landlords and middlemen might be convinced to come to an "Understanding with the tenants, that if their Farms were not neglected, and Corn &ca was below a *Stated price,* then a Fair abatement would be granted."

Concerning his major proposal, for the improvement of communications throughout the country, Carter had more definite ideas. He particularly urged the construction of roads through the mountainous districts from the Silvermines westward to County Limerick. This, he argued, would have numerous benefits. It would provide "A Vast Field of Employment for the Labouring Classes, Now too Numerous to be supported by the Farmers." It would also open an "almost Inaccessible district" which was the "Refuge of all Outlaws, who the Inhabitants from their present *Unprotected* State are forced to harbour." He noted that the moneys expended on public works in the disturbed areas of County Cork earlier in the decade had shown the efficacy of such a program. The constabulary force accompanying the road-builders would provide protection to the farmers, and the work itself would instil habits of industry in the labourers. The road would provide a "Safe and rapid transit for agricultural produce" to markets where farmers could sell their crop at a fair price rather than to "Some forestaller or agent purchasing for a Capitalist." An improved road network would also result in lower prices for coal, which was needed by the people because of the scarcity of turf in many areas but which nearly doubled in price only fifteen miles from the mines at Killenaule because of the difficulty of carriage.

Finally, Carter suggested government sponsorship of manufacturing. He pointed to the example of a Mr Malcomson, who ran a cotton factory and flour and other mills in Clonmel, Carrick-on-Suir, and other places in the southern part of the county: "Doubtless he was induced by the facilities for Trade in this *Improved* part of the County, to Expend a Large Capital in Building and different Commercial Speculations, but the Result has proved that the Systematic annual Employment given by him at Very Moderate wages, has considerably ameliorated the Condition of the Peasantry and Uninterrupted Tranquillity prevails throughout the Whole of that district, Therefore it may be Expected that the Same System would produce a Similar Effect in any other Part of the Country if equally prepared, or improved." Yet, noted Carter, "Without the aid of Funds from Government as formerly granted for Public Works, and advanced to Individuals in business, who gave proper Securities, there is little Prospect of any beneficial Change in this County."[87]

Anglesey requested "a very trifling" sum of money from Peel to commence road works and to establish a few constabulary barracks in Tipperary, and asked that the government "guarantee to such respectable Capitalists as I shall find to establish Factories of Cotton & Woolen in and near the County, shall be indemnified for any loss they may sustain by violence." He noted that the roads through the mountainous regions would be paid for by the county at the next assizes.[88]

The Anglesey Road from Newport to Thurles was commenced that year and was completed in 1830 at a cost of £9857.[89] In addition, Lewis's *Topographical Dictionary* of 1847 notes that the range of hills delineating the southern edge of the valley of the Shannon, from the Keeper east to the Slieve Bloom mountains, formerly "a wild tract of country" with "scarcely any road passable for wheel-carriages," had by that time been opened by two roads constructed by the government.[90]

It is, however, unlikely that the encouragement of manufactures urged by Chief Constable Carter and the marquis of Anglesey was ever adopted as government policy. Lewis noted that the staple manufacture of wool at Clonmel and Carrick-on-Suir had been suppressed by parliament in the eighteenth century in order to protect the English woollen industry. Aside from a few local manufacturing establishments producing blankets and some failed efforts by the London Society in the 1810s and 1820s to stimulate the linen industry in the county, the cloth trade was nearly extinct by the 1840s and "flour is now the staple manufacture." Lewis mentioned "an extensive cotton manufactory at Clonmel, of recent establishment," which may have been Malcomson's, but noted that "the county may be considered to be devoid of MANUFACTURES of importance."[91] Most plans to stimulate the economy by undertaking public works did little for the common people. The Shannon improvements benefited commercial agriculture but provided only temporary employment for those in the immediate vicinity of the works.[92] Ironically, the improved river transport may have facilitated the export of grain during the Famine. North Tipperary remained an overwhelmingly agricultural region offering few alternative sources of employment for a rapidly growing and increasingly impoverished population.

POLARIZATION, EMIGRATION,
AND UNREST

The fatal flaw of an agricultural district is the dependence of its inhabitants upon a single economic sector. In such regions the old Malthusian argument can come close to realization, not in this instance in the simplistic sense of population outstripping food supply, for North Tipperary's economy did not operate at a bare subsistence level, but in the sense that economic and demographic adjustments were insufficient to maintain the standard of living of most residents. The underdevelopment of other sectors of the economy provided no safety valve. In the absence of a radical political solution, the consequences had to be improvement of agricultural productivity, economic diversification, emigration, or increasing impoverishment.

In North Tipperary all of these consequences were realized, but at different levels of society. The gentlemen and large farmers improved their incomes by converting the land to more profitable uses, but as we have seen their actions merely increased the pressure on land use and drove tenants off improving estates onto others that were already overcrowded. To a degree all classes faced economic difficulties in the years before the Famine. Many of the gentry were in debt, and their attempts to expand demesne agriculture were a response to their financial difficulties. The small and middling farmers faced further subdivision of holdings in order to provide for their children. Their landholdings were the only thing keeping them from experiencing the plight of the labouring poor, and many lost their lands in the hard times following the Napoleonic Wars. But it was the poor labourers, the ejected tenants, and the rural smallholders who depended upon labour to supplement their meagre holdings who could find no progressive solution. The gentry could upgrade their estates at the expense of their tenants. The small farmers found the capital to emigrate. But the labourers seized upon maintenance of the *status quo* as their one hope for survival. The disturbances and "outrages" that typified North Tipperary more than any other part of Ireland in the 1840s were the result of the people's attempt to defend a man's right to the land and employment he already had, without regard to the legal right of the landlords to change existing arrangements.

The remainder of this work is a study of emigration to Canada from North Tipperary, emigration which, as we have seen, was disproportionately Protestant, and drawn mostly from the ranks of the small farmers and rural tradesmen. For many of these people the solution to their deteriorating

TABLE 6

Sizes of Holdings by Religion, Rural Dunalley Estate, Modreeny Parish, c1826

	Gentlemen		Partners		Farms > 20 a		Farms 5–20 a		Farms 2–5 a		Holdings < 2a	
	n	%	n	%	n	%	n	%	n	%	n	%
Prot.	3	3	11	10	12	11	52	49	16	15	13	12
RC	1	0.5	1	0.5	10	9	40	35	28	25	33	29

Source: Landholding data: tithe applotment book. The landless are excluded as they were not titheable. Surnames characterized according to religion based upon Modreeny parish register and Yeomanry lists.
Note: Excluding the Townfields of Cloughjordan and lands held under middlemen in Behamore. Irish plantation acres.

economic condition was to sell their goodwill or their leases and emigrate to the new world where land was inexpensive and abundant. When a Cloughjordan gentleman offered them the opportunity of accompanying him to Canada in 1818, applicants outnumbered places, and the 800 or so Protestant families who followed these few dozen pioneers to the Canadas over the next forty years were equal in number to a quarter of the entire Protestant population of the region in 1831.

It is logical that the vicinity of Cloughjordan was the one from which the first group of emigrants departed, for Cloughjordan was set in the largely Protestant portion of the Dunalley estate that had once belonged to the Harrisons. Much of the population was descended from eighteenth-century tenants who had been granted freeholds as lessees for terms of three lives under Lord Dunalley's ancestors. In the early nineteenth century the freeholds had been divided somewhat, and the bulk of the Protestants were small and middling farmers.

The Dunalley estate in Modreeny was a community of small freeholders and, apart from the village of Cloughjordan, was effectively a closed community. The farmers here worked their lands with family labour and did not require a large labouring population. Half of the Protestants living in the rural portion of the estate were middling farmers holding from five to twenty plantation acres. Over half of the Roman Catholics who held land farmed less than five acres, double the proportion of Protestants in this category. The number of landless labourers is unknown. Though most of this group was probably Catholic, the Ordnance Survey maps of 1840 indicate few cottages in this area.

Dunalley was non-resident – he lived south of Nenagh at Kilboy – and in contrast to the estates immediately to the west there was little land in demesne on his Modreeny estate. English investigators would have recognized some characteristics of an open community here, for landlord control was not oppressive and there were several Nonconformist chapels and numerous tradesmen in the village. But the estate was a special type that was found also in England – a freeholders' community. If the occupiers chose to make money by running up cottages on the margins of their holdings for the poor who worked on other estates, the picture of an open community would be complete. In Modreeny the small and middling farmers held onto the land themselves, reclaimed additional patches from bog,[93] and determined to prevent subdivision by sending supernumerary sons to Canada. As a result the Dunalley estate here was remarkably free from ejectments and from outrages in the 1830s and 1840s. Hundreds of residents left for Canada between 1818 and 1855, allowing preservation of the *status quo* by the farming population. The estate remained effectively closed.

On most other estates the Protestant small farmers were not so numerous and did not make up a substantial, concentrated population by themselves. When they emigrated, landlords in such parishes lamented the withering away of a loyal and supportive tenantry. George Atkinson, Esq., of Shinrone slightly overstated the case but summed up the situation well when he reported in 1836 that "the class of substantial farmers is therefore almost annihilated, or, which is the same thing, transported to America; such is the difficulty of an industrious man of some little capital procuring a piece of ground upon which it would be worth his while to employ himself."[94]

CHAPTER FOUR

The Beginnings of Tipperary Protestant Emigration

The two largest Upper Canadian Tipperary settlements, near London and Ottawa, share a common origin. With the exception of a few precursors who sailed to the United States and later headed north to Canada,[1] and a few soldiers in the predominantly Ulster 99th Regiment who settled southwest of the site of Ottawa in Richmond,[2] the migration from Tipperary to Canada began with a scheme of assisted emigration in 1818. Richard Talbot, a gentleman of Cloughjordan, had been grooming his sons for military careers, but was frustrated by the termination of the Napoleonic Wars. He took advantage of a limited period of government-assisted emigration to put together a group of several dozen Protestant families who sailed with him on the ship *Brunswick*.

However, Talbot's venture was not the first attempt to initiate organized migration to Canada from North Tipperary. In 1815 Francis Armstrong Evans of Roscrea wrote to the Colonial Office seeking official support for the establishment of a Protestant colony in Lower Canada. Evans's hurry to get his experiment under way and his lack of planning doomed the exercise to failure, but his aims and expectations were much the same as Talbot's and his story parallels that of the latter in a number of ways.

FRANCIS EVANS'S ABORTIVE ATTEMPT AT GROUP SETTLEMENT, 1815

Francis A. Evans was probably typical of many of the minor gentry who left the British Isles when faced with a deterioration of status following the Napoleonic Wars. He came of a respectable Protestant family which "suffered much for our partiality to Government,"[3] particularly at the hands of the rebels in and after 1798.[4] He studied law for a time though apparently never qualified as a solicitor.[5] He had also held a lieutenancy in the Galway Militia.[6]

While he stated that his treatment at the hands of disaffected parties in Ireland was the principal cause of his decision to emigrate,[7] the few biographical details available suggest that he was a young gentleman who had met with a reversal of fortune or one who found himself unable to secure a place in a county community flooded with half-pay officers returning from the wars seeking civil positions. He was to note later, in his emigrants' guide, that his contemporaries emigrated "with a view of bettering their condition, or to avoid apprehended changes in their circumstances, to which most persons in the middle and lower classes of society are subject in the united kingdoms."[8] He was a resident of Roscrea, where two children were baptized in July 1814.[9]

Evans resolved upon emigration as a solution to his difficulties. He was offered land by a friend resident in Louisiana, but turned it down because of his attachment to the British constitution.[10] He applied to the colonial secretary, Lord Bathurst, early in 1815 for information about emigrating to Canada, and at Mr Goulbourn's request sent up certificates of character from Sir Edward Worth Newenham, an old family acquaintance, and his clergyman, Mr L'Estrange of Roscrea. He also sent up similar certificates on behalf of a number of Protestant inhabitants of his neighbourhood who had expressed an interest in accompanying him.[11]

Evans hoped that the entire party would be provided with free passages to Quebec, but he was soon informed that such "encouragement" to settlers had been suspended for a year. Anxious to be on his way, he wrote the Colonial Office that several of the prospective settlers were prepared to pay their own passages if they could be assured of a grant of land upon arrival.[12] Mr Goulbourn replied on 20 May 1815 that land grants would be made upon arrival in Canada, and that rations would be supplied for a limited time.[13] On 3 June Evans wrote hastily from Dublin that three of the families were sailing on the 5th in a vessel bound for Canada. The other families who had applied thought it "rather late in the year" but would join them the next spring. Evans expressed the hope – a vain one, as it turned out – that "there will be no disappointment on our arrival there."[14]

The emigrants were unable to secure immediate passage on a vessel heading for Quebec, so they embarked on a ship bound for the Gulf of St Lawrence. After wintering in the Gaspé Evans reached Quebec the following spring. He was surprised to discover that he was considered an ordinary settler, eligible for the usual grant of land upon proof of actual settlement and cultivation. Over the winter he had devised a plan to secure a large acreage for himself and a township for his followers on the Bay of Chaleur.[15] His hope that thirty or forty Protestant families would join him the following year[16] evaporated with the rejection of his application for a township grant and as the few families that had accompanied him found employment in the fishery and in lumbering on the Miramichi.[17] Finding his family alone, Evans had his name entered for a land grant in the Drummondville military settlement.[18] He completed the settlement duties for land in Wendover by May 1819, but he found that his "avocations" kept leading him away from the settlement.[19] After two unsuccessful attempts at being a schoolmaster[20] and numerous attempts to secure more suitable land elsewhere, he put his education to use in another way and spent much of his spare time petitioning the government as agent of various settlers in the Eastern Townships. It is probable that he spent his last years in Quebec, where his son was resident in 1833.[21]

In 1830 Evans sent the civil secretary a prospectus of a book he was writing, tentatively entitled *The Emigrants Guide, and Lower Canada Land Owners Directory*.[22] He arranged to have a segment of this projected large volume of advice to emigrants published in Dublin, and made one last attempt to secure a new grant from the government. His last petition, seeking re-examination of his land claims, was dated 1 February 1832.[23] He wrote to his publisher in the spring of 1832, but was dead of cholera at Quebec by the time his letters were received.[24] *The Emigrants' Directory and Guide to Obtain Lands and Effect a Settlement in the Canadas* was published posthumously in 1833.

While Evans's projected settlement of Tipperary Protestants in Lower Canada proved abortive, he successfully planted in the minds of some of his neighbours the idea of emigrating to Canada rather than moving to the United States, the place where the small Tipperary emigration of which we have evidence had hitherto been directed. A few of the people who expressed an interest in accompanying Evans to Canada seized the next opportunity offered when Richard Talbot revived the idea three years later.

RICHARD TALBOT AND THE *BRUNSWICK* EMIGRANTS OF 1818

Richard Talbot, like Francis Evans, chose to emigrate because of reverses of fortune which would have entailed declining social status had he remained in Ireland. He was a son of the late Edward Talbot, a gentleman of Clonloghan and Garrane in the King's County.[25] The Talbots of Garrane were a branch of a family of minor gentry numerous in the King's County panhandle, descended from ancestors who had settled there in the seventeenth century.[26] Richard had married in 1795 the daughter of a neighbouring gentleman, John Baird,[27] and was living at the close of the Napoleonic Wars in the village of Cloughjordan, just across the county boundary into Tipperary from the lands "which had for ages been the abode of his family."[28]

"Once possessed of a handsome competency," he was after the wars "in such circumstances as to preclude the possibility of his continuing in the country, without descending from that sphere of life in which he had been accustomed to move, to one, for the endurance of whose toils and difficulties he was, by his former habits, completely incapacitated." He had served briefly in the county militia and had clung to the hope of maintaining family dignity by securing commissions in the army for his two oldest sons, Edward Allen and John. This plan was frustrated by the conclusion of almost two decades of war with France, and hopes of securing civil offices were dashed by the return from service of thousands of young men with "higher claims" upon government patronage.[29]

As economic depression and unemployment set in following the subsidence of the wartime economy, many Irishmen considered emigrating to the United States.[30] However, like Francis Evans before him, Richard Talbot preferred to remain in British dominions and, early in 1816, he wrote to the Colonial Office to inquire about obtaining land grants in Canada.[31] He was no doubt partially motivated by the residence in the province of his older brother, John, who is probably the "friend ... resident in Canada" to whom Talbot referred in correspondence.[32] Talbot spent the better part of a year arranging for the disposal of his properties, but in December 1817 he applied again through an influential intermediary, the earl of Rosse, a family acquaintance of many years and the proprietor of the town of Birr, then called Parsonstown.[33] Talbot's enclosed petition contained the names of seventy-one "Loyal Protestants" and their families who wished to emigrate with him.[34]

Talbot's timing proved better than Francis Evans's had been. Bathurst replied that while encouragement to individuals had been suspended, the Colonial Office was contemplating sponsorship of group settlements. If a responsible person organized a group of emigrants and paid a £10 deposit for each settler, repayable once the emigrants were located on their lands, the Colonial Office would provide conveyance and arrange for land grants to be made free of expense. The Colonial Office hoped that the deposit would guarantee that the emigrants, or at least their leader, were not totally devoid of means and ensure that the expense to the government of conveying them to the colonies was justified by the emigrants becoming actual settlers rather than moving on to the United States.[35]

This £10 deposit plan was operative with respect to emigration to the Canadas for only the one season. During that time four groups accepted the terms and went to newly opened townships in Upper Canada. Two were English parties, one led by Thomas Milburn of Alston, Cumberland, the other by Captain Francis Spilsbury of Newark, Nottinghamshire. Both groups settled in Peterborough County, the Cumberland group in Smith Township and Spilsbury's Nottinghamshire party in Otonabee. A third group was composed of Protestant Scottish Highlanders from Loch Tayside in Perthshire who proceeded to Beckwith in the Bathurst District under the leadership of John Robertson of Breadalbane. Richard Talbot's party was the only one from Ireland to take advantage of the program.[36]

Within a week of receiving the circular, Talbot responded agreeing to Bathurst's conditions.[37] He sent the colonial secretary a new list of thirty-two committed settlers, and enclosed halves of Irish banknotes to the sum of £320. He stated that he would send the matching halves on receipt of Bathurst's instructions, and asked that a ship be sent to Galway, Limerick, Cork, Waterford, or Dublin to take on his party of 237 people.[38]

It was at this stage that Talbot ran into his first bureaucratic snag. Goulbourn stated that the government had not intended carrying out very large families at the public charge. In what was evidently a last-minute attempt at parsimony, Goulbourn protested that the £10 deposit was considered to cover only one settler, his wife, and two children under twelve or one between twelve and seventeen. All other persons would be charged for, those over seventeen being considered settlers for whom the £10 deposit fee would be charged, and additional persons under seventeen would be allowed upon payment of £3 per head.[39] Talbot replied submitting a new list of forty-four names, each heading a family consisting of no more than four people. By shuffling the applicants' families on paper to make each male over seventeen a head and assigning women and children to them arbitrarily, he was able to keep the additional expenditure down to £120. In a few cases he elevated children to the status of heads of families, realizing that there was little the Colonial Office could do to discover his subterfuge.[40]

On 2 April Mr Goulbourn requested the Naval Commissioners to provide a vessel for conveyance of the Talbot party from Cork to Montreal and requested that the agent at Cork inform Mr Talbot when the vessel would be ready for boarding.[41] The emigrants set out for Cork expectantly and arrived there on 4 May.[42] On 11 June they petitioned Bathurst from Cove noting that the *Brunswick* of 541 tons burthen had only arrived the Monday previous, and that in the meantime the settlers had expended much of their capital in maintaining themselves for nearly six weeks. They also feared that the delay would result in their arrival in the colony too late to cultivate any lands for their support the next year. They therefore requested that arrangements be made for some assistance to be provided upon their arrival in Canada.[43] In reply to Goulbourn's indignant letter demanding an explanation,[44] the Navy Office stated that it engaged all transports by public tender. It had taken time to find and refit a vessel for such a voyage, in part, the commissioners pointedly noted, because the Colonial Office did not furnish all the requisite details about provisioning in its first communication.[45] Goulbourn wrote to Talbot on the 18th expressing Lord Bathurst's regret but denying any reponsibility for the settlers' misfortunes, pointing out that he had in an earlier letter recommended that Talbot communicate directly with the agent for transports at Cork to learn the probable date of arrival of the vessel.[46] The letter never reached Talbot, for the party embarked on the 11th[47] and sailed from the Cove of Cork about 11 o'clock the morning of the 13 June.[48]

The voyage was typical of that of emigrant ships of the period. The journey took forty-three and a half days and the passengers were beset by sea-sickness, particularly during the first fortnight when they faced unfavour-able winds. Most distressing were the deaths of twelve children at sea and the burial of eleven more during the twelve days the ship spent among the islands in the St Lawrence.[49] The *Brunswick* followed the HMS *Iphigenia,* out of Portsmouth, up the river,[50] and the arrival of both ships on 29 July was noted in the Quebec *Gazette* of the succeeding day. The party's first sight of Quebec was obscured by smoke from cannon-fire welcoming the passengers of the *Iphigenia* to Canada, for the new governor, the duke of Richmond, and his entourage were on board.[51]

The party spent five days in Quebec, during which time Richard Talbot presented his requisition for land to the new governor. Richmond introduced him to Col. Cockburn, the deputy quarter-master general, who tried to persuade him to settle in Lower Canada. Talbot and his sons discussed the matter and decided that because of the strangeness of the language, customs, and religion of the population there they would feel more comfortable settling in the upper province.[52]

On 3 August the party left Quebec in the steamer *Telegraph* for Montreal. Finding that their destination, York (Toronto), was 500 miles distant, the party remained in Montreal while Richard's son, Edward Allen Talbot, returned to Quebec to solicit government assistance in conveying the party to Upper Canada on some of the government boats they found idle at Lachine. The duke of Richmond stated that he could not permit the use of the boats without authorization by the Secretary of State's Office, and Edward Talbot was forced to return to his father's settlers at Lachine with the news that the journey onward must be made at their own expense.[53] While at Lachine the oldest member of party, John Spearman Sr, died, the first adult death amongst the party since leaving Ireland.[54] At this point fifteen of the families, fearing the expense of a long journey to York with no final destination determined upon,[55] decided to accept Col. Cockburn's offer of land grants in the military settlement which had just been organized at Richmond on the Upper Canadian side of the Ottawa River. It appears likely that these settlers blamed Talbot for the long and expensive wait at the docks in Cork and for the necessity of paying their own passages into Upper Canada, and were irritated by the continuing uncertainty over where they would settle. Two families chose to remain in Montreal. The remainder of the party, nineteen families and probably Talbot's seven servants, made the 120–mile journey from Montreal to Prescott by Durham boat or batteaux in thirteen days, sleeping on the river bank at night. On 3 September the party embarked for York on the schooner *Caledonia,* arriving there six days later.[56]

Upon reaching York, Richard Talbot consulted with the lieutenant-governor, who gave him a letter of introduction to Surveyor General Ridout, but the latter was not able to suggest a settlement location that seemed satisfactory. Shortly afterwards Richard met Col. Thomas Talbot, the eccentric supervisor of settlement in the London and Western Districts.[57] Col. Talbot recommended that Richard go to the Township of London, then on the northern fringes of civilization. Richard agreed with the recommendation, and arrangements were made to begin the trek anew.

On 11 September the party reboarded the *Caledonia* and sailed to Niagara, and thence seven miles to Queenston whence they crossed by land thirty-six miles to Fort Erie. Here Richard arranged to charter the schooner *Young Phoenix* to convey them the 116 remaining miles to Port Talbot in Yarmouth Township. The captain of the vessel proved undependable and the crew intemperate, and the schooner drifted onto rocks on the American shore forty-five miles from Buffalo.[58] Talbot's son John and servant William Mooney swam ashore with life-lines and succeeded in rescuing the party. However, one of the group, Mrs Benjamin Lewis, succumbed to cold and fatigue. Almost all of the passengers' effects were lost, moreover, and the party spent two weeks staying with farmers near Dunkirk, New York, before sailing across the lake on the vessel *Hummingbird* to Port Talbot. From there Richard Talbot probably wrote to York seeking repayment of the £10 deposits made on behalf of his settlers, as on 7 October Lieutenant-Governor Peregrine Maitland drew bills on the Colonial Office in the amount of £210 for the twenty-one male settlers then actually proceeding on to London.[59] On 19–22 October twenty-five settlers signed receipts acknowledging repayment of the sums concerned.[60] After two weeks in Yarmouth Township Richard Talbot removed to Westminster late in October.[61] While most of the settlers probably spent the winter in Westminster or Yarmouth, Edward and John Talbot left on 26 October with six carriers and scouted out the Township of London. They built a log house on Lot 2, Concession 6, into which the family moved on 2 December 1818.[62]

Both Evans's and Talbot's experiments are interesting as examples of early group settlement schemes, but only Talbot's was of any real consequence. The successful plantation of the Talbot group gave rise to a process of chain migration which brought hundreds more Protestant and Roman Catholic families from Tipperary to two different parts of Upper Canada in succeeding decades. This clustering of settlers sharing a common origin and cultural background had important social and political consequences for the remainder of the century. Evans's experiment failed, and he seems to have been unaware of the successful colonies established by Talbot's followers even though some potential emigrants who had applied to accompany him came with Talbot in 1818. Evans quickly abandoned his plans to establish a settlement, and devoted the remainder of his life to efforts to secure land for himself and fair treatment for the residents of his adopted Eastern Townships.

THE SIGNIFICANCE OF THE
EFFORTS OF EVANS AND TALBOT

In Francis Evans's abortive venture we see foreshadowed a number of the
experiences which Richard Talbot's more successful Tipperary colony
underwent several years later. In both cases the leader resolved upon
emigration, and secured a number of settlers to accompany him in the
expectation that the quantity of land granted to himself as a promoter of
emigration would be enlarged as a reward for his efforts. Both arrived in
Canada without any clear idea of where they would settle and found
themselves at the mercy of government bureaucracy. Both saw large numbers
of their settlers drift away from them before they proceeded to their final
locations. Both came to feel that the government had broken its promises to
them, though Evans was, in the end, probably the more charitable of the two,
realizing that he had perhaps been unrealistic in his expectations and had
obviously made some crucial mistakes himself. Neither Talbot nor Evans was
to achieve the position of importance in the colony which he desired. In both
cases a book was one tangible result of the attempt, one a guide for emigrants
written by Evans in the early 1830s, the other a two-volume travelogue
published by Talbot's eldest son in 1824. But why were the greater
expectations of these two settlement leaders not realized, and what was the
long-term significance of their efforts?

The plans of both Richard Talbot and Francis Evans were to a large degree
thwarted by their lack of a suitable *entrée* into the Canadian political scene. In
applying to the Colonial Office both stressed the respectability and loyalty of
their families and secured impressive local references, fully expecting that
large land grants would be forthcoming. These grants, they hoped, would
enable them to live the accustomed life of a landed gentleman, a life which
was slipping from their grasp at home in the economic and social dislocations
that followed the Napoleonic Wars. The Colonial Office perhaps did not
understand the extent of their aspirations. It certainly did little to explain to
them the full significance of colonial land policies. It could not in any case
have told them that personal acquaintance with the leaders of the colony was a
more important qualification for special treatment than letters of recommendation from other members of the county gentry in Ireland. Neither Talbot nor
Evans had any connections in positions of power in the Canadas. Presented
after their arrival in Quebec with what was in fact the standard Colonial Office
recommendation for a settler's grant, the governor's office tended to regard
them as ordinary settlers to whom lands would be granted merely in
proportion to their demonstrated ability to cultivate. Moreover, as time
passed, any awareness the bureaucrats had of the peculiar circumstances of
their emigration faded, making it even more difficult for them to secure what
they felt had been promised them before they left home.[63]

The expectations of Talbot and Evans also betrayed a fundamental misunderstanding of the role of land ownership in Canadian society. In Ireland land was the basis of the economic and political power of the elite; in Canada it was the basis for the prosperity of the multitude. In Ireland the social and economic dominance of the aristocracy and gentry was solidly based upon ownership of land, which was leased out to the tenantry or worked by labourers. Land was thus the source of the rents which made up the bulk of a gentleman's income, and social and political power flowed from this economic base. In Canada, as Evans soon came to realize and as he pointed out in his *Emigrants' Directory:*

When [a settler] becomes the proprietor of a piece of land, all his work is for his own benefit, no rent or taxes being to be paid: he has the full produce of the soil for his support; and the surplus he can send to market, when and how he pleases, as he is not in dread of the agent coming to distrain him for *the rent,* or the collector of *the county cess,* or the tithe proctor, with many others which are the daily visitors of the farmer in England and Ireland. It is this that makes the Canadian farmer feel *really independent;* – in fact he is the lord and master of *his own* estate, and many that have landed in Quebec *without a pound in the world,* have been able to realize by this course what is here represented, and can now, from their having had themselves substantial proof of its reality, testify that it is not an imaginary picture, but one to be met with in Canada every day.[64]

While Talbot and Evans were aware before leaving Ireland that land in Canada was granted to emigrants generally, they still held to the belief that they could build a new station in life for themselves based on ownership of a larger acreage than the norm. Though Evans recognized the benefits of land ownership for the average settler, who with diligence could build a secure future for himself and his children, he also became painfully aware of how an immigrant with capital, like himself, could rapidly lose the material advantage with which he had begun in the search for what was not to be: "Emigrants who have got any capital should, as soon as possible after landing decide on the part of the country they wish to settle in, and at once proceed to examine it; the distance and delay to be measured by the depth of their purses – that is, if their means be small they must seek for land as near as they can match themselves, and not foolishly exhaust their money in moving to distant places, while suitable situations may be obtained near at hand."[65]

What Evans in essence came to realize was that success for a gentleman who was without political influence rested upon the same footing as for settlers of lesser origins – diligence and intelligent management of resources. If he did not waste his capital aiming to find the unattainable, a gentleman could use it to improve his farm with the assistance of the hired labour many emigrants could not afford. In this manner he could remain materially in advance of his neighbours. In a newly settled area in which an elite was not firmly in control, this prosperity might bring with it some of the status and position the gentleman desired. But in a country in which free grants, and later lands at easy terms of purchase, were open to all, and in which squatting on crown and clergy lands without payment of fees or rents was so common that the government was forced to accommodate it, there was little possibility that a gentleman could maintain his status by renting out lands to farmers on the European model. The demand for tenancy on private holdings in the pioneer period was insufficient to support a landlord class devoid of other forms of income.

Neither Evans nor Talbot reached in Canada the social position at which he aimed. Richard Talbot was a militia officer in London Township, but he never attained even the basic civil appointment of justice of the peace. His son Edward Allen Talbot began a more successful career in the colonies but soon alienated himself from government circles. Like Francis Evans, he wrote a book about his early experiences in the Canadas. *Five Years' Residence in the Canadas* (London 1824), an entertaining but quirky account of his travels in America, went into several English and foreign-language editions. He was made a magistrate for the London District in 1829[66] and was appointed a captain of militia, but in 1830 he was court martialed on charges of non-attendance at muster, though he was acquitted on all but one of five charges. Later that year Edward Allen was once more in bad odour with officialdom after he led a mob which evicted the William Armitage family and burned down their house in London Township in an attempt to reinstate John Ardell, whom Col. Talbot had quite properly dispossessed for absenteeism and non-completion of settlement duties. This incident reflects a typically Tipperary attitude to, and defence of, perceived property rights in this period, but leading such a mob was scarcely something a gentleman would have done in Ireland. Such a resort to extra-legal action suggests that Richard Talbot's family felt increasingly alienated from the provincial administration after Richard's long and losing battle to obtain his large land grant free of fees as he felt he had been promised.[67] After Edward Allen squandered much of his means in publication of his book and in an optimistic attempt to develop a perpetual-motion machine,[68] he was induced to edit a Reform newspaper in London. After his militia services were refused during the Mackenzie rebellion, he left Upper Canada[69] and died in poverty in Lockport, New York, in 1839.[70] His brother John appears to have become embittered by what he felt was the government's shabby treatment of his father. He embraced Reform politics enthusiastically and edited the St Thomas *Liberal* but fled to the United States following the failure of the 1837 Rebellion.[71]

Francis Evans was appointed a commissioner for the trial of small causes in 1824 but this was his only official position.[72] He was not a member of the legislature as has been asserted, this being a misinterpretation by William Kingsford of a statement by Evans's publisher that he had helped to secure to the people of the Eastern Townships "equal advantages with those parts then enjoying the privilege of being Represented in the Provincial Parliament."[73] Nor was he a government land agent, as his publisher assumed.[74] He merely wrote to the government on behalf of neighbours and other settlers. The Executive Council in fact refused an application he made in 1829 on the grounds that he assumed the general character of an agent for several townships without naming any individuals for whom he was authorized to act.[75] Evans made his living in Lower Canada as a schoolmaster, that last resort of many a fallen gentleman, and a profession also pursued by John Talbot for a few years.

Evans was a forerunner who failed to establish in Lower Canada in 1815 the colony that Richard Talbot founded in the upper province three years later. Although Evans appears to have been unaware of the Talbot colony in the London area, there was a link between the two ventures embodied in the several families whose interest in emigrating was aroused by Evans and confirmed by Talbot's more successful efforts.

The stories of both these organized emigration schemes suggest something of the extent of the enthusiasm for postwar emigration that led potential settlers to dispose of their Irish properties and sail for Canada with only the most idealistic of notions about what they would do upon arrival. They also indicate how the Colonial Office in this period was groping for the most effective way of accomplishing its aims. The expense of Talbot's expedition – it cost the British government £1270.12.7[76] – was one of the factors which led to the abandonment of officially assisted emigration within the year, though a few later experiments were made (most notably the Peter Robinson emigrations of 1823 and 1825). The major factor was the realization that the mania for emigration was sufficiently intense in itself to make large numbers of those wanting to go to the Canadas scrape together the passage money without drawing upon the public purse.

However, the major significance of Richard Talbot's group migration lay in its implications for the future direction of emigration from Tipperary and in its implications, too, for the two regions of Upper Canada in which his followers settled. Though Talbot's authority over his followers received a shattering blow soon after arrival when nearly half his party left him, and he never occupied the position of local influence he desired, he nonetheless founded the largest Tipperary community in the Canadas and was indirectly responsible for the establishment of the second largest. That these settlements were to grow more by a snowballing process of chain migration than by design does not diminish the signficance, however unexpected at the time, of Talbot's initiating action.[77]

THE EMIGRANTS OF 1815 AND 1818:
ORIGINS AND CHARACTERIZATION

Richard Talbot's group of settlers was drawn from a wide area within North Tipperary, which suggests that family connections and networks of friends were more important than geographical proximity in determining migration patterns. Though the majority of Talbot's followers came from within a few miles of his residence at Cloughjordan and his former residence in Templeharry parish immediately to the east, knowledge of the expedition spread very quickly to surprisingly distant parishes through these social networks. An examination of the names and residences of the families that applied to accompany Francis Evans in 1815 suggests that the same pattern of information dissemination was operative in the case of that abortive experiment. Most of Evans's applicants came from parishes north and south of his home at Roscrea, to the east of Talbot's Cloughjordan, but in this instance, too, kinship ties extended the geographical source area of the prospective emigrant population beyond the immediate neighbourhood.

None of Evans's settlers appear to have been from his own town of Roscrea but rather were residents of rural parishes in the vicinity, living mostly in the King's County panhandle to the north of the town and in the parishes near the Queen's County border to its south. Francis Evans had interested sixteen families in accompanying him to Canada in 1815. The distribution of these families can be only partly traced, due to the loss of the first of two packets of character certificates Evans forwarded to the Colonial Office. The residences of ten can be identified.[78] Charles Goulding (who later emigrated with Talbot) was a resident of Moneygall in Richard Talbot's neighbourhood.[79] Thomas Howard Jr was also resident on the Minchin estate there, but prior to his marriage to Goulding's sister he had lived eight miles to the southeast at Templemore. William Howard still lived at Templemore, though he had also married a Goulding from Moneygall.[80] Thomas Howard Sr, so noted because he was several years older than Thomas Jr, was possibly somehow related to the others, but he lived in the parish of Bourney, south of Roscrea. He emigrated in 1819 to London Township, where he was known by his full name of Thomas Whitfield Howard.[81] The Richard Shepherd family also lived in Templemore, but the two other Shepherd families for whom Evans sent in certificates, those of William and John, lived at Finnoe, west of Borrisokane, and at Kilfithmone, to the south of Roscrea. William Cheswell lived at Ballymackey. Applicant William Robinson, a shoemaker in Ettagh near Birr, emigrated to Williamsburgh, UC, in the spring of 1823 and after about seven years was able to raise money to bring his family out to settle in West Gwillimbury, north of Toronto. Robinson's father-in-law, the Rev. John Connell of Ettagh, was also among Evans's applicants, but he did not emigrate; he died in 1822, leaving his family in financial difficulties.[82] Apart

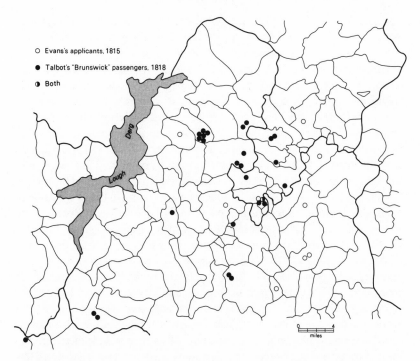

MAP 11   Origins of Evans and Talbot emigrants. Family ties brought prospective emigrants from as far as Limerick, setting the stage for chain migration drawing upon the entire North Tipperary region.

from Evans's own family, residents of Roscrea, the remaining settlers cannot be certainly identified with a place, although several of the surnames are those of families resident mostly between Roscrea and Birr in the King's County panhandle.[83]

The origins of the Talbot settlers cannot all be identified either, but I have ascertained the places of origin of twenty-four of the thirty-eight families with reasonable certainty, as well as the origins of two of the seven servants.[84] Most came from within a six- or seven-mile radius of Talbot's home at Cloughjordan in Modreeny parish, but as in the case of Evans, few came from his own village and none can be identified as his own tenants. That more were not from Modreeny is surprising, for Cloughjordan village was in the heart of the heavily Protestant portion of the Dunalley estate that was the place of origin of hundreds of later emigrants. Only two settlers, William Haskett[85] and William Hodgins, were from there;[86] Haskett was originally of the large Borrisokane family of the name. A half-dozen came from the latter place, which included a market town four miles west of Cloughjordan and also had a large Protestant population. Seven families were from just east of Cloughjordan in the King's County panhandle where Talbot's own ancestral lands were located. Four were from Moneygall and its vicinity, one from Dunkerrin, and two from Shinrone just to the north.

The settlers coming from further away had ties to the region near Talbot's home. William Geary was an estate manager in County Clare but had previously farmed 100 acres in Shinrone and was married to a daughter of the rector of Templeharry, the parish adjacent to Modreeny which included Moneygall.[87] Joseph Hardy was from Killymer, County Galway, but was related to Talbot's wife.[88] Robert Grant, a clothier of Limerick City, had been recently married to a sister of settler Francis Powell, a linen weaver of Newport, on the Limerick border, which was also the birthplace of the servant Edmund Stoney.[89] How these families came to be recruited is not known, though later evidence suggests that the Powells had relatives in Roscrea. The servant William O'Neil whose father farmed near Nenagh is the only identified 1818 emigrant from that town.[90] Two families from the Otway estate, the Siftons and Shouldices, came on the *Brunswick,* the Siftons sending two sons, who were followed by the rest of the family later, and three generations of Shouldices proceeding at once. These families had farmed adjoining freeholds since the 1750s and were well-known to one another.[91] It is possible that one of the Shouldices farmed at Dunkerrin, near Cloughjordan, for several years prior to emigration.[92] This may be how these families came to be recruited. The reply to a diocesan questionnaire of 1820 noted that the Protestants in Monsea parish on the Shannon "have declined in number in consequence to an emigration to Upper Canada in the summer of 1818," but the families concerned cannot be identified because of the destruction of Monsea's parish registers.[93] The residences of Talbot's settlers concentrate on the whole further to the west than those of Evans's applicants, but nonetheless a wide area of North Tipperary and the King's County panhandle was represented in the first migration. This facilitated the spread of information about the government-sponsored migration through the region over the succeeding winter and enabled chain migration from a wide area to commence the next year.

The division of Talbot's party at Lachine split the settlers into two groups fairly representative of the diverse geographical origins of the whole. This facilitated the growth of both the Ottawa and the London settlement concentrations by chain migration from the same parts of Tipperary. The Offaly (King's County) settlers proceeded mostly to London and the identified Borrisokane people went mostly to the Ottawa Valley, but this imbalance was soon redressed by new arrivals. More strikingly, of the two families from Newport, on the Limerick border, the Powells settled in Goulbourn while the Stoneys went to London, and of the former Otway tenants from Glankeen, in the southern mountains, the Shouldices chose the Ottawa Valley while the Siftons remained with Talbot. There was a bit of initial shuffling as Samuel Long and William Mooney left the Talbot Settlement and moved to Huntley Township north of Richmond. The later flow of migration, however, was decidedly in the opposite direction, always from Ottawa to London and never the reverse.

The Talbot settlers were Protestant, loyal to the British crown, and possessed of at least the rudiments of literacy. Most were yeomen farmers of small means who could probably have afforded to emigrate without government assistance.

That these early emigrants were Protestant was partly a consequence of the generally better economic circumstances of the Protestant population of Ireland, but it seems to have been a result also of the deeply ingrained belief, based upon generations of privileged treatment, that it was the loyal Protestant population that the government would wish to assist. Applicants for Colonial Office assistance in the years following the Napoleonic Wars were overwhelmingly Protestants. The government had not stated that only Protestants would be sent to the colonies as settlers, nor had the Colonial Office by 1818 associated the sponsorship of groups like Talbot's with the government's plan to settle the eastern part of Upper Canada with loyal Britons. Had this been the case, the Talbot settlers would have been directed to the military settlements there in the first place. Rather, assisted emigration was intended to help relieve unemployment in Britain and prevent useful citizens from emigrating to the United States. Nevertheless, the perception of the policy in Ireland was that only loyal Protestants were welcome as assisted settlers. One landlord in the region even protested in 1819 that some of the people hoping to secure assistance in proceeding to Canada were Roman Catholics "intent on passing as Protestants."[94] It was not until the Hon. Peter Robinson of Upper Canada secured the support of the British government for a program of assisted emigration of Roman Catholics from a troubled region of County Cork in 1823 that this stereotype broke down. Certainly Talbot stressed in 1817 that all the prospective settlers in his list were "Loyal Protestants ... who I am bold to say, would be ready under My Command to serve his Majesty in defence of their adopted Country as we have heretofore done here against Foreign Invaders, or Domestick Traytors."[95] At least one of the party came to Canada with a personal axe to grind. Samuel Long's father had been murdered at Toomevara in 1816 by several of the local Catholic population for allowing the use of one of his buildings as a barracks. Samuel later asserted that he was "forced to quit that Country for fear of loosing my life also,"[96] but his insertion of an advertisement in the press while at York en route to Port Talbot informing the public of a £50 reward offered by the Dublin Police Office for the apprehension of two suspects who had escaped to America suggests that he may possibly have had other motives.[97]

The privileged status of the Protestant population of Ireland is reflected in the economic circumstances of the *Brunswick* settlers. Though they emigrated because they faced an economic crisis, they were not already in a destitute position. Richard Talbot's obituary termed them "a colony of sturdy yeomanry,"[98] and this is confirmed by the occupations stated in Talbot's lists. Over half the families were headed by farmers. Four families were headed by cabin passengers "of respectability," Talbot, Burton, and Geary being gentlemen while Hardy, a relative of Mrs Talbot, was a saddler.[99] Twelve of the settlers were tradesmen: four smiths, three shoemakers, a painter and glazier, a clothier, two weavers, and a carpenter, and another was a military pensioner.

That the Talbot settlers were not without some means was certainly the opinion of Charles Rolleston, a landlord at Silverhills near Moneygall. He wrote to Lord Bathurst in 1819 to protest against any further government encouragement of emigration: "I am myself well acquainted with those who went in a free ship last year from Cork, they were from my neighbourhood, and some of them went to get rid of their debts and tho able to pay them were induced to take advantage of a free ship to cheat their creditors."[100]

We have figures on the amount of cash brought by eighteen of the settlers who took up land in London, obtained from the results of a questionnaire summarized by Edward Allen Talbot in his book. Most brought amounts equivalent to several years' wages for a day labourer, computed at a rate of eight pence a day, the low rate prevalent in North Tipperary.[101] The amounts would doubtless have been a little larger had not the long delay at Cork awaiting the arrival of the *Brunswick* from Deptford induced needless expense. Nonetheless, most brought £50 (seven) or £100 (six). One brought £75 and three brought less than £50. Only William Geary, a cabin passenger and former estate agent, arrived with more than £100; his capital amounted to three times that sum. All reported that their resources had been entirely exhausted within a few years of arriving in Canada, but the money had allowed them to make a start, and all reported in 1823 that they were "perfectly satisfied with their adopted country."[102] Their resources at the point of emigration compare favourably with those of the Roman Catholic Peter Robinson settlers of 1823. These people were cottiers, reduced farmers, and unemployed labourers and tradesmen, people who were "wretchedly poor" but "not too debilitated or demoralized to succeed as settlers." None of the "Robinsonians" brought more than £10 or £20 and many had no capital at all.[103] All the adult males in Talbot's party were able at least to sign their names, though some did not do it well.[104] However, most of Robinson's settlers were also literate and "knew the rudiments of arithmetic."[105]

It is significant that Talbot's party was composed of families, for family emigration was to be the norm among the settlers who followed them. This circumstance reflects both the economic and social positions of the settlers, in that they were not forced by circumstances to emigrate as individuals or labourers. It also reflects the importance of family structure to an agricultural population. The family as a mechanism for the acquisition and apportionment of land incorporated emigration into its operating system. Of forty adult settlers, nine were unmarried while another thirteen were but recently wed, nine of them having no children as yet and four having only one. These figures, however, disguise several extended-family and three-generation groupings within the party. The young Goulding and Howard families were headed by brothers-in-law. Hodgins and Young, the former recently married and the latter with an infant child, were sons-in-law of the settler John Colbert. Corbett, with two small children, was a son-in-law of Spearman. The Siftons, Richardsons, and O'Neils would become three-generation families in the New World with the arrival of relatives the next year. Gaps in the genealogical record prevent definite statements of kinship, but the pensioner Turner was married to a Haskett, probably a relative of the settler Haskett. It has already been noted that Joseph Hardy was related to Mrs Talbot, while Mrs Delahunt was Jane Guest, probably a close relative of the settler Thomas Guest, and Thomas Stanley from Borrisokane was married to a Hodgins, no doubt related somehow to William Hodgins of Modreeny.[106] In many cases the maiden names of the settlers' wives are still unknown, and it is probable that many more instances of sibling relationships among the settlers remain unsuspected for this reason.

Thus, to a remarkable degree the first shipload of North Tipperary Protestants set the pattern for the chain migration that was to continue for over thirty years. Like the passengers of the *Brunswick,* the later arrivals would be mostly farmers facing declining fortunes. They would travel in family groups and would come out to join relatives already in Canada. Both their places of origin and their destinations were foreshadowed in the pattern established by Richard Talbot's emigrants in 1818. Had the British government been aware that the *Brunswick* experiment would initiate a process of chain migration that would bring thousands of settlers to Upper Canada they would have been better convinced that the expenditure of public funds had been worthwhile.[107] The £10 deposit plan was to become an unrecognized success, for it established the pattern and set the process in motion. Had it been planned that way it could not have succeeded better.

TWO SMALLER SETTLEMENTS:
ESQUESING AND ROUGEMONT

The expedition under Talbot's leadership was, by reason of its size, the most important influence in determining where the major Tipperary colonies would take root and grow, but two other migrations led to the establishment of three other Tipperary colonies in 1818 and 1819. The independent emigration to Lower Canada of three brothers from near Roscrea and the inclusion of two Tipperary expatriates among a group of Irish Methodists moving north from

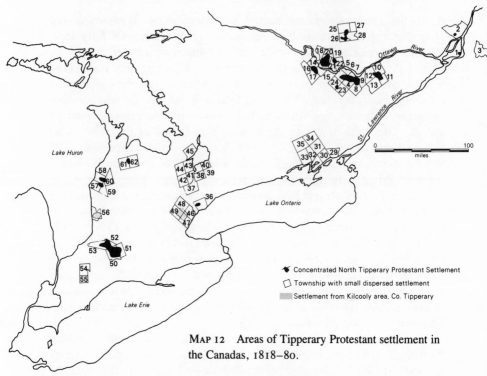

MAP 12   Areas of Tipperary Protestant settlement in the Canadas, 1818–80.

Lower Canada
1 Montreal
2 Mascouche
3 Ste-Marie and St-Césaire

Carp Valley
4 Huntley
5 Fitzroy
6 Torbolton
7 March
8 Goulbourn
9 Nepean

Russell County
10 Cumberland
11 Russell
12 Gloucester
13 Osgoode

Renfrew County
14 Ross
15 Horton

16 Bromley
17 Admaston

Pontiac County
18 Litchfield
19 Clarendon
20 Thorne

North Onslow
21 Bristol
22 Onslow

Lanark County
23 Ramsay
24 Pakenham

Kazabazua Area
25 Wright
26 Aylwin
27 Northfield
28 Hincks

Kingston Area
29 Kingston

30 Ernesttown
31 Camden East
32 Richmond township
33 Tyendinaga
34 Sheffield
35 Hungerford

Toronto Area
36 York
37 King
38 East Gwillimbury
39 North Gwillimbury
40 Georgina
41 West Gwillimbury
42 Tecumseth
43 Innisfil
44 Essa
45 Oro

Halton-Peel
46 Toronto township
47 Trafalgar
48 Chinguacousy

49 Esquesing

London Area
50 London
51 West Nissouri
52 Biddulph
53 McGillivray

Lambton County
54 Brooke
55 Euphemia

Goderich
56 Goderich

Bruce County
57 Huron township
58 Kincardine
59 Kinloss
60 Greenock

Grey County
61 Sullivan
62 Holland

New York gave rise to small clusters of Tipperary settlers west of Toronto and in the seigneuries of Lower Canada. Though a few families emigrated to join friends in these locations, most eventually drifted away or moved on to the larger colonies near Richmond and London.

In the autumn of 1818 the British consul at New York, James Buchanan, a native of County Tyrone, met with some fifty heads of families originally from the British Isles to persuade them to move north to Canada. Most of the group were Methodists and many were from Buchanan's home county in northern Ireland, but among those present was Thomas Reed, a former resident of Borrisokane married to a native of Borris-in-Ossory. He had been in the United States since at least 1810. As a result of the meeting, four men, John Beatty, James Beattie, Joseph Graham, and Reed, went to York in October 1818 and secured a promise of a tract of land for their friends from New York and for relatives from Ireland who would immediately join them. The first party from New York arrived at York in April 1819 and was settled in the northern part of Toronto Township. Reed and Graham's party arrived in June and was settled, with the friends from Ireland, in the southeastern quarter of the nearby and newly surveyed township of Esquesing.[108] Several of the families that emigrated from the North Tipperary region in 1819 joined the Reeds, including his brother John, William Kent from Youghalarra and his son-in-law Robert Howard of Shinrone and Nenagh, and Samuel Watkins from Birr. Thomas Bridge of Roscrea applied for land in Esquesing for himself and his relative Ralph Smith, but Bridge moved instead to the Tipperary colony in Richmond while Howard and Smith settled in Montreal, where Edward Allen Talbot met the latter and married his daughter in 1821.[109]

All of the North Tipperary settlers in Esquesing appear to have been people of some means. Thomas Reed was described as a gentleman of Borrisokane in 1801 when he and his wife Caroline Matilda Gardiner acknowledged receipt of a £200 legacy she had received from her father, Thomas Gardiner of Borris-in-Ossory.[110] Kent was a native of Youghalarra parish, apparently a farmer of Kylebeg and related to the prominent Kents of Garrykennedy in Castletownarra. Kent brought with him two working men and a woman who were bound to him for five years.[111] His son-in-law Howard was born in Nenagh, the son of Robert Howard, a distiller of Shinrone. Howard soon moved to Montreal where he became the partner of a later arrival from Nenagh in the mercantile firm of Howard and Thompson.[112] Watkins was from Birr, married to the daughter of a gentleman of Banagher. Most of the Watkinses left Esquesing in the 1840s and became wealthy merchants in Hamilton.[113] Bridge was a member of a gentry family in Roscrea; Smith was his first cousin once removed, and a member of a Cromwellian family, the Smiths of Glasshouse. Smith's wife was related to the Kents, but the closeness of her relationship to William Kent is unknown.[114] It is possible that emigrants of means and standing shunned Talbot's colony in London Township, but it is more likely that they joined Reed in Esquesing because he had been able to send letters home from New York the previous autumn, whereas Talbot did not reach his new residence till after the close of navigation.

One of Beatty's party was Martin Switzer, a member of a Palatine colony at Kilcooly, some twenty miles south of Roscrea. Switzer had lived for a time in Navan, County Meath, before emigrating to Boston in 1804. Upon coming to Canada he obtained land in Toronto Township. He was implicated in the 1837 Rebellion and returned to the United States thereafter, but he may be considered the founder of the sizeable settlement of Kilcooly Protestants around the site of the later village of Streetsville. As noted before, this was a completely separate social group from the North Tipperary emigrants, with distinctive surnames, places of origin and settlement, and its own migration patterns within Canada.[115] The growth of this colony in the township adjacent to that of the Kents and their friends, with both groups arising by processes of chain migration from the two Tipperary members of a mostly northern Irish Methodist group from New York, is entirely fortuitous, but a fascinating coincidence.[116]

The foundation of another small colony was laid at Rougemont in the parish of St-Césaire near Chambly, Lower Canada, as the result of the independent emigration of three brothers from the Roscrea area in 1818. Joseph, Matthew, and Robert Standish lived just east of the town in Queen's County, where they farmed extensively. They had links with the more central portion of the North Tipperary region, for their father had come from Knockballymeagher in the parish of Bourney, south of Roscrea, and the three brothers were non-resident middlemen over a substantial land-holding in the part of the Ormond plain that was most thickly dotted with landlord demesnes and large farms; they held a lease for three lives renewable forever of 192 acres in Springfield in the parish of Finnoe. Following the death of their father, who had farmed on a large scale and owned a bleach green at Ballytarsna in the parish of Borris-in-Ossory, the three brothers sold out to a fourth and left for Canada around the same time as Talbot's settlers. It is possible that the collapse of the cloth trade in Borris-in-Ossory had something to do with their departure. Two brothers were in St-Césaire by autumn, when Robert purchased land there, but the third, Joseph, moved on to York and joined Thomas Reed (whose wife was from Borris-in-Ossory) in Esquesing Township the following year.[117] In the 1820s several other families, mostly from the Roscrea area, joined the Standishes in Rougemont after living for a time in Montreal.[118]

Thus the North Tipperary colonies near London and Richmond, and in Esquesing and Rougemont, all began in 1818 or 1819 and grew thereafter by chain migration. All drew upon a common source region in Ireland. Though some drew more from one part of the region than another, there were substantial overlaps because of kinship links between the residents of distant parishes. As in the case of the Talbot migration itself, such relationships were more important than geography in determining where emigrants would settle. Family ties facilitated the spread of information throughout the region. When inhabitants of North Tipperary submitted another list of potential emigrants to the government in the spring of 1819, it included the names of people who would settle in all of these Canadian locations, and in a few other places as well. As early as 1819, multilateral kinship links provided the prospective emigrant with a choice of settlement locations in Canada where there were relatives or acquaintances.

CHAPTER FIVE

Chain Migration

The movement of Protestants from North Tipperary that was set in motion by the *Brunswick* emigration in 1818 continued right through the Famine era of the late 1840s and early 1850s with little change in character or destination. Though the decision to emigrate at a particular time was influenced by reflections upon economic and social conditions at home, the locations of family members who had gone before continued to be the major determinants of destination.

THE MOVEMENT CONTINUES: THE 1819 PETITIONS AND THE START OF CHAIN MIGRATION

Before leaving Ireland it had been apparent to Richard Talbot that many more residents of his neighbourhood were interested in emigrating to Canada than could be incorporated in the sponsored group that sailed on the *Brunswick* under the £10 deposit plan. He had written to Earl Bathurst in April 1818 to say that he was considering appointing an agent in Cloughjordan or sending one of his sons back to Ireland in the autumn to make arrangements for a second party to come out in 1819.[1] Since it soon became apparent to Talbot that he had nothing to gain personally by further involvement in sponsoring emigration, nothing came of this idea. Nonetheless, emigration to the Canadas from Tipperary was to continue without Talbot's intervention.

The news of government sponsorship had spread fairly widely in North Tipperary in 1818, as evidenced by the scattering of places from which Talbot's settlers came. Of the seventy-four potential settlers who had applied in 1817, fewer than a dozen had been among those eventually chosen. Some joined in petitioning again in 1819, while others simply appeared in Canada without the preliminary of a letter to the Colonial Office. Some had heard that the government did not contemplate a repetition of the previous year's expedition, while others either did not have updated information or hoped that it was not true. By the beginning of May it was apparent that there was a "very general emigration of the protestants" from this part of Ireland. Landlord Charles Rolleston feared that "the day is not far off, when they [Protestants] will be wanting in this country more than in Canada."[2]

The initial hope of many who wrote to the Colonial Office was that the £10 deposit scheme would be repeated. The new year was only twelve days old when Apollos Hassell wrote from Cloughjordan on behalf of "a number of Loyal Protestants in this neighbourhood" asking for a ship to convey them to Canada, but making no direct reference to the previous year's transactions. The same month Robert Birch, a shoemaker formerly of Roscrea who had evidently moved to Borrisokane after his marriage to a Hodgins of that place (probably a relative of Mrs Thomas Stanley who had sailed the year before), petitioned to state his determination to proceed to Upper Canada as a settler in the spring, and forwarded a list of twelve families "who wish to Acompany me as Settlers." Their surnames suggest that most were from Borrisokane and a few from Roscrea, while some were probably from Ballingarry since the vicar of that parish certified their loyalty and Protestantism along with the Rev. Mr Huleatt of Borrisokane.[3]

In March, Robert Boyd of Moneygall and John Baskerville of Traverston worded a petition alluding to the "necessity [which] alone compels us to leave our native Country" and offered to send £10 for each settler, having "unanimously appointed Robert Boyd our Agent."[4] This petition was a descendant of Apollos Hassell's January letter and Birch's petition from Borrisokane. Few of the names on Birch's list were repeated, but Birch and his brothers appeared on the new list and, despite the statement about Boyd's leadership in the petition, Thomas Hassell signed the list as agent, and his name appeared below that of Apollos on the list. The government offered no assistance, and those who did come found the passage money themselves.

The list of fifty-seven families attached to Boyd's petition is remarkable for the number of settlement locations in Canada that the names represent. Emigrants of later years tended to head for the Ottawa Valley or the London area to a greater extent than did the settlers of 1819 (see Figure 1). As has already been suggested, the solution to this puzzle lies partly in the fact that the Talbots settled in London Township only in December 1818 and most of Talbot's settlers probably did not come up from Yarmouth until the ensuing spring. Thus any letters which might have reached friends at home by the spring of 1819 can have given little encouraging news. Indeed, when the first petitions to the Colonial Office were written in January, no letters of more recent date than the early autumn could have reached Ireland. The settlers who had parted with Talbot at Lachine had, of course, reached the Ottawa Valley earlier in the season and had time to send favourable first impressions home before the close of navigation. Nevertheless, it is likely that those who left early in 1819 were, like those before them, emigrating with no clear idea of where they would settle, but were heartened by the prospect of escaping distressed circumstances in Ireland to become freeholders in Canada. Smaller numbers had received word from Thomas Reed in New York and journeyed to meet him at York. It seems to have taken longer for friends to reach the Standish brothers in Rougemont, for most of the families that joined them in the 1820s spent a couple of years in Montreal first. Once the firm establishment of the Ottawa Valley and London colonies became more widely known, the majority of the region's emigrants left Ireland with one or other of these two destinations in mind, and many visited the Richmond area en route to London. The small clusters of North Tipperary families in Rougemont and Esquesing did not grow signficantly and eventually declined in numbers as some of their residents moved on.

Boyd's list is also remarkable for the wide geographical area at home from which the names were drawn. As in the case of Talbot's party, the distant families no doubt learned of the plan from relatives and friends living near the compilers of the list. Not all emigrated, but given the disappointing response from the government to their request for assisted passage it is striking that about half of the fifty-seven families came out shortly thereafter at their own expense. Some of the remaining families emigrated later. Of the families on the list that can be identified, only a few were from Moneygall itself and none of these appear to have come out. However, the widespread places of residence of the identified families show that ties of kinship had carried the news of official encouragement of the Talbot party throughout North Tipperary.

The petition included a few relatives of people who had been on the *Brunswick*. Henry and Robert O'Neil, father and brother of William who had gone out as a servant with Talbot, submitted a character certificate from the Rev. Henry Bayly, who had been their landlord near Nenagh for upwards of thirty years. Robert remained for some time in Montreal, as did his brother James, while Henry and the rest of the family went on to join William in London Township.[5] Joseph Sifton and his parents and their respective families also came out from Glantane near Castle Otway in this year to join brothers who had gone with Talbot the year before.[6]

Family connections of petitioners extended the Tipperary migration field to the Birr area of King's County. Robert Birch's brother Thomas had recently married a daughter of Lancelot Robinson of Grange, Seirkieran, near Birr, and the family of "Lanty Robinson" along with two other Robinsons appears on the petition. Robinson's wife was herself from Borrisokane, where Robert Birch was living.[7] On arrival in Canada, Robert Birch proceeded to Richmond while the Robinsons secured seigneurial land in Mascouche, north of Montreal, from Mr Pangman, an English-speaking seigneur of an almost entirely French-speaking seigneury. The family claims that Robinson, a carpenter with a large family, could not afford to travel further.[8] Thomas Birch, Lanty Robinson's son-in-law, may have spent a short time with him, for he is recorded in Montreal in 1823, but he soon joined his brother in Richmond and took up land in nearby Nepean.[9] The third brother, George, was refused land in Mascouche and moved between Caledonia on the Ottawa River and Goulbourn for a number of years before eventually moving to the London area.[10] Also from the Birr area came Samuel Watkins and his large family, to join Reed in Esquesing.

Several other families from Borrisokane appear on the 1819 list. John Bull and his four sons, "near neighbours" of Thomas Towers, Esq., and former members of his yeomanry corps, came out in 1819 and settled in York Township near Toronto.[11] Thomas Bull was married to Frances Goulding, and her brother Thomas Goulding of Roscrea settled near the Bulls in York. Goulding, a native of Ardcrony, had been married in Ireland to a sister of Thomas Reed of Esquesing, who helped lead the group of prewar Irish settlers up from New York the same year.[12] Thomas Bull had left Borrisokane and lived in Roscrea near his wife's family for a year or so prior to emigrating.[13] There were four other Goulding families in the list, including Thomas's brothers William and James, smiths, and Samuel, a carpenter.[14] We find Samuel living in Montreal shortly thereafter along with other Gouldings whose relationship has not been determined; after Samuel died his widow moved to Rougemont.[15] James Goulding of Moneygall, who was not on the list, was in York, Upper Canada, by September, and in London shortly thereafter.[16] He was probably a close relative of Charles Goulding of Moneygall who applied to emigrate with Evans in 1815 and went with Talbot in 1818. The Roscrea family was probably more distantly connected with Charles since none of them joined him in London Township. Also from Roscrea were William and Robert Carden, shoemakers who had lived for the last four years in Borris-in-Ossory. William lived in Montreal, where he married, and then moved to Rougemont.[17]

Also taking advantage of the apparent opportunity provided by Boyd's efforts was Adam Prittie, probably from the Silvermines area, going out to join his wife's brother, Andrew Caswell, a Limerick man who had gone to New York and headed north to Canada, settling in Drummond Township in the Perth military settlement in 1816. These Caswells were forerunners of a County Limerick group, partly composed of Palatines from the Nantinan area, that came out by a process of chain migration thereafter and settled mainly in Pakenham and Stafford in the Upper Ottawa Valley. Mary Caswell had, however, married a Tipperary man, and so attempted to join with settlers from that region in order to secure a passage to Canada. Her story provides another interesting early example of how bilineal kinship allowed a couple a choice of alternate migration fields.[18]

Individual petitions and letters add further names to the list of those who inquired in 1819. So far as is known, only William O'Neil of the *Brunswick* passengers had been from Nenagh, the largest market town in North Tipperary, located some nine miles southwest of Cloughjordan, though Joseph Hardy had once lived there. In January 1819 William Cantrell, an apothecary in Nenagh, wrote "at the urgent Request of Several Most respectable Protestant families in this Neighbourhood who are inclined to Embark for Upper Canada this Spring if insured the protection of our Government & the terms as liberal as those granted to many who Sailed last season." Although Cantrell did not emigrate himself, his wife was a sister of Robert Howard, later of Esquesing and Montreal; he may have been writing on Howard's behalf.[19]

Word of the Talbot party's departure had also reached Templemore by the spring of 1819. Families from Templemore, some of whom had moved to Moneygall, had been among those who considered emigrating with Evans in 1815, but no Templemore families appear to have accompanied Talbot. On 17 March 1819 Richard Rud wrote on behalf of twenty Protestant families in Templemore who wished to emigrate to Upper Canada and hoped that the government "will encourage in 1819 as in 1818." He received the usual negative response.[20] On 8 April William Sutherland wrote from the same place saying much the same thing and received the same reply.[21] On 14 April Samuel Howard, late a private in the Wexford Militia but a former and present resident of Templemore, wrote that he had received no benefits since the reduction of his regiment six years before, and "for True pinuary and want of Trade" asked free passage for his family of five children.[22] It is probable that Samuel was related to Thomas T. Howard of Moneygall, a *Brunswick* passenger who had been a resident of Templemore prior to his marriage to Esther Goulding in 1809, at which time he had moved north to his wife's parish. The day before, Samuel Howard's brother-in-law, George T. Fitzgerald, had written that he was "informed that there is agreat [sic] number of persons in this county, has got the grant of free passage to upper canada, I also inquire of Your Lordship Could families in this town Get the grant of free passage And land. if not I further Inquire of your Lordship if ayoung Man goes to canada And pays the passage will he get the grant of land." Fitzgerald explained, "we are here in this town agreat number of stout resolute loyal Subjects to his Magesties Crown when Occasion required we are kean half Idile and Any implyment it is Papists gets it."[23] Fitzgerald, his parents, brothers, and sisters, and Howard, came to Canada on their own resources and settled in London Township.

Residents of the Protestant colony across the river at Mountshannon, County Galway, had been acquainted with some of Richard Talbot's party and also sought to secure assisted passages in 1819. Much of the population of the village of Mountshannon was made up of Protestant labourers who were very poor – so poor, in fact, that most of them proved unable to emigrate when the government refused them assistance. There were, however, a number of farmers in the surrounding countryside who were the descendants of eighteenth-century freeholders. Now facing economic ruin but still possessing interests in small parcels of land, some members of this class were able to emigrate. The clergyman at Mountshannon, James Martin, wrote in March 1819 on behalf of ten families of "Protestant Loyalists" who hoped to "make a deposit in money for each family, as done last year," having "already parted their little holdings in this Country, in expectation of following many of their friends and relations who went out last year and from whom they have had the most favourable accounts."[24] Unfortunately the certificates bearing their names are not in the file, and so the exact interconnections cannot be known. The only member of this group who can be identified positively is John Boucher, a tenant of Sir James Read, Bart., at Mountshannon. The very next day Read wrote in protest to the Colonial Office, stating that the prospective settlers were "endeavouring to quit this country defrauding me of my rent." Read mentioned John Bouchier in particular and asked that no further emigrants from his estate be permitted to leave Ireland without the landlord's permission.[25]

No *Brunswick* emigrants from Mountshannon have been identified, and it is likely that the friends and relations Martin mentioned had resided in Tipperary. Certainly four Clarke brothers from Cregg townland near Mountshannon who emigrated in 1819 had links with the Talbot party. The wife of George Clarke was a daughter of Nicholas Shouldice from the Castle Otway neighbourhood, one of the party that had separated from Talbot at Lachine. One of the Clarkes settled near the Bulls and Gouldings in York Township and two nearby in Tecumseth, one of them soon marrying Thomas Reed's daughter, but George Clarke, stayed in Montreal over the winter by the pregnancy of his wife, settled in 1820 in March Township, the residence of his father-in-law. The godfather of George's daughter born in Montreal that winter was Thomas Acres, probably from Borrisoleigh, near Castle Otway, whose wife was a Holland from Nutgrove, Clonrush, very near Cregg.[26] Thus by 1819 families from the entire North Tipperary region were aware of the departure of Talbot's party and were preparing to follow them.

Of course, not everyone who inquired in 1819 actually emigrated. For some the lack of free passages was a sufficient disincentive. John Baskerville, who wrote the covering letter for the large 1819 list with Robert Boyd, did not come till 1846, whereas Edward Owens of Borrisokane, one of the men on the list, came in 1825. His probable brother William, whose name preceded that of Edward, petitioned again in 1827[27] but seems never to have come. However, a number of his children went to the Ottawa Valley in the 1840s.

Similarly, some of those who did come in 1819 did not bother to petition, but simply paid their fares and left. Among those who settled in the Ottawa Valley were close relatives of *Brunswick* passengers. Frederick William

TABLE 7

Shouldice, Clarke, Holland, and Dyas Families

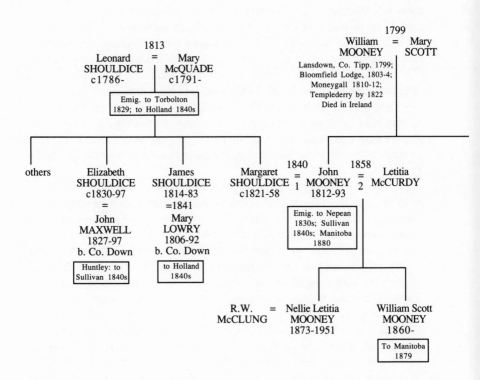

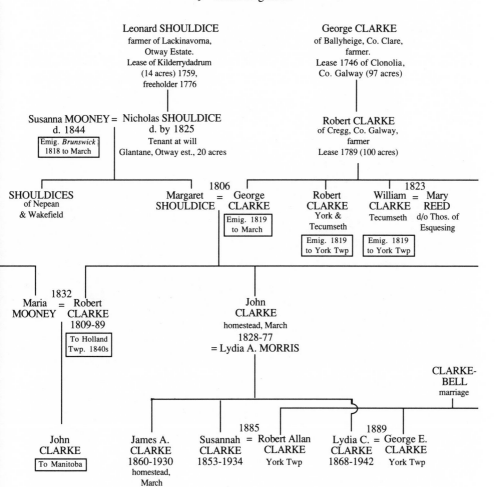

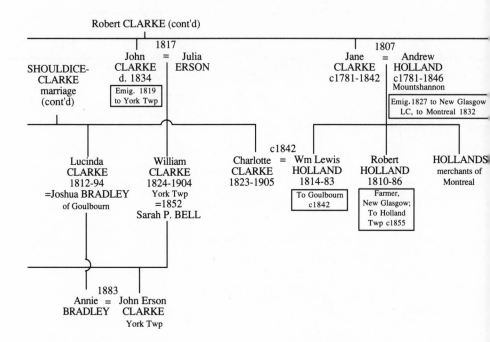

Sources: NLI, 21.F.129, Otway estate map, 1794; NLI, ms 13,000(8), Otway rentals; PRO, Dublin, D.20,368; Registry of Deeds, Dublin, 188/372/126044, 431/151/279607; PRO, Dublin: Killaloe, Newport, Castle Connell, and Templeharry parish registers; PAC, RG 1, L 3, vol. 102, C12/257, reel C-1723; *Nenagh Guardian,* 13 August 1842, 1, col. 1; *Christian Guardian,* 28 April 1886, 267; Nellie McClung, *Clearing in the West* (Toronto 1976); information from Keith Hollier, Nellie Young, Howard Dawson, E. Marjorie Moodie, Jean Kelly, and Marsha Shouldice; Canadian census, parish register, land, and gravestone data.

Note: This table illustrates several points made in the text:

1 Chain migration. Numerous examples of relatives coming out to join earlier emigrants may be traced on the table. The degree of relationship of the Shouldice families is unknown, but Leonard emigrated to join Nicholas's family. John Mooney's emigration was probably stimulated by that of Susanna (Mooney) Shouldice; he may have been her nephew but the relationship has not been proved.

2 Choice of settlement locations with kin present. The Clarkes are related in some degree to the Clarkes of Table 8, and Edward Cox was from the same townland as and no doubt related to the Coxes of Table 12.

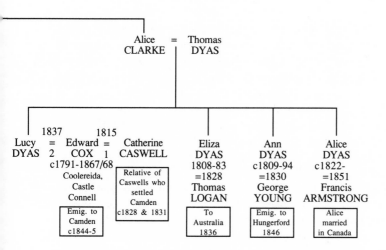

3 Choice of locations widened by bilateral kinship. Migrants moved to maternal and wife's kin as much as to their own. George Clarke separated from his brothers in 1819 and settled in March Twp near his father-in-law while his brothers located near Toronto. George's son Robert moved to Grey County in the 1840s with his wife's family, the Mooneys, and the second Shouldice family, one of whom was the wife of John Mooney. They were joined in the 1850s by Robert Clarke's cousin, Robert Holland from New Glasgow, LC. An Irish cousin, a daughter of Alice (Clarke) Dyas, went to Australia while some of her sisters followed their brother-in-law Edward Cox to the Kingston area of Canada. Cox had considered going out to his wife's relations in Australia but chose instead to join his first wife's Caswell relatives in Canada.

4 Incorporation of non-Tipperary families into the kin and migration network. Several of Leonard Shouldice's children married members of a County Down group resident on the Fitzroy-Huntley border. Some of the relatives of the latter joined in the movement to Grey County.

5 Movement late in the life cycle. Some of the children of Nicholas Shouldice and of the second Leonard were married at the times of their respective moves. Both families are consequently examples of three-generation migration.

6 Cousin marriages reaffirming kin ties despite distance. William L. Holland came to March from Montreal around 1842 and married his first cousin, Charlotte Clarke. After the expansion of the railway network facilitated visiting, three members of the York County Clarkes married second cousins from March in the 1880s. The grandfathers of the couples had parted in Montreal in 1819.

Richardson, who arrived in 1819 with his wife and small family, was a son of William who had come the year before. Thomas Morgan was a brother of William Morgan, and Nathaniel Corbett was doubtless a relative of Patrick. Michael Rivington, progenitor of a large family in Huntley who came in 1819, had been on Talbot's first list of applicants two years previously. William Healy was a carpenter of Moneygall, a village which had sent several *Brunswick* passengers, and his wife was a distant connection of Richard Talbot, though she had married beneath her. Thomas Hodgins and his wife Hetty (Pye) and children came out from Borrisokane to Goulbourn in this year, too.

A number of the 1819 emigrants, including the Siftons, O'Neils, Acres, Richardsons, and Hodginses, came out together on the ship *Camperdown*. In light of the number of individual petitions filed by the Colonial Office that year it is unlikely that it was the only vessel to convey North Tipperary residents to Canada that season, but it was clearly viewed at the time and for some years after as the successor to the *Brunswick*. Richard Talbot's obituary in the *Leinster Express* was later to refer to the "large acession [sic] in 1819" which followed Talbot's party,[28] and the name of the *Camperdown* is one of the very few names of emigrant ships thought sufficiently important to have been preserved in the independent oral traditions of several families. The *Camperdown* sailed from Limerick on 25 June 1819 with 256 settlers, not all from Tipperary, and was described as "one of the best appointed vessels which has cleared out of this port for a long time."[29] She arrived at Quebec on 7 September, apparently having lost only four settlers during the crossing.

Of the 1819 emigrants, about twenty families went to London Township and about a dozen to the Richmond military settlement. Ten remained in Montreal, most for only a few years, moving on to other Tipperary colonies in the Canadas. About the same number settled in York County, north of Toronto, mostly in the Downsview neighbourhood of York Township. A few settled away from their compatriots, often in neighbourhoods that were being opened for settlement when they arrived; the Portts, for example, chose Tyendinaga, near Belleville, where Indian lands were opened to settlers that year.[30] Charles Sifton's son-in-law Joseph Wallis lived in Belleville for a time after arriving in Canada.[31] A few may have been sidetracked en route to somewhere else. Benjamin Tydd, a brewer and distiller from a family of minor gentry in Modreeny who were eighteenth-century middlemen under Lord Dunalley, proceeded to York, as did many of the 1819 arrivals, and petitioned for land.[32] He obtained employment with the Rev. Ralph Leeming in Hamilton, but petitioned again for a building lot at Coote's Paradise (now Dundas).[33] He remained in the Hamilton area and when he died of cholera in 1832 he was gaoler in the town.[34] All of these immigrant settlers but Tydd drew at least a few relatives and friends to their localities in ensuing years, but many such immigrants moved on to the large colonies at Richmond and London. Even Tydd purchased land in West Nissouri, immediately east of London Township, and may have contemplated moving there before his untimely death, as it was his only landholding outside Hamilton.[35] Because the largest number of settlers located in the Ottawa Valley and the London area, however, they continued to be the major settlement areas for North Tipperary Protestants. Chain migration brought Tipperary families into these regions in considerable numbers for the next thirty-five years.

LATER IMMIGRATION FROM
NORTH TIPPERARY

By the early 1820s it was apparent that the Colonial Office had realized that subsidization of emigration was largely unnecessary as substantial numbers of people had proved that they were able to make their way to the colonies without government assistance. For this reason, and also in response to a temporary improvement in the economy at home,[36] the number of petitions to the Colonial Office in quest of aid fell off in this period.[37] In 1819 Lord Bathurst had received twenty-three petitions from the North Tipperary region, two enclosing long lists of prospective emigrants. In 1820 only two petitions were received and in 1821 the same number again. However, newspaper accounts of the Peter Robinson experiments in 1823 and 1825 revived hopes of assisted passage and there was once more a flurry of letters, twelve in 1823, eight in 1824, and thirty in 1825, but these hopes were shortlived. It soon became apparent that the Robinson ventures would not be repeated. Thereafter, petitions came mostly from former soldiers, who remained eligible for free grants in the Canadas after grants were abolished for civilian applicants in 1826, or who wrote to inquire about transferring pension payments to Canada, and from those who felt they had special claims upon the government's favour. In 1826 five petitions were received, three from military pensioners and two from individuals inquiring about the possibility of free ships going out that year. In 1827 eleven letters came in, five from military personnel, one from a policeman, one from a prospective Robinson settler who had been unable to put his affairs in order in time to leave in 1825, one from a brother of Richard Talbot's settler Joseph O'Brien, and the remainder from people who had heard rumours of another free ship or hoped that one would materialize. The numbers continued to decline as it became apparent that free ships were a thing of the past, and the years 1832–4 saw only three such petitions, two from subconstables of police and one from a Protestant schoolmaster.

While the numbers of petitioners are useful as a barometer of public perceptions of government emigration policy and, to some degree, of interest

TABLE 8

Oakley, Long, Clarke, and Flynn Families

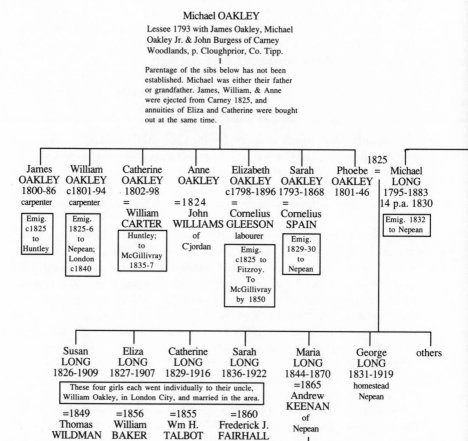

Michael OAKLEY

Lessee 1793 with James Oakley, Michael
Oakley Jr. & John Burgess of Carney
Woodlands, p. Cloughprior, Co. Tipp.

Parentage of the sibs below has not been
established. Michael was either their father
or grandfather. James, William, & Anne
were ejected from Carney 1825, and
annuities of Eliza and Catherine were bought
out at the same time.

| James OAKLEY 1800-86 carpenter | William OAKLEY c1801-94 carpenter | Catherine OAKLEY 1802-98 | Anne OAKLEY | Elizabeth OAKLEY c1798-1896 | Sarah OAKLEY 1793-1868 | Phoebe OAKLEY 1801-46 | 1825 = Michael LONG 1795-1883 14 p.a. 1830 |

Catherine OAKLEY
=
William CARTER
Huntley;
to
McGillivray
1835-7

Anne OAKLEY
=1824
John WILLIAMS
of
C'jordan

Elizabeth OAKLEY
=
Cornelius GLEESON
labourer
Emig. c1825 to Fitzroy. To McGillivray by 1850

Sarah OAKLEY
=
Cornelius SPAIN
Emig. 1829-30 to Nepean

James OAKLEY: Emig. c1825 to Huntley

William OAKLEY: Emig. 1825-6 to Nepean; London c1840

Michael LONG: Emig. 1832 to Nepean

| Susan LONG 1826-1909 | Eliza LONG 1827-1907 | Catherine LONG 1829-1916 | Sarah LONG 1836-1922 | Maria LONG 1844-1870 =1865 Andrew KEENAN of Nepean | George LONG 1831-1919 homestead Nepean | others |

These four girls each went individually to their uncle,
William Oakley, in London City, and married in the area.

| =1849 Thomas WILDMAN | =1856 William BAKER | =1855 Wm H. TALBOT | =1860 Frederick J. FAIRHALL |

To Manitoba under
Thos. Greenway, 1881

William KEENAN
c1868-

Edith KEENAN
1870-

With their great
uncle, Robert Long,
in Stephen Twp. 1871

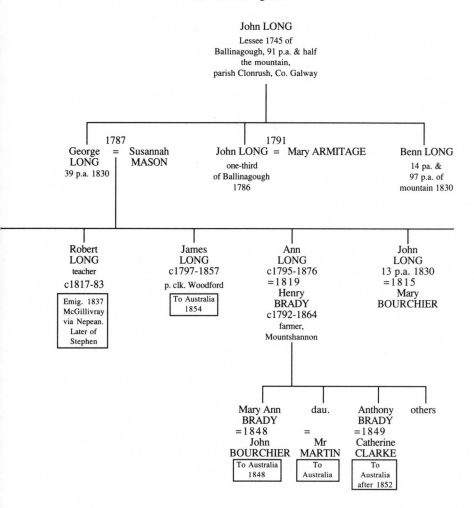

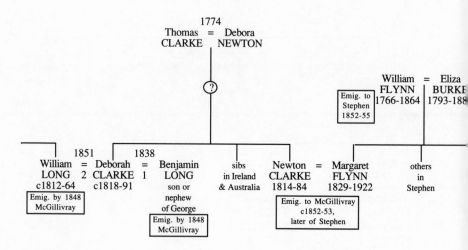

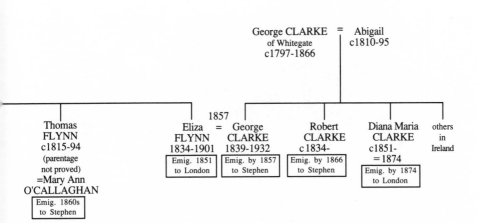

Sources: Registry of Deeds, Dublin, 802/165/541300, 147/194/99370; PRO, Dublin, Mountshannon parish register; Brady and Clarke gravestones at Mountshannon; PRO, Dublin, Index to Killaloe Diocesan marriage licence bonds; M.H. Bourchier, *'Boomagong' and the Bourchier Family* (Tocumwal? 1973); information from Lois Long, Judy Hodgins, and Phyl Simons; Canadian census, land, gravestone, and parish register data.
Note: This table illustrates several points made in the text:

1 Subdivision of property. The large Long property was much subdivided among the descendants of the original lessee by the third generation.

2 Kin ties over distance. The Long, Clarke, and Flynn families of the Mountshannon area became involved in movement to Canada ultimately because of the link established when Michael Long of Ballinagough near Mountshannon married Phoebe Oakley of Carney, on the other side of Lough Derg, in 1825.

3 Bilateral kinship operative in migration. Michael Long emigrated to his wife's brother in Nepean and bought land adjoining the lot Oakley occupied.

4 Chain migration. Chain migration spread from one network of kin to another as the siblings of marriage partners emigrated in turn.

5 Internal chain migration. The move from the Ottawa Valley to McGillivray near London of William Carter and his brothers attracted William's wife's family, the Oakleys, who were followed in turn by Longs. The families who came from Ireland later went directly to the London area, settling in Stephen immediately north of McGillivray. Four of Michael Long's daughters lived with their uncle Oakley in London and married in that area; two of Long's grandchildren lived with their great-uncle Robert Long in Stephen in 1871.

6 Chain migration to Australia from the Mountshannon area. The Bourchiers were followed by Mrs Bourchier's siblings and uncle.

7 Unusually, the Oakley family was of mixed religion, some of the children being raised Roman Catholic and the rest Church of Ireland.

FIGURE 1

Dates of Immigration of Tipperary Protestant Families in the Canadas

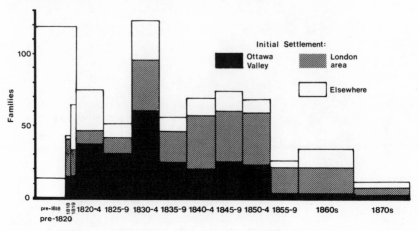

Source: Compiled family files.

in emigration itself, they do not accurately reflect the number of actual emigrants from Tipperary. As we have seen, many people left without writing to the government, and not all those who did inquire in fact left.

Because no passenger lists or nominal immigration returns were preserved on either side of the Atlantic, it is very difficult to determine the number of immigrants from Tipperary that arrived in the province each year. The only way of obtaining this data is to gather together all available information about the individual immigrants who have been identified in order to determine individual dates of immigration as closely as possible. The resulting dates are often approximate at best, though normally they fall within a short range of years. For this reason, immigrants have been grouped together in small time periods to avoid giving a misleading impression of the exactness of the data. In Figure 1 the numbers refer to families, each unaccompanied single emigrant, group of unmarried siblings, or married couple, widow or widower with or without children being counted as one. In all, some 775 Protestant families from the North Tipperary region have been identified as coming to the Canadas in the period covered by this study.

The largest numbers of emigrants to arrive in any individual years seem to have come in 1818 and 1819. However, twelve Tipperary Protestant emigrants were already in the Canadas when the *Brunswick* party arrived in 1818. Six were members of the 99/100 Regiment that was disbanded that year at Quebec. Francis Evans, Thomas Reed, and Richard Talbot's brother John have already been mentioned. Another military man was Lt George Hopper, living at Prescott and soon to be clerk of works for the Grenville Canal. Though not from Tipperary himself, he had a brother in Roscrea whose children would contact him upon reaching Canada.[38] A second Thomas Reid from Tipperary had been working for Philemon Wright in Hull since 1814. Jocelyn Waller, a brother of Sir Robert Waller of Castle Waller in the Union of Newport, arrived at Quebec in 1817 to take up a government posting and would remain in the colony.[39] Forty-two families came out in 1818, thirty-nine of them on the *Brunswick,* and sixty-four more came in 1819. Sources do not allow the exact years of arrival of all later emigrants to be determined, but between 1820 and 1824 another seventy-four families came to the Canadas, and another fifty-one arrived in the second half of the 1820s. More precision is possible concerning the families who settled in the Ottawa Valley in this period. Fifteen families from the *Brunswick* party settled in eastern Upper Canada, and a dozen joined them in 1819. Only three families arrived in 1820, but fourteen came in 1821 and thirteen in 1822. Emigration then dropped off somewhat, with only a dozen arriving during the next three years, and another twenty-one in the last four years of the 1820s. In the early 1830s, however, the number of Tipperary immigrants reached an all-time high, with 123 families arriving in the Canadas between 1830 and 1834. Thereafter immigration was fairly steady, with some sixty to seventy families arriving every five years right through the Famine era. After the mid-1850s, however, the numbers dropped off, with twenty-six families arriving in the late 1850s, thirty-three in the 1860s, and eleven in the following decade. Before 1830 more of the arrivals located in the Ottawa Valley than anywhere else, but by 1840 the majority of the immigrants were settling north of London, where good land was still available in the newly opened townships of the Huron Tract.

The pattern produced by these figures indicates clearly the initial wave of enthusiasm for emigration to Canada that followed hard upon the arrival of the Talbot party. Some of the seventy-four families who arrived in the early 1820s were no doubt motivated by the partial famines and disturbances that marked these years. The high numbers arriving in the early 1830s coincide with the pre-Famine peak years for Irish emigration to Canada in 1831 and 1832. While the general economic explanations no doubt also applied to the Tipperary case, the taut political atmosphere preceding and surrounding Catholic emancipation in 1829 was a significant factor in the decision of many Tipperary Protestants to emigrate in that period. Some families had been directly involved in the disturbances of those tension-filled years. The departure in 1832 of a large connection of Hodginses from Borrisokane and Terryglass was directly related to Catholic reaction to the acquittal of one of their number, James Hodgins, later of Biddulph, a subconstable of police who had been charged with murder after shooting a man during a riot in Borrisokane. It was reported after the incident that the Protestants of the neighbourhood were coming into the town to sleep at night and that many were contemplating emigration.[40]

Information about the places of origin and socio-economic circumstances of emigrants from a particular region is difficult to determine because of the destruction of many Irish records during the Civil War of the 1920s. Sufficient data survives to identify most of the emigrant settlers with the region, but not enough to provide a socio-economic profile based upon individual data. For the same reason exact figures on the numbers and types of emigrants leaving various parishes are not available, but a Parliamentary Commission on the Poor Law that sat in the mid-1830s did gather the subjective impressions of landlords, magistrates, and parochial clergy on these topics. Its 1836 report presents the opinions of these people on the numbers and character of those leaving their parishes during the previous three years. These members of the Protestant establishment may not have been in the best position to know about occurrences among the lower classes, particularly among the Catholic population and the labourers who were not direct tenants. Some frankly admitted their ignorance. The Rev. James Saunderson of Ballingarry and Uskane stated that he "can't say" whether there had been emigrants, that they would have gone "to America, if any," and that none had received assistance to emigrate "that I can hear of,"[41] and the minister at Castletownarra replied to the question on emigration: "don't know of any; maybe some without my knowledge."[42] Nevertheless, the returns are useful for the details they do provide and, scattered though they are, they tend to confirm the patterns indicated by the rough figures compiled from the data on individuals and point to some general conclusions.

Generally speaking, emigration from the North Tipperary region was thought to be predominantly made up of respectable Protestant farm families who had sold their interests in their landholdings and gone to Canada. Typical of the comments were those of the Rev. William B. Fry of Dunkerrin: "A good many left this parish, mostly Protestants, and I fear many more will shortly leave their old habitations, to seek for peace and quietness in every foreign land where they think such is to be obtained ... They have converted their property into specie, and I believe received no other assistance."[43] George Atkinson, Esq., JP, Cloghprior, noted: "There were many families emigrated to Canada, from this and the adjoining parishes, within the last three years; they were of the most decent class of farmers, and possessed far the most money ... They received no assistance; they were people that did not require it."[44]

It is apparent from the returns that, because emigration was predominantly Protestant, emigrants were drawn most heavily from the areas with the largest populations of Protestant farmers and tradesmen, particularly the former. These types of people concentrated most heavily in the barony of Clonlisk in the King's County panhandle and the parishes to its immediate south and especially to its west, in the Cloughjordan-Borrisokane area. George Atkinson, Esq., JP, noted at Shinrone in the King's panhandle: "The number of emigrants from the neighbourhood, though not immediately from this parish, has been considerable. They may almost be said to be exclusively Protestant, the members of any other sect bearing no proportion; they are also mainly confined to the class of respectable yeomen, whose industry has procured for them a small capital; the very description of persons who are most wanted at home, and who, if they even carried nothing with them, would be in themselves a loss ... They have all gone to Canada, and, as far as I know, without receiving or requiring any assistance."[45]

That the emigrants were partly motivated to leave by the disturbances in the countryside and were able to go without assistance by government or landlord was affirmed by a number of witnesses, including the Rev. Mr Fry at Dunkerrin, and the Rev. Mr Gresson at Borrisnafarney and Bourney, who noted that "the only emigrants are the useful industrious yeoman, who has been driven from his native home by fear of the religious and political agitator" and has gone "to the Canadas, in general."[46] A similar comment was made in Templemore, south of the hills below Roscrea. The Carden estate, with its substantial Protestant population centred upon the market town of Templemore, made up much of the parish. The Rev. William N. Falkiner indignantly characterized emigration from this parochial union as follows: "Several very *respectable Protestant families* have left this, *much disgusted* at the situation they were in, unprotected from lawless aggression of mobs, and deserted by Government; *such were their complaints;* they went to Canada."[47]

Specifying the geographical origins of emigrants within the region is difficult because of the uneven survival of records concerning the various parishes. Where a good parish register exists it is possible to identify many of the parish's emigrants from entries of marriage or of baptisms of children. In the absence of a register, however, identifications cannot be as numerous or as certain. In all, 460 of the 775 families identified as coming to Canada from the region between 1803 and 1880 have been linked to a parish. It must be remembered, however, that the origins of fully 40 per cent of emigrants have not been pinpointed, usually because they left a parish before the register commenced, were not married or did not have a child born in a parish with a register, or because identifying information was inconclusive. However, comparison of the data available with Map 3 showing Protestant population concentrations in 1831 and with comments in the Parliamentary Report of 1836 allows us to see where the gaps in our knowledge lie. In order to give some idea of how heavy emigration was from particular parishes, I have added to Table 9 a calculation of emigrating families as a percentage of Protestant families in the parishes in 1831. Because of the continuing ramification of continually resident families and because of internal migration into parishes, these figures cannot be a real measure. They serve purely as an indicator of the proportional magnitude of emigration to Canada from certain parishes for which information is available. Emigration from the region

TABLE 9

Parochial Origins of Protestant Emigrant Families

Parish or Union	Earliest Registers	Protestant Families 1831*	Emigrating Families**	Emigts. as % of Families, 1831
Modreeny	1827	250	100	40
Borrisokane		120	48+	40+
Mountshannon Union		160	28	18
Templeharry Union	1800	100	25	25
Roscrea and Kyle	1784	300	24	8
Templemore Union	1791	145	23	16
Glankeen & Templederry		45	19	42
Castletownarra Union	1802	35	19	54
Nenagh		120	18	15
Birr and Loughkeen	1760	370	18	5
Shinrone Union	1741	250	17	7
Terryglass	1809	30	11	37
Dunkerrin Union	1825	75	11	15
Castle Connell	1824	60	8	13
Newport Union	1780	100	8	8
Aghnameadle	1834	20	5	25
Ogonnelloe	1807	25	5	20
Corbally	1834	100	5	5
Other parishes, < 5 families each	***		68	

* Protestant inhabitants divided by 5. Source: HC (1836) XXXIII.
** Protestant families emigrating to Canada, 1803–80, mostly 1818–55. Parish of origin identified from sources in Ireland and Canada for 460 of 775 families.
*** Registers examined, with dates of commencement: Aglishcloghane (1828), Killaloe (1679), Borris-nafarney (1828), Ettagh (1820), Kilcolman (1839).

generally was fairly heavy, for the 775 families who left, mostly in the generation between 1818 and 1855, represent a quarter of the number of Protestant families in the region in 1831.

The greatest number of Protestant emigrants from one parish noted in the 1836 Parliamentary Report, and the greatest number identified from my files, came from the almost solidly Protestant southeastern portion of the parish of Modreeny, which made up part of the Dunalley estate around Cloughjordan village, whence Richard Talbot's party had departed in 1818. While most of the 1836 parochial returns for the region noted the emigration of a few or a few dozen people, emigration from Modreeny was, by contrast, of major proportions. The Rev. William Homan noted that within the last three years "about 200 Protestants" had left his parish of 4506 people (1258 Protestants in 1831), "generally in comfortable circumstances, and industrious persons" who had gone "to America, and the greater number to Upper Canada." Homan also stated emphatically that the emigrants from his parish were Protestants, the number including "only one Roman Catholic, and he a person of bad character."[48] About 100 of the total of 775 identified Protestant families known to have emigrated to Canada from the North Tipperary region between 1803 and 1880 came from Modreeny parish, or 40 per cent of the parish's Protestant population in 1831. Modreeny's 1258 Protestants in 1831 accounted for 7 to 8 per cent of the Protestant population of the region, while its emigrants accounted for 13 per cent of the regional total. The overrepresentation of residents of Modreeny among the emigrants reflects the fact that the Dunalley estate was home to large numbers of middling freehold farmers who possessed the means to finance their departure. This circumstance is probably more significant than the fact that chain migration from the region was largely set in motion by a resident of the parish, for Richard Talbot appears to have taken with him few actual residents of Modreeny.

Substantial numbers of the identified emigrants also came from parishes in the vicinity of Modreeny. The parish of Borrisokane provided the second-largest number of identified Canadian immigrants. Despite the destruction of its pre-civil registration parish registers, forty-eight families have been identified with it, comprising 40 per cent of the parish's 1831 Protestant population figure. The actual numbers must be much higher. The Protestants of Borrisokane were described in 1820 as "gentry, petty farmers, shopkeepers, & mechanicks"[49] – in other words, few were labourers – and the village was a notable bastion of Orange sympathies. It is unfortunate that the Parliamentary Commission interviewed no witness from Borrisokane. Templeharry and Shinrone unions, in the King's panhandle to the other side of Modreeny, were the homes of about twenty-five and seventeen emigrating families, respectively; both figures are probably fairly comprehensive, as both parishes possess good registers. The Templeharry figure is significant, amounting to 25 per cent of the 1831 population. Dunkerrin union, in contrast, accounted for only eleven families, 15 per cent of the population.

As one moves outwards on the map from Modreeny, the nature of the emigration changes. A number of parishes reported no known emigrants in the 1836 report, while others reported small numbers of poor Roman Catholics bound as often for the United States as for Canada. The Roman Catholic parish priest of Seirkieran, east of Birr, reported that about twenty tradesmen and labourers had gone to America.[50] The rector of Kilmore Union, in the mountains south of Nenagh, a union that included the residence of Lord Dunalley but was a largely Catholic area, stated that four to six families had gone each year, only a third of them Protestants. He stated that the Protestants "generally take with them the means of making a comfortable settlement" but the Catholics "go out as labourers." Most went to Canada.[51] The large and mountainous Church of Ireland parochial union of St John's,

Newport, on the border with County Limerick, also had a small proportion of Protestants in its population. One report stated that about thirty people "generally of the poorer class" had gone to America from Killoscully in that union,[52] and the Rev. John Pennefather reported in greater detail that some fifty or sixty boys and young men and some adults had left the union for Upper Canada and the United States.[53] These emigrants seem to have been mainly Roman Catholic; certainly the Newport Church of Ireland registers which begin in 1780 only permitted the identification of eight families of Canadian immigrants. Though the evidence is too scanty to permit an incontrovertible generalization, Roman Catholic emigration from the North Tipperary region in the early 1830s seems to have been comparatively small numerically, drawn mostly from the poor, overcrowded mountain parishes where the Protestant population was negligible, directed to the United States more often than Protestant emigration, and characterized by the individual departures of young people as well as by family migration.

It is noteworthy that some of the marginal Protestant colonies in largely Catholic areas were almost depopulated by emigration. The numbers of families leaving the Castletownarra and Castle Otway neighbourhoods amounted to about half their 1831 populations. The Castletownarra Roman Catholic register provides evidence that the small numbers of Protestants there, thirty-five families in 1831, intermarried extensively with local Catholic families and that many subsequently converted. The number of Church of Ireland baptisms, which averaged five per year between 1802 and the early 1830s, dropped to one every five years thereafter. The primary valuation of 1850 confirms that almost all of the Protestants who had not converted had left the parish by that time. I have record of many of them in Canada.[54]

It is significant, too, that the major market towns of Birr and Roscrea contributed a much smaller proportion of emigrants to the Canadas than one would predict on the basis of their substantial numbers of Protestant inhabitants alone. Both parishes possess registers dating back to the eighteenth century, but only two dozen emigrant families can be identified with Roscrea[55] and only eighteen with the union of Birr and Loughkeen. The 1821 census for the town and parish of Birr and the adjoining barony of Ballybritt survives, but this source permitted the identification of only some dozen and a half emigrating families in the entire barony.[56] A number of the families who did come to Canada from Birr had personal links with residents of the Ormond baronies, and it is possible that the majority of the inhabitants of the Birr area may have associated themselves more with Offaly-midlands migration patterns rather than with the North Tipperary channels. As many emigrants came from the small Protestant colonies near Castle Otway and in Castletownarra union as came from these two towns. Though Nenagh, the major market town of North Tipperary, was home to only 120 Protestant families in 1831, it was probably a more important source of emigrants than is suggested by the eighteen emigrating families who can be identified, for unlike Birr and Roscrea, Nenagh's registers do not survive. The Parliamentary Commission on the Poor Law strangely failed to canvass opinion there. Protestant emigration from Nenagh, though more important than that from Birr and Roscrea, was certainly less significant than that from the much smaller village of Borrisokane, which had the same Protestant population as Nenagh but contributed nearly three times the number of identified emigrants despite a parallel loss of major documentary sources.

Inniscaltra, on the Galway shore of Lough Derg, was somewhat of an exception in terms of migration patterns as it was in respect to social structure and religious composition. Its numerous Protestant residents included a large number of poor Protestant labourers living in the estate village of Mountshannon, though the neighbouring parish of Clonrush was home to a number of Protestant farming families descended from eighteenth-century freeholders. A comparatively few extended family connections account for the more than two dozen emigrating families identified.[57] Philip Reade, Esq., JP, reported several emigrants to the United States and Canada in the 1836 report, "generally respectable persons of the established Church."[58] Despite several attempts to secure government assistance to emigrate to Canada to join friends who had gone with Talbot, very few names on the lists submitted to the Colonial Office from Mountshannon in the 1820s ever appeared in Canadian Tipperary communities. The few that did often turned up only many years later, possibly as a result of years of saving up the passage money. That some Protestant residents did emigrate to the United States from the Mountshannon area, taking advantage of the lower fares, is probably a reflection of the comparative poverty of the Protestant population there.

The data assembled about North Tipperary emigrants to the Canadas combined with the literary evidence of the Colonial Office petitions and the Parliamentary Report of 1836 do allow some conclusions to be made about the nature of emigration from the region in this period. If the comments made by the gentlemen of Tipperary were true, the chain migration set in motion by Richard Talbot in 1818 had succeeded in diverting Protestant emigration to the Canadas and away from the United States. The consensus of opinion was that the bulk of Protestant emigrants were proceeding to Upper Canada. The landlords also agreed that most of the emigrants were Protestant farmers who could provide their own passage and initial support by disposing of their little properties. Though many of the emigrants are known to have practised trades, emigration was heaviest from Richard Talbot's old neighbourhood where the Protestant population was largest and where the greatest number of middling freehold farmers resided. Smaller numbers came from the towns, where the Protestant population was often comparatively large but was made up for the most part of labourers and poor tradesmen. The substantial village of

Borrisokane is perhaps the one exception to this generalization, though it is not possible to tell how many of the emigrants lived in the village and how many farmed nearby. Many gentlemen viewed the departure of the Protestant families with regret. Though few would have denied that the emigrants faced declining fortunes in Ireland, many would have agreed with Charles Rolleston of Silverhills that the emigrants were on the whole the very sort of loyal, industrious Protestants that the ascendancy would have preferred, had it been possible, to have retained at home.[59]

Roman Catholic emigration from the lowlands of this part of the Shannon Valley where the bulk of the Protestant population resided was evidently still comparatively insignificant in the early 1830s. Greater numbers of Roman Catholics were leaving the crowded, impoverished mountain parishes on the periphery of the area. Such emigration was still directed mostly to the United States and was composed of young, single males more often than of families. The parliamentary reports do not tell the whole story, for communities of North Tipperary Roman Catholic families were forming in Jockvale (Nepean) and Biddulph by the late 1820s and mid-1830s, respectively, adjacent to strong Tipperary Protestant settlements. In both cases, however, the bulk of the Catholic population arrived later.

Substantial Protestant emigration to Canada from North Tipperary continued through the 1840s and into the Famine period. Because the Famine era saw massive emigration from Ireland as a whole and has often been treated as a turning point in both Irish and emigration history, the Famine in North Tipperary and its effects upon Protestant emigration are worthy of separate examination.

THE FAMINE MIGRATION

The story of Protestant emigration to Canada from North Tipperary took no novel twists in the Famine period of the late 1840s. The volume and nature of the emigration remained much the same as in the late 1830s and early 1840s. Most emigrants were small farmers in economically uncertain circumstances going out to join relatives who had preceded them; a few gentlemen and professionals emigrated to the towns of Upper Canada in this period but this, too, was no new phenomenon. The significant changes occurred after the immediate effects of the Famine had subsided. After the mid-1850s Protestant emigrants to the Canadas were much less numerous, went more often to the cities than they had before, and were probably greatly outnumbered by friends and kin going to the new frontier in Australia and New Zealand.

The effects of the Famine in North Tipperary were devastating, but Tipperary was not affected as badly as some other parts of Ireland. There are gradations even of horror and misery.[60] In 1849 300 people died in Nenagh Workhouse every month[61] and in 1851 there were still over 1100 people in the

Union Workhouse at Borrisokane, as many people as resided in the rest of the town.[62] Parochial relief committees, such as the one organized by the clergy and gentry at Mountshannon, met during the Famine to co-ordinate relief and distribute imported corn meal to the poor. At Mountshannon the Church of Ireland rector Mr Huleatt and the Roman Catholic parish priest Mr O'Brien sat as chairman and secretary on the Clonrush Relief Committee which collected subscriptions from the gentry of the neighbourhood, petitioned for shares in various English and overseas relief funds, lobbied for the initiation of public works as "the only substantial means of keeping this dense population from pressing starvation," and arranged for the sale of the meal that was secured from the distribution depots in Galway or Banagher.[63]

The short-term and long-term demographic consequences of the Famine were traumatic in North Tipperary, as in most of southern Ireland. In Silvermines Roman Catholic parish the number of Catholic baptisms dropped from 150 per year in the early 1840s to fifty-three in 1849 and then stabilized at about eighty-five annually.[64] Nonetheless, the actual mortality in Tipperary was not as severe as it was in localities at a distance of two or three days' travel. The Rev. Frederick F. Trench of Modreeny observed that "though there were multitudes around us suffering most severely from insufficiency of food, yet ... there was an immeasurable distance between their state and that of persons dying from extreme hunger."[65] He consequently left his parish in 1847 to organize relief work in the Schull district of County Cork, financing the work with money subscribed largely from "amongst his own friends and relations in Ireland."[66] Excess mortality reached its height in Tipperary only in 1849–50, later than it did in the rest of the country,[67] in a period that more or less coincided with the low in baptisms recorded at Silvermines. More died from "impure and insufficient diet; and fever, dysentery, the crowding in the workhouse, or hardship on the relief works" than from starvation.[68] However, mortality in Tipperary never reached much more than half the level it attained in Clare and Galway, the worst counties in this respect, and Tipperary occupied its accustomed intermediate statistical position between the sorely tried west and the more fortunate east of Ireland.[69]

The reduction of population as a consequence of the Famine was nevertheless of major proportions, particularly since Tipperary was one of the few counties in which the growth rate had continued to increase until the failure of the potato crop. In most parishes the number of people declined by about a third between 1841 and 1851, due to both deaths and departures, and in some of the mountain parishes where the population had been growing most rapidly in the previous decade the decline was much greater (see Map 13). Declines were also heavy in some of the open parishes on the Ormond plain such as Ballygibbon and Cloughprior (which included the Commons of Carney), in Aghnameadle where large-scale evictions cleared the Dawson estate, and across the Shannon in the impoverished Clare border parishes west

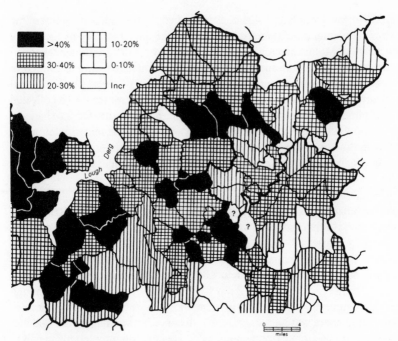

MAP 13   Population decline, 1841–51, by parish. Death during the Famine of the
late 1840s was a class-specific phenomenon. As a man in Roscrea wrote to an
uncle in Canada: "You would Scarcely miss a Soul out of fair or market but the
Country part is wild and unpopulated not a house in Some places within a mile of
each other – like the baseless fabric of a vision that leaves not a wreck behind it"
(Hopper correspondence, Thomas Hayes to Arthur Hopper, Roscrea, 2 Feb.
1852). Death struck most heavily in the crowded mountain parishes where the population had been increasing most rapidly, and evictions followed in the "open"
parishes of the Ormond plain.
Source: HC (1852–3) XCI.

of Mountshannon. The decline was less marked in Templeharry and Shinrone
unions in the King's panhandle, probably because of the high proportion of
Protestant small farmers in their populations, a class that was better able to
weather the Famine years than the poor Catholics. The parochial population
increased only in the parishes that included the towns of Roscrea and Birr and
in the large village of Borrisokane, because of the influx of dispossessed
country people. The population of Templemore decreased only marginally for
the same reason; the fact that it did not increase was probably due to Sir John
Carden's strict control over settlement in the rural parts of his estate. The
population in Nenagh declined by over 20 per cent, but the reason is
unclear.[70]

This period was marked by social disturbances in North Tipperary, in itself
a sign that the people had not sunk to the point where they had lost the will to

resist. The troubles were but an intensification of the endemic violence that had made the region notorious in the early 1840s, and they were caused largely by the increase, in the wake of the Famine, of the evictions that had lain behind much of the earlier discontent. Because immediate lessors were responsible for payment of the poor rate on smallholdings, landlords faced both loss of rental income due to the inability of the tenantry to pay and an unprecedented increase in the poor rates levied against them. Many of the minor gentry who dominated North Tipperary were heavily in debt even before the Famine and witnesses to the Devon Commission in 1844 had noted a number of estates in receivership. Many of these landlords had pursued a policy of eliminating middlemen in order to maximize rents, but as a result they found themselves in the Famine years responsible for paying the poor rates on smallholdings, in the parishes where these still prevailed. The only solution in many cases was to evict the tenants for non-payment of rent and level their houses.[71] Thomas Hayes of Roscrea wrote to his uncle Arthur Hopper in Canada in September 1849 describing conditions in his neighbourhood: "Ireland is at present in an awful State respecting rents and Taxes= As an Idea – There is a 3/4d Three Shillings and four pence in the pound poor rate after being collected and now – There is Three and eight pence more Struck= large quantities of land untenanted and the Tenants Sent to the poorhouse of which it is no disgrace to be an inmate. Robberies and murders Every day transactions of the most glaring Characters taking place – Landlords Shooting= tenants ejecting= auctions of farming Stock and implements of Husbandry every day taking place for rent and arrears of rent."[72]

Cousens has noted that in 1847 the rate of eviction in Tipperary was the highest in Ireland. In that year alone 7.9 per cent of the population was made homeless.[73] In June 1849 one of the most infamous occurrences took place when 567 people were ejected in one day from the estate of the Rev. Massey Dawson in an eviction still remembered as "The Sack of Toomevara." Lenihan, the Limerick historian, noted: "The razed village presented a melancholy spectacle to the eye of the tourist. The long line of destroyed habitations which formed the principal street of the unfortunate place remained as they were eleven months after. The huts which were built against the Chapel walls were tumbled down under the vigorous blows of sundry bailiffs and their inhabitants scattered far and wide over the country."[74]

The class most adversely affected by the Famine was the labouring poor, who accounted for the bulk of the deaths and evictions. The troubles of the Famine years gave the farmers some harrowing moments and burdened them temporarily with heavy poor rates, but they were able to purchase food and were not totally dependent on the potato in any case. The years after the Famine provided them with the opportunity to enlarge their holdings by taking up lands vacated by evicted smallholders and labourers, in some cases laying the foundations of future wealth. The contrasting impact of the Famine and its aftermath on the two classes was sketched vividly in a letter of Thomas Hayes at Roscrea to his uncle in Canada in February 1852: "Old Ireland is Still the Same yet= You would Scarcely miss a Soul out of fair or market but the Country part is wild and unpopulated not a house in Some places within a mile of each other= like the baseless fabric of a vision which leaves not a wreck behind it= You Speak of leaving old Ireland in good time but thank god there are people you left after you, who were not half as well of [sic] as you were and are now worth many thousands of pounds and a good number too and there is not a finer Country in the world for a capitalist than Ireland is at present= hundreds of magnificent estates Selling in Ireland at 10 to 15 and Twenty years purchase according to the Situation of the place leaving a hereditary property for your Son & your Sons Son after you in a Healthy Climate and a fine Soil."[75] The Hayes family were ejected from their lease of their ancestral Sparling lands in Ballinakill for non-payment of rent, but they were able to secure a new lease and after the Famine rapidly accumulated the capital to take a second farm. The losers at Ballinakill were, typically, the poor. The land had formerly been occupied by Hayes and another farmer along with six paupers, but the paupers' houses were thrown down and their six acres let to another man. The problem over Ballinakill, coming when it did, caused the Hayes family a good deal of anxiety, but it ended up not costing them a farthing – *"we were above it – thank god."*[76]

Though the Famine and ensuing eviction and emigration of much of the labouring population allowed the consolidation of farms to proceed at a pace unimagined in the 1840s, farm sizes may also have increased in some areas where labourers had never been common. In six Protestant townlands in the Newtown quarter of the Dunalley estate in Modreeny, the major freeholders' community, farm sizes notably increased by 1854. Since 1826/7 the number of holdings under forty statute acres had decreased from forty-one to nineteen and the number of farms over forty acres had risen from four to twelve. We have record of a large number of former residents of these townlands reaching Canada before the Famine as well as during and after it, and it is impossible to judge whether the increase in farm size here took place before or after the Famine.[77]

Because the farmers saw new opportunities opening to them at home by the early 1850s there was less incentive for members of this class, which included a large proportion of the Protestants, to emigrate, particularly to Upper Canada where the frontier of cheap land was nearing extinction. Soaring poor rates in the immediate aftermath of the Famine may have been an incentive for some farmers to leave in the late 1840s and very early 1850s, but emigration from Tipperary after 1854 attracted mostly the Roman Catholic labourers and smallholders who suffered eviction. Cousens's scattergram of county statistics indicates that Tipperary saw the second-largest percentage of its population evicted between 1851 and 1854 of any county in Ireland and the highest percentage emigrate during the same period; the neighbouring counties of King's and Clare displayed similar patterns.[78] Cousens noted that in North Tipperary, western King's, and eastern Galway, emigration was greater than indigence alone could have encouraged and was probably due to the number of evictions and the presence of a large labouring population that chose emigration over pauperization.[79]

Examination of my list reveals that the number of Protestant arrivals in the late 1840s and early 1850s was approximately the same as in the early 1840s, and only slightly higher than in the late 1830s. Equally significant is the fact that the numbers fell off appreciably after 1854, to only a third of previous levels, and continued to decline thereafter. This suggests that the Famine migration of Protestants was little more than a continuation of the existing situation. The decline in Protestant emigration after 1854 is attributable partly to improving conditions at home and to the effective closing of the frontier in Upper Canada as remaining unsettled lands were taken up, and probably also to the competing attractions of Australia and New Zealand.

The majority of the Protestant emigrants of the Famine era appear not to have been well off. Most of them spent a few years visiting relatives and working in Carleton or Middlesex counties after arriving from Ireland, but very few were able to purchase developed land in these areas. After building up some capital, they moved on to smaller Tipperary communities in Renfrew or Bruce counties where uncleared land was still available. Typical is a Hodgins family that left Ireland in the early 1850s: "Henry Hodgins came to Canada in 1851. His father, also named Henry, died while he was a child. His mother who was a Ralph, died about 2 years before he came to Canada. He sailed from Limerick, on June 14, on board the ship Rhoda Campbell. Seven weeks later he reached Quebec. The following day he came to Montreal. He hired there with a farmer, a French Roman Catholic, for a month for $5.00. At the month's end he came by boat to Hamilton and to London and Biddulph where he worked for eight years."[80] Hodgins and two brothers, who probably came with him, remained in London for several years but in the late 1850s and early 1860s moved to the Tipperary settlement in Kinloss, Bruce County, and acquired land there. Two sisters married Richard Blackwell and Joseph Wasnidge of McGillivray Township, near London, while the family was resident in Middlesex, but the Blackwells joined the Hodginses in Kinloss in 1878.[81]

The vast numbers of Irish arriving in the cities during the Famine years severely strained municipal relief efforts, but most merely passed through. The few North Tipperary Protestant arrivals who actually remained in the cities in this period were mostly people from the higher levels of society, such as Dr Robert Hobbs and Dr Henry Going of London, and Mr R.A. Waller and Mr Charles Cambie, gentlemen of Cromwellian descent who lost their Tipperary estates and moved to Toronto. An extensive connection of

Winnetts and Winders settled in Toronto and London, but they were town people from Killaloe; however, the earliest members of this connection to arrive were two brothers-in-law, William Loane and Stephen Worrall, who came in 1846 and settled in York and Ekfrid Townships.[82] A very few recent immigrants turned up in the towns in the 1852 census, all passing through, such as the Gaynors in Hamilton, widow and children of a prosperous farmer/gentleman of Ballingarry.[83] However, a greater proportion of arrivals after 1854 located in the towns, as will be demonstrated in chapter 7 when we come to consider rural-urban migration.

Cousens has noted that emigration during the Famine years tended on the whole to consist of entire families, for as many women as men left the country during that period.[84] One might question his conclusion, for not all women emigrated with families. Some single women were sent out to Australia and Canada from workhouses. Three parties of paupers from Nenagh Workhouse were assisted to emigrate during the Famine years. In 1849–50 eighty-five orphan girls were selected for free passages to Australia, and thirty young women were sent to Western Australia in 1852. In April 1852 387 inmates, mostly female, were embarked at Limerick for Quebec.[85] The agent at Quebec forwarded 110 of the women on to Bytown, and James Henry Burke, the agent at Bytown, himself of Tipperary descent, reported that all had been engaged as servants in the town or vicinity within two days of arriving.[86] However, as Cousens himself has pointed out, the precarious financial situation of the unions during the crisis prevented much assisted emigration of this kind from taking place and the 5000 who left Ireland annually in this manner made up a miniscule proportion of the more than one million who emigrated in this period.[87] A recent study of emigration from the Limerick Workhouse indicates that many of these assisted Famine migrants were in any case emigrating to join relatives. They frequently applied to the Board of Guardians to make up the difference between money sent by relations abroad and the price of passage. The author concluded that "the end of the journey for the majority ... was a family reunion."[88] Similar annotations on lists of indigent emigrants assisted from Quebec to Montreal in 1846 suggest that a high proportion intended to join relatives already in the Canadas.[89]

Almost all of the Protestant emigrants who reached the Canadas from North Tipperary between 1845 and 1854 seem to have come out to relatives. The kinship connections cannot be documented in every case, but most settled not only in an existing Tipperary community but near someone of the same surname. Typical is the Samuel Farmer family of Cowbawn, Modreeny. Originally of a family of small farmers on the Dunalley estate,[90] Farmer had worked as a labourer at Clonbrone, Birr, in his wife's neighbourhood, before emigrating in the Famine years to join the families of two sisters, Mrs Thomas Dagg and Mrs Thomas Wall, in Huntley Township.[91] He occupied a clergy reserve in the neighbourhood but left it without completing the purchase.[92] He then died, but his sons bought new farms in the eastern part of Gloucester Township which was still being settled. Three nephews, sons of William Farmer of Cowbawn, arrived in the mid-1850s and also took up land in Gloucester, and a niece, Anna Bridget Spooner from Behamore, arrived around the same time and married her cousin Richard Dagg.[93] William's three sons were the last Farmers in Modreeny parish, for William's widow Jane, who was recorded in 1854 letting a house from farmers in Newtown (Guest), died there later the same year.[94]

The Protestants were generally not of the labouring class, the group that felt the horrors of the Famine years most acutely. Some Protestant farmers even benefited from the events of the late 1840s by adding to their Irish landholdings. Some of those who were less prosperous nevertheless did emigrate to Canada, but their numbers were no greater than usual. Those who did come still came out to relatives, though many lacked the means to remain in the established settlements and moved on to areas where land was cheaper after building up some capital. In their second moves, however, they still tended to move from one Tipperary settlement to another. Few settled permanently in the towns and those who did were for the most part distressed gentlemen. However, the early 1850s was the last period in which the old patterns prevailed. Thereafter Protestant emigration to Canada from North Tipperary was of little consequence. The Famine only helped keep open a little longer a migration channel that was soon to close.

EMIGRATION TO AUSTRALIA AND NEW ZEALAND

Protestant emigrants from North Tipperary ceased to come to the Canadas in great numbers by the mid-1850s but emigration from that part of Ireland did not decline proportionally, for it appears that emigration from North Tipperary to Australia and New Zealand began to reach significant levels in the post-Famine years.

Residents of North Tipperary had expressed interest in New South Wales soon after the Napoleonic Wars, at the same time they petitioned the Colonial Office about Upper Canada,[95] but emigration from the British Isles to Australia was insignificant until 1837 when New South Wales ceased to be a penal colony. At least one of North Tipperary's prospective emigrants to Australia chose Canada instead in this period.[96]

After 1837 the number of British emigrants to Australasia tripled and for several years the numbers going there were roughly comparable to those leaving for British North America. The Australian colonies received considerable publicity in the Irish press in the early 1840s, and the *Nenagh Guardian* published numerous items on Australia while ignoring movement to Canada. John Besnard of Cork, agent for the Emigration Company for

Australia, regularly advertised his sailings in the *Guardian,* often in notices headed "Free Emigration," alluding to the New South Wales bounty system which paid the passage of agricultural labourers, craftsmen, and servants needed in the colony.[97] The *Guardian* also gave two columns to the "Emigrants' Farewell Festival" in Cork in 1841,[98] and space to favourable accounts of Mr Besnard's operations[99] and to letters of thanks from passengers on his vessels for Sydney and Port Philip.[100] In the summer of 1842 it published a letter from Thomas and Elzabeth (Dyas) Logan, formerly of Mountshannon, who had emigrated to New South Wales in 1836. Logan had written the letter to encourage his brother-in-law, Edward Cox of Coolereida, Castle Connell, to join him.[101] In 1842 the volume of emigration to New South Wales turned firmly downward, returned to pre-1838 levels, and remained insignificant for some years.[102] In the event Cox chose to join relatives of his first wife on a rocky farm in Camden East, near Kingston, Upper Canada (see Table 7).

Emigration to Australia began to boom in 1853 when the Colonial Office abandoned Edward Gibbon Wakefield's system of settling Australia through the intermediary of "great Companies" and after Tasmania ceased to be a penal colony. The discovery of gold in that decade was a further incentive.[103] That the tide of Tipperary Protestant emigration was turning away from Canada and towards Australasia in this period appears from the fact that brothers and sisters of a number of earlier emigrants to Canada left Ireland and settled in Australia and New Zealand.[104] Several families from Ogonnelloe even left the Ottawa Valley in 1853 and journeyed to New Zealand,[105] and a couple of Hodginses from London Township went to the gold region, one remaining in Australia as a settler.[106]

Though emigration of North Tipperary Protestants to Canada declined after the final impetus provided by the hardships of the Famine years, the movement of these people out of Ireland had merely turned to a new frontier further away.

CONCLUSION

The movement of population from County Tipperary to the Canadas in the nineteenth century is a classic example of chain migration based upon kinship. It began as a government-sponsored experiment but the process immediately became self-generating. Though it is doubtful that the government realized the fact at the time, the experiment's goal of diverting emigration to Canada and away from the United States was realized insofar as North Tipperary was concerned, for the bulk of Protestant emigrants from the region as late as the 1850s left Ireland intending to follow their relatives to Canada. The influence of relatives in determining the origins, volume, direction, and destination of emigration was already apparent in 1818, for the residents of parishes distant from the home of the sponsor, Richard Talbot, were brought into the group that sailed on the *Brunswick* by relatives who lived closer to him. Kin contacts continued to spread news of the Talbot party's government sponsorship throughout the North Tipperary region and were responsible for the widespread petitioning of government early in 1819 and for the heavy emigration from the region that same year. Bilateral kinship and large family size combined to present prospective emigrants as early as 1819 with a wide choice of Canadian settlement locations in which relatives were living. Nonetheless, the presence of the largest numbers of immigrants in the London and Ottawa areas stimulated the majority of later arrivals to locate in those neighbourhoods. Emigration from North Tipperary continued right through the Famine era without any appreciable change in volume, and most of the Famine emigrants came out to relatives who were already in Canada. Compiled information about temporal shifts in the volume of emigration from the region suggests, however, that while the destination to which emigrants proceeded was influenced most strongly by the presence of kin, the timing of the decision to leave Ireland related to domestic economic and social conditions. Even the Famine period may not have been an exception to this generalization, for the volume of emigration to Canada diminished to insignificant proportions in the mid-1850s as the frontier of cheap land in Canada receded and as the Protestants of Tipperary turned to new frontiers in the South Pacific or enlarged their Irish holdings by leasing lands vacated during or after the Famine. The process of chain migration was to continue in the New World, linking the major colonies in the Ottawa and London areas and drawing the populations of the smaller colonies towards them.

CHAPTER SIX

The Major Colonies in Context: Middlesex and Carleton

IRISH SETTLEMENT IN UPPER CANADA

The Irish were the largest ethnic group in Upper Canada (Ontario) in the nineteenth century. Although the Irish lived throughout the province, they made up a clear majority of the population in several important regions. Comparison of the areas of greatest Irish predominance in 1871 with what we know of early settlement history suggests that the areas of heaviest Irish concentration were determined very early and that later immigration and internal migration reaffirmed the existing pattern.[1]

The Irish constituted a second wave of settlement, coming after the Loyalists and Americans who had settled for the most part along the St Lawrence River before the War of 1812. The most heavily Irish areas were in townships well back from the "Front," except in eastern Ontario where the Irish accounted for from 40 to 60 per cent of the populations of many of the riverfront townships. Even there, however, sequence of arrival determined that the Irish took up residence in the back concessions.

An examination of Map 14 reveals several areas in which the Irish proportion of township populations was greater than 60 per cent. All are traceable to settlements commenced at the time of the first large-scale Irish immigration to Upper Canada following the Napoleonic Wars. Several of these concentrations originated in government-organized or government-sponsored emigration and settlement schemes. The greatest concentration was in the Ottawa and Rideau valleys where twenty-nine townships, most centred on the Rideau Canal route, were at least 60 per cent Irish; four contiguous townships (March, Goulbourn, Huntley, and Marlborough, all in Carleton County), were more than 80 per cent Irish. It was here that the British government had constructed the Rideau Canal as a safe inland waterway distant from the American border and here, too, that it had encouraged the settlement of a loyal population following the conclusion of the Napoleonic Wars and the War of 1812. The government had disbanded several regiments in the area, most notably the predominantly Irish 99th or "old 100th" in Goulbourn; established three military settlements, with superintending officers on the spot to co-ordinate military and civilian settlement; aided early colonists with grants of rations and supplies; and planted several sponsored groups of British settlers. Among the latter were two groups of Irish who received outright government assistance: about half of Talbot's group of Tipperary Protestants and the first of two groups of settlers, mostly poor Catholics from County Cork, who were brought out under the supervision of Peter Robinson, brother of the Upper Canadian attorney-general, in 1823. The Irish population of the Rideau townships was supplemented by immigrants who had laboured on the Rideau Canal works in the late 1820s and very early 1830s.

Proceeding westward, a second Irish concentration is evident in the Peterborough area, especially in the townships of Cartwright, Manvers, Cavan, Ops, Douro, and Emily. Irish settlement here dates also from the influx that followed the Napoleonic Wars, stimulated by the settlement of emigrants from Counties Cavan and Monaghan who were sent from New York by the British consul to occupy new townships named for their counties of origin. A second impetus in this region came with the arrival of Peter Robinson's second party in 1825, like the first consisting mostly of poor Catholics from County Cork.[2]

Further west again another concentration of Irish appears north and west of Toronto in York and Simcoe counties, in the townships of Toronto Gore, Albion, Tecumseth, Adjala, Mono, Amamarth, Mulmur, Tossorontio, and Essa. Like the other regions discussed heretofore, northern York and Simcoe counties were opened to settlement after the Napoleonic Wars when Irish settlers began to arrive in considerable numbers.[3] The area north of the capital at York (Toronto) was a favoured area in part because many emigrants had been instructed before leaving Ireland to proceed to York on arrival and apply to the lieutenant-governor for a grant of land.[4] There was group settlement in this region as in the others; a block of land in northern Toronto Township was held open in 1818–19 for the Beatty parties from New York, and an adjacent colony of Protestants from Kilcooly, County Tipperary developed, largely in the 1820s, as a result of the inclusion of one settler from that place among the Beatty immigrants. Delineation of other group settlements of Irish in York and Simcoe awaits the work of other researchers. The most westerly concentration of Irish was located in Biddulph Township, a northern extension of the colony founded in London, immediately to its south, by the remaining half of Richard Talbot's party.

The clusters of residents of Irish origin in more northerly areas in 1871 reflect secondary settlement from the earlier-settled areas already mentioned.

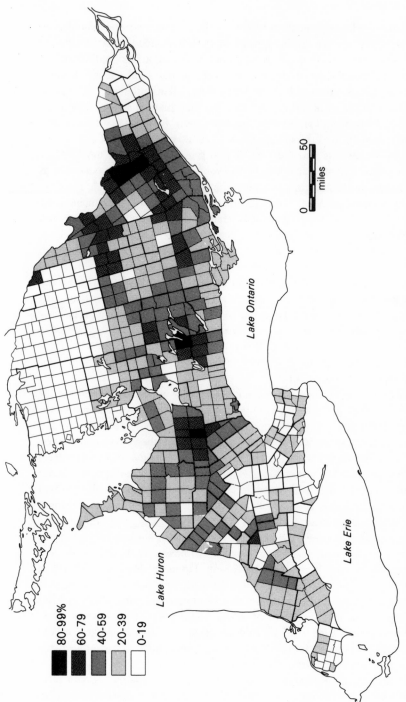

MAP 14 Concentration of population of Irish ethnic origin, by township, 1871. Chain migration supplemented natural increase in perpetuating the locations of the earliest group settlements made in the period following the Napoleonic Wars.

Source: *Census of Canada*, 1871. Adapted and enlarged, with permission, from Glenn J Lockwood, "The Irish in Eastern Ontario: The Social Structure of Montague Township in Lanark County, 1861–1881," MA thesis, University of Ottawa, 1980.

80-99%
60-79
40-59
20-39
0-19

Lake Ontario

Lake Huron

Lake Erie

0   50
miles

A concentration in the Grey County townships of Euphrasia and Holland has been shown by Darrell Norris to have originated in the 1840s, largely by migration from heavily Irish Protestant Peel County near Toronto. Similarly, much of the population of Renfrew County resided for a time in Lanark and Carleton.[5]

Therefore, despite high rates of internal population mobility (or perhaps, in light of the phenomenon of widespread chain migration, because of them), the concentrations of Irish in 1871 continued to be in the areas of the province where the first Irish settlers had made their homes two generations before, or in townships that derived their initial populations from the earlier concentrations. These patterns in themselves suggest that once a migration stream was established it continued to flow into a region for some time, strengthening the existing Irish population. We have seen how the Tipperary Protestant concentrations established near London and Richmond in 1818 grew by such a process of chain migration. In both areas other immigrant groups of varying sizes clustered together in a similar fashion. Government emigration and settlement policy, and the policy of the privately owned Canada Land Company, could initiate such settlements, but their actions merely provided the stimulus for growth that continued whether or not further encouragement was forthcoming.

In both the London and Richmond areas the Tipperary parties were among the first settlers in their immediate vicinities. As friends and relatives emigrated to join them the two largest concentrations of Tipperary Protestants in the province grew from these two small cores, comprising together some three dozen families, helping to give to each region a distinctive Irish loyalist character. The physical, economic, and social environments in which the two groups found themselves in these two widely separated parts of the province were very different one from the other. In the remainder of this chapter I will examine the human environment and place the London and Richmond settlements of the Tipperary Protestants in the context of those who settled around them. The local settlement patterns that resulted from the intersection of the chain migration process, geography, and settlement policy had important implications for the later cultural and political history of the two regions.

SETTLEMENT IN THE UPPER
OTTAWA VALLEY BEFORE 1818

Before 1818 settlement in what is now the Ottawa area was limited to two settlements populated largely by American immigrants: the Rideau Settlement, composed of several dozen farms on either side of the Rideau River in the townships of Marlborough, Oxford, Wolford, and Montague, settled from the south in the 1790s, and Hull Township on the Lower Canadian side of the

Ottawa River where Philemon Wright of Woburn, Massachusetts, had settled a small colonizing group from New England in 1800. Hull's population, which was still small in 1816, included a scattering of Englishmen, Irish, Nova Scotians, and Swedes, many of them hired by the Wrights at Quebec.[6] There was even one Tipperary man, Thomas Reid, who was there by 1814.[7] How he came to be in America is not known. After the conclusion of the wars Hull was swamped by large numbers of immigrants arriving from the British Isles, particularly from Ireland. This same wave of immigrants populated much of the Ottawa Valley. Though a number of the Tipperary Irish found employment for brief periods in Wright's enterprises,[8] none but Reid, who married into Wright's family, settled permanently in Hull.

In 1816 the British government founded the Perth military settlement in an attempt to establish a loyal population of disbanded soldiers and British emigrants near the projected route of the Rideau Canal. A local superintendent, responsible to the Quarter-Master General's Department, was appointed to locate disbanded soldiers and civilian emigrants on their lands. The arrivals in 1816 were largely personnel from disbanded regiments and Scottish mechanics and labourers who had been sent to Quebec the year before. They were settled in the townships of Bathurst, Drummond, Beckwith, South Elmsley, and South Burgess.[9] Settlement in the immediate neighbourhood where the breakaway Talbot settlers were located in 1818 was commenced that same year with the establishment of a second military settlement.

THE RICHMOND MILITARY SETTLEMENT AND THE *BRUNSWICK* EMIGRANTS OF 1818

The members of the Tipperary party were among the first civilians sent to the new military establishment at Richmond.

Early in 1818 the British government decided to offer land to officers and men of the 99th Regiment who wished to remain in Canada upon the return of the corps to England for disbandment.[10] The 99th had been raised in Ireland in 1804 as the 100th Prince Regent's County of Dublin Regiment for colonial service and had immediately been posted to the North American colonies, where it fought through the entire War of 1812. The regiment was renumbered the 99th after postwar disbandments commenced. The unit's long experience in the colonies made it a prime candidate for the government's plan to settle soldiers in the province.[11]

Captain Fowler reported from Perth in July 1818 that the lots in the Perth settlement had been "granted to so great a distance from the Depot at Perth as to render it absolutely necessary to establish another Depot in some other part of the Settlement, previous to putting the 400 Men of the 99th on their Lands, and from whence they may receive their provisions, and Implements wih promptness and facility." Lt-Col. Francis Cockburn, the deputy quarter-master general, recommended to Governor Sir John C. Sherbrooke that a new village be established as close as possible to the River Ottawa, and he suggested a site on the River Jacques (Jock) in the southern part of Goulbourn Township. Cockburn recommended that Captain George Thew Burke of the 99th be appointed secretary and storekeeper.[12] Because he anticipated that it would be some time before the men of the 99th could be placed on their lands, Cockburn in July ordered the regiment to remain at Lachine and be provisioned there while twenty or thirty men proceeded to Richmond with Burke,[13] who was given superintendence of Goulbourn, the eastern half of Beckwith, March and Huntley (which were surveyed in 1820), and the crown reserves in Nepean.[14] The surveys at Richmond were under way by late August.[15]

Cockburn immediately began to recruit civilian emigrants for the military settlement, for it was in July also that he convinced a number of Richard Talbot's party, newly arrived at Montreal, to proceed up the Ottawa to Richmond. His task may have been made easier by the fact that a number of the military settlers ordered to Richmond were known to some of Talbot's party. Captain Burke, the superintendent of the settlement, and Lt Joseph Maxwell, another officer of the 99th who settled there, were both North Tipperary men. Burke was a member of an old Roman Catholic gentry family that had held lands in the vicinity of Borrisoleigh for many centuries, though he was himself a native of Ballyartella in the parish of Dromineer and had converted at least nominally to Anglicanism in order to secure a military commission.[16] Some of Talbot's party may have known Burke, for it is certain that some later arrivals did.[17] Maxwell was born at Roscrea, the son of a gentleman of that parish.[18] There were also three Tipperary Protestants among the enlisted men of the 99th who settled at Richmond. Two, Corporal Arthur Sharpley from Modreeny[19] and Private Henry Hayes from Roscrea,[20] left the settlement in the 1820s but their presence in the encampment at Lachine in 1818 may have allowed them contact with Talbot's followers. The third, Sergeant Andrew Spearman, appears to have been related to some of Talbot's party and he must have played some role in the decision of the latter to abandon Talbot.[21] Some of the emigrants may also have known Thomas Reid, who had been working for Wright in Hull for almost five years by the time the party arrived.

On 11 November, Cockburn reported that seventy-two emigrants who had come to the Canadas under the £10 deposit plan with recommendations from the Colonial Office had been settled at Richmond.[22] About a dozen of these were Talbot's settlers, most of whom Burke shortly afterwards located on the Twelfth Line of Goulbourn in the northeastern corner of the township, near the site of the later hamlet of Hazeldean. The remainder were the Perthshire Scots from Loch Tayside, who were settled by Burke in the northeastern quarter of Beckwith Township to the west.

A third settlement under military administration (Lanark) was established in the region by order of the new governor, the earl of Dalhousie, when he visited Perth and Richmond in August 1820. Dalhousie had just received word from Britain of the government's decision to send out 1200 Scots from Lanarkshire, an attempt to reduce postwar unemployment among the weavers of the Glasgow area. The governor noted ruefully in his journal that "500 of them had arrived at Quebec as soon as Lord B's letters." These Scots were settled in the townships of North Sherbrooke, Dalhousie, Lanark, and Ramsay in 1820 and 1821.[23]

Though there was a large Scottish contingent in the Lanark and Perth settlements and the Perthshire group dominated the northeastern quarter of Beckwith, the vicinity of Richmond itself was mostly settled by Irishmen. Even the soldier settlers of what was soon to become Carleton County were mostly of Irish birth. In 1822 there were 202 officers and men living in the four townships of Goulbourn, Huntley, March, and Nepean. Of these, 135 were men of the 99th, twenty-two had served in the 37th, six in the 60th, and thirty-nine in various other units.[24] Some of the men of the 37th and of the assorted units were English, although a significant number were Irish, and the six men of the 60th were German, but the 99th, which contributed the bulk of the settlers, was predominantly Irish. In 1820 there had been 167 men from the 99th in the settlement, and 400 had initially been expected, but in 1822 only 135 remained. The surviving Regimental Description Book provides us with the birthplaces of all but thirty of the 167 who were actual settlers.[25] The regiment was named the Prince Regent's County of Dublin Regiment, but Dubliners never dominated its ranks and the unit had recruited widely right up to the year of disbandment in order to bring its numbers up to strength. Seven of these soldier settlers were from England and four were natives of Lower Canada, including one French Canadian; one man was born in the army, but the remaining 125 were Irish. Of these 125, seventy-five were from Ulster, mostly the western counties: eighteen were from Derry, fifteen from Tyrone, fifteen from Cavan, and twelve from Fermanagh. Outside Ulster, ten were natives of Dublin and six were from Kildare, but the remainder came from scattered areas of the kingdom. Most of the men of the 99th had been labourers or weavers before enlisting. However, the population of Carleton County received a greater impetus from the early civilian settlers who found their way to the military settlement or were directed to it in its earliest years of settlement.

THE BEGINNINGS OF CHAIN MIGRATION

By 1820 there were a number of civilian emigrants in the Richmond military settlement from parts of Ireland that contributed significant numbers of settlers to the area in succeeding years. A number of these immigrants were men who had come to Upper Canada on their own, but once in Richmond they solicited free passages from Britain for their wives and children. Col. Cockburn promised a number of men passages for their families, but the British government in the end honoured only the nine such requests Cockburn submitted in a list dated 2 May 1820. All nine had settled in Goulbourn:[26]

Jas.[recte Wm.] Cuthbert	Newtownbarry, Co. Wexford	woman & 7 chn
James Keys	Newtownbarry, Co. Wexford	woman & 6 chn
William Morgan	Borrisokane, Co. Tipperary	woman & 5 chn
John Taylor	Roscrea, Co. Tipperary	woman & 3 chn
Martin Nash (37th Foot)	Goran, Co. Kilkenny	woman & 4 chn
Thomas Scharf	Castlecomer, Co. Kilkenny	woman & 3 chn
James Scharf	Old Leighlin, Co. Carlow	woman & 2 chn
Edward Basset	Leighlin Bridge, Co. Carlow	woman & 6 chn
William Kemp	Cavan	woman & 5 chn

It is striking that all these settlers were from what is now the Irish Republic and that only one, the soldier Martin Nash, was Roman Catholic.

The geographical origins of the men in Cockburn's list are fairly representative of the parts of Ireland that contributed most strongly to the population of the region in succeeding decades. Though there is reason to think that Irish settlement in the Toronto and Peterborough areas may have been drawn primarily from Ulster,[27] there was a very large southern Protestant component in the Irish population of eastern Upper Canada. The misapprehension that the Protestant Irish need necessarily have come from Ulster is not new. The editor of the Bytown *Packet* editorialized in 1849 to correct mis-statements in the Montreal *Herald:* "The Herald is again at fault when he asserts that the real Settlers are Protestants, from the North of Ireland. There is a great majority in Carleton, whether Protestant or Catholic from the South of Ireland, and the Herald is, therefore, grossly mistaken when he supposes that they are 'Scotch Irishmen' generally ... You are not Irish ... oh! no; you are a sort of improved, Scotchified Irish!"[28]

The Tipperary colony was not the largest of the southern Irish communities in eastern Upper Canada. Far greater numbers of Protestants came from the southeastern counties of Ireland, and they settled over a much wider area than did their Tipperary counterparts, locating throughout the Rideau basin from the concessions to the rear of Gananoque and Brockville on the St Lawrence northward sixty miles into Carleton County. The first emigrants from the Wexford area arrived in the rear of Elizabethtown in 1809, and about fifteen families were living there and in Leeds and Lansdowne townships by the time the War of 1812 began. When the wars ended in 1815, thousands of their fellow-countrymen joined them, sailing without government assistance from various eastern ports within striking distance of their homes in north Wexford,

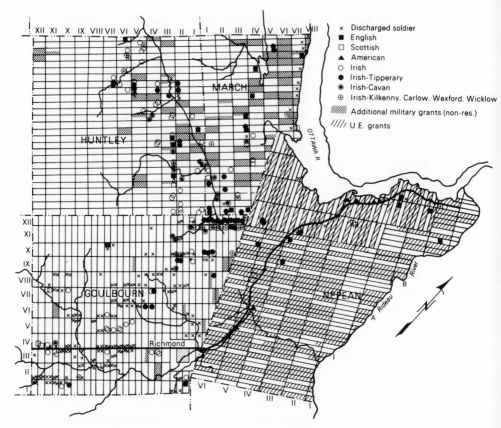

MAP 15   Settlement in western Carleton County, 1822. North Tipperary families moved north up the Carp River Valley from the earliest locations in northeastern Goulbourn, but became interspersed with settlers arriving from other parts of Ireland. Sources: AO, RG 21A, MS 262, 1822 census and assessment rolls; RG 1, MS 154, locations, Richmond military settlement; Carleton County Abstract Indexes to Deeds.

south Wicklow, Carlow, and northeastern Kilkenny. Hundreds purchased lots in the rear of the St Lawrence townships from earlier Loyalist and American residents.

Some of the men on Cockburn's list were among the Wexford settlers who began a second front of settlement, taking up free-grant lands in the new military townships in Lanark and western Carleton counties after 1815. The superintendents of the military settlements responded to the popular demand of immigrants to locate near relatives.[29] Captain Burke settled the South Leinster Irish in southeastern Beckwith in the vicinity of the depot village of Franktown, south of the area occupied by the Perthshire Scots. He also located some with Talbot's party in northeastern Goulbourn. The Franktown area developed as a largely Wexford community, extending southward in the 1830s and 1840s into Montague and North Elmsley townships. Several dozen Wexford families also located north of Goulbourn in the Carp Valley in ensuing years, but greater numbers joined their compatriots in the townships of the Perth and Lanark military settlements. The greatest concentration, however, continued to be in Leeds County to the south where the Wexford population for many years elected one of their own, Ogle R. Gowan, to the legislature as a champion of Orange and Irish interests.[30]

A third group of settlers in Carleton County was represented in Colonel Cockburn's list by William Kemp of Cavan. Several dozen families of Protestant farmers and weavers from the north Cavan parishes of Annagh, Annagelliffe, and Castleterra petitioned the Colonial Office for assistance to emigrate to join relatives in the Richmond military settlement between 1820 and 1822.[31] Though the government refused them aid, most came in any case and settled in Goulbourn, Huntley, March, and Nepean townships, where they were joined by a number of other families from their old neighbourhood who did not bother to petition the government before leaving Ireland. Many of these emigrants were pioneers of Methodism in Carleton County, and their faith, which they adopted in Ireland and not on the Canadian frontier, helped to keep the families close for many generations.[32]

Thus the process of chain migration was by no means peculiarly characteristic of the North Tipperary Irish. It appears rather to have been a very common method by which settlements in Upper Canada were populated.

THE SETTLEMENT PATTERN IN CARLETON COUNTY, 1822

By the time military superintendence of the settlement in what became Carleton County ended in 1822, much of the western part of the county had been occupied. The townships of Fitzroy and Torbolton to the north had not been under military administration, and population there in 1822 was limited to a Leith merchant, Charles Shirreff, and a few followers who had recently settled at the Chats (Fitzroy Harbour).[33] Settlement in Marlborough and North Gower, to the south, was at this period still confined to a narrow strip of occupied farms along the Rideau River. Population there was small and the area occupied approximated the old prewar Rideau settlement. In the 1820s, however, settlement of the northern portions of these townships would proceed as settlers moved south from the military settlement.[34]

It is evident from the map of Carleton County in 1822[35] (Map 15) that most of the soldiers located in Goulbourn, though a scattering lived in other townships. A number of half-pay officers occupied the scenic but thin-soiled Ottawa River front in March Township. The land in the northwestern part of

Goulbourn was poor and that southwest of Richmond village was low and swampy, which accounts for the empty areas there. Much of western Huntley and the northern part of the March-Huntley line were characterized by thin soil and outcrops of rock. For this reason, settlement in these townships initially occupied the fertile lands of the Carp Valley. It is evident from the map that settlement had commenced in Goulbourn and had spread gradually up the Carp Valley after Huntley and March were surveyed in March 1820. The soldiers were assigned acreages by rank, and the sergeants and officers who took up residence in Goulbourn usually took their additional land in Huntley or March. This delayed settlement in the latter townships, but many of these supplemental military grants were sold or regranted because of defaulted taxes in the late 1820s, especially after the abolition of free grants.[36]

Nepean had been surveyed years before and most of the lands there not allocated for crown and clergy reserves had been granted to Loyalists and the children of Loyalists. None of the Loyalists actually took up their grants there. A few Americans had settled in the Ottawa front, offshoots of Wright's Hull settlement. Four of the Tipperary group were located by Burke on crown reserves in the northwestern part of Nepean in 1818. But on the whole Nepean had been granted to absentees and the township was unoccupied. Dalhousie noted in his journal in August 1820: "From Richmond landing place to the village of Richmond, 22 miles, it is almost wholly waste & wild woods, the property of absentees or Crown & Clergy Reserves, but generally in large grants made by the Government of Upper Canada which they can neither recall, nor force into settlement. This Township of Nepean is not one of those given over for the Military settlers & therefore may be considered as a useless waste, a serious difficulty in the way of the prosperity of this part of the Country, & it is mortifying in a greater degree from its possessing the only harbour & approach – by which the great object of these settlements can be attained."[37]

The 1822 settlement map also makes plain that residences of people of a common origin were not immediately contiguous. The reason for this was simply that the area under military superintendence was settled very quickly. Immigrants arriving several years after their friends were unable to secure lots beside them, but were able to acquire land in the neighbourhood. Because most of the early settlers were Irish Protestants, however, these interweaving networks of chain migration did build up a solidly Irish Protestant block that gave to the Carp Valley of Carleton County an Orange flavour it never lost.

Roman Catholics settled in clusters away from the Protestants also because of their later arrival. The Peter Robinson settlers, mostly Roman Catholics from the disturbed north Cork region who were sent to Canada as an experiment in government-sponsored emigration, arrived in 1823, but by that time most of the grantable lands in the area of the military settlements were already located. The "Robinsonians" were therefore located in Pakenham,

Ramsay, and the northwestern corners of Huntley and Goulbourn. Later Irish Catholic settlers also located in western Huntley, with the result that the settlement pattern of that township maps as an Irish Catholic western half on stony land, and an Irish Protestant eastern half in the fertile Carp Valley.

LATER IRISH GROUPS IN CARLETON COUNTY

In surrounding townships several other group settlements were formed in later years. Roman Catholic settlers began arriving from County Tipperary in the late 1820s, although most arrived in the 1830s and 1840s. The earliest arrivals, who are recorded on the 1828 militia list,[38] located in the fifth and sixth concessions of the Rideau front, in the west of Nepean, as settlers began to spread east from Richmond, buying up Loyalist rights after free grants were abolished in 1826. They formed part of an area of mixed religion and ethnicity along the Richmond Road. The rest of this south Nepean area to the east, in the Jockvale neighbourhood along the Jock River, was settled in the 1830s and 1840s almost exclusively by Tipperary Catholics from parishes such as Nenagh, Templemore, Borrisokane, Lorrha, and Kilbarron, in other words from North Tipperary, the same region from which the Tipperary Protestants in the Carp Valley came.[39] The eastern concessions of Nepean along the Rideau River were the last settled, in the 1840s. The "Back Bush" or Merivale area, as it came to be called, received a stimulus from the arrival of a party from western County Down who came in 1842 on the ship *Dolphin,* later joined by friends and relatives.[40]

The Roman Catholic population of western Huntley Township was also largely of Tipperary origin, but my research has not revealed from what part of the county the emigrants came. Most were pre-Famine immigrants.[41]

A North Down group of interrelated Presbyterian families from the neighbourhood of Killinchey, Killyleagh, Comber, and Saintfield formed on the Huntley/Fitzroy line between the later villages of Carp and Kinburn in the area called the Lowry neighbourhood. The Moorhead family began this migration in 1821 but the greater number arrived in the 1840s.[42]

There is also evidence of a small group of Protestants from County Tyrone in the Carp Valley of Huntley. John L. Gourlay has left an account of the arrival of his own family, part of a party of seventeen that left Bytown in 1833, walking out through the stumps of the Richmond Road, stopping for a mid-day meal at William Bell's tavern, spending the night at Billy Bradley's log tavern at Hazeldean, and proceeding to Stittsville the next day and then up the third line of Huntley. The Gourlays were joining friends and relatives from back home: "Samuel Johnston had heard we were coming or dreamed it, for he met us two miles from his house and took us all there to dinner. After dinner, which was a very enjoyable one, all that had relatives, left to find

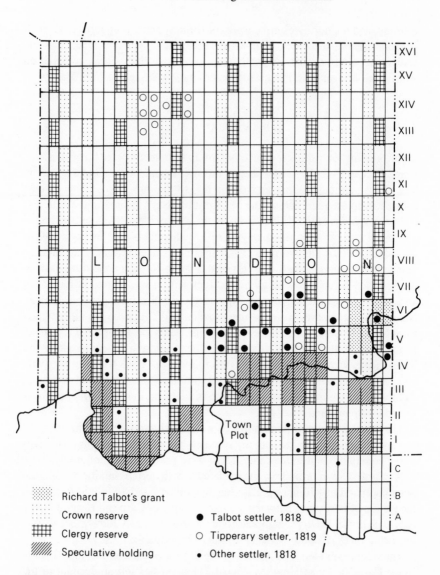

MAP 16 Settlement in London Township, 1818–19. Richard Talbot's immigrants located in the newly surveyed township, and were joined the next year by friends from the homeland.

Sources: Based upon Daniel J. Brock, "Richard Talbot, the Tipperary Irish, and the Formative Years of London Township, 1818–1826," MA thesis, University of Western Ontario, 1969, map 1, 50; locations in F.T. Rosser, *London Township Pioneers* (Belleville 1975).

them, some of whom came to meet them as they departed. Some of us stayed that night with Mr and Mrs Johnston."[43]

Thus arrivals of later Irish immigrants in Carleton County conformed to the earlier patterns. Certain neighbourhoods were dominated by Irish Catholics, in the Jockvale and Corkery instances by Catholics from the same part of Ireland. The Carp remained a mixed community of northern and southern Protestants who gave the Carp Valley a general Protestant Irish character it has never lost, but a character in later generations distinctive of no particular region of the homeland.

GROUP SETTLEMENT IN LONDON TOWNSHIP

Like the Tipperary settlers who took up lands near Richmond, the members of the Richard Talbot party who located in London Township were among the first residents of a newly settled area. Other settlers came from a wide variety of places, many from other locations in British North America and the United States. The Tipperary party and their friends who joined them in later years formed the largest group settlement in the township, but there were several smaller groups that formed distinct neighbourhoods. Because of the rapidity with which London was settled, the Tipperary emigrants did not form a completely solid block in Talbot's vicinity. However, since many arrived in the first few years and no other group in the township approached them in numbers, the Tipperary Protestants formed a more solid concentration in London Township than they did in the Ottawa Valley.

London had originally been intended by Lt-Gov. Simcoe as the site for the capital of Upper Canada. Although the boundaries of the township were roughly laid out and a town plot allocated, the township was not opened for settlement until after the Napoleonic Wars. Only two families were in residence before 1818, having obtained special permission to locate there by agreeing to try growing hemp which the British government required for naval purposes. There were small settlements in townships to the south of London, but the bulk of the population of western Upper Canada still lived along the lakefront and in the Niagara Peninsula.

Col. Thomas Talbot visited Sir Peregrine Maitland at York in August 1818 when Maitland arrived to assume the lieutenant-governorship. Talbot secured permission to add London Township to the vast territory in the western part of the province over which he was the superintendent of settlement. Richard Talbot's Tipperary party, which had reached Quebec the same day as Maitland, arrived at York around the time Col. Talbot did and were immediately recruited as settlers for London. Only the first four and a half concessions had been surveyed by this time and much of this had been granted to speculators and non-resident Loyalist heirs. However, a survey of the eastern halves of concessions 5 and 6 and the front of 7 was immediately ordered to provide lands for the Irish immigrants.

The survey of the township was completed in the spring of 1819 as the flow of settlers into London commenced. By the end of the year the population had jumped from 122 to 503.[44] The friends and relatives from Tipperary who joined the 1818 emigrants this year settled in the neighbourhood of the Talbot party's locations, interspersing among them and locating also in the concessions immediately to their north.

A second Tipperary cluster formed in 1819 in the northwestern part of the township some five miles away. The reason for this is not entirely clear, but sequence of arrival may be part of the explanation. Col. Talbot's laconic system of record-keeping prevents us from specifying the dates of locations closer than the year, if that, but it is possible that these settlers arrived after most of the grantable lands in the immediate vicinity of their compatriots had been located to others. It is also probable that an element of deliberate choice played a part, for the families who located in the northwestern area were members of large connections of O'Neil, Hodgins, and Deacon siblings who may well have located there so that they could secure a large number of farms close together for themselves and for kin who arrived soon afterwards.

Most of the other settlement groups in London Township were fairly small, composed of interrelated families who came together over a number of years. The best known was the Welsh settlement in the northwestern corner of the township, beyond the second Tipperary cluster, near the later post office of Brecon. The Welsh settlement was established by John Matthews, who had lived in Southwold Township since 1817.[45] Matthews returned to Wales and brought out thirty-four relatives from his native Glamorganshire in 1821. They were settled by Colonel Talbot on an 1800–acre reservation at the extremity of the surveyed land in London Township.[46] The settlement attracted Welshmen from the United States and the homeland, some recruited by Matthews after he moved to Stamford near Hamilton in the 1830s. The settlement in the corner of London Township spilled over into the adjoining corners of Biddulph, McGillivray, East Williams, and Lobo. About 175 immigrants, comprising about fifty immigrating families, settled in the neighbourhood by 1851, about an eighth the number of Tipperary families who came to the London area in the same period. The number of inhabitants of Welsh descent remained fairly steady at about 300 between the middle and end of the nineteenth century.[47]

Immediately to the south of the Welsh settlement and somewhat larger was the English settlement, composed of families from the adjoining counties of Cumberland and Northumberland on the Scottish border. The earliest families came in 1818, but friends and relatives continued to arrive through the 1820s and 1830s. By the 1830s the settlement had spilled over into the adjoining township of Lobo.[48]

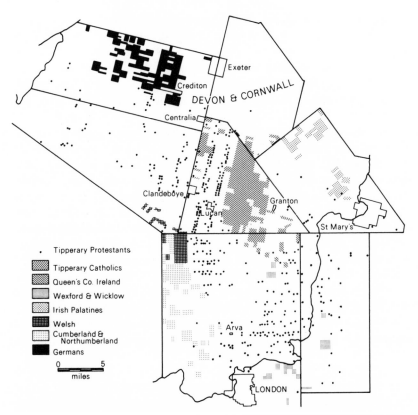

MAP 17 Group settlements in the London area, 1878. The Tipperary settlement was but one of many communities to draw its population from a small area in Europe, but it was probably the largest.
Sources for places of origin are identified in the notes to chapter 6. Locations from Middlesex, Huron, and Perth county atlases.

A small group of Wicklow-Wexford Protestants arrived in London beginning in 1819 and located mostly in the second and third concessions in the southeastern part of the township, across the North Branch of the Thames from the Richard Talbot party, in the neighbourhood called The Grove. Others lived just to the east, in the southern part of West Nissouri. Most of these families, including the Beltons, Dickensons, Doyles, Kinches, Perci-vals, Philpots, Stedmans, Tackaburys, Tukes, Websters, and Williamses, had emigrated to Madison County, New York, before the War of 1812 and came north to London at different times. One such party is known to have arrived in 1831. However, some arrived directly from Ireland as late as 1853. According to one account the movement north from New York was caused by quarrels with Roman Catholics from the same part of Ireland who had settled near them in the United States. According to another version, migrant members of the second emigrant generation simply came in search of land and established a secondary settlement. Many of these Irish settlers were Methodists.[49]

A small group of Irish Protestant families from the Mountmellick, Rosenallis, and Maryborough region of Queen's County settled in the northeastern corner of London Township and the adjoining South Boundary Concession of Biddulph. This group consisted of several large family connections, primarily the Langfords, Garretts, Westmans, and Parkinsons, with such other families as the Gowans and Lawlors, some of whom settled near Toronto.[50] Despite the closeness of the parishes of origin of these emigrants to the easternmost parishes of the North Tipperary region, and the propinquity of their settlement location in Canada to the largest North Tipperary colony in the Canadas, there appears to have been no connection between the two, for the Queen's County cluster was located at the far end of Biddulph from the Tipperary Protestant group and was separated from them by empty lands that later filled up with Tipperary Catholics.[51]

Despite the rapidity of settlement in London Township, it still proved possible for immigrants to settle near relatives and friends they came to join. As a result, London Township's population was composed in large part of a number of extended kin groups, most of which originated in the earliest years of settlement but received the bulk of their membership in later years as a consequence of chain migration.

GROUP SETTLEMENT IN THE SOUTHERN HURON TRACT

The Tipperary settlement in Biddulph and McGillivray, while adjacent to the earlier settlement in London Township, was not under the superintendence of Col. Thomas Talbot but rather was part of the unsurveyed lands of the Huron Tract sold by the government to the Canada Company in the late 1820s. The Canada Company was a private corporation headquartered in England which was formed in 1824 for the purpose of purchasing the crown and clergy reserves in Upper Canada for resale to settlers at a profit. The million-acre Huron Tract was sold to the company in lieu of the clergy reserves after Bishop Strachan was successful in opposing their alienation.[52]

While a positive policy of encouraging group settlements may not have been followed by the Canada Company, the company did facilitate the settlement of old-world neighbours together by its system of appointing local agents, and its officers certainly recognized that chain migration was a major mechanism driving forward the settlement process. The company's most active efforts at recruiting settlers in Europe were directed towards encouraging German emigration to the Huron Tract. An agent named Rischmuller was appointed by the commissioners to engage German settlers, and in 1844 he brought nine families to Stratford from New York State. Rischmuller did little more, but a German community grew up at Stratford despite his inactivity as the settlers already there wrote home. Just as the single party brought to Canada by Richard Talbot in 1818 stimulated Tipperary settlement in two parts of the province, so chain migration enlarged communities in the Huron Tract that began with small numbers. The Canada Company's commissioner, Frederick Widder, "was convinced that the majority of all immigrants were influenced by reports from acquaintances in the New World."[53]

The Canada Company had agents in a number of European centres and these representatives frequently sent parties of settlers to Canada,[54] but of equal importance were the local agents who oversaw settlement of the various townships and gave the immigrants their locations.[55] These representatives were sometimes selected once a pattern of regional and national origins was observable among the early settlers of a locality. The Devonshire settlement around the appropriately named town of Exeter had its origin in the settlement of John Balkwill near the site of the town early in 1831. Balkwill returned to England to encourage friends to emigrate. He was joined in Canada in 1832 by his brother-in-law William May, George Snell, and a number of his own brothers, who settled along the London and Goderich Road either side of the Usborne/Stephen line. "Their influence on friends at home subsequently prevailed to such an extent that that whole section of the township was settled up by natives of the old English Shire."[56] One of the Balkwill brothers who came in 1835 was rewarded for his diligence in encouraging settlement by being appointed constable and agent for the company for Usborne Township.[57]

Settlements of people from ethnically distinctive regions, such as the states of Germany, or clusters of French Canadians or Scots are readily noticeable, but identification of settlements of people from a particular part of England or Ireland or most especially from other parts of the Canadas requires detailed research at the individual level. H.J. Johnston nonetheless identified ten group settlements in the five eastern townships of the Huron Tract.[58] Stafford Johnston has more recently demonstrated that such ethnic clusters sometimes drew their populations from very small areas of the source countries. Through detailed research he has shown that a Hessian cluster in the Easthopes, with a secondary settlement in the next generation near Alsfeldt in Normanby Township, Grey County, came from Kreis Alsfeld, an administrative unit measuring some eighteen by twelve miles, in Oberhessen. He has also pointed out some other concentrations of Germans in the Huron Tract that appear to have derived similarly from geographically restricted source areas.[59]

The pattern in the seven southwestern townships of the tract was similar, and identified groups have been mapped in Map 17. Statistics compiled on a township basis emphasize some of the settlements, such as the Irish domination in Biddulph and the Scottish concentration in Williams, but

TABLE 10

Ethnic Settlement in the Southwestern Huron Tract, 1852

Township	English		German		Irish		Scotch		Total
	n	%	n	%	n	%	n	%	
Stephen	247	57.7	28	6.5	131	30.6	9	2.1	428
Hay	42	10.5	76	19.0	118	29.6	135	33.8	399
Usborne	370	38.9	14	1.5	264	27.7	281	29.5	952
Williams	111	7.5	1	0.1	85	5.7	1197	80.4	1489
Biddulph	50	4.6			953	87.1	43	3.9	1094
McGillivray	236	24.4			410	42.4	259	26.8	966

Source: Census of Upper Canada, 1851–2. Birthplaces of non-native born, by township.

census boundaries disguise internal geographical divisions of a municipality between settlement groups and artificially subdivide communities that extended over township boundaries.

Though the areas covered by these ethnic settlements crossed township boundaries, they were normally centred in one municipality. Tipperary Protestants and Tipperary Catholics occupied distinct halves of Biddulph while groups from several parts of Scotland occupied various concessions in Williams. Scots also settled further north in the Hensall area. Germans occupied western Hay and the adjacent north-central part of Stephen, separated by swamp from the very large group of English settlers from Devon and Cornwall who occupied eastern Stephen and most of Usborne. Settlements of migrants from particular parts of the earlier-settled regions of Upper Canada are impossible to pick out without extensive research, but may well have existed here as they did elsewhere.[60]

THE PALATINES OF BLANSHARD

A small group settlement in Blanshard Township deserves special mention, for some of its members were from North Tipperary though they emigrated with relatives from North Limerick and were really part of a separate group, the Irish Palatines. The Palatines were Germans who had come to Ireland in 1709 as refugees from principalities torn by political and religious warfare. Several thousand were taken to Ireland by a committee of landlords to form the nuclei of Protestant colonies on estates there. The greater number shortly went to England in expectation of being sent to America, but about 250 families remained to be settled in rural areas of Ireland. The largest group were sent to the Southwell estate near Rathkeale in County Limerick.[61] Descendants spread out from the Rathkeale area, a few scattering into North

TABLE 11
Ethnic Settlement in the Southwestern Huron Tract, 1871

Township	English		German		Irish		Scotch		
	n	%	n	%	n	%	n	%	Total
Stephen	1716	39.5	763	17.5	1217	28.6	497	11.4	4349
Hay	363	9.3	1974	50.7	556	14.3	661	17.0	3897
Usborne	2027	52.9	44	1.1	912	23.8	830	21.7	3831
West Williams	1047	30.6	225	6.6	545	15.9	1569	45.8	3427
East Williams	384	13.5	22	0.8	237	8.3	2156	75.6	2853
Biddulph	478	11.4	10	0.2	3293	78.4	298	7.1	4198
McGillivray	1632	35.0	161	3.5	1758	37.7	847	18.2	4658

Source: Census of Ontario, 1871. Ethnic origin by township.

Tipperary, and a considerable number settling at Kilcooly, County Tipperary, in the 1770s.[62] Clusters of Palatines are found in many parts of Ontario, a few interrelated families always settling together. This dispersed settlement pattern, however, belies extensive internal mobility and contact with friends settled elsewhere in the province. Some came as Loyalists from the United States, where they had lived for a generation, but a great many also came to Upper Canada directly from Ireland.

The Palatine families who settled in Blanshard Township, Perth County, are of particular interest because of their proximity to the Tipperary colony that grew up in Biddulph, just to the north of London. Blanshard, like Biddulph, was a township settled by the Canada Company. It was opened about ten years later, in 1841, but it was occupied very rapidly.[63] The 1842 census roll records twenty families, with a population of seventy-seven, whereas that of 1845 notes 222 families and 972 people.[64]

Some of the Sparling families who settled in Blanshard were from the northwestern border areas of Tipperary, but the fact that they settled just north of Biddulph, which had the largest Tipperary population in Upper Canada, may have been coincidence. These Sparlings were only several decades removed from the Adare area of County Limerick, and they were joined later by Sparling relatives from that county and from the Kilcooly area of Tipperary, many of whom had lived elsewhere in the province before moving to Blanshard.[65] Other Palatine families in Blanshard included the Benners, Brethours, Delmages, Doupes, Legears, Millers, Reynards, St Johns, Shiers, Spierans, Switzers, and Teskeys. From further afield in Upper Canada came also the Sparrows and Morphys from Beckwith (Lanark County), the latter family including the widow of the founder of Carleton Place, first known as Morphy's Falls.[66] Many of these families were among the very early settlers of Blanshard. The first Palatines in Blanshard settled together along the

Mitchell Road just northwest of St Mary's townsite. Later arrivals located to the west in the 2nd and 3rd Concessions, east of Kirkton.[67]

There were a number of North Tipperary families in Blanshard and the town of St Mary's, but none seem to have had any particular association with the Palatines there. Some were early London settlers with large families who came in quest of additional land for their children. John Blackwell and Philip P. Harding were two such. Both remained only a short time in Blanshard, and later moved further north, perhaps as a result of the rapidity with which land was snapped up in Blanshard. Others were late arrivals, such as the Hayeses and their relatives the Willises and Drapers, who found the land in London and Biddulph mostly taken up, and therefore settled just over the line into Blanshard at Prospect Hill. Still others were short-distance migrants whose parents lived in the Tipperary communities immediately to the south, in Biddulph or London. They moved to Blanshard in search of farms as they came of age, or set up in business in the town of St Mary's.

A few Palatine families had a longer residential history in North Tipperary than did the Sparlings of the Killaloe neighbourhood. The most notable were the Switzers of Templederry, who had connections with Nenagh and Birr[68] and were related to the Siftons who had come to London in 1818. That these people were part of the Tipperary group is demonstrated by the fact of their settlement in London and West Nissouri, closer to the North Tipperary heartland, rather than in the Palatine colony in Blanshard.

The migrations of the Limerick Palatines and their descendants intersected in places with those of the North Tipperary people, but they were really a distinct group. Nevertheless, they displayed, both in Ireland and in Canada, group, chain, and gravitational settlement patterns similar to those which have been traced for the North Tipperary Protestants. Only the locations were different.

THE TIPPERARY SETTLEMENTS IN BIDDULPH AND MCGILLIVRAY

The Tipperary Protestant settlement in Biddulph and McGillivray was an extension northward of the quite solid Tipperary cluster in the northwestern corner of London Township, immediately east of the Welsh settlement. Although Biddulph had originally been intended for a colony of free blacks from the United States, the black settlement failed to grow and the Irish who were immigrating to join friends in London were allowed to locate in Biddulph and, within a few years, dominated it. One of the Tipperary settlers was appointed local agent by the Canada Company and recruited settlers both for the Protestant settlement that grew up in the western half of the township and for the Roman Catholic Tipperary colony immediately to its east. Irish settlement began in Biddulph in 1833,[69] but most of the available land was taken up between 1835 and 1842 in the case of the Protestant settlement, and in the ten years following 1842 in the case of the Catholic settlement. After 1842 most Tipperary Protestants reaching Biddulph moved on to adjoining townships or to Tipperary settlements further north to secure land.

The earliest settlers in the southern part of the Huron Tract occupied lands along the roads built by the Canada Company.[70] As in the townships further north, the Wilberforce settlement and early white settlement in Biddulph and McGillivray occupied a thin band of land on either side of the London and Goderich Road. Only a few of these settlers who took up most of the lots along the portion of the road that followed the township line between Biddulph and McGillivray were from Tipperary, though one, Robert Hodgins, kept one of the first inns there on the McGillivray side.[71] This mixed settlement pattern remained typical of the road ever after, as most of the lots along it were taken up by the time Tipperary settlement in the townships began in earnest.

The Tipperary settlement in Biddulph was a continuation of the settlement in the northwestern part of London Township. The first farms claimed in the early 1830s were just over the line from London's 16th Concession. The first land taken up in Biddulph by a Tipperary Protestant was in fact purchased to enlarge an adjoining London Township farm. James Stanley had emigrated in 1822 and lived from 1824 on the northern edge of London Township. In 1832 he purchased two Biddulph lots that adjoined his farm.[72] The first Tipperary Irish actually to settle in Biddulph were probably the brothers John and Thomas Coursey who purchased Lot 37, Con. 2, and Lot 38, Con. 3, on 27 April 1833. They were brothers about nineteen and twenty-five years of age, sons of Richard Coursey, who had held one and a quarter Irish acres in Clonbrennan, parish of Dunkerrin. The father is said to have been robbed and killed at Dundas in 1832 en route to London.[73] Two other farms were taken up in July 1833 by Thomas Atkinson and Martha (Spencer), who emigrated from Shinrone that year or the year before,[74] and by Adam Hodgins, who had emigrated in 1831 and applied unsuccessfully to purchase a lot in London Township which he mistakenly believed was a clergy reserve.[75] Hodgins is said to have assisted in the survey of Biddulph. He agreed to buy a lot adjacent to Stanley's land in 1833. The only purchaser in 1834 was George Carter, who arrived from the Ottawa Valley and purchased a lot north of the site of Clandeboye village.

Although documentation of the precise date is lacking, it was probably in 1835 that James Hodgins, Adam's brother, was appointed Biddulph agent by the Canada Company. "Big Jim" had been a subconstable of police stationed at Borrisokane and Roscrea until 1832 when he had emigrated to Canada, fearing for his safety because of widespread discontent at his acquittal by a Protestant jury following his shooting of a Roman Catholic at Borrisokane in 1829.[76] Hodgins is said to have "arranged passage for many friends and relatives who wished to emigrate to Canada." His first party is said to have left

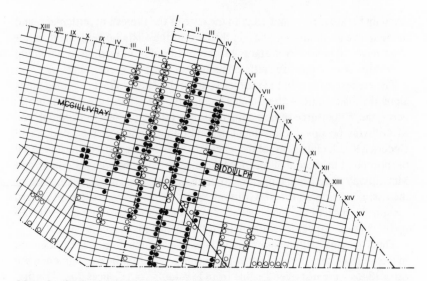

MAP 18   Settlement in Biddulph and McGillivray, 1842. Tipperary Protestants were located in western Biddulph by James Hodgins, a Finnoe man employed as the local Canada Company agent. Friends from the Ottawa Valley settled in McGillivray to the west.
Source: UWO, Huron District census and assessment rolls, 1842.

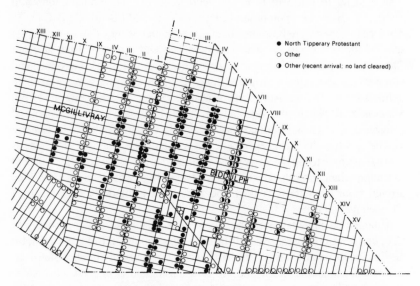

MAP 19   Settlement in Biddulph and McGillivray, 1845. By 1845 Tipperary Catholics were settling in substantial numbers east of the "Roman Line."
Source: UWO, Huron District census and assessment rolls, 1845.

Ireland in April 1835 and to have included many settlers named Hodgins as well as the Scillys.[77] Certainly land allocations were particularly heavy between September 1835 and July 1836, with many of the recipients being named Hodgins or Atkinson or being related to one or the other of these two families.[78]

In the later 1830s and early 1840s Protestants from Tipperary occupied most of the 2nd through 5th concessions. Some also settled in family clusters in McGillivray Township on the other side of the London and Goderich Road. In 1842 the eastern half of Biddulph was still unoccupied, apart from several members of the small Queen's County group in London Township who had taken up six lots on the South Boundary and several families of Irish Roman Catholics in the southernmost lots of concessions 7 and 8. These last were the first of the Tipperary Catholic settlers who, during the remainder of the 1840s and into the 1850s, took up lots in concessions 6 through 11.

Few of the Protestants immigrating in the 1840s and 1850s located in Biddulph, for the concessions allocated to them had been largely occupied by 1842. Though eleven new arrivals obtained Canada Company contracts or leases there in 1840–2, only eight did so in the next dozen years. Most of these lots were in the upper five lots of concessions 2 and 3 and in the North Boundary concession. Two new settlers purchased land in Biddulph from existing residents, one secured a farm by marrying an heiress, and three remained in the township without land. One of these, Jonas Poe, occupied fifty acres for many years before finally leasing it formally from the Canada Company in 1882.[79] Twelve immigrant Tipperary settlers occupied land in McGillivray between 1840 and 1854, but only three of these settled after 1850 and of these three one purchased from a speculator, one from his brother, and one never purchased but worked as a labourer. Nine settled in Blanshard Township, mostly around Prospect Hill, adjoining London Township. Three of the immigrants who located in Huron County acquired land in Stephen just north of the last allocated Biddulph lots and one located in Usborne, while three families settled in Tuckersmith, after a time in McGillivray, and five left for Bruce County to acquire land.[80] Thus the concentrated North Tipperary Protestant settlement in Biddulph was mostly settled in the short period between 1835 and 1842. Those who arrived later found the concessions allocated to their compatriots fully settled and were forced to locate in scattered clusters in nearby townships, or to work in Biddulph for a time and then move to northern Huron or to Bruce County.

It is curious that James Hodgins, who left Ireland after shooting a Roman Catholic, reserved the centre of the township for Tipperary Catholics and settled them there in significant numbers beginning at precisely the time the filling up of the western concessions forced many of his fellow Protestants to locate elsewhere. Hodgins is said to have visited Ireland in 1842 and again in

1844 to recruit settlers, but this cannot be documented.[81] A newspaper account at the time of the Donnelly murders in 1880 summarized the history of the Catholic settlement as follows:

During the first ten years subsequent to the land coming onto the market a good portion of the frontier part of the township was located chiefly by Irish Protestants, but not until after the year 1840 was there any land taken up or settled upon in the 6, 7, 8, 9 and 10th concessions. This is the portion which now forms the disturbed district. Subsequent to the last named date these concessions began to fill up with emigrants from Ireland. They were brought here on the representations of a man named Jas. Hodgins, who, at the time, was acting as the Canada Company's agent in the Township. About 1845 there might be a dozen families settled there, and they formed the nucleus of what is now widely known as the Catholic Settlement.[82]

The 6th to 11th concessions were occupied successively from west to east, with settlement proceeding northward from the London Township side, but no Protestant received allocations of land in these concessions even after lots in the western concessions of Biddulph had been completely taken up.[83] Of course, the sequence of occupation may explain this paradox, for once the most westerly concession allocated to the Roman Catholics had been settled, Protestants may have preferred to locate in McGillivray, to the west, rather than to settle among the Catholics or in a concession separated from their compatriots by the "Roman Line."

Most of the Tipperary Protestants who came to Biddulph directly from Ireland therefore arrived before the Canada Company changed its land policy in 1842 from one of one-fifth down and four instalments to an easier lease-to-purchase arrangement involving no down-payment. The old policy was less attractive to prospective settlers than the contemporary government policy which allowed ten years' credit. Clarence Karr has asserted that the Canada Company's more restrictive practice in this period attracted only settlers with "considerable means"[84] whom he termed "the 'aristocrats' of the emigrants." The new leasing policy of 1842 allowed "almost penniless, often illiterate pioneers" to make no down-payment and pay twelve increasing annual instalments with an option to purchase or renew at the end of that time.[85]

Certainly the Tipperary Catholics and the later Protestant immigrants must have benefited from the new leasing system, and it is probably not coincidence that the arrival of the generally poorer Catholics coincided with this change in policy. Karr's characterization of the earlier settlers accords well with the general descriptions of the Protestant emigrants leaving Tipperary as small farmers and "sturdy yeomanry" with the means to finance their own departure from Ireland. The fact that large numbers of Tipperary Protestants chose to take up land in the Huron Tract when it was supposedly more easily available elsewhere in Upper Canada confirms the attraction of friends and kin already there.

But how well does Karr's characterization of the early settlers of the Huron Tract really describe the Tipperary Protestants? Karr reprinted a table showing statistics on the various townships of the Huron Tract in 1840. The average wealth of the ninety settlers in Biddulph upon coming to the district had been only £20, less than half the average found in most townships.[86] Biddulph's population included the Tipperary Protestants, the twenty or so Wilberforce black families, and the settlers along the London and Goderich Road, but one would expect the blacks to have been less well off than the Irish and the settlers along the major road in the district to have had somewhat more money than the norm. The bulk of the Tipperary Protestant emigrants could afford to make down-payments of £10 or £12 for the privilege of settling near their friends, but it is questionable whether they could have met their financial obligations had the Canadà Company insisted upon payments being made when due. In fact, payments according to the schedule of instalments were not enforced, despite efforts by Widder in 1841 to sue delinquents for payment.[87] Of the sixty allocations of land to Tipperary Protestants that were made in Biddulph and McGillivray before 1840, only thirteen were fully paid for before the terms of the contracts expired.[88] Two properties were transfered to assignees before the final instalments were required, but in forty-five of the sixty instances the final payments were made and the deeds issued some years later, in many cases as late as the mid-1850s. In the meantime, the occupiers built up considerable arrears of interest which they also had to pay off before they could secure their deeds. Some settlers had only paid the down-payment or cleared away some of the interest by the time their five instalments were legally due. These pieces of evidence suggest that the Tipperary Protestants who settled in Biddulph were able to finance their passage from Ireland and make a down-payment on lands in Canada, for most appear to have done this soon after arriving in the country, but that they had only moderate means, less than the average settler in the district. Richard Talbot's settlers in 1818 had brought about £50 each but even those who brought £100 reported that they had fully expended their savings during their first few years in the country.[89] However, for emigrants from Tipperary the accumulation of arrears was not a new phenomenon.

By 1842 lands in the Huron Tract had become more attractive in their own right. Huron was no longer so far beyond the normal frontier of settlement as it had been in the 1830s, and the terms of the new lease policy were liberal. Later arrivals continued to lease lands, under the company's new policy, in adjoining townships, while some of those who arrived later still worked in the neighbourhood until they could afford to purchase from the crown in Bruce County, aided by the restoration of the credit system for sale of crown lands in 1852.

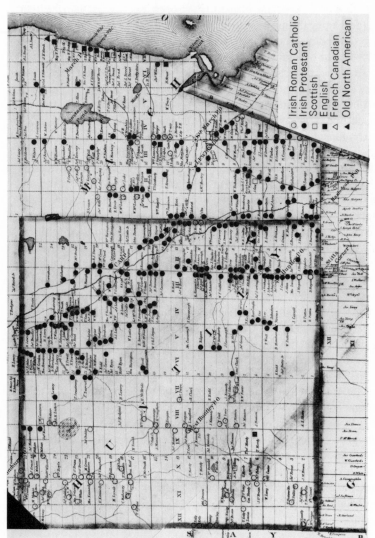

MAP 20 Ethnic settlement pattern in Huntley and March, 1863. Irish Catholics occupied the stony lands of west Huntley and Protestants the fertile Carp Valley, but early arrival helps explain the Protestant advantage (compare map 15). The mixed pattern in northwestern March reflects settlement in the 1840s both by newly arrived Irish Catholics and by the children of earlier Protestant families living to the south.
Source: H.F. Walling, Map of the County of Carleton, 1863; 1861 census.

CONTRASTING SETTLEMENT
PATTERNS

The geographical settlement patterns in the London and Richmond areas, although clustered, were very different each from the other. The Richmond segment of the *Brunswick* group was mostly placed in the first instance on the Twelfth Line of Goulbourn, in the northeastern corner of the township, and the major concentration of Tipperary settlement developed north from this original nucleus. Incoming Tipperary people in the next few years settled on the Third Line of Huntley and in the Carp Valley plain west of the later village of Carp, as well as to the east in the South March area. By the late 1820s most of the reasonably useable crown land in March, Huntley, and Goulbourn had been located, and immigrants were settling north up the Carp in Fitzroy Township.

The important point is that the Tipperary settlement in the Ottawa area, though mostly in the Carp Valley, was not in a solid block. Western Carleton County was also settled by chain migration from a concentration of Protestant population in south Leinster on the borders of Counties Kilkenny, Carlow, Wexford, and Wicklow. The arrivals in eastern Upper Canada from this region were more numerous than those from North Tipperary. The pattern was also complicated by the migration of Protestants from several adjoining parishes in north Cavan, followed in later years by small groups from Down, Tyrone, and probably other places. With two out of every seven lots set aside for reserves and immigrants arriving at a steady pace from several parts of Ireland, the chances of a settler's brother arriving a year later and finding a lot available next door were fairly slim, though the chances of obtaining one in the neighbourhood were good.

The settlement pattern in Carleton County included a number of areas of a religiously homogeneous nature. The Jockvale area of Nepean and the Corkery area of West Huntley were almost exclusively Tipperary Catholic communities. The Merivale area was home to the south Down settlers of the 1840s, but the comparatively late settlement of this neighbourhood also attracted children of Irish Protestant families in the Carp Valley. Some other Irish Protestant groups, notably the north Down group in the Lowry neighbourhood of the Huntley-Fitzroy Line, settled in relatively restricted but not exclusive neighbourhoods, but in Huntley and Fitzroy generally Irish Protestants from several areas were intermixed indiscriminately by their sequence of arrival. Nonetheless, Huntley's residential pattern maps as a striking division into a solidly Irish Protestant eastern half, in the Carp Valley, and a later-settled but equally concentrated Irish Catholic western half that grew up where some of the Peter Robinson emigrants of 1823 were located. The author of the Carleton County atlas commented in 1879 upon the

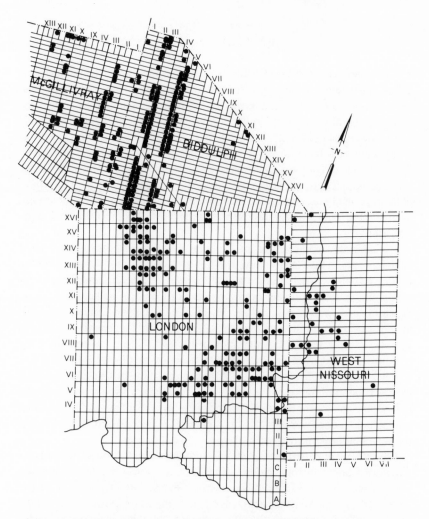

MAP 21   North Tipperary Protestant settlement in the London area, 1862. Large numbers, but a less diffuse settlement pattern than that of 1878 (map 17). Immigration diminished as the supply of cheap land vanished, but farmers continued to buy land near home for their sons.
Source: locations from Hermon, New Map of the County of Huron, and Tremaine's Map of the County of Middlesex, 1862.

continuing contrast in material as well as religious circumstances between the two halves of the township:

In the section of the Township referred to [the western half] there is not the semblance of a village; the great majority of the houses and outbuildings are of a description to which the word wretched might fitly be applied, and a very great bulk of the "land" (or rather of the surface, as there is not much land to be found in some localities) would rival the Rocky Mountains, if not in their picturesque effect and natural grandeur, at least in the "rocky" character and absolute worthlessness for agricultural purposes of its surface; while the general effect caused by the "great fire," which left nothing of value of what was once a dense forest, is one of desolation and dreary solitude. Altogether, one is inclined to pity those who were so unwise or so unfortunate as to have located in such a place as Western Huntley.

The author was enthusiastic about the Carp settlement in the eastern part of Huntley, which was "the oldest settled portion of the Township. From its advantages of location and fertility of soil it suffered no drawbacks in the progress of its development, but increased and improved from the very first, until it is now a fertile valley of cultivated fields, covered with superior residences, and exhibiting on every hand proofs of wealth and prosperity among its inhabitants such as class it with the most favored sections of the Province."[90] The physical segregation of Protestants and Catholics helped to preserve the social cleavage that was based in Huntley on the differential land quality in the two neighourhoods as well on upon historical background, and to maintain the tensions between the two religious groups. However, the Protestants from various parts of Ireland readily intermarried and developed a general Protestant Irish-Canadian identity.[91]

The distribution pattern of the various settlement groups in London Township was similar to that in the Ottawa Valley, though somewhat more concentrated. The Tipperary Protestants who came under Richard Talbot formed a large but not exclusive cluster in the southeastern part of the township, and other settlement groups in the township similarly formed highly regionalized clusters that were nevertheless interspersed with farms occupied by residents of different origins. The second Tipperary cluster that began in the northwestern part of the township in 1819 was more densely settled.

It was in the township of Biddulph, however, that the settlement pattern was most highly concentrated. In the Huron Tract there were no reserves to interrupt the contiguity of settlement. Indeed, the Canada Company itself appears to have indirectly encouraged the development of exclusive neighbourhoods by appointing its local settlement agents from the ranks of early settlers who displayed interest in recruiting friends and relatives from their places of origin, such as Balkwill of the Devonshire settlement and Hodgins who recruited for Biddulph.

Thus ethnicity-religion maps of Huntley and Biddulph (Maps 17 and 20) seem to depict similar settlement patterns, but they conceal equally fundamental differences. In Biddulph, both Orange and Green halves of the township were the results of movement from County Tipperary. In Huntley the Protestant half was made up of amalgams of peoples from very different regions of Ireland. The result was that the cultural characteristics of the people of Biddulph were less diluted by contact with neighbours from other backgrounds. It is probable that the continuance of disturbances in Biddulph into the 1880s, long after the boisterousness of the Ottawa Valley settlement had quieted down, is related to the cultural homogeneity of the Biddulph settlements, and to the fact that most of the Roman Catholic population of Biddulph had left Tipperary in the 1840s, the decade in which disturbances there were most severe.

CHAPTER SEVEN

Internal Migration

Donald Akenson has pointed out that the Irish in Upper Canada were predominantly a rural people, at least as rural as the general population.[1] He accepted that they may have clustered in the cities in the first instance, but posited that "eventually most of them settled in rural areas" through a "multi-stage (and in some instances multi-generational) migration" from the ports where they disembarked.[2] In the case of the group at hand there was very little initial settlement in the cities. I have already noted that only gentlemen and professionals tended to settle in the cities in the first instance. Most Tipperary Protestants appear to have been particularly single-minded in their preference for rural residences. Very few stayed in cities or towns for more than a winter upon arrival, and most proceeded immediately onto the land, or at least to a rural area if not immediately onto an available lot. This movement was of course facilitated after 1819 by acquaintance with settlers who were already in Canada; most new arrivals came with at least a preliminary destination already in mind. Even those who had been tradesmen in Ireland sought farms. Of course, many tradesmen in North Tipperary were also small farmers and in such a highly agricultural economy as that of southern Ireland no one was far from the land. However, a small cluster of Tipperary Protestants did form in Montreal in the migration period, and this centre therefore bears further examination. We must also look at the move into the cities of Ottawa and London from the Tipperary colonies in their hinterlands to judge the nature as well as the volume of such movement, and take a look at the reaction of the residents of Biddulph to the foundation of the town of Lucan in their midst in the 1850s.

We should examine the destinations of those who left their initial rural settlement locations. One can distinguish four types of internal migration between rural communities. First was gravitation migration, in which people of Tipperary origin who had settled in isolated locations or smaller colonies migrated to areas where there were other people of similar origin, generally larger colonies. Increasingly common after mid-century was the second type, individual chain migration of families in which a family would move to an area where no Tipperary settlers were already resident, but would be accompanied or followed there by some of their own kin and friends. Where enough families moved to an area in this way they formed secondary settlements, the third variety. Such secondary settlements were created by movement from an area of early concentrated settlement, and could involve either long-distance, kin-based migration or relatively short-distance, neigh-bourhood movement in which people from one part of a district moved to populate another, with kin ties operating only as a secondary mechanism. A fourth type, movement which involved dropping out of the chain-migration pattern completely, was very uncommon for North Tipperary Protestants.

The desire to establish themselves upon the land reflected the reason most of these emigrants came to Canada in the first place. Akenson has noted that Irish Protestants in particular demonstrated a "noteworthy aggressiveness in the acquisition of land"; they were "land hungry" immigrants with a mania for acquisition that was "intense, single-minded, and beyond mere economic calculation." Akenson's assertion is not consciously Weberian, for he sees the roots of this aggressiveness lying in the Protestants' attitudes to the Irish political and tenurial systems rather than in their Protestantism itself. Acquiring secure title to land in Ireland made one "comfortable, if not rich," but also served as "a bulwark against the hostile natives who surrounded them."[3] Nonetheless, if this aggressiveness was rooted in observation of the Irish situation, it is difficult to understand why the Irish Catholics would not have been equally acquisitive upon reaching Canada. Indeed, one might expect as much, for land-hunger is stereotypical of peasant attitudes, whether expressed in the admonition of Duddy Kravitz's Zeyda that "A man without land is nobody"[4] or in Woody Allen's satirization of a Russian peasant father, demented by a life of fruitless toil, proudly displaying to his imprisoned son a piece of turf and a model house as the realization of his dreams.[5] Akenson's statistics show that the Irish Catholics were only slightly less rural than Irish Protestants in Upper Canada and it is likely that they were no less "land-hungry." The difference lies probably in the lesser degree of success Catholics had in acquiring good land in rural areas. Akenson cites a study of successful Peter Robinson settlers near Peterborough and his own recent studies indicate that Catholic Irish became prosperous in some parts of Upper Canada.[6] But the story is not everywhere the same. Certainly in one of the two areas of the province upon which this study has most closely focused, Carleton County, Catholics occupied poor lands that offered little prospect for prosperity. In both the London and Ottawa areas, the Protestants began arriving earlier than the Catholics. The rapidity of early settlement on the best lands forced later arrivals, both Protestant and Catholic, to locate on poor soils and, as we shall see, this circumstance forced the Protestants at least into renewed migration a generation after initial settlement.

Chapter 8 will explore the motivations behind acquisition of landed property by Tipperary Protestants in the Canadas. First we must look at where the quest led them.

AN URBAN CLUSTER: THE TIPPERARY PROTESTANTS IN MONTREAL

Since 1818 there have always been small numbers of North Tipperary Protestants in the city of Montreal, although the nature of their settlement there has varied over time. These people represent essentially four types of urban settlement. First were sojourners, emigrants passing through the city en route to somewhere else who paused long enough to have a child baptized or buried,[7] to marry someone they met on board ship, or who remained in the city over the winter before proceeding on to the land in the spring.[8] Second, some emigrants lived and worked in the city for a few years to accumulate some capital before moving on to the land. The majority of the early Tipperary emigrants who clustered in Montreal fell into this category. A third type were business and professional men who were attracted to the city primarily for business reasons, examples of what Gordon Darroch has termed career migration.[9] Finally, there were those who came into the city from the countryside. Since rural-urban migration was generally a later phenomenon while the first three types were characteristic of those arriving directly from Ireland, rural-urban migration will be considered separately later in this chapter. These types of urban settlement have been classified on the basis of motivation for urban residence, but the people in each category did not constitute separate groups. Those passing through contacted those who were merchants there and some merchants, while drawn to Montreal by business opportunities, also had relatives in the city or initiated some chain migration in their wake.

Two of Richard Talbot's settlers of 1818 remained with their families in Montreal when the rest of the *Brunswick* party departed for Richmond and London. William Burton, a gentleman from Shinrone, opened a store in the city and Thomas Delahunt from the same parish practised his trade of blacksmithing there. A number of families joined them in succeeding years. Among the families there by 1825 was that of Arthur Hopper, a jeweller from Roscrea who came in 1822 and moved on to Huntley in 1835. He was a relative of William Burton's wife, and Burton moved to Goulbourn about the time Hopper went to adjoining Huntley Township.[10] Ralph Smith, a gentleman of Roscrea whose daughter Edward Allen Talbot married in

Montreal in 1821, came to Canada in 1819 with his kinsman Thomas Bridge, who unsuccessfully applied for land for both in the little Tipperary colony in Esquesing. Smith later left Montreal and opened the first brewery in Hull.[11] Robert Howard went to Esquesing in 1819, with his father-in-law William Kent, but he left the Toronto area almost immediately and became a merchant in Montreal in partnership with William Harte Thompson, a cousin of Burton's wife, who settled with his father at Richmond. Howard conducted the important Montreal arm of the business and the Howards remained Montreal residents after the partnership ended.[12]

The gentry and merchants came out initially to join Burton, but a number of more humble folk contacted Thomas Delahunt upon arriving in the city. Most of them remained only a short time. Those from farming backgrounds worked in the city as labourers or sawyers for several years and in the mid- to late 1820s moved on to rural Tipperary colonies elsewhere in Upper and Lower Canada. Even most of the carpenters and shoemakers moved on to farms after a few years in the city. Francis Abbott from Aglishcloghane parish, Freeman Blackwell, and Delahunt were listed one after another in the 1825 census. The former two worked as sawyers in Montreal for several years before moving to Carleton County around 1828.[13] James O'Neil, who lived in Montreal for a few years before joining his brothers in London, was recorded next door to John and Watson Litle, brothers from County Monaghan. John later married the widow of O'Neil's brother Robert and moved to Bytown.[14] Samuel Goulding was a carpenter and coachmaker in the city, but after his death in 1825 at the age of thirty-two his widow joined relatives in the small Tipperary colony in Rougemont.[15]

Though business associations, family relationships, and chains of godparenthood convey the impression of two distinct class-based groups of Tipperary Protestants in the city, the members of these two social levels shared common residential and migrational patterns and were united by their common interest in the Orange Order. The 1825 census unfortunately does not give street addresses, but almost all of the North Tipperary immigrants are recorded in the space of a few pages in the central part of the old city and parish of Montreal. They must all have lived close to one another. Members of the group are credited with establishing one of Canada's early civilian Orange lodges in the city in the late 1820s. Arthur Hopper, William Burton, and Francis Abbott were three of the four founders whose names have come down to us. Burton returned to Ireland to obtain a charter for the lodge. When Ogle R. Gowan, the Wexford Orangeman, arrived from Dublin en route to Brockville in 1829, a son was baptized at Christ Church, Montreal, with William and Elizabeth Maria Burton as sponsors. When Gowan established the Grand Lodge of British North America in Brockville the next year Burton was selected as deputy grand treasurer of the order.[16]

By 1831 some of these residents had moved on to rural areas and a few others had arrived in the city, but the initial cluster had broken up and those remaining lived on various streets in the old parish of Montreal. Delahunt was a blacksmith in rue St-Antoine, where the recent arrival Benjamin Boake of Nenagh was a labourer.[17] O'Neil was a servant in rue du College.[18] Robert Howard kept his store in Place d'Armes, while Burton's was in rue St-Joseph.[19] Two new arrivals, Francis and Nicholas Bethel, were respectively a jeweller in St Paul street and a shoemaker in rue des Fortifications.[20] The jeweller was at 84 St Paul Street in July 1830, and Arthur Hopper, also a jeweller, was addressed there in 1832. If the two were not in business together one must have succeeded the other in the property. In 1831 Hopper was living outside the city as a farmer in the Côte St-Antoine.[21] A sister of Richard and George Hayes who had settled in London in 1819 advertised for them in the press in 1830, giving Bethel's address. It appears likely that she was Mrs Moses Coates.[22] Coates was certainly in Montreal in June 1831 when he was a witness, with Robert Hodgins, at the marriage of Thomas Hodgins to Robert's sister Ann. The Hodginses were merely passing through Montreal, and Robert and his brothers spent several years with Coates in Huntley before they all moved on to Biddulph and McGillivray.

Though the residential concentration was less marked in 1831, the personal connections with other people from North Tipperary continued. Boake's son James was a witness to the marriage of John R. Stanley, a steamboat steward whose wife had died in the General Hospital soon after the family arrived from Modreeny in 1830. Stanley's second wife was Clarinda Sides, a resident of Montreal but daughter of a tailor in Templemore.[23] The Boakes soon left Montreal to join cousins who had settled in York Township near Toronto some years before.[24] Parish registers of the 1820s and 1830s provide evidence in the names of parties, sponsors, and witnesses of the temporary residence in the city of other North Tipperary families passing through or living there for a couple of years: Colbert and Dagg relatives of Abbott's wife; Powells, Nappers, and Spearmans, some of whom obtained land in Hemmingford, Lower Canada; Whitten relatives of the Delahunts; Ashtons, Evanses, Gouldings, and Cardens who soon joined the Standishes at Rougemont; Hills and Lewises, blacksmiths and carriagemakers in Montreal, some of whom went to London; Ardells, Englands, Ginnises, Mossops, Hasketts, and Hollands.

Very few of the humbler folk remained in Montreal, preferring to move on to the land, and scarcely any of the North Tipperary Protestants who emigrated later appear to have settled in the city. A very few are identifiable in the 1861 census, such as John Spearman, a plasterer from Cloughjordan who apparently converted to Catholicism after his marriage and was confirmed in that faith by marriage to a second Roman Catholic wife in Montreal in 1850. In 1861 he was living in the basement of a brick house in Colborne Street.[25] Some of those who did settle in Montreal later continued earlier patterns by

TABLE 12

Grant, Powell, Cox, and Morris Families

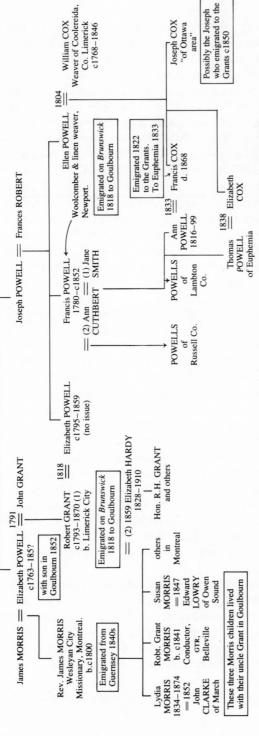

Sources: R.E. Cox, *The Families of Francis and Ann Cox* (Beaconsfield 1972); R.H. Grant, "Biography of Robert Grant, 1793–1870," typescript courtesy Hon. R.A. Bell; PRO, Dublin, Stradbally and Newport parish registers; indexes to Killaloe and Cashel diocesan marriage licence bonds; *Commemorative Biographical Record of the County of Lambton* (Toronto 1906), 321–2, 752–3; various Canadian parish, census, land, and gravestone records.

Note: This genealogical table illustrates several points made in the text:

1 Chain migration. Several of the Cox children came out in the 1820s to their uncle, Robert Grant, who had emigrated in 1818. Joseph Cox may be the relative whose family lived with the Grants upon arriving from Ireland around 1850, but another Joseph Cox settled on the Gatineau River and it is unclear who is meant. Three of the Morris children from Montreal lived for a time with their uncle Grant in Goulbourn, two marrying in the neighbourhood.

2 Assistance for kin. Robert Grant became wealthy through country store-keeping and supported large numbers of relatives in his household.

3 Cousin marriage. This table includes three instances of first cousin marriages: Grant and his first wife, and two marriages between Cox and Powell cousins. After living with the Grants for a number of years, the Coxes accompanied the children of Francis Powell's first marriage to Euphemia, Lambton County, in the 1830s.

4 Moves late in life to provide for children. Powell's second family moved with him to Russell, east of Ottawa, just before he died c1852.

moving to or establishing contact with rural communities where they had relatives. James Morris, a half-brother of *Brunswick* passenger Robert Grant of Hazeldean, emigrated in the 1840s or 1850s after a residence in Guernsey and was a Methodist city missionary living in St James Street. Several of his children lived with their Ottawa Valley uncle, however, and married in that district.[26]

The merchant class, too, who formed the bulk of the later Montrealers of Tipperary Protestant origin, were not drawn to the city by totally economic considerations. The Holland family of Montreal illustrates the point that even the mercantile families of Canada's financial capital shared in the kin-based patterns of migration and assistance. Andrew Holland of Mountshannon, a member of a family of middlemen and minor landlords in Clonrush parish, moved into Montreal in 1832 from New Glasgow, Lower Canada, where he had first settled, turning his farm over to his eldest son, Robert. Robert later moved to Holland Township, Grey County, where his cousin Robert Clarke had settled some years before. The remaining Holland brothers became merchants in Montreal, except for William Lewis Holland, a wheelwright, who went to the Ottawa Valley after his uncle George Clarke died and married the latter's daughter Charlotte. John Holland, a partner in Holland and Mathewson in Montreal, loaned mortgage money to William and later died while visiting his cousin, Nicholas Clarke, at Manotick near Ottawa.[27]

John Haskett of London Township provides a rare example of eastward migration. This move must have been prompted by family as much as by business concerns. John was a son of William Haskett, a painter who emigrated on the *Brunswick* in 1818 and settled in London Township. In the early 1860s John was a partner in Montreal with Samuel Goulding Haskett, son of Thomas Haskett, a painter of Borrisokane and Moneygall who emigrated in the 1850s to Nanticoke in Norfolk County, where Samuel was a merchant and postmaster fom 1854 to 1862. The two painters were probably brothers. For several years in the early 1860s John was a partner in his cousin Samuel's fruit and provision business in Commissioners Street, Montreal, though the partnership lasted only a few years. In 1871 John was a corn merchant in Ingersoll. The two cousins must have been in contact even before they went into business together for both had married daughters of Jacob Irwin of Montreal in the early 1850s.[28] There were a few examples of career migration that were apparently unaffected by kinship considerations, such as the residence in the city of Dr Samuel Waller, late of Quebec, brother of Sir Edmond Waller and son of Jocelyn Waller, who had come to Canada to take up a government appointment,[29] and the retirement there of gentleman Jackson Wray.[30] Andrew Hayes, son of a Dublin relative of Mrs Arthur Hopper, came to the city after the Hoppers left it, apparently motivated solely by business considerations.[31]

Some studies have suggested that "the greater the distance moved, the higher [was] their occupational status,"[32] but far more farmers of North

Tipperary background made the 400 or 500 mile journey from Lower Canada or the Ottawa Valley to London than replicated the Hasketts' movement in the opposite direction. It is true that business considerations took merchants, doctors, and brewers to locations where they had no kin,[33] but the known instances suggest that kinship influenced the movements of these classes as it did those of the farmers.

THE IMPERMANENCE OF THE SMALL COMMUNITIES

I have already explained how the Tipperary Protestants who followed the Talbot party to Canada in 1819 settled in numerous locations in Upper and Lower Canada because many left Ireland before the destination of the *Brunswick* migrants became known. Chain migration in subsequent years led to the growth of small colonies of Tipperary Protestants in some of these areas, but later immigration was directed more often to the largest colonies at Richmond and London. In time, residents in these smaller colonies gravitated to join their compatriots in these two locations while others spread throughout the hinterlands of their immediate areas, leaving only a few families in these early locations.

One colony that initially showed some strength was the one established by Robert and Matthew Standish at Rougemont in Rouville County, Lower Canada, in 1818. A number of families, largely from the Roscrea area, joined them in the 1820s, often using Montreal as a staging area where they spent several years before proceeding to the countryside. Though some two dozen families settled here in this period, most had moved on by the 1840s. Arthur Hopper of Roscrea and Montreal owned lots on the South West River and sold some to his brother-in-law, Benjamin Sparling, who settled upon them. Sparling moved to Bolton Township in the 1840s.[34] In 1822 the heirs of Benjamin Blackall of Garden Hill, County Limerick, sold their interests in Knockagarry and emigrated to Montreal.[35] By 1826 the families of Edward, John, and Waltho Blackall, and their brothers-in-law John Haskett and Thomas Patrick, were in the parish of Ste Marie de Monnoir. In 1833 the Hasketts and Patricks moved to London Township where Haskett had relatives living.[36] The Blackalls moved to other parts of Lower Canada, some to Iberville County. A carpenter named Walter Blackall of that place (b. LC c1830), son of one of the three brothers, moved to London in the 1860s and rented an acre from his cousin, Thomas Patrick Jr.[37] In 1871 a John Blackall, widower, a stone mason, was living with Thomas Patrick's brother George.[38]

Other residents of the Rougemont area moved directly to London or Biddulph after only a brief residence in Lower Canada. Matthew Standish's wife Rebecca Stanley corresponded in the 1830s with a relative, Joseph Dobbs of Abbeyleix.[39] Some of the Dobbs apparently came out to

Rougemont, for Francis Alexander and his wife Mary Dobbs were in Ste Marie in the late 1830s.[40] Several years later they settled on a farm in Biddulph beside Mary's parents, James (c1772–1851) and Mary Dobbs, who came to Canada in 1835 but reached Biddulph only in 1840; they probably spent the intervening years in Ste Marie, too. Several other families who lived near Rougemont also left, but they did not go to other Tipperary colonies. These families included the Ashtons, Boates, Evanses, Crookeses, and Mottasheds, and the Masons, Mossops, and Smiths at nearby Chambly. By 1852 only four families of Standishes, three of Cardens, one Evans, and one Ashton remained in a mostly French-Canadian area.[41] Most of the children of William Carden, who was an innkeeper in St-Césaire village, lived for a time in Bytown where William Jr was a partner with his brother-in-law, William Cousens, in a store on Wellington Street.[42] The colony at Rougemont has not completely disappeared, for Standish descendants reside in the area still.

Another very small colony was formed, beginning in 1819, at Mascouche, north of Montreal, by the Robinsons and Alexanders from Seirkieran and Kinnitty. Joined later by additional Robinsons and intermarried with the Edgehills of Rawdon, these families were the only Protestants apart from the seigneur in a seigneury populated by French Canadians. Several of the Alexanders moved to London Township in the 1840s, and the use of characteristic given names in the family of Francis Alexander of Ste Marie and Biddulph suggests a relationship with the Mascouche family.[43] Some of the Robinsons moved away, but some connections with distant kin were retained. Thomas and Lancelot Robinson corresponded with their cousin John Haskett of London. In 1860 Tom wrote about his family: "now i will tell you whare my brothers and Sisters are liveing Sarah lives in Otawa John went from ohio to Canses 4 years ago and it did not agree with his health So he Died 2 years ago last October. William lives In Hastings C.W. 60 miles from Madoc. Josept is in Illinois but i Cannot tell whare now as he moves about a good deal Richard lives far away in oregon he is not Married he was away for 21 years and never Wrote to us for that time he told us at last were he was So i Cannot tell much about him he writes when the humer takes him but Says very litle. Lanty and family are all well."[44] William Robinson settled on the Hastings Road, one of the colonization roads constructed by the government of Canada West in the 1850s to lure settlers onto the Canadian Shield as the frontier of cultivable land receded. One of William's sons, William Jr, went to the nearest Tipperary colony in the Ottawa Valley in 1866 to marry a distant cousin, Mary Jane Armstrong, whose Irish grandmother had been a Haskett.[45] Richard Robinson in Oregon corresponded in later years with his niece Ann Jane Alexander. In 1878 Ann Jane migrated with her first-cousin husband to join her uncle in Oregon but died there the next year of the "typhoid and pneumonia fever" that had plagued the family since their arrival and been a constant topic in their letters home.[46]

The Kingston area of Upper Canada was not a centre of Tipperary Protestant population, and the few North Tipperary Protestant families who settled there formed several distinct familial clusters. Aside from John Ardell and Mary (Dagg) who resided in Frontenac County for a short time in 1819 before moving on to London Township,[47] the first and only major residents in the vicinity of the city itself were several members of the Armitage family of Modreeny. The Armitages' presence drew friends and relatives to the area for a time, but all moved on to London, as did several of the Armitages themselves. John Armitage and Ann (Robinson) arrived in Canada with their infant son in 1827 and settled in Kingston Township. John's brother James, who may have come with them, proceeded on to the London area by 1836 and in 1840 purchased land in Biddulph. Another brother, William, left his farm in Burnwood, Modreeny, in 1829–31 and obtained land in London Township. In 1831 Francis Armitage, probably an older brother of the others, arrived from Ireland and bought land in Ernesttown, near Odessa. His eldest son John purchased the other half of Francis's lot three years later. In 1839 Francis sold his farm to his son Rody and moved to Tyendinaga, near Belleville, where he purchased land for his three younger sons.[48]

The presence of the Armitages attracted a number of other families who paused for a while en route to London from Ireland, but none stayed for any appreciable length of time. In 1835–6 two Hodgins families from County Tipperary passed through Kingston. In 1837–8 Joseph Thompson and James Dagg, immigrants from Modreeny who were married to Ardell or McArdell sisters, arrived at Ernesttown and had children baptized at St George's Church, with Francis Armitage's children John and Susan as sponsors to the Dagg infant. Within a few years the Thompsons and Daggs moved on to Biddulph. Francis Sadleir, a young man from Finnoe whose mother was a Robinson, said to have been a cousin of old John Armitage's wife, lived in the Kingston area briefly before moving to Biddulph; he belonged to a Kingston Orange lodge from 1847 to 1849.[49]

The Armitages themselves did not all remain in the Kingston area. John moved to Biddulph in 1849 after his house and barns in Kingston Township were destroyed by fire and purchased his brother James's Canada Company contract.[50] Francis's son Rody moved to Biddulph in 1852 after his house, too, was burned.[51] Francis's oldest son John remained and became a prominent farmer in Ernesttown but he, too, sought out Tipperary compatriots for in 1841 he married Annie Guest, daughter of Thomas Guest of Oxford on Rideau. The Guests were residentially one of the closest Tipperary families to the Armitages, though they lived some sixty-five miles away.[52]

Francis Armitage's farm in Tyendinaga, near Belleville, was very close to that of his executor John Portt,[53] a member of a King's County family whose presence may have drawn Armitage to the township when he began to look for additional land. The Portts came to Canada in 1819 and to Tyendinaga the following year at the time when the interior part of the township, formerly part of an Indian reserve, was opened to white settlement. William Portt had six sons and several daughters. Of the boys only the youngest, James, appears to have had any sons who survived past the age of twenty, so none of this Portt family migrated far in the second generation. The Portts remained almost the only North Tipperary family in the Belleville area, though in the 1820s a few members of the Sifton family moved east from London, but they soon returned whence they came.[54] Whether they were influenced in their move by the Portt family is unknown.

Direct ties with the London colony were established by relatives of the Portts who arrived from Ireland later. James Porte of Mount Heaton near Roscrea brought his four children to Deseronto in 1837 and moved on to Biddulph, where his wife's family had relatives, in 1839. His eldest son William, later the postmaster of Lucan, married a Belleville girl in 1851.[55] Another Porte from King's County came to London soon after James, apparently bypassing Tyendinaga. Gilbert Porte, son of the parish clerk of Kinnitty, emigrated to London in 1841 and was a shoemaker in that city.[56] His brother Robert came in 1849 and after living with Gilbert for a few years became a bootmaker in Biddulph and later a merchant at Parkhill.[57] The last Portes to come settled not far from the Tyendinaga family and were probably influenced by them. The family of Thomas Porte, who had moved from his native King's County to County Wexford some years before, came to Canada in the early 1850s and settled at Picton in Prince Edward County.[58]

Finally, a number of interrelated families from the western edge of the North Tipperary region settled in Camden East Township and its vicinity. The settlement of these families in Camden was determined by the relationship of one of the earliest of the families to a group of Palatine settlers from County Limerick who had made Camden their home.[59] The family connections of the Caswell family of Youghalarra, the first of whom was in Camden by 1828, extended the web of kinship eastward from Limerick into the Tipperary study area.[60] Richard Long's wife was a Caswell, as had been the first wife of Edward Cox of Coolereida, County Limerick.[61] The latter's second wife, who emigrated with him, was a Dyas from Mountshannon, and several of her relatives also settled in townships near Camden.

The Camden area families illustrate the point that many emigrants had a choice of settlement locations where relatives already lived. Relatives of the Caswells had settled in Drummond Township near Perth in 1816[62] and earlier members of the Cox family of Coolereida had emigrated to Upper Canada to join Grant relatives from Limerick and Powell relatives from Newport, County Tipperary; they had lived in the Ottawa Valley but by the 1840s were in Lambton County. Lucy (Dyas) Cox was a daughter of Thomas Dyas and Alice Clarke, who lived in the vicinity of Mountshannon, County Galway. Her mother Alice was a daughter of Robert Clarke, a freeholder of Cregg,

Clonrush, the father of four Clarke brothers who had emigrated to Canada in 1819, three settling in York and Tecumseth near Toronto, and the fourth, George, near his wife's family, the Shouldices, in March Township on the Ottawa River. I have already recounted how the Coxes chose to come out to the Caswells rather than go to Lucy's sister Eliza and her husband Thomas Logan in Australia.[63]

Near Toronto, as in the Kingston area, the comparatively few residents of North Tipperary origin formed several groups. In these cases, however, migratory links with the London area were quite weak. One Toronto area cluster was in the Downsview neighbourhood of York Township, where one of the small colonies was formed in 1819, the other in the northern part of York County and the southern half of Simcoe, roughly between Newmarket and Barrie. This second cluster was formed by kin and relatives of kin of William Robinson, one of Francis Evans's 1815 applicants, who brought his family to West Gwillimbury from King's County in the 1820s to join his wife's cousin, James Wallace, who had come in 1819.[64] Both groups had weak links with the larger Tipperary colonies though, as we shall see, the Clarkes in York Township kept in contact with their cousins near Ottawa and reaffirmed the relationship by repeated intermarriage in the 1880s. Because both groups near Toronto were relatively small, these families formed no significant secondary settlements elsewhere, though members of the families usually moved with close relatives when they left the region. Most remained in the hinterland of Toronto by 1881, but the families tended to scatter through the northern townships, probably due to the high demand and consequently high prices for land throughout the region and especially in the vicinity of the metropolis.

The Boakes, Bulls, Clarkes, Reeds, and Gouldings near Downsview in York Township intermarried with one another and with the few remaining families who located in Esquesing in 1819. After the early years there appear to have been few contacts with London, though the Rev. Edmund Stoney, a *Brunswick* passenger, served on the Yonge Street Circuit in 1833–4 and became well-known to the Methodists among the Downsview group,[65] and John Boake Jr moved to London Township around 1871.[66] Most of the members of these families who left Downsview spread north into Simcoe and Wellington counties. Edward Boake bought land for two sons in Whitchurch, near Newmarket, while several of John's children moved to Essa near Barrie. In 1883 three of Edward's sons and their cousin Edward W., son of John, went to Yorkton in what is now Saskatchewan. The Clarkes had actually been located for land in Tecumseth and two of the four brothers settled there; their children scattered north into Simcoe County. The Bulls remained mostly in York Township, the city of Toronto, and Toronto and Etobicoke townships to its west. In Esquesing the Kents[67] and Watkinses moved into Hamilton in the 1840s, where the latter became wealthy merchants. Many of the Standishes remained in Esquesing or in Erin to its north during the period of this study but others moved with Reed and Going relatives in the 1860s and 1870s to Huron, Greenock, and Culross townships in Bruce County, east of the Tipperary colony at Bervie with which they seem not to have associated. Though most of the Reeds went to Bruce County, Thomas established his eldest son on a farm in Toronto Township near home and the latter's cousin John H. Reed went to Artemesia in Grey County in the 1860s.[68]

The families who grouped loosely in the northern area, particularly in the Gwillimburys, were mostly from western Queen's County and the King's County panhandle as well as from the adjacent Cloughjordan area, though the Baskervilles and probably the Corbetts were from Youghalarra on the Shannon. The Ardills and Knowltons, Williamses, Sheppards and Whitfords located in North Gwillimbury, the Ashburys there and in York Township, the Baskervilles across Lake Simcoe in Oro, the Corbetts in North Gwillimbury and Georgina, the Morans in the latter place, the Carters in King, the Longs in West and East Gwillimbury, the Lewises, Wallaces, and Robinsons in West Gwillimbury, and the Stanleys, Woods, and Worrells at least temporarily in the city of Toronto after their arrival in the Famine period.[69] The only link with the Tipperary settlement near London was forged by brothers George and Arthur Brown who moved to McGillivray and ran a store at Brinsley. Arthur in 1862 married a Richardson whose family had moved there from the Ottawa Valley colony.[70] However, a number of the Woods, Searsons, and Carters moved to Brooke Township, Lambton County, in the 1850s.[71] Others moved northwards, as occurred also among the Downsview people. Some of the second generation of the Robinsons moved into Innisfil in the 1840s, and the third to Wallace and Maryborough twenty years later.[72]

No early cluster of Tipperary Protestants formed in Toronto in the 1820s and 1830s as had in Montreal, but Toronto was then a much smaller centre. Nonetheless, a few gentlemen and prosperous merchants established themselves in the city at various times. The first of these was George Kingsmill of Templemore, a former soldier who came to Toronto in 1829 and ran a provision store in Market Street. He later became high bailiff and an aide to Sir Francis Bond Head during the Mackenzie Rebellion.[73] Kingsmill was an uncle of Thomas Frazer Kingsmill who came to London in 1865 via Georgia and Toronto and established the well-known London department store, Kingsmill's.[74] Also with a connection to the London area was Frederick Falkiner, a gentleman from Borrisokane who came to York Township and Toronto in the late 1840s. After his death his widow moved to London and a son married a daughter of Dr Robert Hobbs of that place, formerly of Borrisokane;[75] other sons lived in Beverley and New Zealand.[76] Another merchant in Toronto was Rice Lewis from Nenagh, who established a large hardware company in the 1840s. Lewis's second wife was a Watkins from Birr, probably related to the Hamilton family. His sons moved where business

TABLE 13

Major Destinations of Internal Migration by Tipperary Protestant Families Settled in the Ottawa Valley

	1825–9	1830–4	1835–9	1840–4	1845–9	1850–4	1855–9	1860–4	1865–9	1870–4	1875–80	Total
Clarendon	4	1	7	2	1	2						17
London area		1	19	17	7	1	1	2	1			49
North Onslow			1	6	2	1		1				11
Chatsworth (Grey)				7	1		1					9
Cobden (Renfrew)					3	4	2	1				10
Kincardine (Bruce)						21						21
Russell County					2	7	6	3	2	1	2	23
Kazabazua (Gatineau)						9		6				15
City of Ottawa	1		3	3	3	2	3	4		3	8	30
Total												185

Sources: Compiled family files, census, and land records.

took them: John to Kidderminster, England, where he was a carpet manufacturer, Charles W. to New York.[77] Generally the merchants and gentlemen of Toronto moved as the interests of their careers dictated but, as we have seen, career considerations were not completely independent of the influences of kinship ties. A few other families, apparently unrelated to the major groups, scattered in various places: the Beynons in King and Vaughan, the Englands in Tecumseth (some later moving to Morris in Huron County), the Morphys, Mossops, and Charles Cambie (a civil servant, later of Quebec and Ottawa) in the city, and families of gentlemen like the Coxes in Erindale and the Youngs in Scarborough.

There was a tendency for many of those who settled in the small Tipperary colonies in Upper and Lower Canada to gravitate in time to the larger colonies, particularly the largest, in the London area, where most had relatives, but this gravitation was most common in the first and second generations. The move was usually made by immigrant families who became dissatisfied or left to obtain land for their children, or by children who went to western relatives in search of land. However, not all made such a move. In every case at least a few became sufficiently successful to remain where they had first settled. When seeking land, new generations tended less often to move to London. More frequently they remained in the general area of the minor colony, often moving into townships to the rear of where their parents had first settled.

THE MOVEMENT OF TIPPERARY SETTLERS WITHIN AND FROM THE OTTAWA VALLEY

As in the case of the smaller communities, some families in the major Tipperary colony in the Ottawa Valley gravitated to the London area, some fifty in number. However, the settlers resident near the future capital also formed several secondary settlements within the valley itself and migrated through the mechanism of chain migration to other locations beyond its boundaries.

A considerable amount of local migration was not really migration at all, because it consisted merely of a move from one township to the next, often leaving the mover only a couple of concessions or at most a few miles from where he began. This is the case, for example, with Huntley families who purchased lands for their sons in Fitzroy. In terms of medium- and long-distance movement, however, different areas were favoured in different periods, as Table 13 suggests. The selection of a given area was usually influenced to some degree by government land policy, as it was when the Shouldices and their relatives took advantage of the offer of free fifty-acre

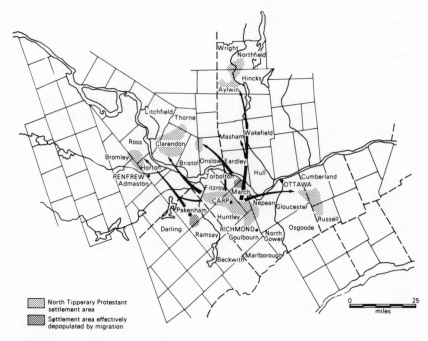

North Tipperary Protestant
settlement area

Settlement area effectively
depopulated by migration

0   25
miles

MAP 22   Primary and secondary settlements in the Ottawa Valley. Much of the
valley was settled by members of new generations leaving the earliest settlement
area in western Carleton County.

grants on the Garafraxa Road in the early 1840s,[78] but sometimes it was
simply a matter of an area opening at a opportune time – Russell County in the
1840s, for example.

The information, companionship, and assistance provided by kin were
instrumental in all the medium and longer distance moves, but in the case of
the former, that is, moves to more distant areas still within the Ottawa Valley,
the migrants were not confined to interrelated families of Tipperary descent.
Rather, such migration was a neighbourhood phenomenon. Thus one finds
Clarendon Township around Shawville in the late 1820s and 1830s, western
Russell County from the late 1840s onwards, and the Kazabazua area of the
Gatineau Valley in the 1850s and 1860s receiving influxes of western
Carleton County families, mostly Irish Protestant, but not exclusively of
Tipperary origin.

Clarendon was the earliest of the secondary settlements within the Ottawa
Valley. Thomas Hodgins of Goulbourn and late of Borrisokane is said to have
been one of the two men who first scouted out the area in 1821,[79] but the major
stimulus to settlement there was the activity of James Prendergast, a former
ensign of the 99th, who became settlement agent in order to secure a
percentage of the land. Prendergast recruited heavily among former soldiers

and other settlers in the Richmond military settlement, many of whom were already securely established on lands there, some of fair agricultural potential.[80] In the early 1830s the movement of recent arrivals in Carleton up to Clarendon was further stimulated by the slowness of the Crown Lands Department in responding to requests for the sale of such clergy reserves as had been allocated for disposal in 1827. Hamnett Pinhey of March, the local agent for sales, wrote to Peter Robinson, the commissioner, in 1833: "I understood from Mr McNaughton, a month or two ago, that in conformity to your desire, he had surveyed and transmitted to you his Evaluations of the respective Clergy reserves as particularized in my Schedule left with you; am looking out for your promised letter on the subject; but the inconvenient proximity of the Lower province to us is such, that if applicants do not very speedily get located here, they are ferried across, and *fixed* as our neighbours opposite call it, in Clarendon and other Lower Canadian townships."[81] The movement to Clarendon was thus not specific to any one of the groups of Irish immigrants that made up the older townships' population. The 1851 census of Clarendon reads like a roster of early Huntley families, Tipperary and non-Tipperary alike.

In later years more recent areas of settlement within the Ottawa Valley supplanted Clarendon as the destination of internal migrants. Like those who moved to Clarendon, the farmers who formed a secondary settlement in western Russell County beginning in the late 1840s and those who went up the Gatineau River to Kazabazua in the next decade were drawn from the general population of west Carleton and not solely from the settlers of Tipperary background. In all three locations the Carletonians created solid neighbourhoods of Irish Protestants adjacent to areas of Catholic settlement, reminiscent of the settlement pattern in Huntley.

On the Ontario side, much of the land east of the Rideau River was settled comparatively late. Settlers began to enter Gloucester and Osgoode in considerable numbers only in the 1830s, while the eastern part of Gloucester and much of Russell County were settled only in the 1840s to 1860s, the western townships by the mostly Irish Protestant Carleton County people and the eastern parts by French Canadians. Chad Gaffield has already explained how areas of anglophone and francophone settlement in Prescott and Russell counties reflected the farming practices of the people, which in turn were related to drainage conditions. The Irish favoured the sandy, well-drained lands while the French Canadians' knowledge of drainage techniques and other ways of managing wet land allowed them to develop the imperfectly drained soils.[82] This may be illustrated by comparing the modern County Soil Map with the settlement pattern of Russell Township shown on the 1862 County Map.[83] The road from Russell village north to Bearbrook passes through a band of Vars gravelly sand, described in the Soil Survey as undulating, well-drained, and excellent cropland. The Irish Protestant

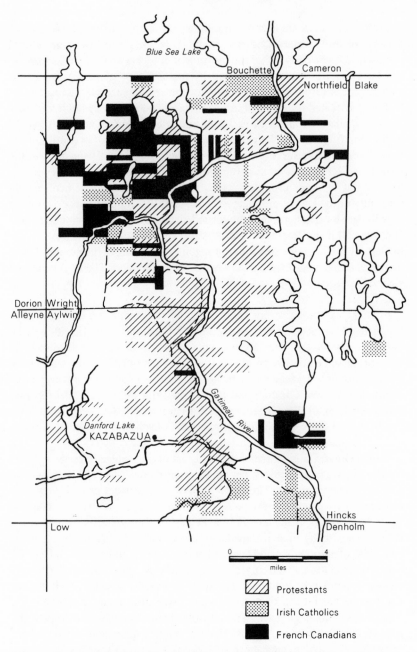

MAP 23 Settlement patterns: Gatineau River. Protestant Irish moving north into Quebec province from western Carleton County recreated near Kazabazua the clustered settlement pattern of the Carp Valley.

Source: Patents to end of 1871 in *List of Lands Granted in the Province of Quebec* (Quebec 1891).

settlement of the early 1860s was centred on this soil, with an additional clustering in the southwestern corner of the township on Grenville loam of similar description. The French-Canadian population was settled along the banks of the Castor River in the Embrun area, very few of them as yet venturing far back from the river.

The move to Russell was not a response to the government's reinstatement in 1852 of the credit system for purchasing crown land. For eleven years the demand for cash payment had made acquisition of crown lands difficult for many farmers,[84] and a perusal of the Crown Lands Department's Township Papers reveals a very great number of Tipperary farmers in western Carleton County making deposits in 1853 and 1854 to purchase crown lands near their homes or inferior but inexpensive land in Renfrew County. However, the move to Russell began in the late 1840s, before the new policy came into force. Even after 1852 the incoming settlers most often purchased from private individuals, mostly speculators or non-resident owners. Although most of these resided in neighbouring townships, a few were well-known speculators like Peter McGill.

In the 1850s settlers moved up the Gatineau River beyond Wakefield in greater numbers than before, with numerous sons of Carleton County farmers obtaining land especially on the western side of the river around Aylwin, Kazabazua, and Danford Lake, some forty miles north of Ottawa. In his *History of the Ottawa Valley,* the Rev. J.L. Gourlay, a Presbyterian clergyman, described his first missionary tour to this area in the autumn of 1856. At that time Low was "a forest with few patches cleared" and the present site of Kazabazua was still forested.[85] He described the farms along Danford Creek west of Kazabazua as they appeared in 1896: "The farms have passably good buildings, respectable, and the fields generally in a good state of cultivation. Crops often fine, hay in all the samples of hardy grasses is very abundant, oats, barley, rye, even spring wheat and Indian corn can be made profitable crops on the elevated table lands and fertile valleys."[86] He regarded the farms to the north around Aylwin village as good, but noted that there was only one "level from end to end and not broken by rocks and mountains." Beyond the Pickanock River, which flows into the Gatineau from the west beyond Aylwin, in the Blue Sea Lake region, the country was only "thinly occupied" with the residents being "sometimes ... in sight of each other, in other parts not so near and the vision obscured by hills around which the road takes many a wind and turn."[87] The land here was rough, and some of the families who had moved into this area in the 1850s and 1860s moved on to the Bruce Peninsula, the last frontier of southern Ontario, twenty years later.[88] These Gatineau townships, indeed, received almost their full complement of settlers by 1870, for the 1881 census reveals few new families.

In looking at long-distance migration which took Tipperary people out of the Ottawa Valley before Confederation, we find a rather different phenomenon from the pattern that characterized movement within the valley. The

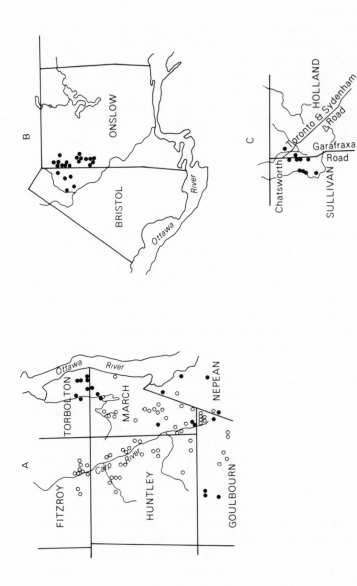

MAP 24 Kin network migration, I. The black dots represent the settlers who, after a generation on marginal lands in Torbolton, moved in the late 1840s and early 1850s with relatives from the major Carp Valley concentration to several secondary locations: North Onslow, some twenty miles away on the Lower Canadian side of the Ottawa, others to the Garafraxa Road near Owen Sound, and several families to Picton, New Zealand (not shown). There should be more black dots in Torbolton, where the lot numbers of several squatters are not known. The white dots represent Tipperary settlers who did not participate in these movements.

Sources: (A) Abstract Indexes; AO, RG I, C-IV, Township Papers; (B) 1871 census; (C) 1861 census.

longer movements did not draw from a neighbourhood area within which kin links operated as a stimulus to chain migration so much as from extended kinship networks themselves. In the case of the Ottawa Valley Tipperary settlers, the migrations were specific to the Tipperary families and to certain families from other parts of Ireland with whom the Tipperary people had married during their residence in the Ottawa Valley. Even where the majority of individual families migrating to a particular destination had clustered in Ottawa Valley locations, they were joined in the move by relatives who did not live near at hand. There were several movements of this type.

One of the smaller migrations involved the Powell and Cox families of Goulbourn and the Wall family of Beckwith, eight miles to the west. The Powells were from Newport on the western border of North Tipperary, and their Cox cousins had lived not far from there. The Walls, however, had lived thirty miles to the east in Roscrea. The Powells and Walls appear to have shared relatives in the Sheppard family, who came out from Ireland to join their kin in 1840–2 after the earlier group had moved west. By moving west, relatives who had lived some distance apart in Ireland, and beyond daily contact with one another in their first Canadian homes, came together in a newly settled area where they were able to secure neighbouring farms. In this case the new residence was in Euphemia Township, Lambton County, and the families were settled there by 1838.[89]

Strikingly parallel migratory patterns characterized two groups that arrived, one or two families at a time, and settled in two areas of marginal land in the Ottawa Valley beginning in the 1820s, at a distance from the major concentration of Tipperary population in the more fertile Carp Valley. The movements of both these kin networks are represented on the accompanying sets of maps. One group consisted of Shouldice, Taylor, Fuller, Young, Rutledge, and Armitage families who settled on the March-Torbolton line; their Mooney, Clarke, and Taylor relatives settled in Goulbourn at the southern end of the Carp Valley concentration. Most of these families were from Youghalarra parish on the River Shannon, from Ogonnelloe across the river in Clare, and from Mountshannon in Galway. The Shouldices were from the Otway estate over twenty miles away near Borrisoleigh. The connection was provided by the Clarkes and Mooneys, whose Irish migrations had linked the two areas.[90] The other network of families lived in Lanark County on the Ramsay-Pakenham line, and consisted of families with some tie to the parish of Modreeny, County Tipperary, with the addition of a few families from Borrisokane. Fourteen surnames were borne by members of this group, but six of the original heads of family were married to Daggs.[91] A few of these families lived first in the Carp Valley and, as in the case of the Torbolton group, some continued to reside there until they rejoined their relatives in renewed migration.

Through chain migration both groups built up communities in areas that

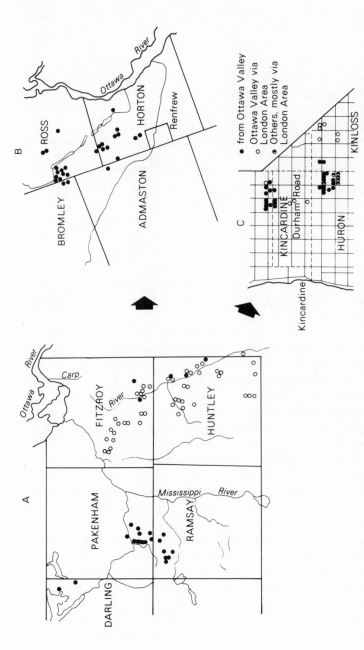

MAP 25 Kin network migration, 2. This second group settled on marginal lands in the Ottawa Valley, this time on the Ramsay-Pakenham line, moved in the late 1840s and early 1850s, again with some relatives from the Carp Valley (where some of the Pakenham settlers had also briefly resided), to the Cobden area of Renfrew County and the Kincardine area of Bruce County. The Kincardine settlers were joined by families from around London, some of whom had once lived in the Ottawa Valley. Most of the families involved in these migrations were from Modreeny parish, County Tipperary.

Sources: (A) 1842 and 1852 censuses; Abstract Indexes to Deeds; AO, RG 1, C-IV, Townships Papers; Land Records Index; (B) 1871 census; (C) 1861 census.

Legend (map C):
- from Ottawa Valley
- Ottawa Valley via London Area
- Others, mostly via London Area

were marginal in terms both of soil quality and of proximity to the major Tipperary community in the valley. As sons came of age they took up land nearby because, despite its poor quality, it was near their parents' farms.[92] Both groups intermarried heavily within their individual networks, but they also expanded the social boundaries of their kin groups by associating with extended families of non-Tipperary origin which thereafter married repeatedly into the Tipperary families and shared their later migratory habits. In the case of the Ramsay network the family was the Peevers of County Kerry, who moved with them to Renfrew County from Huntley. The Torbolton group linked up with the Majors from County Cork, many of whom later moved to the Quebec side of the Ottawa with them, and with a number of County Down Presbyterians resident in the Lowry neighbourhood on the Huntley-Fitzroy line.

After a generation in the Ottawa Valley the two networks began to move away as they had come, a few families at a time. The Torbolton-centred network began to move just before 1840 and the Ramsay one not quite ten years later. Though their destinations were different, the pattern was the same. Each group divided and moved to more than one destination. The Torbolton network moved partly to Grey County in the early 1840s, taking up free grants along the Garafraxa Road near Chatsworth with some members of the North Down group with whom they had intermarried while in the valley, and partly across the Ottawa and into the interior, settling in a tight cluster at North Onslow. The Fuller family, with some Taylor cousins, left Torbolton in the early 1850s for New Zealand.[93] The Ramsay group split between the Bervie area, east of Kincardine in Bruce County, which was being opened in the early 1850s, and the Cobden area, north of Renfrew. In both places they formed new clusters, with fathers and adult sons taking up adjoining lots. Close kin ties usually won out over more distant ones in determining which family went to each location, though some families like the Blackwells split between Ottawa Valley and external settlement areas. Kinship was bilateral, as some families moved with the mother's relatives, others with the father's, some with the husband's and some with the wife's. In the case of both networks the original colonies all but disappeared, leaving only the James Armitage family in Torbolton and the Richard Stanley and Edward Owens families in Pakenham, along with several married sisters of the latter.

The cohesiveness of these family networks was reinforced by intermarriage which continued after the groups left their initial settlement locations. Of twenty-eight marriages involving Tipperary Protestants in the Bruce County marriage register[94] between 1859 and 1867, sixteen were endogamous. Put another way, thirty-two people married within the network, seven married other Irish Protestants, one married a girl from England and another one from the United States. The origins of three partners are at present unknown. None married into the initially predominant Scots Presbyterian group. The proportion marrying endogamously was higher in the early years: eighteen of twenty people in 1859–61, ten of fourteen in 1862–4, but only four of ten in 1865–7. In Cobden and North Onslow, endogamy was extensive but was supplemented by marriage with closely neighbouring families from other parts of Ireland. The result of marrying neighbours in the new communities, of course, was a close association of kinship with place, as the tight clustering of the North Onslow group, depicted in Map 24, shows.[95]

The largest of the chain migrations west involved the movement of Tipperary families from the Carp Valley core to the other major nucleus of Tipperary settlement north of London. Some of the fifty families who left the Ottawa Valley for "New London" in the 1830s and early 1840s settled in Biddulph, and a few obtained land in Blanshard, to the northeast, which filled up rapidly in the mid-1840s, but most settled in McGillivray, to the west of Biddulph, which was not occupied so quickly. In Biddulph the Tipperary settlers were dominant and filled up much of the township in solid Protestant and Catholics blocks, as already demonstrated. In McGillivray the Ottawa Valley migrants clustered by family on adjoining farms on whatever concessions were being opened when they happened to arrive. Almost all of McGillivray's Tipperary population in 1852 had, in fact, formerly lived in the Ottawa Valley, though in later decades they were outnumbered as settlers of Tipperary origin diffused into the township from London and Biddulph.

Tipperary settlement in the Ottawa region thus spread up the corridor of good land in the Carp Valley from the initial clustering near the site of Hazeldean in the northeastern corner of Goulbourn Township, and then took the form of secondary settlements in pockets of the Ottawa Valley that were settled later. The largest of these secondary settlements were formed by neighbourhood migration, so that new clusters of Huntley and Fitzroy families formed in Clarendon, Russell, and the Gatineau, while smaller, familial-based clusters were formed at Cobden and North Onslow. The settlement pattern within the Carp Valley diffused somewhat, as the 1879 county atlas illustrates, but settlement there from the beginning was composed of Irish Protestants from several parts of the homeland and there was no distinct Tipperary block, but rather a block of residents of Irish Protestant origin in general.

EXPANSION OUTWARD FROM THE LONDON-BIDDULPH CORES

Movement within the London area was different from that within the Ottawa Valley. I have already outlined how initial settlement spread from London Township north into Biddulph and McGillivray once those townships were opened to occupation by the Canada Company in the 1830s. The movement of residents of Tipperary origin within the Middlesex-Huron-Perth County area continued to follow a general northward direction, following the chronology of settlement, but there was also a gradual diffusion of population outwards from the London-Biddulph cores, as a comparison of Maps 17 and 21 illustrates. Characteristic was the movement from the core area directly north into Stephen, where there were only three families of male Tipperary descent resident in 1852, but twelve in 1861, twenty-two in 1871, and thirty-nine ten years later. Some of this net rise is accounted for by natural increase, but forty-two families of Tipperary descent actually moved into the township between the 1840s and 1881. Ten of these were late arrivals directly from Ireland, mostly members of the Flynn and Clarke families from near Mountshannon in Galway, but twenty-nine families moved north from Biddulph and McGillivray, in about equal numbers.

The most likely reason for the differences in the internal migration patterns in the Ottawa Valley and the London region is the nature of the soil and the topography of the two areas. The Ottawa Valley is a rugged region with patches of good soil in the river valleys, wide areas of uncultivable rocky hills, and large expanses of thin, stony soils. Many of these latter areas were settled at one time but later abandoned, but nevertheless it was these topographical constraints which prevented the frontier from spreading in an even progression northward from the initial settlement locations around Richmond and Perth. Later generations passed over intervening lands that had been taken up or which were uncultivable to form secondary settlements northwest, north, and east of Ottawa. Around London, indeed in western Ontario generally, the soil is almost all of high quality and the topography flat or gently rolling. The general movement of settlement in the region which concerns us was northward from London, along the London-Goderich Road and then east and west from that major northward transportation route. While the initial occupation of the lands in Huron County was largely complete by the 1870s, movement outward from London continued as farmers and their sons bought farms as close to home as they could find them and as tradesmen located in the new villages and towns of the region. The settlement pattern in 1881 was therefore more diffused than it had been initially but was still clearly centred upon the original cores.

Because land quality posed no constraints and settlement progressed essentially in one northward direction (though West Nissouri was also settled largely by eastward movement from London), no secondary settlements formed in the three counties. The only major Canadian secondary settlement formed by Tipperary Protestants from the London area was that in the Bervie neighbourhood of Bruce County, east of Kincardine, some eighty miles north of London. As already indicated, this settlement also drew upon the Ottawa Valley colonies.

THE SECONDARY SETTLEMENT
NEAR KINCARDINE

Settlement in the Kincardine area was initiated by the decision of the government in 1848 to run a colonization road from the site of Durham in Simcoe County to the mouth of the Penetangore River on Lake Huron, where the town of Kincardine now stands. Fifty-acre lots were offered as free grants in two concessions on either side of the Durham Road.[96] The remainder of the townships in the vicinity beyond these four ranges were surveyed in 1850–2.[97] These additional lands, upon which most of the Tipperary settlers in Bruce County located, were offered for sale in 1851 and in the "Big Sale" of 1854.[98]

A major secondary settlement of Tipperary Protestants developed here and while the absence of surviving correspondence prevents us from tracing the communications that drew people together, it is striking that the Kincardine colony drew both from the London and Ottawa areas. The first settlers of Tipperary origin, who came to Kincardine Township in 1850–1, were John Portis and James Armitage from Biddulph, John Hayes from London Township, Richard Remmington from Huntley, and Edward Stanley and his sons Henry and James from Pakenham, who boarded in the township over the winter of 1851–2; the rest of the family joined them in the spring. It is likely that a number of other families had already decided upon locations as census enumerators noted that the majority of lots in the rear of Huron Township had been "taken up by parties who intend coming on in the spring as soon as the navigation opens."[99] In some cases the movement to Bruce County reunited families that had parted years before. William Dagg who came from Pakenham was an uncle of the Daggs who moved up from Biddulph; both had emigrated from Ballysteena, Modreeny, in the 1830s.[100] The Morgans and Walls who moved north from Middlesex had been there only a few years and were originally from the Ottawa Valley. William Morgan was the only *Brunswick* passenger to reach Bruce County. The greatest number of families arrived during the 1850s (thirty-five), but half of those coming from Middlesex and Huron arrived in the 1860s and 1870s. By the 1880s, however, some families were again on the move, this time to the Prairie West, seeking land for a new generation.

Map 25 illustrates the curious settlement pattern that resulted from the chronology of occupation. The free grant lands had been taken up by the Scots and other early arrivals within a few years of the opening of the area to settlement, and so all but the earliest of the Tipperary families located beyond the Durham Road concessions on the crown and school lands that the government offered for sale. The odd result was the establishment of two clusters in the Bervie neighbourhood separated by several miles of earlier-

TABLE 14
Origins of North Tipperary Migrant Families to Bruce County, 1849–81

	To 1852	To 1861	To 1871	To 1881	Total
London area	3	13	7	10	33
Ottawa area	3	18			21
Ireland		4	2	1	7
Total	6	35	9	11	61

Sources: Compiled family files, census, and land records.

settled territory. In several cases, such as the Collinses, Stanleys, and Morgans, fathers and adult sons took up adjoining farms.

RURAL-URBAN MIGRATION

Rural-urban movement is a particular form of internal migration. Though it generally constituted a form of medium- or short-distance movement, its nature was somewhat different from the rural pattern and so it deserves to be treated separately. Several types of migrants from the countryside may be distinguished. First there were those who practised non-agricultural occupations and for whom movement from village to city or the reverse was simply a move from one level of central place to another. Second were apprentices from the countryside, who did not always remain in the city after learning their trades. Third were widows and retired people who moved into the city after a life on the farm. There are a few examples of retirement to the city but this seems to have been largely a twentieth-century phenomenon. However, it became fairly common for farmers to retire to the larger villages and smaller towns, such as Lucan and St Marys, by the 1870s. Finally, there were those who could be called the "true" rural-urban migrants, for it is these people that historians usually have in mind when they discuss the topic: those who came into the city from working farms, either farmers who lost or gave up their lands, or farmers' sons who came into the city seeking first careers or first jobs. The major cities that could be expected to have drawn Tipperary Protestants from the countryside were those that grew up near the major areas of settlement: Ottawa and London. We must also look at the smaller town of Lucan, which arose in the middle of the Biddulph Tipperary colony as a result of the coming of the railway in the late 1850s, for Lucan by 1881 attracted more rural inmigrants than did the vastly larger city.[101]

Considering its size and its proximity to the centre of Tipperary population in the Ottawa Valley, the city of Ottawa exercised a very weak pull on the farming families of the group under investigation. In the early decades of Bytown's existence the town was a commercial centre for the lumber business

TABLE 15
Families of Male North Tipperary Descent
Resident in Bruce County, 1852–81

	1852	1861	1871	1881
Kincardine	6	19	24	41
Town			3	10
Kinloss		12	19	31
Huron		15	20	30
Greenock		6	9	7
Brant		1	5	*
Elderslie		1	2	*
Lucknow vge				1
Total	6	54	82	120

Sources: Compiled family files, census, and land records.
* census not seen.

and for the forwarding trade and passenger traffic on the Ottawa River and Rideau Canal. Even after the large sawmills opened in the 1850s only a few farmers' sons abandoned the seasonal round of agriculture in summer and timbering in winter for full-time occupations in the lumber mills. We can see a somewhat greater tendency for young men to move to the city after Confederation, but this movement was still very small and it was not industrially oriented. This circumstance underlines the heavily rural nature of families of Tipperary Protestant descent in the valley.

A dozen Tipperary families had lived in Ottawa from their first arrival in the region, so far as I can determine. All but one were there by 1852. Only one was a labourer in Corktown; most of the rest had followed non-agricultural occupations before coming to Bytown, and of course continued to do so once they arrived.

Up to 1881 only thirty migrant families of the group in question moved in from the rural parts of the valley. Nine of these had lived in nearby villages immediately prior to moving to the city, and seventeen were drawn from the townships of Carleton County, though not all from farming occupations. Four came from further away, but three of these had once lived not far from the city. A half dozen came into the city every decade beginning in the late 1830s, but the nature of the movement changed by the 1860s, and the small numbers increased in the 1870s when eleven moved from the countryside to the city, including the new suburbs in Nepean Township to the city's west.

Some of the early movement in the 1830s and 1840s was accounted for by a shuffling of village populations as officials and merchants responded to the growing importance of Bytown. Another migrant in this period was a widow from South March, and four were young men entering the town as apprentices, three of them members of one family. We cannot know, of course, how many young men from the countryside were apprenticed in Bytown and then left again between censuses. Frank Jones of March Township served his apprenticeship as a cabinet maker there with Kennedy and Blyth, for example, but he is not included in the figures because he left the valley in 1849 and plied his trade at Clandeboye, north of London. The important point is that few farmers' sons moved into the town permanently in this period.

Most of the immigrants of the 1850s were people already established in non-agricultural occupations in the surrounding townships and villages. For them the move was one of several from one level of central place to another. By the 1860s, however, most of the immigrants were young men from the farms moving in to take up new, often first, careers. However, none became general labourers, and only a couple worked in industry. Their trades in 1881 were agricultural implement dealer, flour merchant, foreman, two hotel keepers, barrister, agent, millman, and servant. Some were obviously upwardly mobile, like the barrister John Hodgins, son of a Huntley farmer who had sent him to Toronto for an education.

Family ties seem to have exercised little influence in attracting most of these people into the city, though I must except the merchants from this generalization.[102] For most, of course, this move did not take them far from their places of origin, and the movement was the rural-urban equivalent of a move to a neighbouring township, though it did immerse them in a new way of life. The psychological impact was probably not as great as it would have been had the rural-urban migrants secured industrial employment. Of greater importance was the weakness of the urban attraction for the Tipperary population in this period.

The pattern of migration into the City of London was in some ways quite different from that into Ottawa. Nearly three times as many families moved into London in the period of this study (to 1881) as moved into the eastern city, 114 as opposed to forty-two, but this difference in volume is not as significant as it at first appears. Though Ottawa was the larger of the two centres by 1871,[103] the population of Tipperary Protestant origin by that year was some two and a half times larger in the immediate hinterland of London and much more concentrated geographically, so the greater migration into the latter city largely reflected the fact that it had a greater rural base from which to draw.

To a small extent the greater numbers moving into London also reflected the fact that immigration directly from Tipperary continued into London much longer than it did into Ottawa. All but one of the dozen families who came into Ottawa directly from Ireland arrived by 1852, when the city was still the town of Bytown, whereas only two of the nine Tipperary families who lived in London in 1842 had come into the town immediately after

TABLE 16

Numbers of Male-Descended Heads of Families of Tipperary Protestant Origin in Ottawa and London Areas, Rural and Urban, 1821–81

	Carleton County			London Area*			London Area as % of Carleton Co.
	Rural	City	% Urban	Rural	City	% Urban	
1821	49	0		42	0		86
1831	69	2	2.8	74	0		104
1842	114	5	4.2	188	8	2.1	161
1852	132	14	9.6	283	8	2.7	199
1861	165	14	7.8	382	33	7.9	232
1871	183	24	11.6	488	56	10.3	263
1881	203	23	10.2	489	90	15.5	256

Sources: 1842–81: PAC, RG 31, census returns. 1842 Biddulph and McGillivray: UWO, Huron District census and assessment rolls; 1821–31 and London Twp and City, 1852–61: surviving and legible census plus calculations from compiled family files.
* London Township, West Nissouri, Biddulph, McGillivray, and Lucan.

immigrating.[104] However, in the 1840s six of the seven families arriving in the city were directly from overseas, and the heaviest such movement came in the 1850s when fifteen of twenty-eight arriving families were new immigrants. A half dozen arrived from Ireland even in the 1860s, and a similar number in the 1870s. By mid-century increasing numbers of immigrants were bypassing the Ottawa Valley, where land of reasonable quality and price had long ago been snapped up, and proceeding directly to western Ontario, as has already been indicated. Even upon reaching the latter region, late arrivals found that rural opportunities were limited and a few located in the city. That the types of occupations followed in the city by Irish immigrants declined notably in status and prosperity as time passed probably relates to this factor. Of the six who reached London in the 1840s, three were merchants and one a merchant's clerk, one a doctor, and the sixth a painter. The arrivals of the 1850s were mostly tradesmen, though three were poor shoemakers, two were widows, and one a labourer. Those who arrived after 1860, however, were widows, gardeners, clerks, labourers, and railway workers. Nonetheless, those who settled initially in the city tended to stay there. Of the twenty-three who arrived in the city before 1860 all but three remained, with two of the three exceptions locating on farms in London Township and West Nissouri. Even most of the Irish families who arrived in the 1860s were still in the city in 1881.

Those who came into the city of London from the countryside came predominantly from neighbouring London Township and to a much lesser extent from West Nissouri to its east. Most were farmers' sons who came in to take up a trade or keep store though, as in Ottawa, one or two in each decade were widows or professional men. However, three became hotel keepers in the 1860s and another three in the 1870s, taking advantage of the city's expansion. One of the latter was already in the city in 1871 as an apprentice carriage maker, but apparently he found the prospects of hotel keeping more promising. Two families came in from Biddulph in the 1860s and six in the 1870s, but these were not headed by farmers' sons seeking their fortunes in the city. Almost all had been tradesmen or shopkeepers in Biddulph or its growing village of Lucan ten years earlier. The rural inmigrants of the 1870s were in general still farmers' sons or rural tradesmen, but a half dozen had once been farmers nearby. Whether they moved to the city after losing their farms, or whether they sold them at a profit to developers as London spread outward, is uncertain. The fact that most entered respectable trades or businesses in the city suggests that the latter may have been the case.

Of considerable importance, however, is the fact that the percentage of Tipperary residents in the London area not living on farms was increasing more rapidly than was the equivalent figure for the Ottawa area. In 1861 almost identical proportions of those in the most concentrated areas of Tipperary settlement lived in the two cities: just under 8 per cent. In 1881 just over 10 per cent lived in Ottawa while 15.5 per cent in the London area lived in that city.[105]

As already stated, most of London's inmigrants were from London Township and West Nissouri. That few people came into London and its suburbs from Biddulph before 1881 was largely due to the rapid growth of the town of Lucan in the heart of the Tipperary Protestant settlement in the 1860s and 1870s. If one includes residents of Lucan as well as of London in the "urban" category in 1881, then the proportion of Tipperary Protestant families in that area living off the farm rises to nearly one-quarter of the whole.[106]

Lucan was a town that grew with the coming of the Grand Trunk Railway. It largely supplanted the earlier village of Ireland (now Clandeboye), which in 1852 was a small cross-roads village located where the Proof Line Road from London turned north towards Goderich at the town line of McGillivray. The village of Ireland and surrounding farmland were purchased in 1850 from William McConnell, the original settler, by James C. Macklin, who began selling lots the following year and registered an ambitious subdivision plan in 1852.[107] However, in 1853, in expectation of the railway passing through Biddulph, Sheriff John McDonald and the Hon. Donald McDonald of Toronto purchased Lot 6 on the Proof Line two and a half miles east of Ireland and laid out the village of Marystown, named for Sheriff McDonald's wife, the following year. At the auction of lots in 1855, twenty-eight of the thirty-nine purchasers were local Tipperary Protestants.[108] However, uncer-

TABLE 17
Movement of Tipperary Protestant Families into Lucan

Origin	1855–61	1861–71	1871–81
Already on the site	2		
From Ireland		5	
From Ottawa Valley	1	2	
From nearby villages		4	2
From parental home	4	23	12
Former farmers	1	11	4
Widows		3	6
Women marrying villagers		2	6
Other		1	1
Total	8	51	31

Source: ms census returns.

tainty as to the route the rail line would follow deterred anyone from actually building on the site until the late 1850s. Bernard Stanley, the young son of a farmer who lived just over the line in London Township, built the first substantial house in 1859; in time he became one of the village's wealthiest entrepreneurs. The 1862 county map shows twenty-two buildings in Marystown, by then renamed Lucan, all on Main Street except for the Grand Trunk Railroad Station, which was northeast of the village.[109] The McDonalds registered their plan in 1863. With the rail line established, Lucan grew rapidly and was the residence of 155 families in 1871 (population 695), the year it was incorporated as a town, and 189 families ten years later (population 1015). The slowing of the growth rate was due both to the economic depression of the 1870s and to a number of notorious incidents of incendiarism.[110] In 1861 there were already eight families of Tipperary Protestant descent[111] in the infant settlement, but fifty-one families of North Tipperary background moved in during the 1860s and another thirty-one in the next ten years. In both decades just under half were sons who came of age and left farms in Biddulph and London to earn a livelihood in the new town. The next largest category were farmers themselves, some of whom turned their homestead over to a son and retired to the town. The rest were men attracted into the new centre by the economic opportunities there, of whom the Hawkshaws who came in to run a stage line are an example. It is clear from the figures cited that Lucan also attracted considerable numbers of non-Tipperary inmigrants from beyond the township.

The rise of Lucan was a fortunate occurrence for Biddulph residents. The town became the centre of the township's grain and cattle trade and was a

TABLE 18
Male-Descended Families of Tipperary
Protestant Origin in Towns of London Area, 1881

Lucan	47	Strathroy (1871)	4
St Marys	19	Southampton	2
Exeter	7	Seaforth (1871)	2
Ailsa Craig	6	Clinton	1
Park Hill	6		

Source: 1881 census.

tremendous boost to local economic development.[112] Moreover, it provided the opportunity for dozens of sons of local farmers to leave their parental farms to keep store or practise a trade without leaving the neighbourhood. I have already noted that lands in the western part of Biddulph were almost completely taken up by 1842. The growth of a town in the township twenty years later helped to keep close to home sons who might otherwise have been forced to leave the neighbourhood.

The growth of Lucan expanded the local range of economic opportunities, but for some it was a staging point for their departure from the area. Of the fifty-one Tipperary heads of families who came into the town in the 1860s, nineteen were still there in 1881, five had died, two had gone to live with children in Stephen Township, two had taken farms in Biddulph, and one had moved into London Township and three to the city or its suburbs. The remaining nineteen, a third of the total, left for more distant places. Of the twenty-four farmers' sons who came into Lucan in the 1860s, twelve were still there in 1881, two died by that year, and ten left. There seems to be nothing to distinguish those who left from those who remained. The destination of four of the ten is known. "Buckley" John Hodgins, who had worked in a store in London in the 1850s and in 1861 lived in Biddulph with his parents-in-law, returned to the city, where he was bookkeeper and traveller for Scandrett & Fitzgerald's grocery, a business run by a Tipperary man and his brother-in-law.[113] Arthur Rollins left Lucan in 1879 to help found a town in Manitoba, grocer George Atkinson became an insurance agent in London, and farmer Adam H. Hodgins became a pumpmaker in the Tipperary colony at Bervie near Kincardine.

The cities drew increasing numbers of rural people during the period of this study, but in the case of Ottawa the numbers remained relatively insignificant when contrasted with the 90 per cent of Carleton County residents of Tipperary Protestant descent who remained in the countryside, a proportion that would be much higher if the considerable numbers living in more distant townships of the valley were included. In the London area where there were greater numbers of Tipperary families, the percentage of area residents living in the city rose more rapidly in the 1870s, and would perhaps have been greater still had not the town of Lucan been born in Biddulph two decades earlier. In both cases some of those who moved into the cities were rural tradesmen, and very few took to industrial occupations, but growing numbers of inmigrants were farmers' sons who took to trades or mercantile pursuits as an alternative to becoming farmers. Partly this was due to the full settlement of surrounding rural townships, which made land purchases increasingly expensive, and partly it was due to the increasing opportunities provided by the proliferation of a town and village network stimulated by the railway boom. Both these phenomena were particularly noticeable in the London area, where the local rural movement of the Tipperary Protestant population took the form of a gradual fanning out from the central concentrations as farmers who were able bought developed farms for their sons as close at hand as they could.[114] In the Ottawa area, in contrast, the formation of secondary settlements in newly occupied pockets of the valley outside Carleton County continued into the 1860s, both reducing somewhat the pressures on the land in the older townships and providing a local alternative for young men to moving into Ottawa. This difference in also reflected in the fact that the numbers of Tipperary families increased much more rapidly in the London area than in Carleton County. The numbers in both were about equal in 1821 and 1831, but by 1851 there were twice as many Tipperary Protestant families near London as near Ottawa, and twenty years later there were two and a half times as many.[115] Partly this was because immigration from Ireland continued to flow into London longer than it did into Ottawa, but after 1842 most immigrants proceeded further north to get land after a few years working in London or Biddulph. Mostly it reflected intensification through natural increase of the already concentrated settlement pattern there.

Similarly, the Ottawa Valley did not see the development of new and prosperous railway towns in this period to anything like the extent that this occurred around London. In the 1860s and 1870s most of the small towns and villages in North Middlesex and South Huron became the residences of several shopkeepers or blacksmiths who had come from farms in Biddulph, McGillivray, or London.[116] The most notable example of advantage being taken of the opportunity provided by the growth of local rail centres is Lucan. The citizens of Lucan largely practised traditional rural occupations such as country storekeeping, blacksmithing, and carpenter work, but some learned new occupations, for example, telegraph operating, and the growth of the town provided the opportunity for some merchants, like Bernard Stanley, to become wealthy local entrepreneurs. However, life in Lucan was transitional for many. Some rural people began their business careers there but then moved on to another place. Some returned to farming, sometimes in the west, like Arthur Rollins. Others moved on to larger centres. It is idle to speculate whether Lucan's population might have been more stable if the disturbances and incidents of arson that marked the 1870s had not occurred. Studies of other communities suggest that the mobility levels of Lucan's population were not unusual, but the fact that the destinations of the majority of those leaving Lucan have not been determined is a change from previous experience, as Ontarians of Tipperary Protestant descent had heretofore tended to migrate to predictable locations. Whether it was town life or fear of violence that drove these families from Lucan remains undetermined.

That the tendency of the Tipperary Irish to move into towns and cities was greater in the London area than it was in the Ottawa Valley probably related more to local differences in terms of land availability, quality, price, and demand than it did to inclination. When they did go into the cities, residents of both areas practised traditional occupations in the trades and mercantile sectors and continued to shun industrial employment.

LONG-DISTANCE CONTACT AND THE COMING OF THE RAILWAY

The growth of the railway network was of greater importance in influencing migrational habits than was the growth of the cities in the years with which this study is concerned. The linking of major centres by rail lines in the 1850s facilitated visiting between distant communities, though the rigorous demands of the farm calendar limited the use farmers could make of the new transportation improvements. The impact of the railway upon migration patterns only became apparent in the late 1870s when cheap excursions to the Prairie West made individual exploration and inspection of possible settlement locations a reality for more than the adventurous few and reduced dependence upon distant kin for information about possible future homes. At the same time, however, the greater ease of visiting that the railway brought helped to cement ties between branches of families that had separated years before. In some cases marriages between first and second cousins living hundreds of miles apart resulted from these visits.

These considerations raise the question of the role of correspondence and visiting in maintaining family solidarity despite extensive internal migration both before and after the coming of the railway. In the early years many did not write when the prospect of ever seeing distant kin again seemed dim, and the high postage rates must also have discouraged frequent correspondence in the case of poor families. However, letters must nevertheless have been readily exchanged when members of a family began to seek land elsewhere.

Both visiting and correspondence seem to have received an impetus from the extension of the province's railway network. Fred Richardson's first letter to nephew Frank Jones near London in 1858 contained the news of events that had occurred since the Joneses had left March Township in 1849. Jones had sent Richardson a letter through the latter's "friend Old mr. Abbott" who had gone out to visit his son Thomas in Biddulph. We have only two of Richardson's letters, and he seems not to have written frequently, for he noted in 1860 that "I neglected Answering your letter. the reason was I did not See that I had any thing to Communicate to you more than what had passed by in personal Interview with you and now that I Do write Do not Know of Any Material Occurance Since you have been hear ... I will write to you as soon as Aney Material Changes takes plase."[117]

The railway opened up the possibility of visits for some, but the constraints of farm work prevented most men from taking advantage of the opportunity. Richardson wrote Jones in 1858 that "It is very Possible that your Aunt and myself Would take a ride on the Iron horse to see ye at Some future Day as both of us has a Desire to see ye All," but in 1860 he noted that "We are So Situated untill Some Change takes plase It would be Impossible for us to Quite home for that lienth of time But hopes to Vissit ye yet if we are Sparred."[118] Jones was a cabinetmaker and so was not bound by the limitations on casual movement imposed by agricultural life. He made several visits to the Ottawa Valley, on one occasion arriving inconveniently at harvest time, for which he later offered his apologies.

For the same reason, long-distance visiting was often done by the females of the family. Jones wrote to his cousin Richard Richardson in 1882 that "there are some visitors going down to see you and the other friends in March – For a long time Mrs John Lewis and my wife have talked over the matter of going down together to see the friends, and at last have concluded to do so – and then George Lewis wife has made up her mind that she would go too. Mrs Wm Acres has taken suddenly ill so her daughter Mrs John Lewis has started on monday last for her old home – and Mrs George Lewis and Mrs Jones, are to leave here on tuesday next." Jones expected them to stop first at Ashton at the home of John Shore, whose wife was an Acres. "Mr Shore I suppose will take them down to March. Mrs Lewis I suppose to her Uncles Mr George Acres, and my wife to your place ... If it is not asking too much of you I would like you would take Mrs Jones to Ottawa some day while she is at your place, and let her see the city from its more interesting points, Parliment buildings, Falls, Lovers walk, &c."[119]

If family circumstances were appropriate, visits were sometimes of a different nature, involving work with the host family for months at a time. Four daughters of Michael Long of Nepean, whose wife had died when the children were young, made such visits to their uncle William Oakley in London city, and married in that district. Despite urging by his brothers in Huron County, who said that the land was better in western Ontario and would better repay his labour, Mike never made the move himself. He had only one son to provide for.[120]

Not everyone wrote, of course, or visited. Not everyone was literate and thus able to correspond, others did not know what to say, and still others were not inclined to try. With a kinship network as wide as most of these people possessed, moreover, even those living relatively close to one another could be selective in their recurrent associations. John Shore Jr (b. 1858), who was raised at Ashton, twelve miles from his mother's Acres relatives at Hazeldean, recalled later that "my mother and myself generally made an annual trip down through March, Huntley and Torbolton to see my Grandfather and Grandmother, and mother's sisters and their families." Only once did he see his uncle William Acres, who lived twenty miles away in Torbolton, though he lived until Shore was twenty-nine. Yet it is remarkable how often relatives are mentioned in recounting his life story. He mentions his father buying a horse from Uncle James Mulligan, and himself detouring on the way home from St Catharines Collegiate Institute in 1880 to visit his nieces in McGillivray; his sister had married one of the second cousins there. A first cousin, George Bradley, lived with the Shores for a time as a young man and learned the carpenter's trade from Shore's father. Many of the contacts were by members of the family who taught school. It appears to have been common practice for local farmers to recruit teachers from among young relatives who had secured a certificate, and who boarded with their own relatives. Thus Shore's sister Frances boarded with uncle William Acres in 1871 while teaching in "their School." John Shore himself first "engaged as a Teacher in the School on Henry Slack's farm" and "boarded and lodged with my sister, Annie, who was then Mrs Slack." Around the turn of the century his daughter Gertrude taught in a school near Edward Leach's in North Gower; another of Shore's sisters was married to Leach.[121] Though casual visiting may have been limited by distance, personal preference, or the constraints of farm work, kin could often be enlisted to provide mutually beneficial exchanges of services when the need arose.

Though one could pick and choose the more distant kin with whom one associated, some families enjoyed the new mobility the railway provided and renewed ties with distant relatives. George Clarke had emigrated in 1819 with three brothers who secured locations in the new township of Tecumseth, north of Toronto.[122] George was "staid at Montreal by the confinement of his wife" over the following winter, and in the spring proceeded on to March Township where his wife's family was already living. He died in 1839, and the homestead went to his second-youngest son, John; the remaining sons scattered in the region or moved west with relatives. John had only one surviving son, who succeeded to the farm, but no fewer than four of John's children married relatives. Two married Bradley first cousins who lived

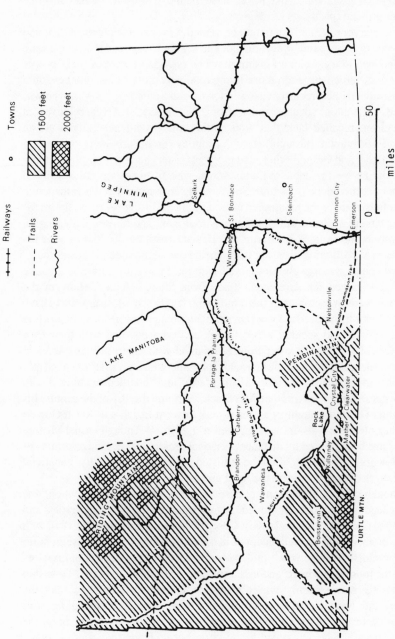

MAP 26 Southern Manitoba, 1881, showing routes and locations mentioned in the text. Manitoba provided a new frontier of farmland in the late 1870s for those who could not obtain it in Ontario. Many residents of Huron and Middlesex counties followed Exeter's Thomas Greenway to Crystal City.

Source: Adapted from Thomas R. Weir, ed., *Economic Atlas of Manitoba* (Winnipeg 1960).

close at hand, but in the 1880s two of the sisters married second cousins from York Township who were grandsons of George Clarke's brother John, from whom he had parted in Montreal in 1819. Another Bradley married a third of the York Clarkes. Although we have no surviving correspondence, the Clarkes obviously maintained and consolidated family ties despite great distances, for a long period.[123] A similar series of marriages were celebrated between the Lewis family of McGillivray and Acres cousins in the Ottawa Valley in the same period, and two children of Daniel Neil of Biddulph married Neil cousins from Fitzroy.[124] In this way at least the new technology reinforced an older way of life.

THE BEGINNINGS OF MIGRATION TO THE PRAIRIE WEST

The railways also helped to stimulate a new exodus to the west in the 1870s, though at the time the movement began the rail lines could carry the new pioneers only part of the way to their destinations. The migration of people from rural Ontario to the Prairie West was a massive movement that had poor economic conditions and the end of Ontario's frontier as a stimulus, and chain migration as a mechanism and incentive. The movement was not one specific to the families who have been the subject of this study, along with their new relatives of other cultural backgrounds. Rather, it was a massive exodus of rural Ontarians for whom a new frontier of available land was past due. Like the establishment of secondary settlements in the Ottawa Valley, the migration to Manitoba can be viewed as neighbourhood migration by residents of an older community, irrespective of background, with the major difference being one of scale. In this case the source neighbourhood was all of Ontario. However, there was some tendency for settlers from particular parts of Ontario to cluster and, as in the case of neighbourhood migration, chain migration based on kinship still played a role in bringing relatives in the wake of the first settlers. The westward movement was just beginning at the time this study ends, but by 1881 the pattern for the future was already being established.

The movement of families of Tipperary origin from western Ontario was part of a general exodus to south-central and southwestern Manitoba that was stimulated and facilitated by the actions and encouragement of a man who played an important role in the development of Manitoba.[125] The Hon. Thomas Greenway, the former member of parliament for South Huron and a member of the Devon and Cornwall settlement, visited southern Manitoba in 1878 and decided to settle in the vicinity of Crystal Creek in the Rock Lake district near the American border.[126] Early in 1879 he and seven other western Ontario men organized themselves as the Rock Lake Colonization Company, agreed to work together for their first year in the west, and set out for

Manitoba. They reached the railhead at Emerson via the United States around
1 April and proceeded overland along the Boundary Commission Trail to
Crystal Creek, where they founded a town with the ambitious name of Crystal
City.[127]

In 1879 Greenway began running emigrant excursions on the Great
Western Railway from various points in western Ontario to St Boniface in
cooperation with other Ontario entrepreneurs, including R.W. Prittie of
Toronto[128] and Robert Patterson, the GWR agent at Paris, Ontario. Cars from
centres like Paris and Kincardine were added to the trains at London, and
additional passengers boarded at Komoka, Glencoe, Chatham, and Windsor.[129] Greenway, associates, or members of his family accompanied each
trainload of passengers. The emigrants were drawn from all over western
Ontario but especially from the counties of Bruce, Huron, Wellington, and
Grey.[130] Greenway particularly directed the passengers to his newly
established town of Crystal City and the adjoining Rock Lake and Turtle
Mountain districts.[131] Though only surveyed in November 1879, Crystal City
possessed by the following March a store, boarding house, blacksmith shop,
two agricultural implement warehouses, and Methodist and Bible Christian
churches – the denominations favoured by the Devonshire settlers of Huron
County. There was already a daily mail, with one of Greenway's partners in
the Rock Lake Colonization Company as postmaster.[132] In September 1881
Greenway established the first newspaper in southern Manitoba, the *Rock
Lake Herald*, which he used to promote Crystal City as "the centre of the
finest farming districts in Manitoba or the north-west." "If you want to make
money," gushed the *Herald*, "locate in Crystal City."[133] Greenway also
organized exhibits of agricultural produce from Manitoba throughout western
Ontario to convince farmers of the advantages of locating in the region.[134]

Some families of Tipperary descent were among the trainloads of Ontario
farmers and mechanics that left London every few weeks in this period. While
the movement to the Turtle Mountain District was a general one from
southwestern Ontario that was stimulated by Greenway's advertizing and
promotion, the role of kinship, as in earlier migrations, appears to have been
paramount in influencing individual decisions to go. "Word passed from one
enthusiastic homesteader to his relatives and friends was … the most effective
advertising and kept a stream of settlers coming to the Turtle Mountain region
until by 1900 there was very little government land left."[135] Such was the
judgment of a western local historian, who noted examples of chain migration
to various parts of the district from Gananoque, Oxford County, and
Ormstown, Quebec, as well as Exeter and Lucan, and concluded that "these
migrations of families and friends are an outstanding feature of western
settlement."[136]

The importance of kinship networks in stimulating the westward migration is easily documented. Arthur Rollins, a Lucan livery-stable keeper who was one of Greenway's original seven partners, had previous ties with the Greenways; his brother, Dr James A. Rollins of Stephen, had married one.[137] Joseph, Robert, and Arthur Rollins went with Greenway's first party in 1879; Robert operated the first general store in Crystal City. Joseph's family arrived in the summer of 1880, and younger brother Frank arrived in 1881. Later in the decade nephews Ardagh (the census calls him James Ardell Rollins) and Edgar, sons of William Rollins of Stephen, joined their uncles.[138] Orange Howard, a grandson of *Brunswick* passenger Thomas T. Howard, arrived in the Turtle Mountain area from London Township in 1879 when he was twenty-one and was joined a year or two later by his older brother Albert. Orange homesteaded near Mather while Albert remained for some years at Crystal City. Sister Essie came west to keep house for Orange, and in 1883 brother Tom brought his family by railway through St Paul to Emerson, then by land to Orange at Crystal City. After a year with Orange, Tom homesteaded near Mather. Sister Abigail came out to teach school and married in the district; finally, in the early 1900s, Annie and Esther came to Mather where they worked as dressmakers; this was Essie's second move west.[139] Frederick Fairhall's family stayed with their old acquaintances the Blackwells after reaching Manitoba.[140] Thomas Fox, who left Lucan for Moncton in 1870 and later lived in Windsor, went to Winnipeg in 1878 and brought his family west the following year. In 1880 he was joined by his brother James and his nephews John and Albert Armitage. In 1882 William Ryan's family stayed with the Foxes when they arrived from Lucan.[141] Ryan's cousin Caleb Ryan obtained entry for a homestead near William the same year.[142] Other London area families in the Crystal City district that had Tipperary connections were those of William Hodgins, a Lucan constable who came to Killarney around 1885,[143] Joseph Rogers of Stephen, a settler of 1879 whose wife was a Hodgins,[144] and the Caughlins.

The causes of migration to Manitoba echoed the reasons for leaving Ireland sixty years earlier. Settlers interviewed as they were boarding the emigrant cars in 1880 emphasized that lack of work and declining wages in Ontario had induced them to try farming in the west.[145] The general financial depression of the 1870s paralleled the post-Napoleonic slump that had earlier caused their fathers and grandfathers to consider emigration to Canada. Unemployment explained the migration of tradesmen, but the movement of farmers and farmers' sons was explained by the fact that "the counties of Bruce, Huron, Wellington, and Grey, the last of the Queen's Bush available in Ontario, had reached the hiving stage when the young men must seek new land elsewhere."[146] A redundant population had also been a major underlying cause of the movement from Tipperary to Upper Canada. Other families who left Biddulph in the early 1880s did so to escape the chronic disturbances there that were brought to national attention by the Donnelly murders near Lucan in 1880. Samuel Blackwell had had a harrowing experience in 1875 when a tenant and his friends appeared at his door one night with blackened faces and threatened to hang him if he did not sign a receipt for the unpaid rent. [147] Local disturbances had also been a cause of the departure of "respectable Protestant families" from North Tipperary in the 1820s and 1830s. As in the earlier migration, too, the opening of a new frontier, the adoption by government of a free land policy, and the initiation of chain migration by an expedition organized by a local gentleman also characterized the exodus from southwestern Ontario to Manitoba.

The desire for land was, however, the paramount reason for the movement, just as chain migration was its major mechanism. Many of the migrants of Tipperary origin who left the Lucan area had owned no land in Ontario or very inadequate acreages. Joseph Rollins in 1871 rented 100 acres in Biddulph, and brother Frank was then still at home; brother Arthur rented his livery stable in Lucan village. The parents of the Howard family in 1871 owned only a two-and-a-half-acre lot off the Proof Line Road in London Township. Joseph Atkinson, who came to Arthur Rollins's in Crystal City in 1882, had lived with his brother Alex the year before, and his brother-in-law James Dempsey, with whom Atkinson went west, was recorded in 1881 as a farm labourer living with his parents-in-law in Biddulph. [148] Daniel Neil owned ten acres in McGillivray in 1871; I have not located the rest of the family, but sons Francis and Robert were in Manitoba ten years later. [149] John McIntyre and Ann (Caughlin), a daughter of Edward Caughlin who had come to Biddulph from Cooraclevin in Dunkerrin in 1834 or 1835, owned a small farm of twenty-five acres in Lobo before moving west. Ann's brother Thomas Caughlin, who brought his family west in the spring of 1880, had been a tenant farmer in East Williams. [150] Their brother-in-law George Mayo, who sent for his family in October 1881, had been a tenant farmer of seventy acres in Biddulph ten years earlier. In 1881 the Mayos were listed in the census of London Township; George was already in the west. He met his family at Emerson with a wagon and four oxen, but had only $2.50 cash and had to work threshing to obtain the money to release his freight. After a year with the McIntyres the Mayos moved into a dugout with a sod roof. [151] For a poor family like the Mayos the prospect of a free homestead in the west offered the only appealing escape from the high land prices in the London area.

Western historian Aileen Garland has pointed out that "few of the men who came out from Lucan were young." [152] The Armitage and Howard brothers were only in their twenties when they moved west, as were Caleb Ryan and

James Fox, but most of the rest were in their early forties. Samuel Blackwell was seventy-five and his brother George even older. Garland judged that William Ryan at thirty-eight was "older than the average homesteader."[153] As in Ontario earlier, families with insufficient property sometimes moved to a frontier of cheap land as the children became old enough to cause parents anxiety about their ability to provide for their establishment in life.

A well-documented Tipperary family that moved to Manitoba in this period was that of John Mooney of Sullivan Township near Owen Sound. The Mooneys settled in southwestern Manitoba, about forty-five miles northwest of Crystal City, but their move owed nothing to Thomas Greenway's promotional campaign. While most of the settlers in the Rock Lake and Turtle Mountain regions went by rail through the United States to Emerson and then west along the Boundary Commission Trail to Crystal City, the Mooneys went by steamer from Owen Sound to Duluth, and thence by rail to St Boniface. From there they journeyed by wagon along the Assiniboine River to Portage la Prairie and over the Yellow Quill Trail to the junction of the Assiniboine and the Souris, where they located in the vicinity of Wawanesa.[154] Mooney had been part of the group from Carleton County that had moved to Grey County in the 1840s. His son Will, in his late teens when he moved west, had read books and newspaper articles about Manitoba and listened receptively to the stories brought back by Michael Lowery, a member of a former Ottawa Valley family who had left Grey for the west in 1878 and came back to be married.[155] The land in Sullivan was stony – "the stones lay over our farm like flocks of sheep," daughter Nellie later wrote[156] – and Will went west in 1879 after hitting a stone with the plough once too often. He joined a survey party to explore the territory and entered homestead locations for himself, his father, and his brother George.[157] Though the Mooneys were not followed to the west by other relatives, they visited several old acquaintances en route and when Will met the family in Winnipeg he was accompanied by his cousin, John Clarke.[158]

A dozen Tipperary families also found their way to Manitoba from the Ottawa Valley by 1881, all from Carleton County. All but two settled in different municipalities, and few in the Rock Lake district, but chain migration at the family level is, as usual, easily documented from family histories. Joseph Baskerville of Gloucester Township moved to Dominion City, near Emerson, in 1878.[159] In the same year his nephew Thomas Baskerville, the second son of John Baskerville Jr of Gloucester, moved west to Nelsonville, north of Morden.[160] In 1882 the latter's older brother homesteaded near Boissevain. He died in Idaho a few years later and his claim was take up by the third brother, Robert, who had gone to Montana around 1879 and later to Idaho, where he remained until his business failed. The two youngest, David and George, remained in Ontario until 1905 when they, too, went to Boissevain. A number of the family's Birch cousins from Cumberland Township moved to Carberry, Manitoba, in 1885, and another, George Wilton Jr, worked for a time for Robert Baskerville in the United States.[161]

None of the dozen Ottawa Valley families who were in the west by 1881 were from the Quebec side of the Ottawa. Residents of the Clarendon area had spread north into North Clarendon and Thorne in the 1840s and 1850s and the frontier of useable land there was largely exhausted at that time. However, very few of the Tipperary families left the region before 1880. One or two families went to each of Carleton County, Ottawa City, Huron, Bruce, Wisconsin, and New York State, mostly in the 1860s. The 1881 census shows that a great many of the families formed in the late 1840s and early 1850s were still intact, with children nearly thirty years old still living at home. Clearly a flood of the younger generation would soon be released. Similarly, the Kazabazua area had been fully settled by 1871, but few left in the succeeding decade. A few interrelated families from the Wakefield area went to Bruce County in the 1870s, but most remained on the Gatineau for the time being.

Later in the 1880s, movement from Pontiac County became heavy. Local newspapers like the *Shawville Equity* noted departures and visits home, printed general articles on westward migration, advertisements for the railway companies, letters from former residents in the west, and scathing attacks on supposedly misleading advertising about the advantages of settling in Nebraska and the Dakotas. Local residents joined the CPR's farmers' excursions or colonists' specials that left Arnprior on the western side of the Ottawa, and every week the *Equity* reported families or young farmers moving west or making an exploratory trip.[162]

As in the case of emigrants from Carleton County, those who left the Pontiac went to many different destinations. A major reason for this was that the cheap railway excursions made it possible for the first time for intending settlers to scout out possible locations themselves rather than to depend upon letters from relatives who had gone before them. It was common in the 1880s and 1890s for a young man to make several such trips before finding land he liked; he then came home to make preparations for a permanent move west. Silas Richardson, second son of Richard Richardson Jr and great-grandson of William, the *Brunswick* passenger, lived in the United States for a time in the late 1880s but returned to his native Clarendon, "where he will permanently reside," in April 1889.[163] But by the end of June he was gone again, on a rail excursion from Ottawa to Calgary. He wrote a letter to the editors of his hometown paper, including a description of the extensive farm near Calgary of Oliver Ingram, husband of his father's first cousin, who had left Litchfield Township some years before,[164] and continued his journey, eventually reaching the Washington Territory. After extensive travels in the western states and British Columbia he purchased a farm about fifty miles from Edmonton and returned to Clarendon in January 1894.[165] In February he married Emma Eades of Radford,[166] and a few weeks later he loaded his horses, cattle, and farm implements on the train at Sand Point for the long journey to his farm at Pakan, NWT.[167] The new ease of travel and communications by no means eliminated chain migration; indeed it facilitated contact with relatives who lived at a distance. But by reducing travel time and expense the railway excursions eliminated the irreversibility of a decision to move to a location and the necessity of relying upon the advice of third parties in choosing it. Long-distance migration became more like career migration in that family ties became only one consideration among many in choosing a place to live.

MIGRATION TO THE
UNITED STATES

The destination of westward migration was not confined in the 1870s and 1880s to the new province of Manitoba. One enterprising farmer from McGillivray, Gilbert Carter, moved his family to Prince Albert, NWT, around 1880 and became a grain merchant,[168] but large numbers of people from western Ontario also moved into the American west. Settlement in the northern border areas of the Dakota Territory may be considered part of the same migration as that to Manitoba, for the international boundary posed little restriction to free movement back and forth. Residents along the border with North Dakota have always shopped and picked berries south of the line. By 1883 the first settlers had entered the Sarles and Hannah districts of North Dakota, which are immediately south of the Rock Lake district. A number of families in the Crystal City and Pilot Mound areas moved across the border to take up free homesteads there, including a number of sons of the early Manitoba settlers who had been under age when their families came west, such as Mervyn Rollins, who was about thirteen when the family joined his father Joseph in 1880.[169] Other families who had settled on the American side of the line later moved across to Manitoba. Joseph Wall's family, originally from the Tipperary colony near Kincardine, settled in Pembina County, south of the old railhead at Emerson, in 1881 but in the 1890s moved to Clearwater, Manitoba. Mrs Wall's nephew, Francis James Collins, had preceded them to Manitoba and in the mid-1880s had carried the mail from Emerson to Crystal City. Wall was followed to Manitoba in the early years of the twentieth century by his brothers Silas and George.[170]

The destinations of Tipperary Protestants residing in eastern Upper Canada before 1870 were predominantly the Tipperary colonies in the western part of the province, but a few instances of movement to each of the successive American frontiers have turned up. However, movement from the London area to the United States was probably more significant. In the early 1840s the families of John Gray and John McGuffin (whose wife was a daughter of Samuel Howard of London Township) moved to Ogle County, Illinois, as did that of Thomas Guest Jr of Oxford-on-Rideau in eastern Upper Canada.[171] Movement from western Ontario to Michigan, particularly the eastern counties of Huron, Sanilac, St Clair, and Lapeer, is known to have been particularly heavy from the 1830s onwards.[172] The same emigrant trains that took the residents of western Ontario to Manitoba carried others bound for Dakota and Nebraska. One passenger estimated in 1880 that ten times as many people were leaving Elgin County for the midwestern states as for Manitoba.[173] Some examples of chain migration at the family level are in evidence, and a secondary settlement of Tipperary Catholics from Jockvale in Carleton County has recently been documented in the vicinity of Petersville, Clinton County, Iowa, from as early as the 1850s.[174] Whether any significant secondary settlements of Tipperary Protestants were established in the United States by migrants from the Canadas remains to be seen.

CONCLUSION

The Tipperary Protestants in 1881 remained a rural people in Ontario as they had been in Ireland. A quarter of those in the London area by that date lived in the city itself or in Lucan, but a quarter of the Protestant population of North Tipperary had lived in towns and villages fifty years earlier.[175] In the Ottawa Valley, where there was less pressure on the land, only 10 per cent of the families of Tipperary Protestant descent were urban dwellers. The evidence suggests that emigrants from North Tipperary were overly representative of the class of middling farmers, which partially explains the rural bias in Canada. The aim of all but gentlemen and merchants upon arriving in Canada seems to have been to locate on a farm as quickly as possible. The only early urban cluster discovered, that in Montreal, broke up by the 1830s after a decade of existence as its members moved to rural communities. Later Tipperary inhabitants of the city were on the whole merchants drawn to it for financial and commercial reasons, but even these residents practised family chain migration as did families in the rural areas.

The rural dwellers were mobile, like many of the residents of nineteenth-century Canada. However, their movements from one community to another did not make them rootless wanderers.[176] Most made a move of more than a few miles only once or twice in a lifetime. One of the most mobile, *Brunswick* passenger William Morgan, earned the nickname "the Rattler," but even he moved only five times in his sixty-eight years, only three times any great distance: from Borrisokane to the Ottawa Valley in 1818, from Huntley to McGillivray in 1839, and to Kincardine in 1854. Each of his moves took him to a major Tipperary colony where he was never without friends.[177]

The North Tipperary Protestants in the Canadas demonstrated all three varieties of group settlement which Price has defined as typical of immigrant ethnic groups. Organized group settlement instigated by Richard Talbot initiated the overseas movement and established the cores of the major colonies that grew thereafter by chain migration. James Hodgins is also said to have organized emigration to Biddulph in the 1840s, though this is poorly documented. The exodus to Manitoba that began in the late 1870s with Greenway's railway excursions may also be regarded as organized group settlement. Chain migration was the mechanism by which clusters of Tipperary families increased and declined. Gravitation migration, in which settlers sharing a common background came together in new locations, occurred time and again, as residents of the small colonies drifted to London and as residents of both the Ottawa and London groups colonized Bruce County east of Kincardine.[178] There was also a dispersing effect in the areas of existing colonies as farmers purchased lands for the new generation a little further from the parental homesteads and as tradesmen and merchants moved to nearby villages. But settlement remained centred upon the original cores of Tipperary population.

The family was the major influence in chain migration. Friends were no doubt a factor, but friendship is hard to document. In any case relatives can normally be identified in communities to which a migrant was going, or if not a proven relative at least someone sharing a surname or a wife's surname. Maternal and wife's kin were just as likely to attract migrants as paternal relatives. Because most families were large and many had residents in several places most migrants could choose between a number of locations and still be assured of kin being present to welcome and assist them.

While the vast majority of Tipperary Protestants moved with or to join kin, within the Ottawa Valley I have noted examples of migration from an entire neighbourhood, irrespective of origin, to settle newly opened parts of the valley, with kin ties operating at a secondary level within the context of a general movement. Later the movement to the Prairies operated similarly. A major factor in diminishing the reliance upon kin in the selection of new settlement locations must have been the possibility of personal inspection. The secondary settlements in the Ottawa Valley were close enough to the Carp to permit a viewing, and the initiation of relatively cheap railway excursions permitted tentative exploration of possible locations in the Prairie West.

Rather than move to a distant community where one had kin and then move to another if it proved not to answer expectations, potential migrants were able to explore much of the Canadian and American west firsthand before making a firm commitment to move. Even so, chain migration did not become a thing of the past. A little Middlesex Tipperary community formed near Crystal City, Manitoba, but it was small and its members were scattered over a large range of territory. Kinship remained important but by the 1880s was no longer the major influence in determining settlement location.

Migration and Family Economic Strategies

THE RURAL IDEAL

The previous chapters have demonstrated that migration was largely a family affair. People moved in families, moved with kin, and moved to join kin, and we have seen how people of North Tipperary Protestant origin practised group, chain, and gravitational patterns of migration to and within the Canadas in the nineteenth century. The direction, destination, and to some extent the volume of movements were clearly determined by family considerations, with both the elementary family and bilateral kin serving as channels for information and assistance and as an important source of psychological support in adjusting to life in a new location, but the timing and causes of internal movements have yet to be considered. These considerations, too, are intimately linked with the family, but in this context with the family as the primary unit of production, and as the major mechanism of intergenerational transfer of land, the means of production in an agricultural society.

Though the basic domestic unit, as in all societies,[1] was the elementary family of husband, wife, and children, there was an important lineal aspect to the family farm. Because land was always expensive to obtain (we have already seen how Biddulph farmers took many years to finish paying for their land)[2] and became increasingly costly as a region became populated and the land improved, parental assistance in the acquisition of land by the new generation was necessary or at the very least highly desirable as such help greatly eased the burden borne by new families. The family was not merely an economic unit. Parents' behaviour demonstrated that they felt strongly the obligation to provide for their children's futures, even if the form such provision took implied geographical separation. Where such separation proved unavoidable, the migratory systems already outlined helped to reduce the psychological effects of distance by ensuring that kin were never far away.

The ideal, of course, was to provide for one's children in such a way as to keep them close at hand. A large family of sons labouring on the home place permitted the improvement and cultivation of a large acreage without the expense of hiring labour. In this ideal case, sons did without money they could have earned by working elsewhere because they knew that they would be provided for out of the family accumulation, in the form of a developed farm nearby, if all went well. The system saved the sons considerable money, for they were able to plow profits back into improvement and expansion of holdings rather than spend them on buying the land or making mortgage payments. Though the cost to sons of working family land in expectation of gaining title was a substantial loss of independence to parental control and guidance, the system often facilitated early marriage by minimizing the cost of setting up a farm. Sons often built homes on additional farms still owned by their fathers. Very few sons seem to have indicated displeasure at restricted independence by leaving. Indeed, the major causes of departure for sons provided for by their fathers at an early stage in life were inadequacy of the acreage for comfortable support (fifty acres in many cases seems to have been too little) and an opportunity to follow a more profitable, non-agricultural occupation. Both of these circumstances were comparatively rare. The prevalence of chain migration suggests, moreover, that family ties were valued in this society, and I have met with very few examples of independent wanderlust.

The discussion of family strategies of heirship which follows is based upon my compiled genealogical files and the reconstruction of the sequence of land dealings of families of North Tipperary descent who lived on the Ontario side of the Ottawa River from initial settlement up to 1881. The ideal came closest to realization among the Tipperary Protestants of the Ottawa Valley in the family of Frederick William Richardson. Richardson, a shoemaker from Borrisokane, had come from Ireland in 1819 with his wife and two daughters, joining his parents and siblings who had come on the *Brunswick* the year before.[3] In 1828, three years after the birth of his eldest son, Richardson bought an additional hundred acres from the Canada Company near his homestead in March Township, and his purchases pretty nearly kept pace with the births of his five younger sons in succeeding years. In all, in addition to his free grant, he purchased 300 acres from the Canada Company, 200 from the University of Toronto, part of the lands reserved for the profit of the proposed King's College, and 300 from fellow Tipperary settlers, including 100 from his brother-in-law, Thomas Somerville. Richardson retained ownership of all the family holdings until shortly before his death in 1879 at the age of eighty-four,[4] but he apportioned the land among his sons, and in 1862, following the death of his wife, he made legal provision for eventual transfer of title by entering into bonds guaranteeing that each son would receive the land he occupied.[5] Each of the six sons lived on a different lot after he married, but the father retained title and they worked the lands together. Living so close to one another, it was an almost communal arrangement.[6] In 1858 Richardson explained his system and philosophy in a letter to his nephew Frank Jones near London:

We Carry on farming as We Did when you were hear but better Equiped with Mashinery and farming Implements. the boys both Married and Single workes through Each other Still Allowing me to guide them, advise in particular affairs. as long as the[y] unite in their business as the[y] Do the[y] will remain a Sollid firm in farming which has Always been my Studdy in farming pursuits ... I have built good Out offisces of Stone Since you were hear which makes the rock look like a fortress. you Know I am not fond of hurding money as long as i Can make both Ends meet i am Satisfied. As yet thank goodness i am Not Afflicted With Either balif or Sherrif. If my Stock of Cattle horses and Sheep were to be Sold the[y] would fetch a hansome Sum, but we must not Exult at our prosperrety as the wise Disposer of Events is Always Able to Change our Situation As he thinks fit.[7]

The Richardson sons all married young, three at twenty-two and the rest at twenty-three, twenty-four, and twenty-five years of age. Each built a house on his own allocation prior to marrying. The 1852 census records William, who married in 1847, in a log house with his young family and a female servant, and the rest of the family living at home in the father's single-story stone house. The family's prosperity by the 1850s was such that some built of stone immediately. The corner stone of Richard's house was dated 1857; Richard married the following January.[8] In 1860 Fred wrote to Jones that "Thomas has his house Nearly finished inside of Course when finished he will be on the lookout for Some Stray Sqaw [sic] for a Companion."[9] Three months later Thomas married a distant relative. By 1861 all but the youngest of the Richardsons were living in their own homes and had 325 of their 900 acres clear, 244 of them under crop, eighty-one in pasturage, and four occupied by gardens or orchards.[10] Richardson lived to see his land divided among six sons and his two eldest grandsons, all in prosperous circumstances.

In less extreme examples of this version of the devolutionary system, sons had to wait for a gift of land until the father was willing to retire from farming with suitable support for himself and his wife in their old age, or at least until he felt he could release a suitable acreage to a son without materially harming the well-being of the family remaining at home and his own and his wife's old-age security. To shorten the waiting period, sons who acquired a farm at marriage often purchased their land from their parent rather than receiving it as a gift. By so doing they reimbursed the family against future income lost by giving up the land, but nevertheless obtained a farm in a desirable location and often at less than market value. An outright gift, in the legal form of a sale for "love and $1" or five shillings, bestowed when a son was still relatively young, was most common where a father had few children to provide for or had become reasonably well-to-do.

Older sons were normally provided for as they became able, and the homestead almost always went to the youngest or second-youngest, who had less time to wait, with maintenance of the parents by the inheriting son made a charge on the property if title was transferred while the parents were living.[11] The Ontario practice approximated ultimogeniture except in special circumstances. Sometimes when a father died leaving a young family he adopted the logical testamentary expedient of allowing the eldest son to take over management and ownership as soon as he was old enough, and ordering him to provide for the younger siblings *in loco parentis*. This is the logic of the so-called "Canadian system" whereby one heir inherits and pays off the rest.[12] This strategy was neither peculiarly Canadian nor a general system. Rather, it was a devolutionary strategy peculiar to one stage in the life cycle, found almost exclusively in cases where the father died leaving younger children at home and unprovided for with land, education, or trade.[13] Even in these circumstances many fathers chose to leave their homesteads to their widows for life and then to the youngest son. In other cases the executors controlled the property until the youngest son was of age.

LINEALITY OF LAND AND PROVISION FOR WIDOWS

The principle that land descended in the male line explains the nature of the provisions made for widows, daughters, and stepsons, but not the fact that such provision was felt to be both just and necessary. As Goody has pointed out, any form of endowment of females from the parental estate reduces the patrimony to some degree and, by withdrawing capital, threatens the principle of maintaining the integrity of landholdings for male heirs, yet "the estate is always subject to the claims of other siblings" even though such shares are not equal to that of the inheritor(s) of the land.[14]

The testamentary provisions made in the Ottawa Valley for widows allowed the women as much freedom and control as was possible without endangering the principle that the farm must revert to a male heir of the late husband after her death. In over half the wills of Ottawa Valley residents of North Tipperary origin whose wives survived them the widows retained control of the homestead for life, even though this often meant denying the inheriting son title for decades.[15] In another fifth of the cases the widow was provided with a house or absolute control over specified rooms along with detailed provisions for her support and maintenance. In another 10 per cent of cases, cash or an annuity was provided which, cross-checking with census returns indicates, enabled the widow to live independently. There was no

TABLE 19
Provisions for Widows in Wills of Men
of North Tipperary Protestant Descent, Ottawa Valley

Control of homestead for life	26
Rooms or house, and support or annuity	9
Cash or annuity	5
Portion of land	4
Equal share with children	3
Use of house with son, and support	3
Support from proceeds of sale	1
Use of cash for life	1
Total	52

Sources: AO, Carleton County Surrogate Court will registers, Land
Registry wills, and General Registers.

significant change over time in the provisions made for wives evident in the
wills examined, which dated from 1826 to about 1890.

It was not uncommon for wives to be allowed to dispose of the livestock and
household furnishings as they saw fit. Animals and furnishings were, with
cash, the most common kind of dowry women brought to a marriage in the
first half of the century, and they were frequently allowed disposal of the same
categories of property.

The sometimes elaborate provisions made for widows in wills and
maintenance agreements when they were not given lifetime control over the
homestead were also a direct result of the practice of transmitting land to male
children. By making various arrangements for support, elderly people were
able to live in their own homes independently until they died. When formerly
landowning farmers or their widows did live with children, however, they
normally lived with sons rather than daughters, as is perhaps more common
today. This was the case when the widow retained control of the homestead
for life with reversion to a son, the most common arrangement, but it was also
the usual state of affairs when title was passed to the son while his father was
living or upon his death. In the days before social security the only ways a
farmer could guarantee adequate support in his old age without retaining
control of property until his death were to sell the land and live off the
proceeds or to charge support against the homestead, and sometimes other
lands, when he passed them to the next generation. There was no way a farmer
could enforce support of a widow by his son-in-law. If a man wanted to
guarantee his wife's support after his death he therefore had little option but to
make her the responsibility of their son, as a condition upon inheritance of the
farm. It has long been a commonplace that widows frequently co-operate
better with homemaking daughters they have themselves raised than with

daughters-in-law who have imbibed another woman's ideas about how to run a household. The possibility of conflict between the women was probably the reason for the frequently elaborate provisions in wills and maintenance agreements obliging the son to pay annuities, to provide his mother with absolute control of certain rooms and use of a cow and firewood, or even to build her a new house somewhere on the property if the generations found they could not live together. John Colbert Jr of Goulbourn made such a provision for his wife in 1862. His son John was not yet married, so the future circumstances in which his widow would find herself were indeterminate:

My Beloved Wife Jane Colbert to get her support from my son John in this her present house of residence so long as they can agree and should they disagree he my son John is to build her a comfortable house upon the corner of Lot No. thirty in the twelfth Concession of Goulbourn ... one acre and a half of land to be attached to said house and said Land to be well fenced properly tilled and manured from year to year also ten Pounds H. cy per Annum her bed and bedding and whatever household furniture she may require also a Cow and the feed of her Cow winter and summer and whatever wood she may require ... the wood to be left at her Door ready to put into her stove those provisions in event of her not marrying again to remain binding on my son John during her natural life.[16]

As it happened, John III died unmarried in 1876 and the property reverted to his mother's absolute control under the new intestacy law.

The lineal principle in the transmission of land also lies behind the fact that where wives were entrusted with management of the homestead, their control ceased in the event of remarriage. The "cutting off" of a widow if she married again was not an arbitrary action by a jealous husband anxious to enforce his wife's fidelity even from beyond the grave, as it has sometimes been portrayed.[17] Rather, it was a recognition of the danger of a farmer's children being deprived of their patrimony in favour of a second husband or his children. Because of the rigid demarcation of sexual roles in the nineteenth century it followed that a woman remarrying would be provided for by her second husband and that therefore the continuance of her support from the estate of her first husband would be superfluous. I have seen one example of a cash bequest to a widow in lieu of life interest in the event of remarriage, but in this instance there were no surviving children and the farm was to revert in any case to the testator's brothers.[18] More normally the woman's maintenance ceased totally upon remarriage.

That there was a very real danger of a landowner's children being effectively disinherited by remarriage is demonstrated by the several instances of landless young men who obtained land by marrying widows with farms. Thomas Acres Jr married Martha Clarke, the widow of Alexander

Johnston of Huntley. Johnston had been a squatter on a clergy reserve, but he died in the mid-1830s shortly after agreeing with Peter Robinson on a purchase price. Payments made by the widow were temporarily lost during a period of maladministration in the Crown Lands Office, and in 1848 her representative, Hamnett Pinhey, was still attempting to have her recognized as the purchaser.[19] Martha had remarried within a year of her husband's death, in about 1837, to Thomas Acres Jr, whose father had been unable to provide him with land. When the clergy reserve sale was finally made in 1850, the patent was issued in Acres's name.[20] When he died in 1861 he left the homestead to his son Thomas. His step-daughter's husband, John Dawson, was an executor of Acres's will (Acres called him a "friend"), as was Mrs Acres's brother, but his stepson Alexander Johnston Jr received only a cash bequest of $12 and is said by the family to have gone to the United States.[21] Acres had taken over his wife's debts upon marrying her[22] and no doubt was the person who really paid the instalments on the farm, but the exclusion of the stepson from the land that had come to Acres from his father is nonetheless notable.

PROVISIONS FOR STEPSONS

The lineality of landed property is also reflected in the nature of provisions made for stepsons. As in Acres's case, the common bequest to a stepson was one of cash, not land, even when a stepfather like John Boucher had land in ample supply and the stepsons had no expectation of an inheritance from the estates of their own fathers. In numerous cases, of course, stepchildren were not provided for since they were the children of a marriage cut short by death. In several of the examples of stepchildren that could be cited (Dorrington/ Cavanagh, Scott/Morgan, Ardill/Rivington) the orphans or children of a first wife were raised by maternal kin. In one interesting example of a widow remarrying, the children appear to have been raised by kin of the first husband, with the family farm being properly reserved for them despite the evident want of the second husband and his children.[23] The instance of Andrew Dugas giving land to one of his Cavanagh stepsons is unique in this study.[24]

PROVISIONS FOR DAUGHTERS

Daughters were entitled to a share of the family substance if there was sufficient to go around, but in farming families their portions did not consist of land and were seldom equal in cash value to those of their brothers.[25] Land was given to daughters either before or after the father's death only in unusual circumstances, if a daughter married a poor tradesman, for example,[26] or if a married daughter was moving back to be closer to home.[27] In such cases, however, land was given or sold to daughters or sons-in-law by farmers only if it could be spared by the sons.

The assumption that most women would marry was reflected in the fact that girls most often received their portions in the form of a dowry given at marriage. Each new marriage and the ensuing establishment of a new elementary family was thus endowed, ideally, by the families of both bride and groom, with the groom obtaining land from his father (though title might not be immediately given) and the beginnings of household furnishings and livestock being provided by the bride's family.[28] We have evidence of the form taken by dowries only in the wills left by testators with daughters still at home. When all children still at home were provided for in a will, the bequest of a dollar to married daughters, as to older sons, is a fairly sure indication that they had already received their portions. The most common dowry was one which enabled a new bride to set up housekeeping, and consisted of some combination of cash, furniture, and livestock. In wills we find reference to dowries consisting of $80 and a bed or bedding on marriage or leaving home permanently,[29] $40 and a bedstead and bedding,[30] and several cows or sheep and a sewing machine.[31] John Barber, a poor farmer in Fitzroy, left his daughters Elizabeth, Catherine, Ellen, and Mary cows called Dandy, Curly, Cherry, and Pinkey.[32] Sometimes daughters were merely left cash to be paid them at marriage, especially if the girls were very young when the will was made.

A cash sum became the most common form of provision after 1870, perhaps reflecting recognition that the average age of females at marriage was rising, more girls were remaining unmarried, and many were spending at least a few years as teachers upon leaving home. In these circumstances the old form of endowment, which was most suitable for girls who could reasonably be expected to marry young and within the farm community, was decreasingly appropriate. Though cash endowments were by far the norm in this period, some fathers went beyond that in recognizing new possibilities. One girl was given the option of attending the Normal School to train as a teacher, and it became fairly common to insist that daughters receive an education. John Clarke provided his daughters with $80 or equivalent and schooling at least six months per year to age fifteen. Clarke followed earlier custom, however, in making the dowry conditional upon the agreement of a majority of his executors and son James Albert (thirteen when his father died) to the girls' choice of marriage partner. Since the executors were Clarke's nephews John Kemp and Albert Bradley and his brother-in-law William Richardson, the group that met to pass judgment upon the girls' choices constituted an effective family council. Three girls lessened the odds by marrying cousins.[33]

The emphasis upon the male line in transmission of real estate explains much about the provisions accorded stepchildren and wider kin as well as widows and daughters. Though descent of landed property was lineal, though ideally partible, among males, an obligation was also felt towards female relations. We have already noted how bilateral kin were of considerable significance in the context of migration. Men were quite as likely to move with or to join their wives' or mothers' relatives as their own or their fathers'. The deeply felt obligation to provide a start in life for all one's children reflected this bilaterality of kinship also, but because land was transmitted from father to sons, other forms of provision had to be made for widows, daughters, and stepsons.

ASSISTANCE FOR EXTRA-FAMILIAL KIN

Though the devolution of land was strictly from father to sons, obligation was felt to assist more distant kin in other ways. Such assistance extended also to affines (relatives by marriage). Some farmers left cash bequests to orphaned nieces.[34] Sometimes the children of deceased daughters were raised by their maternal grandparents when the fathers remarried.[35] Adopted children also received cash bequests.[36] Thomas Birch, a well-to-do Nepean farmer, left money to bury his unfortunate brother Robert, whose many sons had never recovered from Robert's bankruptcy. Birch did not help out his nephews by providing them with land, but we cannot know whether or not he ever gave them cash assistance. Frederick William Richardson was responsible for apprenticing his wife's nephew Frank Jones, a "poor boy" whose farming father could not provide for him. The successful cabinet-maker Jones recalled this timely assistance: "I have never forgotten your Fathers Kindness to me, in using his influence to get me into a place at Kennedy & Blyths ... since I came here to the west, I have been enabled to get, by means of my trade, and God's blessing a good livelihood, and a good competence for old age, if my wife or I needs it and something to give my children as they may settle themselves. You know that much depends on a lucky start in life, now for a very poor boy, I have had that lucky start, and to Your Father, and my Uncle I owe much, very much concerning that beginning."[37]

The Jones family also serves as a good example of the ways in which family members assisted one another even when distance prevented their participation in local labour exchanges and similar workaday services. After Frank Jones's sister Mary and her husband Joseph Glenney left western Upper Canada for Michigan in the early 1850s, Jones corresponded with Glenney about the possibility of acquiring wild lands in Michigan, and Frank and Mary's wandering brother Robert also spent some time with the Glenneys.[38] In May 1862 Mary wrote to Francis about sending her daughter Maria back to London to learn the weaving trade: "And now Fransis I am going to ask one favour of you it will be some trouble but no expense this is getting a great Sheep Country & there is no Weavers here I want you to make some enquiries & see who wee Can send Maria to to learn the trade her Father says she ought to learn it in six months and she is very apt to pick up anything She has got education to do her I dare Say as much as you got I was going to Send her over this Sumer but thought it better Consult you & Jane first as I know you will do what you Can to favour my views."[39] After Glenney joined the 22nd Michigan Infantry later that year he continued to write to Jones from army camps in the southern states asking his assistance in procuring sheep for Mary back home in Michigan.[40] The Jones and Glenney families continued to visit back and forth for the remainder of their lives after Joseph died of wounds received at Chickamauga.[41] Mary returned to McGillivray to comfort Frank when his wife died and visited on numerous other occasions.[42]

A noteworthy feature of the Jones correspondence is that travelling relatives were always asked to report on land quality and prices. Frank Jones's brother Thomas reported on this topic from the west coast in the 1850s, and Glenney not only answered questions about government land-sales policy in Michigan but wrote enticing descriptions of Kentucky when he was encamped there during the Civil War.[43]

Obligations to kin are most noticeably reflected in the extended households of those most materially able to honour the obligation. The 1852 census recorded large households in the families of the two wealthiest Tipperary settlers of Carleton County, William Hodgins and Robert Grant, and also in that of George T. Burke of Bytown, the former superintendent of the Richmond military settlement and in 1852 the county registrar. Hodgins's testamentary provisions for his vast landholdings extended exclusively to his immediate family, but among the eight labourers and servants living with him in 1852 were three Hodginses, whose relationship remains undetermined: Henry, son of Richard of Huntley, and Adam and Thomas, sons of Thomas of Huntley.[44]

Grant assisted and gave shelter to a large number of his own and his wife's relatives.[45] In 1852 Grant and his first wife shared their household with Grant's eighty-nine-year-old mother, his niece Lydia Morris from Montreal, Joseph Cox, a cousin of some degree recently arrived from Ireland, and the latter's wife and two sons, Timothy McKey, a Roman Catholic whose surname nonetheless leads one to speculate that he may have been a brother of Cox's wife, who was a Mackey, and Margaret Farmer, daughter of a Huntley family from Modreeny of no known kinship to the Grants.[46] By 1861 Grant had remarried and was a parent for the first time, but his household still included more distant kin: Robert Grant Morris, a nephew up from Montreal, and Frances Cox, daughter of Joseph who now farmed in Huntley, along with two Catholic servant girls.[47]

Family memoirs indicate that kin arriving in Canada generally proceeded to the Grants. Several of the children of Mrs Grant's sister, Ellen Cox, arrived in 1822 and remained until they moved to Lambton County with Powell cousins in the 1830s. At least one of the children of Mrs Grant's brother, Francis Powell, who had come with the Grants on the *Brunswick* in 1818, lived with the Grants after Powell's first wife died, and Joseph Cox's son Frank later worked for R.H. Grant as his father had done for Grant's father.[48] The Grants also assisted Joseph Cox in building up substantial landholdings in Huntley by loaning him money on mortgage. Robert Powell of Huntley lived for many years on land owned by Grant there and finally purchased it in 1862.[49] Grant's son recalled that Powell did "considerable business with my father and afterwards with my mother" but was uncertain of the relationship. Grant's niece, Lydia Morris, who was listed with him in the census, came up from Montreal to care for her ailing aunt and in 1852 married a neighbour. Her brother Bobby, who lived with the Grants "many years," was later a conductor on the Grand Trunk Railway, living in Belleville.[50] Another of the Morrises, Susan, probably lived with the Grants in the 1840s, for she was of Goulbourn at her marriage in 1847 to Edward Lowry who had returned for her from Grey County, where he had gone after selling his farm in Huntley to Robert Grant earlier that year.[51]

George Burke was impecunious but held prestigious local offices.[52] His household in Bytown in 1852 included his sons James and Milo, another Milo who was probably his brother, three orphaned granddaughters named Fogarty, his daughter Mary, his deputy-registrar Thomas Jones, and a woman named Norah Burke, possibly a sister; she later lived with Burke's married daughter on Allumette Island.[53] Burke's son George R. also maintained an extended household, living with his widowed sister-in-law, Lizzie (Fogarty) Thompson, and his own widowed daughter.[54] The Burkes continually intermarried with the Fogartys, as they had done in Ireland for generations.[55]

More distant relatives – siblings, nephews, nieces, and cousins – like stepsons and daughters were felt to have no claim upon the lands of a farmer. An obligation to assist them nevertheless existed, and the obligation seems to have increased with one's ability to help. Jones's expression of gratitude to his uncle reminds us, however, that such aid, while often necessary and hoped for, deserved proper appreciation when it was forthcoming. Not every farmer was able to provide adequately for his own family, let alone to provide assistance to his own or his wife's less fortunate relatives.

CLASS DIFFERENCES IN THE DEVOLUTION OF LANDED PROPERTY

The ideals outlined above were those of the farming population. Those practising non-agricultural occupations and those living in the cities exhibited different patterns of property devolution, and social class also played a role in determining the actions a father took in distributing his property. For non-farmers and city residents, land did not constitute the means of production and so there was less incentive in these cases to preserve it for sons. Non-farmers generally provided for their daughters by ordering the sale of town or village lots and division of the proceeds among the girls or by leaving them such properties. Gentlemen such as Joseph Maxwell (d. 1847) and R.Y. Greene (d. 1882) had large farms but they, too, placed their daughters on a par with their sons, Maxwell by leaving them equal shares in the family lands,[56] Greene by giving them a portion in cash equal to that given to his younger sons.

The effective ultimogeniture practised by the farming population also stands in contrast to the British gentry's preference for primogeniture, or passing the landed estate to the eldest son. The British aristocratic system, which was shared by the upper levels of the landed gentry and supported by common law, favoured primogeniture as the method of ensuring continuity of the line, for the lands from which the family derived its title, prestige, and income passed to the eldest son in each generation ensuring that subdivision of the ancestral patrimony would not, in a few generations, reduce a once-prosperous family to a position where its social, economic, and political pretensions lost their reality. I have noted in an earlier chapter nonetheless[57] how the numerous and increasingly cash-starved minor gentry of North Tipperary practised subdivision of their properties in the early nineteenth centry as a method of providing for their children. However, such apportionment often followed the usual Irish practice of granting a term, life, or hereditary interest in land rather than alienating the land itself. As a consequence of the Cromwellian and later confiscations and the increase of population, most land in Ireland was in fact held from someone else, no matter how long the tenure, how easy the terms, or how minimal the rent. Holding of land in fee was relatively uncommon. The accumulation of encumbrances was in the long run disastrous, however, and many estates were disposed of in the mid-nineteenth century by the landed estates courts that were established to clarify and buy out encumbrances and facilitate the sale of encumbered properties.

Such attitudes carried over, to some extent, when members of these classes emigrated to Canada where land was not a source of power in the same way. The assumption that the essential part of the patrimony belonged by general accord to the eldest son is reflected in the Canadian will of Charles Cambie, a descendant of Colonel Solomon Cambie, a Cromwellian grantee,[58] but more immediately the heir, as eldest son of the eldest son, to his grandfather Solomon's (d. 1792) estate of Castletown.[59] Charles Cambie's eldest son was left without his expected inheritance because Castletown was sold under the encumbered estates court. Cambie could only leave him his household furniture, should his wife not otherwise dispose of it, and his prayer "that he, as well as all my children, may have a better inheritance, one that is 'incorruptible, undefiled, and that passeth not away, reserved in heaven for us.'"[60]

Other gentleman left their Canadian homesteads and estates to their eldest sons even when the latter had taken urban occupations and would not, in the event, return to the homestead to live. Whereas most local farmers in such a situation would have left the homestead to a younger son who was still at home and not provided for, gentlemen sometimes gave the younger sons cash and bequeathed the land to the eldest out of principle. Robert Young Greene of March, formerly a gentleman of Castle Connell and Modreeny, expressed his belief in 1882 that it was his "first, earthly duty to make a just & equitable division of whatever I now possess or may hereafter become possessed of between my wife Mary Jane Greene & my children or their heirs." His belief in just and equitable division included a conviction that the family homestead in March, Knocknacree, should go to his eldest son. Accordingly, following the death of his wife, Greene's eldest son Godfrey Benning inherited the 300–acre homestead on the riverfront of March with its contents and livestock, and the six other children received $600 in cash from GB and an equal share of the father's other real and personal estate. R.Y. Greene had been active in the mortgage market but had not bought up other lands, so the residue was effectively personal estate. The sixth son Harold was to receive "an English & Commercial Education" so that he would be "placed in the same position as his brothers except" GB.[61] At least two of the other sons became lawyers and, despite inheriting the homestead, GB continued to live in Ottawa where he was the secretary-treasurer of the Upper Ottawa Improvement Company.[62]

Greene's old-world aristocratic belief in primogeniture of family lands was shared by some other members of the March gentry who were not of Tipperary origin, such as Hamnett Pinhey, an English gentleman who anticipated his later testamentary arrangements by naming his Canadian estate Horaceville, after the eldest son who was to inherit it. Greene's father-in-law, Captain John Benning Monk, gave farms to each of his sons, but he left the homestead to the eldest, who was a lawyer in Bytown, and he entailed each property to descend in the male line of each of his sons.[63] However, as already indicated, some Canadian gentlemen of Tipperary origin, like Maxwell, divided their lands or proceeds from their sale equally among sons and daughters. This was not in keeping with the aristocratic tradition, but neither was it common Canadian rural practice.

In other respects gentry practices were simplified in Canada as a result of the simple tenurial structure here. People of any social standing in Ireland – merchants, large farmers and middlemen, and gentlemen – had formalized dowry arrangements in written marriage settlements that were often enrolled in the Registry of Deeds. The Irish marriage settlement, in its simplest form, represented an attempt by the bride's family to protect its investment, and its daughter's interests, by guaranteeing that in the event of the groom's death the bride and her children would be provided for out of his lands, in consideration of the dowry that had been conveyed to him with the bride.[64] A common arrangement was to put the groom's property into the trusteeship of the bride's relatives for her use after her husband's death, with reversion to the children of the marriage, but guaranteeing to the husband the use of the property during his lifetime.[65]

Jack Goody has pointed out that dowry practices are usually class-specific, with the working classes seldom employing them and provisions becoming increasingly elaborate as one proceeds up the social ladder.[66] At the lower levels of Irish society, among the small and middling freehold farmers and tenants at will, one finds, as among Canadian farming families, no registered marriage settlements. The dowries bestowed by these classes were insufficient to entitle the bride's family to expect the groom's to guarantee family lands to her use or profit. Rather, it was left to the husbands to provide for their wives and children and the dowry, which in Canada consisted typically of cash, bed, and cow in the early nineteenth century, was simply a contribution by the bride's kin towards the setting up of the new household and a recognition that daughters had rights to a share in the parental estate, though not one that threatened the integrity of real estate as a patrimony for her brothers. Marriage settlements were uncommon even at higher levels of society in English Canada where their most common purpose was to declare separate the properties two parties brought to a second marriage late in life, in order to preserve inheritances for the two existing families. The only example I have found involving Tipperary settlers of the Ottawa Valley was that between Coll McDonnell and Mary Emily Burke in 1852. McDonnell settled £1000 secured on his lands in Bytown to Miss Burke's brothers in trust to satisfy her claims on his estate after his death. This was possibly an attempt to preserve the remainder of McDonnell's property to existing heirs, for he had been married before. Since he was a lumber merchant, however, a participant in a volatile trade, the settlement may have been intended, as were some Irish settlements, to protect Miss Burke from the effects of bankruptcy as much as from those of death.[67]

Similarly, the encumbrancing of lands with annuities or rent charges was commonly practised in Canada only as a way of providing for a widow. Sometimes when the surviving children were under age the heir to the land was obligated to compensate his siblings, but this took the form of a cash payment or a fixed number of instalments. However, annuities left to widows were very seldom heritable and were never granted in perpetuity to the heirs of the original recipient, as they frequently were in Ireland, conformably with the principle in marriage settlements of ensuring the well-being of the children of a daughter's marriage as well as of the daughter herself.[68] An excellent Irish example of extensive encumbrancing and the problems to which this practice led is found in the will of an ancestor of a number of emigrants to Canada, Edward Hart, a substantial farmer of Cowlowly in the parish of Rathdowney, just east of Roscrea. Hart leased this 159-acre property in 1737 for lives renewable forever at an annual rent of £136.18.5 stg and re-entry fines of £18.10.7 on the fall of each life. At the time of his death in 1789 the property generated, through subletting, profits of £79.19.1 annually, after paying the rent and the collector's fee. Hart left the property entirely to his eldest and only surviving son Charles who was non-resident, living at Tinderry. However, most of the profits were eliminated by eight perpetual annuities, some imposed as parts of his daughters' marriage settlements and ratifed by will. Four were payable to daughters or sons-in-law with reversion to their heirs, one to his widow for life with reversion to a granddaughter, one to a granddaughter and another to a great-granddaughter who was then just a child, and one to a son-in-law to pay off an unpaid portion of a marriage settlement, with reversion to four sons and one daughter of a deceased son of the testator. Annuities were a convenient way of paying off a large capital sum in instalments charged upon land as well as of insuring a continuing income to one's descendants. Rent charges were also purchaseable, a fact which both simplified and confused matters. Hart's great-grandson Samuel Dudley, for example, in 1841 purchased from his second cousin Ellinor Hopper Swinburn for £41 the £5 annuity she had been bequeathed by her great-grandfather when a child in 1789, and in turn sold it in 1854 to William H. Harte, a descendant of Charles, the heir to the property; WH was making a concerted effort to buy up the by then much-subdivided annuities as the encumbrances were a constant drain on the income of the land, were increasingly difficult to pay owing to the difficulty of keeping track of heirs to miniscule proportions, and would eventually hamper attempts to sell portions of the property. Cowlowly was loaded with further encumbrances intended to provide for wives in the nineteenth century and eventually passed to the landed estates courts in order to untie the tangle. Encumbrancing land with annuities was a strategy of heirship used especially by merchants and large farmers who, like Hart, were middlemen, holding sufficient lands that they could sublet part of them at a profit rent that in turn provided the cash for the annuities. Middling and smaller farmers did not have this convenient but potentially ruinous course open to them and turned to actual subdivision of the land to provide for their children, at least until the prospect of emigration offered an alternative solution.[69]

A few Canadian immigrants did attempt to create other forms of life estate but such testamentary provisions were often ignored. Michael Rivington's will left his lands to his sons' male and female children rather than to his sons directly, but the sons later disposed of the properties as if their father's will had never been made.[70] J.R. Stanley left his Nepean farm to his son John for twenty years and then to John's older brother Robert. However, Robert mortgaged and lost the property long before John's term was up.[71] In Canada life estates and annuities were uncommon, apart from those initiated to support the widows of the testators. Here absolute freehold title in fee simple was the standard tenure, rather than the uses and interests that prevailed in Ireland. The inheritance strategy of encumbrancing a property with annuities did not survive the Atlantic crossing.

TENSIONS BETWEEN LAW AND PRACTICE

The devolutionary system practised by farm families in Upper Canada/ Ontario in the nineteenth century had an inherent logic, but there existed a continual tension between law and practice. The law more closely approximated the practices of the gentry and the city-dwellers than it did those of the larger rural population. The belief of rural people in their own concept of just division was deeply ingrained, however, and they made wills to ensure that land went to the proper recipients or came to agreements among themselves in cases of intestacy to overcome legal dictates with which they were not in sympathy.

It was eminently sensible that a homestead would in most cases become the property of the youngest son while others would be given or sold land as they married or be provided for in some other way, and that daughters would receive dowries of cash and goods which would complement the land that their husbands would receive. However, the English common law prevailing in the province before 1852 dictated that in cases of intestacy all property went to the eldest son. The new intestacy law which became effective in that year recognized the principle of equal division but reflected urban rather than rural practices in that it made property equally divisible among all issue both male and female. This did not conform to rural custom in two respects: it denied that land should go to males only and it did not recognize that in most circumstances the homestead should go to the youngest son. The act recognized that some members of a family might wish to buy out the interests of the others, but it stated that parties authorized to make partitions of real . estate would give preference to the person who would have been heir-at-law had Section 22 and subsequent sections of the act never been passed – in other words, a reversion to the principle of primogeniture.[72]

The tension between law and practice was a primary motivation for making a will, but we must examine instances of private family arrangements made in the event of intestacy to judge how deeply opinion ran. In the case of George Clarke who died in 1839 there was a will but it provided only for the life estate of his wife and the support and education of his three youngest children in the event of her remarriage. Clarke also forbade the sale of the homestead unless all the family agreed. The arrangements made within the family are somewhat confusing, but they indicate nonetheless that the sons believed that they all were entitled by right to an interest in the homestead, even though the law of primogeniture would have made the eldest son the heir upon his mother's death.[73] The father's intention may have been that the land go to the second-youngest son, John, who in fact received it; the will provided that the children be educated until John, the second-youngest, was twenty-one. In any event the second son sold his interest to John in 1848 for £10, and the eldest sold his to the third brother, George, for £5 in 1850, both fairly nominal sums. George sold his own and Robert's share to John for £120 the year following, and probably used the money to buy his tavern in Bells Corners. The youngest son never did sell his interest but went to Clarendon with a cousin and became a merchant, farmer, and eventually crown timber agent.

The desire to provide dowries for daughters and farms for all sons if possible also operated in cases of intestacy after 1852, with the legal preference for the eldest male being conveniently ignored. Thomas Rivington of Huntley had bought up 700 acres, including 200 in Russell upon which he had placed his eldest son, Michael, though without releasing title to him, before he died intestate in 1855. The second son struck out on his own almost immediately and most of the heirs recognized Michael's right to the Cumberland lands by quitting claim for a nominal five shillings, though younger brother Thomas appears to have held out until 1864 and then stung Michael for $400. The third son William, the eldest still at home, stepped into his father's shoes and held 500 acres, including the homestead, for his two youngest brothers, George and Robert, and in the meantime purchased two 100–acre farms in Nepean for his brothers Richard and Thomas. William sold the 500 acres to George and Robert for $1000 but, perhaps in recognition of his actions *in loco parentis,* they gave 100 acres back to him after he failed in a storekeeping venture in Carp in 1877. The lands were mostly sold back and forth and while the boys' payments and earnings may have cancelled out, the daughters clearly ended up with a cash surplus.

The law also lagged behind reality in that the land registration process made no specific provision for the registration of maintenance agreements, an important oversight considering that early inheritance was often made contingent upon the support of aged parents. As a result of this circumstance a wide variety of legal expedients were resorted to, but some agreements continued to go unregistered, sometimes resulting in suits in Chancery to establish title. The simplest procedure was to write in agreements for maintenance as conditions upon a sale, but lawyers seem to have resisted doing this unless the support took the form of a fairly straightforward annuity,[74] and even then this option was not resorted to as often as one might expect. More often the agreement was disguised in some other legal form, frequently as a mortgage. An example is the sale for $1 by George Morgan Sr of 100 acres in March to his son William in 1880 and William's subsequent mortgaging of the property to his father, the consideration being the payment by William of $100 per year for fourteen years, plus 6 per cent interest on any arrears. Maintenance agreements were also registered as bonds, trust deeds, and life leases which, extending for longer than seven years, were registrable under the act. I have even seen an instrument registered as a will that was in fact a premortem contract.[75] When Arthur Hopper purchased lands for his three younger sons in Nepean in 1845 each of the boys entered into an agreement to pay his parents £10 per year for life. The document was not registered at the time but it was inserted in the county General Register many years later.[76] The "GR" was instituted by the Registry Act of 1865 to facilitate the registration of wills and powers of attorney which could not be indexed in the normal manner, which was by lot and concession, because no specific lands were mentioned.[77] The general registers were used for several decades in Carleton County to record other types of instruments not specified by the act, such as naturalizations, charters of lodges, and financial statements of joint-stock companies. The statutory contents of general registers were later expanded, but still excluded maintenance agreements and most of the types of instruments just cited.[78] Registration of maintenance agreements in the GR was not an ideal solution in any case because it physically separated the agreement from the indexed instruments recording title to the land upon which it was a charge. In yet another instance the Court of Chancery ordered that an unregistered agreement be considered a lien upon the property.

We have a few instances in which Chancery suits between members of a family were the result of an unregistered agreement, the legal validity of which was unclear to the family. The action just cited, in which the sons were confirmed in their title while the father's rights were declared to be a lien upon the land, resulted from conflict over an unregistered agreement.[79] A similar action was initiated in 1875 by Joseph Gleeson, who sued his father for possession of the homestead, citing an unregistered agreement in which the father had turned the land over to him for an annuity or rent charge. The parties settled out of court in 1876, with Joseph paying his father $156 in arrears and agreeing to pay an annual rent charge of $40. Two years later old Michael Gleeson released title and guaranteed his support by using a combination of three types of legal instrument. First he sold the farm to Joseph for $2000, and Joseph mortgaged it to his father for the same sum payable in twenty annual instalments without interest. On the same day Michael leased from Joseph a two-acre house lot on the property for one cent per year.[80]

Despite the difficulties posed by the tensions between the practices the rural people found most practically useful and the assumptions of the legal system, which were based upon gentry and urban practices, most rural dwellers found it possible to make their own arrangements to ensure that property descended

TABLE 20

Establishment of Sons by 1881 in 141 Families
on the Upper Canadian Side of the Ottawa River

Land from father, grandfather, stepfather	231
in father's lifetime 134	
by inheritance 88	
both 2	
Free grant	16
Married heiress with land	3
Purchased land	74
Tenant farmer	5
Labourer	7
Trade	52
Profession	17
Migrated without securing land before going	46
Total	451

Source: Compiled family and property files.
Note: The individual's situation noted is his first secure establishment; for example, if he purchased land and then lost it and became a tenant farmer he is included in the former category, but if a tenant farmer who became a landowner, then in the latter. Thus, tenant farmers in this table are those who remained such. This table excludes entire families that migrated and families that had no sons.

as they wished. But wanting to do something was not the same thing as achieving it. It remains to consider how successful they were in achieving their aims.

IDEAL AND REALITY: STRATEGIES OF HEIRSHIP IN THE OTTAWA VALLEY

How realistic was the ideal of passing lands on to one's sons? Of the 451 sons in 141 families who lived on the Ontario side of the Ottawa Valley in the period covered by this study and who were set up independent of their parents by 1881, just over half obtained their initial stake of land from their fathers, 136 while their fathers were living and eighty-eight by inheritance. Another 15 per cent purchased lands in the area, though whether with parental assistance or not it is usually impossible to say. Still another 15 per cent took up a trade or profession, fifty-two becoming tradesmen and seventeen professionals. The selection of these options was normally assisted by parents, for entry into trades and professions customarily followed apprenticeship or education from a young age. Thus, putting sons to a trade may also be regarded as a strategy of heirship. Only 10 per cent of sons left the region as young men without acquiring land there; some whose fate I have not discovered may, of course, have learned a trade before leaving to practise it elsewhere. Professionals are more easily traced.

However, while half of the sons coming of age in the period studied, in the sense of leaving home or being set up in life, were provided with land by the family, fewer than a fifth of families were able to provide for all of their sons in this way, though 7 per cent had no sons to provide for at all. A closer analysis of the provisions or lack of provisions made for sons suggests the difficulty of realizing the ideal and the circumstances that led to adoption of various alternatives. Thirty-six of the families that came to the Ontario shore of the Ottawa, about one in six, provided land in the region for all of their sons. Of these, half had only one or two to provide for. Given the comments made already about the importance of arriving early to secure good land, it is striking that even those who had one or two sons to set up on farms tended to be early settlers who located on good lands in the Carp Valley. None were resident in marginal areas.[81]

A FARM FOR EVERY SON: POSSIBILITIES AND PROBLEMS

Frederick William Richardson was not the only farmer from Tipperary to provide a farm for every son of a large family,[82] although the extent of communal arrangements and parental control may have been unique to the Richardsons. Denis Cavanagh of Huntley bought up 500 acres in addition to his 100–acre grant, and bequeathed 100 acres to each of his sons, to George "the lot he now lives on," and the homestead to the youngest. Cavanagh had purchased two of the lots from brothers-in-law who were moving west to "New London." As in the case of Richardson and Somerville,[83] this kind of arrangement benefited both those who moved and those who stayed behind. The migrant received the cash with which to buy more land at a cheaper price in his new home, and the relative who remained behind obtained a nearby farm on which he could settle a son later. Denis Cavanagh's brother John also became an extensive landowner. He received a free grant but purchased another 800 acres, mostly Canada Company, clergy reserve, and crown lands. John's eldest son bought crown lands on his own in the 1850s, but his father bailed him out of debt in the 1860s and gave him additional property. This did not prevent him from mortgaging anew, and he sold out and went to Manitoba in 1876. John also gave his remaining three sons generous acreages in Huntley, the youngest receiving the homestead as a second farm in 1873 when the father was about seventy-seven years old. Several other farmers who achieved these ends, despite having large families to provide for, were Thomas Birtch, who provided land for most of his eight sons and helped the others acquire it, and John Boucher, father of twenty-three children, who gave farms to four sons during his lifetime and bequeathed land to three others. Only the last of his eight surviving sons, who was three when his father died, received a bequest of cash and an education. I have already related how Thomas Rivington of Huntley bought up 700 acres and how the oldest son still at home stepped into his shoes when Rivington died in 1855 and held 500 acres, including the homestead, for his two youngest brothers, George and Robert, and in the meantime purchased two 100–acre farms in Nepean for his brothers Richard and Thomas.[84] James Hodgins bought up 893 acres in Huntley and gave farms to five of his six surviving sons. His residence and that of his fourth son, Adam, were proudly illustrated in the Carleton County atlas in 1879, which also featured biographies of both men and a portrait of James.[85] The sixth son, John Hodgins, was educated at the County Grammar School and in Toronto and headed the Ottawa legal firm of Hodgins, Kidd, and Rutherford; he was a candidate for the legislature in 1883.[86] Edward Owens of Fitzroy, who came from Borrisokane in 1825, overcame the death of his wife two years after their arrival, leaving five children aged seventeen to three, and was able to provide all four of his sons with farms before he died in 1855. John Reid bought his first land in Huntley from the Canada Company only in 1836, but despite this late start he began to add to his holdings in 1863 by purchasing from neighbours and was able to leave 100–acre farms to three sons, having already given one to his second son before his death. Reid's obituary in 1891 noted that he was "one of the most wealthy farmers in Huntley, having purchased for his sons four of the best farms in the district."[87] A member of the second generation, George H. Acres, was able to provide land for all of his sons, buying lands for the four oldest in Osgoode and leaving the 200–acre homestead that he had himself inherited to his son, Holly (Adam Holland Acres), who was elected to the provincial legislature for twenty-five years.[88]

How did these men manage to amass such large acreages? It is notable that all but one of these successful farmers lived in the most fertile part of the region, the Carp Valley. The exception, Birtch, left his original Goulbourn homestead in 1838 for a more desirable farm on the Richmond Road in Nepean, the main road into Bytown from the west. By 1861 the property values there were among the highest in the county, and Birtch's younger sons profitted in the 1870s by subdividing and selling lots in "Birchton" as the suburbs of the City of Ottawa expanded westward.[89] No one who settled in marginal areas built up equivalent acreages of poor-quality land, though it would have been cheaper to have done so in such an area. Good quality land was more expensive but its profits were also greater, and those who settled on poor lands did so of necessity and had little capital to finance even basic improvements. Of the prosperous farmers cited, Richardson, who came closest to realizing the ideal, had the largest share of poor land, for parts of all his farms lay on the shallow soils broken by rock outcrops that trace the eastern limit of the Carp Valley and rise to become low rocky hills a few miles to the north. Richardson's house and that of his son Tom were built upon and against the rock and Richardson himself noted that when he constructed stone outbuildings, the homestead looked "like a fortress."[90] But the remainder of his lands consisted of the flat, fertile soil of the Carp Valley and made up in productivity what the other portions lacked.[91] The Richardsons' communal co-operation made the most of the good land: in 1861 they had 325 acres under cultivation. These farmers also arrived early. The exception was Reid, who must have made good use of his initial homestead. Many were able to purchase the first few of their additional lands in the pioneer period when uncleared land was still relatively inexpensive.

The very size of their families was also of benefit to these successful farmers, though the children would probably have been more of a burden than a help had the farms been of small potential for improvement. At first children were mouths to feed even on fertile land, but in propitious circumstances having six sons to help with the chores later enabled an established farmer to cultivate a greater acreage without hiring labour.

Nonetheless, many of the pioneer settlers who achieved considerable financial success did so through engaging in profitable non-agricultural enterprises or by-employments, not carpentering or shoemaking, which at best might provide a welcome supplemental income, but in timbering, storekeeping, or tavernkeeping. Richardson emigrated as a shoemaker, but farmed in Canada and engaged as a young man in taking out timber.[92] John Boucher skipped to Canada in 1819 without paying his rent but became quite successful here. He managed to provide land for seven sons by engaging in tavernkeeping for many years, a fairly common route to moderate fortune in pioneer society.[93] James Hodgins, who came to Huntley with his father as a boy in 1821, was given 100 acres by his father on coming of age several years later, but partly through timbering operations built up his holdings to 893 acres, despite a bankruptcy in 1844.[94]

The two wealthiest of the North Tipperary emigrants in the Ottawa Valley, William Hodgins and Robert Grant, were both early arrivals; they came on the *Brunswick* with little in 1818 and settled in the Hazeldean neighbourhood. Both made their fortunes in business, put their money into land, and retired to their farms. Hodgins was a member of the freeholding family of that name who lived at Newtown in Modreeny parish. His fortune was based partly upon country storekeeping and partly upon timber dealings.[95] One agreement survives which explains the nature of his lumbering operations. On 1 May 1843 he paid John Mooney (Nellie McClung's father) £6 for the right to cut pine timber on his land just west of the Stoney Swamp in Nepean for twenty-one years.[96] There is also a record of him teaming for Hamnett Pinhey during an election campaign, and it is probable that he also used his waggons in provisioning the lumber camps.[97] These operations were the safest ways of profiting from the volatile timber trade. Such small operators avoided the large timber merchants' ruinous dilemma of expending capital during the winter before news of the state of the British market arrived with the first spring shipping from Liverpool. Hodgins invested heavily in land, purchasing three lots in March and Huntley in the 1820s in addition to his 100–acre free grant in Goulbourn. He continued to amass property, his holdings reaching 1000 acres in 1837, 2000 in 1844, 3000 in 1848, and 4000 in 1853. In the latter year he retired from any active farming he may have been engaged in and gave 480 acres near his home at Hazeldean to his only surviving son, John. John's farm in 1861 was one of the most prosperous in the region. He rented out 100 acres in March, but he farmed the 380 acres in Goulbourn, of which 270 acres were under cultivation, over 200 of that in pasturage for his forty steers and heifers, twenty-one cows, twenty-nine horses, forty sheep, and fourteen pigs. The farm was valued at $22,000,[98] an amount exceeded in western Carleton County only by some of the large, well-stocked farms on the Richmond Road in Nepean, such as Aylen's ($34,300), Thomson's ($26,250), and William Bell's ($24,000), or William Byers's at Twin Elm ($50,000). Hodgins's farm was one of only five in the county to be pictured in an inset on Walling's 1863 map, Byers's and Aylen's being two of the others.[99]

Grant, formerly a clothier in Limerick, kept store at Hazeldean and bought potash.[100] His store appears to have operated between 1838 and 1847. His son later recorded what he knew of his father's business: "During his first years in Canada he worked with the Wrights in Hull in the summer months, coming out to his farm in the winter and working to get a clearance, he later branched into the lumber business, taking his square timber to Quebec, and also started a general store in connection with his lumbering. He seemed to have a decided propensity for investing in farm property, as he had holdings in almost every section of Carleton County and some even in Quebec province."[101] Grant's property grew from 200 acres in 1838 to 1000 ten years later and to 2000 in 1857. The majority of his lands were in Goulbourn, Huntley, and Nepean, though he did own farms in Torbolton, March, Fitzroy, North Gower, Marlborough, Gloucester, and Beckwith. He was still owner of some 1500 acres when he died in the Great Fire that swept western Carleton County in August 1870. One account states that he suffocated and burned trying to rescue money from his house.[102] Needless to say both Hodgins's and Grant's landholdings far exceeded the needs of their immediate families. Both families continued to farm at Hazeldean, and remained community leaders. Grant's eldest son and two of Hodgins's grandsons were elected to the provincial and federal legislatures.

Though a number of immigrants who arrived with little became highly successful for the reasons suggested and were able to pass on developed farms to their sons, there were risks inherent in striving to provide farms for a large family and not all succeeded in the attempt. Trying to settle a large number of sons on the land meant putting one's resources into land purchases at the expense of alternative strategies that could help sons make a living if the gamble failed. William Mooney, a *Brunswick* passenger who helped rescue his fellow-travellers when Richard Talbot's party was shipwrecked on the Lakes,[103] left London after a few years and came east to Huntley where he eventually settled a large family on farms in the neighbourhood. However, he divided the land too finely, several sons receiving only fifty acres. The Mooneys' small holdings could ill support the financial demands of the troubled 1870s. One son lost his farm but regained another, two disposed of their farms and made brief attempts at storekeeping, at least one of which ended in insolvency, in 1876. Two ended the decade living on lands purchased in their wives' names, whether to avoid creditors or actually purchased with their wives' capital it is impossible to say. The youngest son, Robert, sold his land in 1873 and worked as a farm labourer, living with his wealthy father-in-law, Richard Kidd, who had developed the site of Carp village on land that initially belonged to his father-in-law, William Hodgins. Had Mooney foreseen that the acreages he could give to his sons would be insufficient to guarantee their security, he could have made alternate provisions for some of them, but as matters stood he left them with little alternative to farming.

Excessive subdivision was only one way in which such a plan could be thwarted. A change in economic circumstances easily destroyed what had begun well and dealt a devastating blow to the children's futures. The early death of the family head could have a similar effect if his resources were over-extended. Robert Birtch, whom we have already met as the representative of a group of potential emigrants who petitioned the Colonial Office for "encouragement" in 1819, and brother of Tom, the successful Nepean farmer, made a good start in the New World but suffered financial reverses in the late 1840s from which his family never recovered. An innkeeper and merchant in Richmond, Birtch owned 336 1/2 acres of land by 1844, and shortly afterward provided one son with a town lot and three others with 200 acres between them in North Gower. He had earlier sold a farm to his brother, George, who had had singularly bad luck settling down. However, Robert became indebted to Edward Malloch, a prominent merchant, politician, and regional land shark, and his remaining lands were sold in 1850 to repay the debt. He lived latterly on land belonging to his son-in-law and was buried with money left for that purpose by his more prosperous brother. The future life experiences of all his sons were adversely affected by Robert's misfortunes. The eldest was a life-long tenant farmer, first in North Gower and later in Nepean, bequeathing only personal property by his will in 1877. The second son laboured in various townships in Carleton and Russell counties for some twenty years after his marriage but eventually moved his family away. He returned briefly in 1875 when he was sixty years old and was in Goulbourn long enough, again as a labourer, to be arrested and convicted of theft. He served six months in the county gaol.[104] The third sold his part interest in the North Gower lot his father had purchased to buy a park lot in Richmond and was a farmer of two acres in Richmond in 1861 (just before he bought the ten-acre park lot, which he sold in 1866) and of seven acres in Marlborough ten years later. In 1881 his widow was caretaker of the school in Richmond. The fourth son, Robert, was educated at the local Grammar School in the years when the family's fortunes were on the rise[105] and became an Anglican clergyman in Cobourg and Toronto, though apparently an impecunious one as it was his wife who bought out his brothers' interests in the North Gower property. The fifth and sixth sons, William and Adam John, were the "Birtch Brothers," merchants in Richmond. William was a shoemaker, merchant, potash manufacturer, and hotelkeeper, but sold out in 1863[106] and became a tenant farmer in Wawanosh, Huron County. He moved again and died in Manitoba in 1891. Adam J. purchased some of his father's lands when they were auctioned to pay his debts, but he was forced to sell in the 1860s and was recorded as a farm labourer in the 1881 census. He died in Ottawa in 1896. Some of the sons attempted to improve their lot by migrating, but by the time William moved to Wawanosh the frontier of cheap land in Canada West was nearly exhausted and he moved again when new lands in Manitoba became available.

Other immigrants made a good start but had their program of acquisition cut short by death rather than by business reverses. In merely practical terms such a turn of events was a greater crisis than insolvency because it robbed the family of the breadwinner rather than just of accumulated possessions. Thomas Stanley, a black and white smith from Borrisokane who came on the *Brunswick* in 1818, lived and practised his trade in Richmond village but died in 1836 at the age of sixty. Two of his six surviving sons were then of age but none, as yet, were married. Stanley had sold his 100–acre free grant, but retained two-and-a-half town lots and two park lots in Richmond (22 1/2a), and he had recently bought a 200–acre clergy reserve in Nepean, though he had not finished paying for it when he died. Stanley willed a park lot in Richmond to his second son, Thomas, after the death of his wife, and the remainder of his property to his four younger sons equally. In 1842 his widow wrote to the Crown Lands Department that she was experiencing "great difficulty in rearing a small and helpless family and the times having been so bad, I could not have paid up as I could have wished."[107] She died in 1845 and her sons endured the additional expense of laying claim to the clergy reserve before the Heir and Devisee Commission.[108] Title was finally issued in 1856, twenty-five years after Stanley first claimed the lot.

The burden of having to pay off the purchase of their father's most substantial property combined with its inadequacy for supporting four sons to prevent most of the children from achieving a secure station in life. The eldest son, Samuel, required no assistance from his father, for he was one of the children raised to artificial adult status in 1818 when Richard Talbot adjusted the free list of *Brunswick* passengers. As a settler under Talbot he therefore received his own free grant which he sold to buy land in Fitzroy, selling it in turn and moving to the Gatineau in the mid-1850s to obtain farms for his sons there. As the eldest he inherited his mother's village property under the intestacy law, but he signed it over to his brother James. The second son, Thomas Jr, was raised to be a blacksmith like his father, and received a free grant of a town lot in Richmond and inherited the park lot, but he aspired to own farmland, probably to provide for his own sons, so he sold these properties in 1843 and purchased 100 acres in Huntley. He lost this farm for debt, though his son redeemed it for a time. The third son, James, inherited a quarter share in his father's lands and, upon partition, bought out his brothers' rights to half of the Nepean clergy reserve, and also paid for a village lot for his mother in Richmond. However, he apparently worked as the tavernkeeper in the hotel of his kinsman, J.R. Stanley of Bytown, following the latter's death. He seems to have been the only one of the younger sons to have achieved a position of relative security, for he left money to erect gravestones to his parents and brother, though this apparent luxury may merely have reflected his relatively simple family obligations at the time of his premature death. In his will he ordered his lands sold for the benefit of his wife and son but his only son died soon after him. William, the fourth son, bought out his brothers' interests in the village properties but sold them and bought a forty-acre farm in North Gower. Not surprisingly, this proved too small to be viable and he was recorded as a tenant farmer in the 1871 census. In 1872 he purchased 100 acres near Thomas in Huntley, but lost it to a mortgagee in 1884. He was of March at his death in 1898. The son Robert was illiterate and lost his half of the clergy reserve in 1871 and moved back to Richmond. The sixth[109] and youngest son, John, obtained a park lot when he and his brothers partitioned their inheritance in 1847, but this was nothing upon which to build a future. He was living with his sister, Mrs Green, in Fitzroy in 1852 (aged twenty-two), but three years later sold his park lot to the Presbyterian church and went to the United States, where he was still living in 1909. The untimely death of the father of a large family in this way robbed children of an adequate start in life and was a blow from which they never recovered. Most of the Stanleys remained in the area, struggling to make a living as labourers and tenants, evidence that migrationally "stable" families were not necessarily more "successful" than those who moved.

ALTERNATIVES

Migration as a Strategy of Heirship

Most of the successful farmers discussed above managed to obtain land for their sons in the immediate vicinity of the homestead. Some, however, purchased lands for some of their children at a distance, sacrificing the satisfactions of geographical proximity to the obligation to provide for their sons. A number of Huntley families bought in the neighbouring township of Fitzroy, which was occupied later, but most of these lands were not far from the Huntley homesteads. Birtch bought for several of his sons in Cumberland Township, east of Ottawa, which was being settled in the 1840s through 1860s, largely by Carleton County residents. Thomas Rivington also bought land for his eldest son there, and a Goulbourn tenant farmer, Ben Butler, bought there for his son Richard, though the latter sold the land and chose to live on his wife's farm closer to home. George Acres of Hazeldean bought lands for his four oldest sons in Osgoode in the 1870s. Even if proximity had to be sacrificed, the obligation to provide for one's children was very strong.

Buying land in distant places with the intention of settling sons there appears from several studies to have been a fairly common practice among eighteenth-century New Englanders and among residents of the northern states in the nineteenth century,[110] but I have found no example of this among the Tipperary group. If fathers bought for their sons in a new area they generally made the move with them or had the land entered in the sons' names from the beginning, thus hiding the nature of the transaction. When Arthur Hopper of Huntley bought for his three sons in Nepean, for example, his name did not appear in the deeds and his role is disclosed only in a letter he wrote to the attorney general seeking permission to purchase adjoining lands.[111]

However, it was increasingly difficult to obtain land of any quality in the Ottawa area. It has already been noted that after 1830 London began to supplant the valley as the major Tipperary settlement area. The most fertile land in the Ottawa area was disposed of by the crown during the free-grant era and the race for clergy reserves in the 1830s turned to frustration because of frequent changes of policy regarding sales and inept management by the Crown Lands Department. The acquisition of developed land became increasingly expensive as population rose and the demand for land increased. Many late arrivals settled on poor lands for a time and later left, or merely passed through after visiting relatives and learning of better prospects in Tipperary colonies in western Ontario.

Most people who made decisions to migrate made the choice at one of two stages in the life cycle. Some fifty settlers, about a fifth of the immigrant generation, left the area unmarried or with a family of young children. These are the first-generation equivalent of the young migrant sons who left later because they could not be provided for by their fathers. Another fifth of the families remained until the older children were fully grown or nearly so and then departed as a group. In these situations the inability to secure sufficient property or in some other way to guarantee a livelihood for one's self or one's children lay behind the decision to move on.

Forty-six settlers migrated either unmarried or while their families were still young. Moves made prior to marriage or with a family of young children cannot be viewed as inheritance strategies since these moves were not made to secure extra land for children but rather to acquire primary lands for the heads of these families. Almost all of the people who left at these stages of the life cycle obtained no land while in Carleton or Lanark or left because they were defeated in their efforts to secure title. A handful, such as Robert Long who stopped en route from Ireland to McGillivray to visit his brother Michael,[112] and Charles Piper who had a child baptised in March Township in 1847,[113] were just passing through visiting relatives or scouting out possible settlement locations, and moved on to the London area in short order. A few were Tipperary soldiers of the old 100th leaving the military settlement, like many of their compatriots in arms, after discovering that an agricultural life was not for them. Six were merchants or professionals who followed the dictates of business in deciding upon their future residences, while ten moved on to Clarendon in the 1820s and 1830s, some of them giving up good claims in Carleton County for reasons alluded to in a previous chapter.[114] The remaining two dozen or so were landless immigrants, each with his own story. Blaney Cherry from Kyleashinnaun, Modreeny, rented a farm in Fitzroy from his wife's aunt in the early 1840s and then worked for one of the Burritts in Marlborough, with his brother-in-law Moses Wall, before moving west and taking a job in Dundas near Hamilton.[115] Moses Coates lived in Huntley in the late 1830s, where he was recorded as a customer in the account book of Arthur Hopper's store. He returned to Ireland, but came again, this time to the London area, in the 1860s, where he was a labourer in 1871 and a mail carrier ten years later.[116] The family of Luke Hogan, a stonemason from Borrisokane and latterly of Terryglass, was assisted by the Montreal Emigrant Society upon their arrival in 1832, and Hogan lived in Nepean for about ten years, constructing chimneys for all and sundry before moving to Eardley and settling on a farm there.[117]

Among the migrants, family economic strategies were of obvious importance in the case of forty-five families that moved late in the life cycle, that is, when the older children were about to come of age or when some had in fact already married. Such a move, often a three-generation one, was a late attempt both to maintain family solidarity and to provide for all the sons despite the father's failure to secure land for them in the current place of residence. Even those children who were already established on land usually sold out in these cases and accompanied their kin to the new frontier, though in several instances one of the older sons or married daughters remained behind.[118] The aim of securing land for one's sons was thus achieved by the act of migration, for the money obtained by selling a partially developed farm or farms in the Ottawa Valley was sufficient to pay at least a down-payment on lands for all the family elsewhere. Such migrating family connections must be viewed as more "successful" than families that remained in one place at the expense of seeing most of their children descend into poverty.[119]

A number of families displayed this multi-generational pattern, among them the Carters of Goulbourn and Huntley, who moved to McGillivray in the 1830s to provide for the younger sons after the father was killed by a falling tree; the Abbott Lewis connection of Goulbourn and Huntley, whose move to McGillivray, like that of the Carters, included some married daughters but in his case left the eldest son in the Ottawa Valley; and the family of Francis Neil Sr, who moved on to London frustrated by his efforts to obtain deeds to his clergy reserves in Fitzroy, the only land "suitable for sale" in western Carleton County when he arrived from Ireland in 1831.[120]

This three-generation or late-life-cycle move was particularly typical of those like Neil who arrived after free grants were discontinued, which in the Ottawa Valley coincided more or less with the exhaustion of supplies of land of reasonable quality in the townships initially opened under the military administration, apart from the reserves. This pattern is thus especially characteristic of the two subcolonies that located in marginal areas after the good land in the Carp Valley was largely allocated: the group on the Ramsay-Pakenham line, which included the Collinses, and that on the March-Torbolton line. Almost all of the members of these two colonies migrated in this way around 1850, a generation after arriving, as previously recounted. Many had had trouble securing title to land in these locations, partly due to their own poverty and that of the soil, but partly, too, to incompetence and mismanagement in the Crown Lands Department.

Edward Collins had come to Canada in 1822 aged about forty-six with his wife and at least five children, the eldest in his early twenties. The oldest son, Henry, remained in Ireland, married there, and occupied one acre in Newtown (Guest), Modreeny. He followed the family to Canada in 1831–2 with his wife and three or four young children. Edward had moved frequently in Ireland and came to Canada as his sons were coming of age, perhaps turning over his smallholding to son Henry before emigrating.[121]

The Collins family mostly secured land for the first and second generations in Ramsay. Edward received two grants. Henry inherited his father's farm but sold it to Richard, contracting for a clergy reserve in 1847 for himself but never receiving title. Thomas got a grant also but sold it and lived in Kitley. Francis improved and applied for a clergy reserve in 1828, signed the contract in 1847 and received title in 1854, selling it the next year and moving west. Richard came of age in 1837 and six years later inherited 100 acres from his father and bought another 100 from Henry. Henry's son Edward married in 1849 and in 1854 bought 100 acres for $120 from the Wylie trustees, but sold it and moved west, too. The lands were all close together, apart from Thomas's farm in distant Kitley, but, as Francis noted in 1828 when he applied to buy his clergy reserve, the land was of poor quality: "Indeed it [7/6 per acre] is as much as it is worthe. Only that it is convenient to my fathers Land I would not give so much."[122] Francis planned to chop six more acres that summer "which I will Condense to potash for to pay your honr." He received title twenty-six years after making his first application.

Some members of the second generation had acquired title to farms that could only with difficulty support them and provided little hope of settling the members of the third generation securely around them as they came of age. The opening of Bruce County to settlement in the closing years of the 1840s and the settlement there in 1851–2 of a few Tipperary emigrants from the London and Carp areas provided hope of a solution. When the Collinses made the move west in 1854–5 six of the grandsons of the original Edward, who had died in 1843,[123] were aged eighteen or over. The party that went west in these years numbered fifty-one, including the families of two of Henry's sons-in-law, one of whom actually went in 1852, as well as the young family of John Blackwell, a brother of Henry's daughter-in-law. Blackwell, son of an old Ramsay Tipperary settler, had not met the settlement duties on lands in Renfrew County, where his father had moved his family for the same reason the Collinses went to Kincardine, and forfeited his deposit.[124] When the widow Deborah Collins, who had been living with a daughter, moved to Bruce County in her eighties, the three-generation move west became a four-generation one.[125]

Migration as a deliberate strategy of heirship was not a new opportunity that the Tipperary Irish seized in Canada, but rather a variation on an older theme. Emigration was incorporated into family economic strategies by many North Tipperary Protestants who viewed it as a method of making new lives for their children while avoiding further subdivision of their Irish leaseholds.

It was the responsibility of parents to equip their children to emigrate. Thus William Haskett of Gaulross, Borrisokane, wrote to his brother Thomas in "New London," Upper Canada in 1834: "You would wish that I would be with you as you wrote for me to go out this season but I could not go with my finger in me mouth into that country my father is not able to send me."[126] Two seasons later, however, his father Joseph sent Tom both brother William and various articles to ease his life in the new land: "My dear son you may expect Wm out next year if the Lord spares his life and I expect you will wright to me as soon as you receive this and direct us what kind of close to bring out ... let me know what colour is worn there and whether long or short or is there any short jackets worn. You said to take out some delf. But you will be pleased to let me know what kind you mean and let me know in particular what kind of ... seeds you mean to go out to you likewise." Letters inquired also about economic prospects for remaining members of the family, and about preparations that should be made at home to ready children to earn a living in the new land: "Dear Son send me an account of the sheep in that country, their sise or wait and Dear Son we would wish to know the produce of your ground. Let me know how many barrels of corn of every sort is to the acre. Likewise how many barrels of potatoes is to the acre. Tell me is there such things as schools in that country. Is Dress Making a good business then the way I can improve Mary ann before she goes to that country. Can a single man do well or is he better with a wife when he lands there." By sending his children to Canada as they came of age, Joseph avoided subdividing the twenty-two acres in Gaulross he had inherited from his father, who had been a freeholder there in 1776.[127]

The emigrants did not always expect the separation from the older generation to be permanent. Many expected their parents to join them. Joseph Haskett wrote to Tom in 1835: "as for myself and family I am not determined on going out next season against the time Wm. is going out and I will be a better judge of what time I will be able to go." In the end, Joseph remained at home, and several of his younger children went to New Zealand. Similarly, Johnny Neil of Croghan near Birr expected his father Dan to come out to him in the Ottawa Valley. Though he was joined by several brothers, the parents remained in Ireland.[128] In 1849 Thomas Haskett still hoped that his mother-in-law Mrs White would join his family in London, but his sister conveyed the message that "she is too old to go out to you."[129]

Sometimes a farmer turned over his holding to one of the sons and took the rest of the family to Canada. George Carter, whose family repeated in Canada this practice of moving late in the life cycle, was a farmer on the Otway estate at Fantane in the parish of Glankeen, where he was a tenant at will of twenty Irish acres at a rental of £23.10 per annum. In 1821 he turned over his farm to his eldest son Thomas[130] and migrated with his remaining children, the eldest of whom were also reaching adult age. Indeed the second son, George Jr, married at about age twenty-one just before the family emigrated.[131] The father and sons George and William all obtained free grants in the Richmond military settlement.

Though it was logical in the Carter example for the farm to be given to the eldest son, this was by no means an invariable pattern. In other instances the process more closely resembled that commonly found in Canada later in which the older sons left home first, leaving the home place to the youngest. This was the case with the Sifton family, also from the Otway estate. Joseph Sifton had leased forty-four Irish acres in Gurtadrahawn for three lives in 1760,[132] and in 1806 his son Charles held both this land and a lease for the term of his own life of a further sixty acres in East Glantane. The two eldest sons, Joseph and Bamlet, married in Ireland and presumably both took up portions of their father's lands there; certainly Bamlet occupied the Glantane property in 1824.[133] The next two sons, Charles and John, who were both unmarried at the time, emigrated on the *Brunswick* in 1818, and their favourable report brought out the parents, brother Joseph and his family, sister Rebecca and her husband Joseph Wallis, and the remainder of the unmarried siblings the next year. Bamlet brought his family in 1832.[134] According to family tradition the youngest son, Robert, came close to inheriting the ancestral homestead. A descendant recalled: "Am certain Robert was the youngest son being 10 years old when he came with his parents to this country. His father Charles was a Tinnent Farmer for Col. Ottway. The lease was a hundred year one running from father to youngest son. At this time the older son or sons of Charles had left Ireland. Col. Ottway wanted Charles to renew the lease for Robert the youngest son he refused now that part of his family had left Ireland and he with the remaining ones were going follow them to America."[135] The lease was one for lives, not 100 years, and the terms of the lease did not specify which heir was to inherit possession, but it may be significant that the Sifton family later assumed that the youngest was to be heir. Certainly Robert Sifton did not take over the lease to Gurtadrahawn, which was in the hands of John Ardil ("late C. Siftons") in 1824.[136]

Evidence on inheritance practices among the tenantry in North Tipperary is extremely fragmentary, for complete runs of registered deeds for any one freehold property are very rare. These documents do not in any case always record subdivision within a family. As in Canada, there was no hard and fast rule that dictated how land should be passed on, though custom often assumes an importance beyond its original practical foundations.[137] We have already seen in the Canadian context how customary practices and the provisions of the law were at odds, and we know that in Ireland the forbidding of subdivision both by law and by many landlords proved unenforceable. Determining whether the balance between preferences approximating primogeniture, ultimogeniture, and partibility altered over time as emigration increasingly removed farming families from competition for Irish lands depends upon the analysis of better runs of estate records than currently exist for North Tipperary in the public domain.[138] The tithe applotments of the 1820s and 1830s and the Primary Valuation of the early 1850s are too far apart to be much help in answering this question, and more importantly it is hard to know whether to assign credit for the evident consolidation of holdings noted in freeholders' communities by 1850 to emigration or to the Famine of the 1840s. However, since the farming classes escaped the Famine relatively unscathed, unlike the labouring poor, it is likely that the Famine consolidated an existing trend against subdivision by farmers which was made possible by the heavy emigration of members of this class. Whether the eldest son or the youngest succeeded to the tenancy, the important point is that emigration became a key mechanism by which subdivision was avoided. The Dunalley estate in Modreeny remained a community of substantial freeholders in large part because at least 100 Protestant families departed for Canada between 1818 and the mid-1850s, leaving more land to be divided among those who remained behind. It was only natural that some families adopted internal migration within Canada as a strategy of heirship for similar reasons.

Purchase of Land by Sons

Of course, it was not always possible for a farmer to provide all his sons with land, but moving the whole family to a new frontier was not always an ideal solution either, especially if a father had sufficient resources to develop his own land and provide farms for at least some of his sons. Some sons purchased land. Altogether we find fourteen instances in which fathers provided land for some children while others bought land, usually the older boys. This pattern was most evident in established families living in the old and fertile areas of settlement, the Hazeldean neighbourhood and the Carp Valley, as was also the case with the prosperous farmers who were able to provide farms for all their sons. In some cases, however, there is evidence that the father was unable to provide for some of those who bought. Thomas Acres of March was a carpenter as well as a farmer, but carpentering was not a prosperous by-employment and his two eldest sons wrote in 1832 for a clergy reserve in Torbolton, noting that their father had eleven children at home to support.[139] The government's auction policy defeated this attempt, but Thomas was able to provide his eldest with a clergy reserve sixteen years later, while the second son married a widow who held her husband's goodwill to a farm. The third son inherited the homestead and was able to provide well for his five sons, but the fourth brother rented the old Hopper farm at South March, which had formerly belonged to the brother of his wife's stepmother, though he also bought land in Huntley.[140]

However, the purchase of land by some sons does not necessarily reflect parental inability to provide land, for the land may in some instances have been purchased with the father's assistance. Where there is evidence that this was the case, the families have been included in other categories. In other instances, purchases by the sons reflected fortuitous changes in land policy, particularly the adoption by the government in the 1850s of a policy of instalment sales of crown lands on easy terms with low down-payments. This facilitated the acquisition of property by those with little capital,[141] though available lots close to home tended to be of poor quality and again we cannot eliminate the possibility that the down-payment may have been provided by the father.

In seven cases all sons bought land in the area, and in eight some purchased while others became tradesmen. In both these categories the people concerned were often children of poor families, so parental assistance in these instances likely failed. In nine cases sons migrated leaving the parents behind, a similar suggestion of poverty. However, even if parental assistance failed in all of the twenty-nine instances in which at least some sons had to buy land (which, as already explained, is unlikely), these cases were outnumbered by those in which all sons were provided for (thirty-six such cases) and nearly equalled by those in which the whole clan moved to a new location. In a further twenty-three instances fathers provided for landless sons by raising them for a trade.

Trades and Professions

Providing lands for as many sons as one was able and seeing that others were apprenticed to a trade or given a cash stake to go into some form of business was another heirship compromise, but one which required some foresight. Twenty-three fathers provided land for some sons, either by bequest or by early transfer, while raising other sons to a trade or profession. Four of these fathers and another nine who raised sons to trades only and did not give them land were themselves tradesmen or professionals who put their sons into occupations similar to their own. In a few cases some of the sons became farmers like their fathers while others were educated for the professions, a sure sign of high aspirations and some financial success, even if the prestigious occupation was reserved for a younger child whose education became the culmination of a lifetime of hard work by the older members of the family.

Among the farming families, training for non-agricultural occupations aside from the professions seems not to have been a desired alternative but rather an option resorted to if the family lacked the resources to provide land to make farmers of all the sons. Putting a younger son to a trade was a fairly common strategy adopted in cases where the father died prematurely and was unable to complete his projected program of land acquisition. One finds apprenticeship to a trade, often at the option of the child, with a cash bequest the alternate choice, in the wills of fathers who died leaving young children, as in the case of Thomas Hodgins of Huntley who gave land to his eldest son in his lifetime, willed land to two more, and left money to the last two along with instructions that they be put to a trade. [142] More often the decisions were made by the survivors, who reached a practical solution to the problem at hand.

Tradesmen often raised their children to be tradesmen, since this was by far the most inexpensive option open to them. A poor blacksmith or carpenter, often lacking land himself, had little other way to prepare his sons to earn a livelihood, and training them himself avoided the expenses involved in putting a boy out to a local craftsman to learn a trade. Necessity was probably at least as important as choice in leading members of succeeding generations to follow their fathers into trades. A contrasting example, however, is provided by Samuel Hawkshaw, who first appeared in the Ottawa Valley in the mid-1830s as a shoemaker in Fitzroy Harbour village, [143] and later followed that trade in March Township, where he rented ten acres. He was listed in 1871 and 1881 as a farmer in Huntley Township, but he never owned any land. Three of his seven sons became carpenters and two were blacksmiths. Another was listed as an apprentice in 1871 but was gone ten years later. Only the second son, James, may have been a farmer. He purchased fifty acres in Torbolton several years before his marriage in 1865, but he died in 1868 at the age of twenty-eight without local records ever recording his occupation. It is interesting that none of the sons became shoemakers like their father.

Of course, not all tradesmen were poor. John Nicholson, a cabinetmaker from Templemore, was in Fitzroy Harbour as early as 1837, and he later owned quite extensive village property there. His sons, too, followed non-agricultural occupations. James, the eldest, followed in his father's footsteps, and Edmund may have also, for though he was a blacksmith as a young man he inherited his father's shop tools and machinery. The youngest son, Henry, became a printer in England.[144] Larger enterprises, such as distilling and brewing, required a fair outlay of capital. Ralph Smith has been credited with operating in Hull the first brewery in the Ottawa area. During visits to Ireland he was able to draw upon the expertise of his Birch cousins who operated an extensive brewery at Roscrea.[145] Smith's distant cousin Isaac also operated a brewery in Bytown, as did George R. Burke, son of Captain Burke of the military settlement. None of these operations proved profitable in the end. For some the practice of a trade was a step up. Joshua Dudley, a labourer who came to Fitzroy Township in the Famine period of the late 1840s, moved to Pembroke in the 1860s and was a labourer there. Nevertheless, his eldest son became a wheelwright and carriagemaker in Pembroke, his second son a blacksmith, and the third was a bookkeeper in 1881 at the age of twenty-three.

Some city people were really rural people at heart and bought farms for their sons rather than continue them in urban businesses. J.R. Stanley, a native of Borrisokane, was a servant in Modreeny parish before leaving Ireland in 1830. He worked initially as a steward on a steamboat in the Montreal area but soon came to the Ottawa Valley and secured interest in lands near his first wife's family in Fitzroy. He opened a store and hotel in Bytown and lost the Fitzroy lands to creditors during the 1837 financial crisis. However, he bought farmland in Nepean for two sons, and another farmed near an uncle in Osgoode.[146] Stanley's son-in-law Jonathan Mossop, also from Borrisokane, was tollkeeper on the Union Suspension Bridge between Hull and Bytown of which Stanley was lessee of the bridge tolls, but he retired to a farm in Osgoode just before he died.[147]

Ironically, sons raised to non-agricultural occupations frequently ended their careers in more prosperous and prominent circumstances than their farming brothers, if the occupation was chosen carefully. The siblings who continued farming were soon caught in the same dilemma their fathers had faced: how to buy up land for their sons when they themselves had had little enough of a head start because of their own fathers' limited means. The developing Canadian economy and the rising non-rural sector, however, provided opportunities for those who entered the right trades. Blacksmiths only occasionally became foundry-owners and carpenters sometimes became contractors. We do have examples of the latter phenomenon among the Tipperary group. Apprenticeship to these trades or the dead-end craft of shoemaking was the most financially achievable option for the poor farmer. Country merchants and innkeepers, in contrast, often achieved prosperity and local prominence, rising with the development of rural villages at local crossroads and railway depots. A remarkable instance is the family of Benjamin D. Butler, a lifelong tenant farmer who rented land in Goulbourn from William Hodgins, probably a close relative of Butler's wife. Butler's farm was a prosperous one, though he never owned it.[148] He purchased land for his fourth son, Richard, but his remaining five sons became merchants and hotelkeepers. The eldest, William Henry, "struck out for himself" at fifteen years of age and learned the tanning trade, and became a merchant, postmaster for fifty-two years, justice of the peace, and reeve in Richmond. His was a nineteenth-century success story, and his biography and a cut of his store were duly included in the county atlas in 1879. He may have suffered later reverses, for in his old age he was a shoemaker in Ottawa.[149] His brother John was a hotelkeeper in Carp, and his two youngest brothers both kept hotels called the Butler House. Thomas's opened in Ottawa in 1879, where he later was an alderman and unsuccessful mayoralty candidate,[150] and James ran a hotel at Stittsville for twenty-five years.[151] The third son, Ben Jr, had the kind of unsuccessful career one might more have expected of the landless son of a tenant farmer. He clerked in Richmond and later at Carp with John while still a young man but in 1864, during his sojourn in Huntley, he fathered an illegitimate daughter and was acquitted of poisoning a second girl he had impregnated.[152] He appears, not surprisingly, to have left the neighbourhood after that, but by 1881 he had returned. He was married with three children in that year, but the family all lived with that of his brother James, the later Stittsville hotelkeeper, and the elderly parents on the old rented homestead. Ben Jr died at the Butler House in Ottawa ten years later.[153]

It was probably the productivity of a well-improved farm, and possibly lenient treatment because of his wife's kinship to the landlord, that allowed Butler to establish most of his sons in secure businesses, even though he was only a tenant farmer. In other instances, personal connections and the stimulus of evangelical religion laid the groundwork for successful careers by the sons of struggling farmers. Frank Abbott from Cloonawillan, Aglish-cloghane, was not well off and spent his first few years in Canada working as a sawyer in Montreal.[154] He came to Nepean around 1828 and arranged with the occupant of a clergy reserve to get half of the latter's lease. After the occupier was killed by a falling tree, Abbott managed to substantiate his claim against assertions of the widow with the aid of local gentleman Hamnett

Pinhey. He was unable to acquire extra lands for his sons until 1854, when he mortgaged the homestead he had already settled on his seventh and youngest son Adam to buy farms for his third and sixth sons. The eldest had in the meantime gone to Biddulph in 1840, married there, and taken land from the Canada Company. Frank provided for three sons by apprenticing them to trades in Bytown in the late 1840s. Francis Jr learned the carpenter's trade and worked as a foreman on the works of the Rideau Canal, retiring as paymaster, and served on Ottawa City Council, the Board of Education, and as an original trustee of the Protestant Hospital.[155] Frank used his connections in the Orange Order to apprentice sons John B. and Richard as printers on the *Ottawa Advocate* newspaper, operated by prominent local Orangemen Dawson Kerr and W.P. Lett. During his residence in Montreal, Abbott had helped found one of the first civilian Orange lodges in Canada in conjunction with his fellow Tipperary emigrés Arthur Hopper and William Burton.[156] John later edited newspapers in Simcoe and St Marys[157] and Richard helped establish the Ottawa *Monarchist,* became deputy sheriff of Carleton County, and was latterly a contractor.[158]

Richard Groves, a carpenter from Cloughjordan, and his brother John, appear to have been influenced by their espousal of Methodist progressive self-help doctrine to have high ambitions for their youngest sons.[159] Both managed to buy farms in Fitzroy in the 1840s, some years after emigrating, and gave land to some sons, and raised the rest to trades. However, Richard's two youngest sons became doctors, Dr George Hodgins Groves of Carp, a McGill graduate and onetime nominee for the House of Commons, and Dr Wesley Groves of Quyon.[160] John's youngest also was a doctor, Dr J. Wilson Groves (b. 1850), a Toronto graduate and a skin specialist in Ottawa who earlier practised in Manotick.[161]

CONCLUSION

Migration, devolution of land, and apprenticeship were all strategies of heirship. One cannot examine migration without attempting to understand its causes in this context and without at least briefly looking at the alternatives. A very large proportion of the Protestants of North Tipperary emigrated because the only alternative, subdivision of holdings, was highly unattractive. That the majority settled in two communities in Upper Canada is again a testimony to the importance of family in the lives of these people. Providing for their children was the most important goal these settlers shared and their achievement of this aim should be the major measure of their success or failure. Because most had large families, few were able to provide land for all their sons, but half of the young men coming of age in non-migratory families living on the Ontario side of the Ottawa Valley during the study period were provided with farms by their parents. Some sons purchased land and it is reasonable to expect that in at least some cases they did so with parental assistance. Parents were also largely responsible for putting sons to a trade, even when the choice of trade was left to the son, because of the young age at which apprenticeship began. About a fifth of all families studied in that region, a quarter of those who remained for any significant length of time, adopted migration as a strategy of heirship, selling lands and using the money to buy more and cheaper land further west. Fifteen of the families who adopted this plan did so essentially at the last minute, migrating as multi-generational groups. Another fifth of the immigrating generation moved on because they could not secure lands even for the first generation, but most of these people were able to secure property at their immediate destination. Even when it proved necessary to apprentice sons to a trade this seldom took children out of a rural environment. Comparatively few moved into the city by 1881. The Ontario descendants of North Tipperary Protestants were still at heart a rural people. The flood of movement into Manitoba, the beginnings of which have been traced, is a testimony to the tenaciousness of the rural way of life.

CHAPTER NINE

Conclusions

MIGRATION AND HEIRSHIP

North Tipperary is not a part of Ireland that stands out in the existing literature as one that contributed large numbers of emigrants to nineteenth-century Canada nor, buried as it is deep in the heart of southern Ireland, has it been recognized as an area which contributed significantly to the numbers of emigrant Protestants who made up two-thirds of Upper Canada's Irish population. Though Protestants made up only 8.5 per cent of North Tipperary's people in 1831, they formed (and still form) one of the largest clusters of non-Catholic population in the south. Also, emigration from the region, particularly before the 1840s, was mostly Protestant. The 775 families that left for the Canadas during the period covered by this study, most in the generation between 1818 and 1855, were equal to a quarter of the Protestant population of the region in 1831.

The significance of Tipperary Protestant emigration becomes apparent in a regional context for, as we have seen, the migrations of the Tipperary people continued to follow the earliest-established channels of movement between localities in the two countries. The largest primary settlements of North Tipperary Protestants were north of London and in the Carp Valley west of Ottawa, areas 400 miles apart but intimately connected by the relationships and movements of their residents.

The predominance of Protestants in North Tipperary emigration in this period was the result of socio-economic circumstances that predisposed this group to leave and also made emigration by them possible. The emigrants were rural as well as Protestant, for town-dwellers were under-represented among the migrants at both ends of the route. Those who left were the middling farmers and tradesmen, who faced declining status and prosperity in an overpopulated agricultural region. By leaving Ireland they hoped to preserve or recover, as emigrant farmers, the status and economic well-being that was slipping from their grasp at home as further subdivision of already-reduced holdings became the only way of accommodating the rising generation. One must not exaggerate the economic standing of the emigrants. That the residents of Biddulph in 1840 were among the poorest in the Huron Tract suggests that many of those who came had the means to emigrate and make a down-payment on land but little more. Nonetheless the aim they sought, on both sides of the Atlantic, was to provide a secure future for their children by establishing their sons on farms of a size adequate to support a family and by seeing their daughters married to the sons of other farmers.

Emigration may appear in retrospect to have been the natural solution to the problems these people faced, but such a major decision required a catalyst to stimulate action. The initial incentive was provided by the British government's short-lived £10 deposit plan of sponsored group emigration, which was seized upon by a Tipperary gentleman, Richard Talbot, as the answer to his own problem of declining status. Once the process of migration was begun, the channel remained open as long as opportunity to acquire farms at reasonable prices existed at the western end. A few small settlements were formed distant from the two largest colonies, mostly in 1819 by emigrants who left Ireland before receiving word of where their friends who left with Talbot in 1818 had gone, but the members of these small settlements mostly moved on to London in later years. After the mid-1830s immigrants went more often to London than to the Ottawa Valley, as the good land in the Ottawa area had been granted away by that time. Within another ten years most of the land had also been alienated in London Township and in the Canada Company's Township of Biddulph to its north, where settlement of Tipperary people had been encouraged by James Hodgins, one of their own. Later arrivals remained for a time in these primary settlements, but after gaining a small capital they moved on to acquire lands in secondary settlements in newly opened areas. In other ways the Tipperary Protestants who emigrated in the Famine era were little different from their brothers who emigrated earlier. Almost all the Famine era migrants seem to have come out to relatives already in Canada. A small number settled in the cities, but after the mid-1850s Protestant emigration from North Tipperary turned from Canada to new frontiers in Australia and New Zealand.

The Canadian secondary settlements were formed by people from the primary settlements in the London vicinity and especially by those in the Carp Valley. Members of Carleton County families successively settled Clarendon in the 1820s and 1830s, Russell in the late 1840s and 1850s, and the Kazabazua area on the Gatineau River in the 1850s and 1860s. In this regional migration the family was a mechanism subsidiary to the neighbourhood and these secondary settlements were therefore not composed exclusively of Tipperary families but also of members of the other Irish Protestant groups that had settled in the Carp Valley. Kinship was the major mechanism, however, in the movement of the smaller clusters of Tipperary families who deserted their initial farms on marginal lands in Ramsay and Torbolton after a generation and moved to form new secondary settlements at Cobden and North Onslow in the late 1840s and 1850s. Kinship was also the dominant mechanism in movement out of the region, for in such instances personal inspection of available lands was seldom possible because of the distances involved and the difficulty of transportation; the advice and encouragement of relatives assumed great importance. The primary settlement near London, more specifically the newly settled township of McGillivray to its northwest, was also the major external secondary settlement for the Tipperary people of the Ottawa Valley. The colony at Bervie, near Kincardine in Bruce County, was formed in the 1850s by migrants from both major primary settlements, while smaller clusters were formed by small networks of kin from the Ottawa Valley at Chatsworth near Owen Sound, in Lambton County, and in Marlborough province on the South Island of New Zealand. Aside from the Bervie colony, the London group estabished no secondary settlements in Canada. Farmers continued to buy farms for their sons as near as possible to their homesteads, with the result that the settlement pattern gradually diffused outwards from the initial core. Around London, however, the Tipperary people were more numerous than those around Ottawa, more concentrated, and lived in a region of better quality land that was in great demand. One result was that more of these families moved into the city than was the case in the Ottawa Valley. There also appears to have been much greater movement to the United States from around London, though whether these migrants formed clustered secondary settlements there remains undetermined.

The arrival of the railways changed these migrational patterns by permitting personal exploratory trips to distant areas with potential for settlement. This type of journey only became common when farmers' excursion fares were introduced in the late 1870s to facilitate settlement of the new Canadian west. Chain migration by families remained common, but small groups of kin tended to settle in various areas of Manitoba that caught their fancy. A group of Biddulph families scattered in the general vicinity of Crystal City, but they were part of a general migration from western Ontario stimulated by the colonizing efforts of the former Huron member of parliament, Thomas Greenway. Conversely, the extension of the railway network from the 1850s onwards also strengthened ties between distant relatives by facilitating visiting, though such travel was still restricted by the demands of farm work. Visits by non-farmers, women, and young people, sometimes for extended periods in which the visitors worked with the host families, renewed personal associations with relatives who had parted many years earlier and extended this sense of family to new generations. In some families multiple cousin and second-cousin marriages resulted from these visits in the 1880s.

The channels migration took during most of the period with which this study is concerned were determined by the information, advice, and assistance given by family members who had moved previously, and the Tipperary Protestants illustrate the various types of group, chain, and gravitational migration discussed by theorists of population movement. The timing of the moves related to economic and social conditions that were also linked with family. Underlying both external and internal migration was the desire to build a secure future for one's children. Because this was so, it makes little sense to discuss population movement without also examining strategies of heirship, for migration itself was often conceived in these terms.

The kinship system that operated among these settlers had an internal logic to its operation that makes sense of itself, but the logic of the system was worked out within the context of local circumstances and is best understood in those terms. The aims, however, seem to have remained constant. In the context of migration, kinship was an operative mechanism on a bilateral level, for the people studied were as likely to move with female or maternal kin as with male relatives. In terms of the devolution of land, however, property was strictly heritable in the male line. Land was ideally partible between all one's sons but this was possible in practice only when a farmer had become fairly prosperous. Avoiding ruinous subdivision was a major reason why these Irish farmers had adopted emigration as a strategy of heirship in the early nineteenth century. Ideally, sons were rewarded with lands as a free gift in return for the labour they had devoted to the family farm, but in practice most parents required some monetary compensation against lost income when turning property over to children.

In practice, older sons were provided for as they came of age, either with additional lands or by providing training for a trade. The homestead normally went to the youngest son, who had the least time to wait till his father's retirement. This effective ultimogeniture was sensible in the context of Canadian farms and Canadian life expectancies, but at higher levels of society, amongst the immigrant gentry, a bias towards the British system of primogeniture prevailed, reflecting a concern to preserve the homestead for the eldest son who would carry on the family name and authority, ignoring the fact that status and position in these families was no longer based upon land-holding as it had been in Ireland. In the towns, too, where land did not constitute the means of production, a different system prevailed in which real estate or the proceeds from its sale were divided equally among sons and daughters. The intestacy law in Upper Canada reflected the aristocratic system before 1852 and the urban system thereafter, causing farmers to use wills, maintenance agreements (the importance of which was not reflected in the Registry Act), and private family arrangements to ensure that property devolved as they intended.

The principle of male descent of property determined the provisions made for stepsons and women. Stepsons were outside the male line and were in theory provided for by their own fathers. Because in practice their fathers had often died before securing sufficient land for the next generation, these sons were frequently left landless, but could expect no more than a cash bequest from their stepfathers, no matter how prosperous the latter were. There was a strong belief nonetheless in the propriety of helping to establish all one's children in life. The provision to daughters was complementary to that given to sons, for girls received dowries of cash, goods, and livestock to help them set up a household on the land received from their husbands' families. This was a traditional form of dowry in Britain, which was superseded in Canada in the mid-nineteenth century by cash dowries, or sometimes by education, a reflection of changing circumstances as land became more expensive and the likelihood of all girls marrying farmers or even marrying at all declined. Widows were often given control over the same types of goods they had brought to the marriage, but they were also given the greatest possible control over their husbands' estates consistent with the principle of preserving the land for male heirs. In fully half the wills examined, widows were given control of the farm for life. This was by far the most common form of provision, but the next most common option, that of guaranteeing them rooms or a house plus support, also ensured them a secure future. When widows were left to the care of a son (for only a son inheriting land could be legally obligated to provide for his mother), elaborate testamentary provisions or maintenance agreements spelled out what the women's rights were in the event of disagreement between the generations. That a widow's provision ceased upon remarriage again reflected the lineality of landed property, for the women were provided for by their new husbands and the land therefore reverted to the male heirs of the first marriage. The explanation lies in the logic of an integrated system of family economic strategies, not in some bizarre wish to enforce fidelity from beyond the grave.

Migration operated within this context of heirship strategies and was only one of a number of methods adopted, according to circumstances, to ensure the future of the family. Alternatives to partible inheritance were necessary because not all families were able to secure sufficient land to set up all their sons on viable holdings. In nineteenth-century Canada, however, unlike the Tipperary these people had left, other options were open. Sons could be put to a trade or could operate a shop or tavern in the expanding village network, thanks to the developing economy. Changes in government land policy and, until the 1860s, colonization of new frontiers or pockets of unsettled land, enabled the purchase of farms by young men or their movement to other rural areas where relatives suggested a bargain was to be had. Some farmers became prosperous, largely as a result of arriving early enough to secure good land and buying up more while it was still relatively inexpensive, using the profits of the farm or supplementing their income from the revenues of tavernkeeping or timber contracting. Some of these farmers began educating sons for the professions by mid-century.

Some fifty of the Tipperary families who came to the Ottawa Valley, a fifth of the total, left fairly quickly because they failed to obtain land there. Another fifth of the inmigrants remained for a generation but failed to secure sufficient land for the sons and preserved family solidarity by selling out and moving to a frontier of cheap land when the new generation began to come of age. This sometimes became a multi-generational migration when the move was put off until after some of the children had married. The families who remained on the Ontario side of the Ottawa Valley were successful in seeing most of their sons established within the region, one way or another. Only 10 per cent of the sons of these families left without obtaining land while more than half received farms from their fathers. Twenty per cent received free grants or bought land, whether with parental assistance or not it is impossible to say. Another 15 per cent entered the trades or professions, probably with parental assistance. Though a detailed investigation of devolutionary patterns in the London area was not undertaken, it is evident that in that populous area of first-class land a much greater proportion of the population had to leave farming than was the case in the Ottawa Valley. By 1881 nearly a quarter of the Tipperary families in or near London lived in the city or in the town of Lucan, whereas only 10 per cent of Carleton residents lived in Ottawa. Though the urbanization of these rural families no doubt continued, they did not work in industry and large numbers of the landless flooded into Manitoba and the west in the 1880s, continuing the search for rural land.

There were inevitably a few loners who operated outside the family system and did not even feel the need to maintain a link with their relatives back home. We have the last letter that a wanderer, Frank Jones's brother Robert, sent back: "I was sprse to think that you should take curage to right to me but I am glad that you have don so, but it was a chance that I got your letter, for I have not been in Oakland for tow years ... I have not heard from any for the last three or four years, and it seem to me that I did not care to heare from them, I do not know how rote the last letter, nor did I care, but if you wish to right to me a gaine let me know how all the fox is right soon for I may not stop long theare."[1] The fact that such letters were kept, however, suggests that the families left behind cared to hear from the brothers and sisters in service in England, or the brothers in California or Oregon. What is remarkable about the Tipperary settlers is how few were loners and true transients, and how few people I have lost track of in my research. Most of the missing people are individuals rather than partners in a family unit, emphasizing again the point that it was families who made the trek along the beaten path where others of their kind had gone before. We are fortunate to have the thoughts of wanderers like Robert Jones about his lifestyle, but for a young man of Tipperary Protestant descent they were unusual ideas to have.

A WIDER SIGNIFICANCE

The practice of chain migration was by no means unique to the people who have been the subject of this study. I have already pointed out many examples of clustered settlements in the London and Ottawa areas that drew their populations from parts of England and Germany as well as from other areas of Ireland. Among at least some of these groups chain migration continued to operate internally as it did among the Tipperary Irish. Sometimes this took the form of neighbourhood migration, as it did among the residents of Peel that Norris traced to Euphrasia Township, or the inhabitants of Lanark who followed their member of parliament, Malcolm Cameron, to Sarnia. In other cases internal migration related more closely to kinship and created secondary settlements of families drawn from single parts of Ireland who had initially resided elsewhere in Canada. The large Wexford group in eastern Ontario, for example, gave birth to secondary settlements in Stafford Township, Renfrew County,[2] and Brooke Township, Lambton County, around mid-century. Most of the inhabitants of these new clusters had lived in Beckwith for a generation.[3] Similarly, the Kilcooly Protestants of the Streetsville neighbourhood formed a secondary settlement beginning in the 1830s in Goderich Township, at the opposite end of the Huron Tract from the North Tipperary primary settlement in Biddulph.[4]

For this reason the experiences of the Tipperary Protestants are of wider relevance in evaluating some of the assertions made by historians about Irish emigration in general and Protestant emigration in particular. Kerby Miller, in his important and stimulating study of Irish emigration to North America based on a close study of a vast collection of emigrants' letters, considers chain migration to have been characteristic of the most impoverished Irish Catholics,[5] rooted in a communitarian world of "clachan settlements, rundale and joint tenancies, partible inheritance, and other customs which materially reinforced archaic 'dependent' or 'interdependent' outlooks, including strong communal and familial inhibitions against individual initiative and improvement,"[6] and in which "a profound parochialism and inertia ... reflected a general Catholic worldview emphasizing stasis rather than action."[7] Catholics from the more commercialized eastern districts came during the early nineteenth century to share what he took to be the more individualist Protestant attitude.[8] He notes that after about 1820 Irish Protestants in the United States were increasingly reluctant to burden themselves with emigrant relatives and urged that the newcomers make their own way.[9] Miller views emigration among the Protestants not as a family economic strategy but as a refuge for the disinherited,[10] and notes that fathers stifled rebellion by non-inheriting children by instilling in them a sense of inferiority and submissiveness. Moreover, the families of strong farmers drew "rigid social lines between themselves and less fortunate relations."[11]

All of this seems foreign to the experience of the Tipperary Protestants. The patterns of migration and settlement I have traced indicate that precedent was the major motive force in settlement selection. Once the initial incentive was provided by the £10 deposit plan of sponsored group emigration, the migration channel remained open as long as opportunity to acquire farms existed at the western end. Chain migration continued to be a major factor in later generations as secondary settlements were formed by people from the first settlement locations. If chain migration was characteristic of impoverished Catholics from the most traditional and communitarian parts of Ireland, it was no less evident among large numbers of Protestant Irish who settled in Canada.

Miller does acknowledge that Quakers and Ulster-American farmers assisted relatives more readily than urban Protestants, "knowing they could always feed and employ the newcomers as laborers on their holdings."[12] But since Akenson has demonstrated that the vast majority of the Irish in Ontario, both Protestant and Catholic, were farmers, one should not be content to dispose of such experiences in a sentence as exceptional and conclude with Miller that the Protestant Irish in America generally took an instrumental attitude to business, kinship, and inheritance. Among the Tipperary emigrants it was the most successful who were best able to honour moral obligations to assist less fortunate relatives, and their households were often temporary homes, sometimes for years, to various newly arrived kin. Nor was the line between businessmen and farmers so clear-cut in early nineteenth-century Canada as Miller appears to think it was in the United States. The most successful farmers achieved their status by engaging in non-agricultural occupations such as store- and tavernkeeping, timbering and provisioning, ploughing the capital so generated back into the land. Many small merchants and tradesmen continued to move among hamlets, villages, towns, and cities as opportunity dictated, as they had in Ireland, and in the period with which this study is concerned the large majority of Tipperary people abroad retained a strong preference for a rural way of life.

The objectives of the Tipperary Protestants in coming to Canada – seeking to improve their condition and to preserve a privleged status enjoyed at home – are those Miller notes as typical of a comparatively small number of "voluntary exiles" who were "no longer bound to the traditional, communalistic constraints of Gaelic peasant culture."[13] However, in following to America relatives who had already emigrated, "settl[ing] in communal or family groups rather than as solitary figures," and being "ambitious for themselves and their children," they resembled another type of emigrant Miller feels trod the line between "traditional and modern patterns of thinking and behaving." Miller states that such people were fundamentally mistaken in thinking that such communalistic ideals had a place in America. Those who succeeded were "assimilated to the bourgeois values characteristic of life in the New World." But more were to become disillusioned. The Catholics among them, noted Miller, became the "most devoted and bitter adherents" of the Irish-American nationalist movement.[14]

Though Miller's study addresses emigration to Canada as well as movement to the United States, the comments he makes here typify the traditional view of the Irish in America. The example of the Tipperary Protestants demonstrates that the experience of the Irish in Canada was vastly different, and one feels that the experiences of the Irish who settled in rural parts of the United States will prove, too, to resemble the Canadian patterns. In nineteenth-century Canada, and in the United States, the basic rural unit of production was the family farm of a hundred or a couple of hundred acres, not the large capital-intensive agricultural enterprise employing large numbers of labourers. In the Ottawa Valley a very few extensive farms were operated by timber barons such as Philemon Wright, John Egan & Co., and George Bryson[15] to produce animals and foodstuffs for the shanties, but even there hay and produce purchased in small quantities from thousands of individual farmers were far more important in firing the engines of the timber trade and stimulating high prices and agricultural prosperity in the valley.[16] Capital-intensive agriculture, though strengthening on the demesnes of North Tipperary in the second quarter of the nineteenth century, no more made the transition to Canada than did the landlord-tenant system in which it was rooted.[17] Miller also underestimates the extent to which family priorities were compatible with the demands of commercialized agriculture. It was the family farm and the neighbourhood co-operative cheese factory that responded to new technology and changes in international market demands to facilitate the shift from a wheat-based mixed economy to one focusing upon dairy production in the last four decades of the nineteenth century.[18]

To the Tipperary Protestant emigrants, success did not necessitate "assimilation to bourgeois values." They aimed at providing a competence for their children and, as we have seen, most succeeded in accomplishing this goal within a rural context. A few farmers, such as William Hodgins and Robert Grant of the *Brunswick* party, became phenomenally successful in the new land, and established farms that were regarded as large and progressive within their own region. A few such as the Sifton family eventually left agriculture to become successful in other arenas, but to most success was achieved when an acreage was secured which could be divided into farms of average size for the next generation, or when other provisions could be made to ensure them an honest living.

Deficiencies of American census records hinder historians in their attempts to discover whether the rural or the urban experience was more typical of Irish Americans.[19] But even should the experiences of the Irish in the United States be found to resemble the patterns asserted by Miller, the Tipperary Protestant experience argues against as neat a dichotomization between Protestant and

Catholic, modern and traditional, individualist and communitarian, as he puts forth.

This study cannot address Miller's assertion that Irish Catholics viewed emigration as exile while Protestants generally saw it in more positive terms. Nonetheless, it is clear from examining the migration, settlement, and inheritance patterns outlined in this study that family was of considerable importance to Protestant as well as to Catholic emigrants. One must remember that as a consequence of extensive chain migration an emigrant often ended up with more relatives in Canada than he had in Ireland, and this circumstance was reinforced by the births of new generations and the deaths of the old. Richard Talbot is a case in point. His obituary noted that he came of a family once numerous in the King's County, but by the time of his death no longer represented there. However, several branches followed him to London Township and intermarriage in succeeding generations gave birth to a complex web of kinship connections in the new land.

Among a comparatively small and regionalized emigrant group composed largely of farmers, literary remains are understandably meagre. However, an exchange of poetry between first- and second-generation members of two Tipperary families in western Ontario is illuminating as it reveals two very different attitudes to the homeland. The exchange reflects not a mentality of exile, but rather a fondness for the home of his youth by an emigrant of 1837, and abhorrence of contemporary Irish political violence by a Canadian-born friend who knew Ireland only by reputation. When some recent immigrants proposed a visit home in 1883 to see their friends, John S. Atkinson of Biddulph (1811–1884) published a poem "Erin" in the *Lucan Enterprise* in which he wished them well and urged them to bring back Irish wives "to add to our blessings and people our land." But though he expressed affectionate remembrance of the scenes of his childhood, he realized that his love for Ireland was largely nostalgia for his own personal past: "who is THERE left to greet me with one welcome smile?"

In his poetic response, Leonard D. Stanley of St Marys (1855–1934) questioned how Atkinson could retain any affection for "a land tortured for ages / With dynamite fiends spreading terror and woe / ... Her crimes twenty centuries can not efface." He concluded: "Away with you, Erin, I love you no more." In the exchanges that followed Atkinson replied that Stanley "only knows Ireland by hearsay, but did not grow up among the generous hearted people." He drew a parallel to the Holy Land, also the site of much bloodshed dating back to the days of Eden, and noted that "vile assassins" stalked not Ireland alone, for "by their hands on this side of the ocean, / Fell Lincoln and Garfield and Darcey Magee." Stanley protested that comparisons with primitive eras were specious and that it was an Irishman who had killed Irish-Canadian politician D'Arcy McGee. Stanley was at heart a British Canadian, with attitudes that incorporated strong elements of Irish Protestant defensiveness. To him Ireland was a land in which "true British laws are respected not nearly" and "love for Britannia" did not fill loyal hearts. Moreover, Irishmen (by whom he clearly meant Irish Catholics) exported their troubles:

For wherever you find an Irishman planted
If whiskey indeed can be got in the land,
With unceasing tumult that place will be haunted,
And Donnybrook fairs will be ever on hand ...
Where'er you may find them, no matter what nation –
They're constantly raising a hulla-balloo.

Atkinson countered that he loved England no less for the Gunpowder plot, the Cato Street conspiracy, and the attempts on the life of Queen Victoria, and he took the same attitude towards Ireland: "loving his country while hating her crimes." His judgment of contemporary Irish Catholics was more generous than Stanley's, reflecting his conviction that acts of terrorism were the responsibility of a minority with whom the bulk of Irishmen were not in sympathy:

You think Pat is less loyal than Sandy his neighbor,
And that Britain might look on the Irish as foes,
But look back a few months to the famed Tel-el-Keber,
Was the Shamrock led there by the thistle or rose.

Nonetheless, to both poets Ireland was British, and they accepted loyalty to the crown as a given. Atkinson's attachment was not to Ireland as a nation but to a fondly remembered boyhood home. Both correspondents knew that their country now was Canada. It was loyal, it was British, and round about them the families with whom their ancestors had associated for two centuries had sunk new roots. Both knew that to them Ireland, not Canada, would be the land of exile.[20]

Appendices

This list is a revision of that appearing in Daniel J. Brock, "Richard Talbot, The Tipperary Irish, and the Formative Years of London Township, 1818–1826," MA thesis, University of Western Ontario, 1969, 167–71, and drawing upon extensive genealogical research in Ireland and Canada. Places of initial settlement: L = London Township; G = Goulbourn; M = Montreal. Cash = amount brought according to E.A. Talbot, *Five Years' Residence in the Canadas* (London 1824), II: 198. Names in italic are settlers entitled to land grants and for whom the £10 deposit was made; this part of the list is drawn from CO 384/3, f. 549, PAC, reel B-877. Ages are approximate, according to the best available information.

Cabin Passengers

L   TALBOT, *Richard* Esq. 46, gentleman, Cloughjordan; Lydia (Baird) 43; *Edward Allen* 23; *John* 20; Margaret ?; Esther 10; Lydia 8; Freeman 7; Sarah 6; Hannah 3.

M   BURTON, Mr *William* 30, gentleman, Shinrone; Elizabeth Maria (Harte) 31; Elizabeth Maria 6.

L £300   GEARY, Mr *William* 38, gentleman, estate manager, County Clare, late farmer of 100 acres, Clonlisk, Shinrone; Elizabeth (Jones) 43; *John Jones* 10; Sarah Mary 9; Ann 6; *William Jones* 5; Eliza 4.

L   HARDY, *Joseph* ?, saddler, Killymer, County Galway, formerly of Nenagh; Sarah ( ) ?; Joseph North 18; Deborah ?

Settlers

G   COLBERT, *John* 50, farmer, Ballingarry; Ann ( ) ?; Ann 19; Mary 15; Frances 12; daughter ?

G   COLBERT, *William* ?, farmer, Ballingarry; Mrs ?; Mary 18; Ann 12; John 8; daughter ?

G   CORBETT, *Patrick* 29, shoemaker; Elizabeth (Spearman) 23; John 2; William 1.

M   DELAHUNT, *Thomas* ?, smith, Shinrone; Jane (Guest) ?; William 6; John 4; Editha 4; Katherine 1.

L £30   FOSTER, *George* 30, farmer; Margaret (Piper) 32; John 2.

L £100   GOULDING, *Charles* 34, whitesmith, Moneygall; Ann (Shoebottom) 20; James 6 months (died at sea).

G   GRANT, *Robert* 25, clothier, Limerick City; Elizabeth (Powell) 23.

L £100   GRAY, *Folliott* ?, farmer, once of Moneygall, Templeharry; Mary ( ) ?; Alice Letitia 10; William ?

L £50   GRAY, *John* ?, farmer.

L £100   GUEST, *Thomas* ?, farmer; Elizabeth ( ) ?; daughter 6; Robert 4.

L £100   HASKETT, *William* 36, painter and glazier, Cloughjordan; Mary (Sharman) 26; son 12 (died at sea); Thomas 8; Robert ?; Eliza 4.

?   HAYES, *William* ?, whitesmith.

G   HODGINS, *William* 29, farmer, Newtown, Modreeny; Susan (Colbert) 21.

L £50   HOWARD, *Thomas T.* ?; farmer and weaver, Moneygall; Esther (Goulding) ?; James 3; John 1.

L £50   HOWAY, *Thomas* ?, farmer, probably Borrisokane.

L £50   HOWAY, James ?, farmer, probably Borrisokane.

L £50   KEAYS, *Robert* 39, shoemaker; Elizabeth (Pratt) 33; Maria 8; Henry 1; one other.

L   LEWIS, *Benjamin* ?, farmer, Mrs ?.

L £75   LEWIS, *Francis* 34, farmer; Sarah ( ) 16.

G   LEWIS, *John* 31, farmer; Mary (Sheppard) 18 (carrying John, born 23 September 1818).

G   LONEY, *Richard* ?, farmer; Mrs. ?; Edward 12; son ?; 1 or 2 daughters.

L   LONG, *Samuel* ?, farmer, Toomevara.

G   MORGAN, *William* 19, farmer, Borrisokane.

L?   OLIVE, *James* ?, farmer.

L £100   O'BRIEN, *Joseph* 32, farmer, Garrane, Templeharry; Charity (Ardell) 29; James 3; Mary Ann 1.

G   POWELL, *Francis* 38, woolcomber and linen weaver, Newport; Jane (Smith) ?; Joseph 9; John 7; Mary 6; Thomas 4; Ann 2.

L £50   RALPH, *Robert* 27, farmer.

G   RICHARDSON, *William* ?, shoemaker, Borrisokane; Mary ( ) ?; William Ferdinand 16; Richard 14; Mary 8; Thomas 5; Ann ?

G   SHOULDICE, *James* 31, farmer, probably Fifteen Acres, Dunkerrin; Jane (Boyd) 28; Nicholas 7; Joseph 5; possibly Elizabeth 3 and Robert 1, both of whom died young, possibly at sea.

G   SHOULDICE, *Nicholas* ?, farmer, Glantane West, Glankeen; Susanna (Mooney) ?; *John* ?; George 21; Jane 21; Martha ?; son ?; Susanna ?

L   SIFTON, *John* ?, carpenter, Glantane East, Glankeen.

L   SIFTON, Charles ?, Glantane East, Glankeen.

G   SPEARMAN, *John,* "the oldest member of the party," farmer, Borrisokane; Elizabeth ( ) ?; *John Jr.* 32; three children unidentified.

G   STANLEY, *Thomas* 42, black and white smith, Red Gate, Shinrone, formerly of Borrisokane; Elizabeth (Hodgins) 34; *Samuel* 8; Maria 8; James 7 (died Quebec City 30 July 1818); Thomas 6; probably Eliza ?; Catherine ?; Ellen 2 months (born Cork).

L £100   TURNER, *John* ?, pensioner; Margaret (Haskett?) ?

G   YOUNG, *Robert* 27, farmer; Sarah (Colbert) 22; John 6 months.

Servants

BROOKS, Thomas.

L £50   EVANS, William.

L   MOONEY, William.

L £50   O'NEIL, William 22, Nenagh.

L   PHALEN, John.

L   RODGERS, Peter.

L   STONEY, Edmund 29, Newport; Jane ( ) 18.

APPENDIX B: BIRCH PETITION, 1819

[CO 384/4, f. 31, PAC, reel B-877.]

Bs.OKeane Jan. 1819.

Right Honle. Earl Bathurst.

My Lord

I having determined to proceed to Upper Canada as early as possible in the ensuing Spring provided his Majesties government give me any encouragement – I take the liberty of Sending your Lordship A list of persons who wish to Acompany me as Settlers and for whose Loyalty & Fidelity I have procured (I hope) Satisfactory testimony – I therefore beg your Lordships transmitting to me as soon as possible the exact degree of encouragement which I am to expect from your Lordship. Your reply will be thankfully recd. by your Lordships most obt. & very Humble Servt.

Robt. Birch.

The undernamed persons with their Families consist of persons who are all protestants & Strictly Loyal as may appear to your Lordship by the anexed testimony –

No. Setters [sic] Names	Males	Females	Total No.
1 Robt. Birch	5	3	8
2 Wm. Hobbs	3	2	5
3 Georg Birch	3	2	5
4 John Ardil	2	2	4
5 John Ralph	4	4	8
6 Addam Ralph	5	3	8
7 John Hodgins	3	4	7
8 Elliot White	5	1	6
9 John Allaway	3	1	4
10 John Ballard	2	5	7
11 Robt. Evans	3	2	5
12 Richd. McGinnis	2	2	4
13 Richd. White	1	1	2
	41	32	73

We the undersigned Certify that We know the above Named men to be Protestants and believe them to be truly Loyal to the British Government.

Thos. Towers	Majte. for Co. Tipp.
Hugh Huleatt	Curate of Borisokene
J. Conolly	Vicar of Ballingarry, Justice of the peace for the County of Tipperary
Wm. Haskett	Church Ward.
J.W. Newenham	Termount[?], Justice of the peace for Cty Galway.

APPENDIX C: BOYD-BASKERVILLE PETITION, 1819

[CO 384/4, ff. 106–7, PAC, reel B-877. Residence and settlement location added from other sources.]

To The Rt. Honble Earl Bathurst C.M.

May it please your Lordship

We His Majesty's most Loyal and Most Dutiful Subjects beg leave to state to Your

Lordship that necessity alone compels us to leave our native Country, but though We are providentialley called from home, We are not the less Loyal on that Account, but wish to serve with the Same Zeal in Canada that we have done in Ireland.

We further pray that your Lordship May be pleased to order that a Ship be Sent to receive us at Cork or any other port, your Lordship may think proper (On the receipt of Your Lordships favorable Answer We shall immediately Send £10 for each Settler, We have unanimously appointed Robert Boyd our Agent, as Gentleman of tried[?] loyalty and well known for his peaceable behaviour & Conciliating Manners –

P.S. If the P.C. shall be of opinion that 60 Settlers & their families are too many, the number shall be Reduced So as to meet your Lordships Commands.

We Remain
Your Lordships most Obdt. & Most Dutiful Servants
John Baskerville
Robert Boyd

Settlers	Wives	Children Under Age Male	Female	[Residence]	[Settled]
Armitage John	Jane				
James				Nenagh	York town
Benjn.	Mary				
James					
Baskerville John	Sarah	4		Traverston	Gloucester 1846
Bull John	Mary		1	Borrisokane	York Township
Thomas	Frances	1	2	Roscrea	York Twp 1820
Bathw.	Elizabeth		2	Borrisokane	York Township
Edward				Borrisokane	York Township
Boyd Robert				Moneygall	
Joseph	Mary	1	2		
Birch Robert	Susannah*	4	2	Borrisokane	Richmond
Thomas	Jane*	2	1	Roscrea	Montreal & Richmond
George	Catherine*	2	3	Roscrea	Caledonia
Carden William				Borris-in-Ossory	Rigaud LC
Robert	Ann				
Golding William	Jane*				
Thomas	Mary*	1	1	Roscrea	
William Junr.	Alice*	5		Roscrea	
James	Catherine*	1	1	Roscrea	
Samuel				Roscrea	Montreal
Hassell Thomas	Dorothy	2	1	Modreeny	
Apollos	Harriett			Modreeny	
Holland George	Catherine	4	2	Modreeny	

Hasset John	Fanny	3	5		
Arthur	Catherine		1	Silverhills	d. Ire. 1847
Howe James	Margaret	2	4	Modreeny	
Harding Robert	Mary			Carrigatoher	London Twp
Hodgins William	Elizabeth	2	3		
William Junr.	Catherine		1		
Jones Francis					
Lewis John	Mary				Modreeny?
William	Jane	3	3	Modreeny?	McGillivray c1836?
John Junr.	Mary	1	2	Modreeny	
John Benjn.	Frances	2	1		
Thomas	Mary		2		
John	Ann	3	2		
Lloyd George					
Neill Robert	Mary			Nenagh	Montreal
Henry	Catherine			Nenagh	London Twp
Owen William	Sarah	2	3	Borrisokane	d. Ireland
Edward	Eliza	3	1	Borrisokane	Fitzroy 1825
[P]rettie Adam	Mary		1	Mucklin	Drummond
Reid John	–	3	3	King's Co.?	Esquesing
Robinson Lanty	–	3	2	Sierkeiran	Mascouche
John	–	3	1		
George	–	2	3		Mascouche?
Shouldice John	Jane	2	1		
Joseph					
Sifton Joseph	Catherine	2		Glantane	London Twp
Charles	Rebecca	5	2	Glantane	London Twp
Tidd Benjamin				Modreeny	Barton
Walker Joseph	Elizabeth	1	5	Modreeny	Quebec City
Watkins Samuel		3	3	Birr	Esquesing
Samuel Junr.		3	3	Birr	Esquesing
Willis Wm.	Sarah	1	2		
Williams John					
Ardil John	Mary				
Hodgins Richard	Catherine	2	2		Huntley 1822?
Brenan John	Jane	2	1		

Direct To Mr. Robert Boyd, Moneygale post office, Kings County.

Clough Jordan March 29th 1819.

We certify that the within Mentioned Persons are Protestants and they are Known to us as our parishioners and have never had reason to question their Loyalty or peaceable behaviour. Please to refer to the enclosed certificates.

[blank]

I certify that the signatures of the different Clergymen are in their own hand Writing.

Thos. Hawkins
Dean of Clonfert
April 5th 1819.

P.S. The settlers nominated in this memorial have been carefully selected from numerous applications on the behalf of others equally desirous of emigrating to His Majesty's dominions in Upper Canada. Should it be the intention of His Majesty's Ministers to extend the encouragement, the number of settlers that have already applied are not less than one hundred & fifty.

Thomas Hassell,
Agent.

* The names of the Birch wives are given incorrectly; they should be Eleanor, Sarah, and Sarah, respectively. The names of the Gouldings' wives appear to be given incorrectly also.]

APPENDIX D: THE KILCOOLY PALATINES AND THEIR CANADIAN COLONIES

Within County Tipperary was another area of Protestant settlement, some twenty miles south of Roscrea, separated from the North Tipperary settlement region by a low sweep of mountains. These Protestants lived at places such as Littleton and Killenaule, and a few came from adjoining parishes in County Kilkenny, but they were especially numerous on the Barker estate at Kilcooly. They were of diverse origins but many were of Palatine descent. In 1772 Sir William Barker of Kilcooly Abbey, "with a view to establishing a Protestant Colony on his estate," induced Palatine families from the Rathkeale area of County Limerick to move to his lands by offering them generous terms on freehold leases. Five families, those of Paul Smeltzer, Adam Baker, Daniel Ruckle, John Switzer, and Sebastian Lawrence, took a lease in Newpark. These surnames were to become familiar in areas of Palatine settlement in Upper Canada.[1] The Protestant population of Kilcooly parish also included the descendants of miners brought from the north of England to work the coal fields at New Birmingham. Other Protestant tenants were attracted to the Barker estate from the neighbouring county of Kilkenny. An 1829 pew list for the parish church records the familiar Palatine surnames Bible, Dolmage, Glazier, Miller, Ruckle, Smeltzer, Sparling, and Young, and other names Archbold, Baldwin, Barry, Block, Caesar, Churchill, Deeves, Douglass, Groves, Hayden, Hill, Magee, Mason, Parker, Semple, Sloan, Steep, Sutliffe, Thompson, and Whitty.[2] With the exception of the common names like Hill and Thompson, this is a very different list from one which could be compiled in the North Tipperary parishes.[3]

As already recounted, the first Palatine of a Kilcooly family to emigrate to Canada appears to have been Martin Switzer, who went to the United States in 1804 and in 1819 moved north to Toronto Township with the Beatty party from New York. He was joined in the 1820s by some of his brothers and by numerous other families, and a colony arose in the vicinity of the village of Streetsville where the townships of Toronto, Chinguacousy, Trafalgar, and Esquesing met.[4] This Tipperary community gave root to a secondary settlement in Goderich Township at the northern end of Huron County where a Methodist appointment was named Tipperary. A number of families from the Streetsville neighbourhood were already there by 1835, and ten years later there were some thirty families in the new region.[5] Thus Huron County was home to two Tipperary Protestant communities: a settlement of North Tipperary families in Biddulph and McGillivray at its southern extremity, and a secondary settlement of Kilcooly emigrants near Goderich at its northern end.

Like North Tipperary, the Kilcooly region suffered disturbances in the early nineteenth century. The Palatines and other Protestants in Kilcooly were sometimes attacked because of their conspicuous presence as a privileged minority. Their ancestors had, after all, been brought to the Barker estate for the express purpose of building up a Protestant tenantry.[6] Elements of this violent style of life in Ireland were carried over into Canada. Nicholas Flood Davin recounted the story of the Streetsville settlement this way: "The greater part of a township near Streetsville, County of Peel, is settled by emigrants from 'Gallant Tipperary.' They used to be called some years ago the 'Town-line blazers' … They were accustomed to come down to town with their guns, a practice which I hope they have discontinued. 'One old boy,' writes a correspondent, 'would come down, and when he took a glass too much he would say: 'Do you think you could box a Cole or a Cantlan? No! nor by –– could you box old Rowley himself.'"[7]

One popular account of this era described the Blazers as "ruffians [who] terrorized the district," led by John Miller, who "set himself as a petty king of this part of Peel and ruled with an iron hand."[8] Other accounts describe them as Tipperary Orangemen who, under the leadership of Harry Cole,[9] partook of cheap whiskey and became "famous over the country as fighters," cleaning out Streetsville's barrooms on a regular basis.[10] Cole, who was in Toronto Township by 1829 and whose brother Peter settled in Goderich, was founder of the first Orange Lodge in his district, led his Orange band in breaking up Mackenzie's political meetings in the area, and during the 1837 Rebellion became Captain of a local militia unit. In 1838 he was arrested for attempting to rape a twelve-year-old girl. Although he was convicted and served half his sentence of two years at hard labour, he may have been the victim of a malicious accusation. Friends submitted a petition bearing 688 signatures praying for his release and he was pardoned on 7 June 1840.[11]

By contrast, some members of the Streetsville Tipperary community were peaceful, law-abiding Methodists, many of them descendants of John Wesley's Irish Palatine converts. Charles Bowles of Chinguacousy, born in Tipperary in 1797, was the son and grandson of Palatine Methodist women[12] and members of the Caesar, Dolmage, Perdue, Sparrow, Switzer, and Webster families were converted in Ireland.[13] One source attributes the demise of the Townline Blazers to the conversion of John Miller.[14]

In a number of ways, therefore, the Kilcooly Protestants were very like their compatriots from North Tipperary. Both formed considerable Protestant concentrations in largely Roman Catholic areas in the homeland and emigrated to populate specific neighbourhoods, following relatives and friends who had preceded them. They formed secondary settlements in newer parts of Upper Canada, the Streetsville people in Goderich and the North Tipperary families in Bruce County. Both groups imported their at times lawless lifestyles and a willingness to resort to violence to achieve personal and political ends. However, both groups included members whose principal interest was spiritual advancement, converts to Methodism prior to emigration.

A few Kilcooly families had family connections with Templemore, the market town between Kilcooly and Roscrea,[15] and one emigrant, John Cantelon, had moved from Kilcooly to North Tipperary, married a Haskett, and lived for a time in Templeharry parish.[16] However, upon emigrating to Canada in 1841 they settled with his relatives in Goderich rather than near any kin Mrs Cantelon might have had in the North Tipperary settlements near London.[17] There is very little overlap in the lists of surnames found among the two groups, and their migratory patterns, while similar in nature, took them to different locations. Like the Palatines of Blanshard, the Tipperary Irish of Streetsville and Goderich were an emigrant group distinct from their North Tipperary fellow-countrymen.

Notes

1 Donald Akenson discusses the limitations of the aggregate emigration statistics in "Ontario: Whatever Happened to the Irish?" in D.H. Akenson, ed., *Canadian Papers in Rural History* 3 (1982): 204–56. Official passenger lists of those arriving at the port of Quebec begin only in 1865, and for other ports manifests commence even later. Some early lists are included in Colonial Office correspondence files, but they are few and often are really lists of prospective emigrants rather than of those who left Britain. There is a Public Archives of Canada (PAC) Finding Aid to these lists, which are in CO 384. Pre-1865 passenger lists scattered through various collections in the PAC have been referenced in the General Index under the heading "Canada: Emigration/Immigration." Of some use in this study were the Passage Book for 1832 of the Montreal Emigrant Society (PAC, Governor General's Office, RG 7, G 18, vol. 46, microfilm, reel H-962), lists of those provisioned upon arrival at Montreal, 1846, compiled by James Allison, emigrant agent there (PAC, Neilson Collection, MG 24, B 1, vol. 21), and the Destination Registers maintained by the Quebec Agency of the Ontario government in the 1870s (Archives of Ontario (AO), RG 11, ser. M, vols. 8 & 9). However, all of these cover only special categories of immigrants and very short time periods, and only a few North Tipperary families were located in each.
2 C.J. Houston and W.J. Smyth, "The Irish Abroad: Better Questions through a Better Source, the Canadian Census," *Irish Geography* 13 (1980): 1–19; Akenson, "Whatever Happened?" 204–56. Akenson emphasizes the successful rural settlement of both Protestant and Catholic Irish in nineteenth-century Ontario, whereas Smyth and Houston stress that a greater proportion of Catholics settled in towns and cities. The urban Catholics were, nonetheless, clearly a minority.
3 Studies of population mobility have turned up high rates of departure from var-

ious communities. Katz and Gagan suggested in the 1970s that the highly
mobile society depicted was very different from the stable, rooted communities
of families that were assumed to be the popular stereotype, and asserted that
many of Canada's nineteenth-century inhabitants were rootless wanderers. Mays
reclassified some of Gagan's data that had yielded the first evidences of
extensive movement and suggested, on the basis of a family reconstitution study,
the presence of a sizeable core of permanent families amidst the hustle and
bustle of short-term residents. The new intimation was that in a real sense these
core families *were* the local community. However, this study, too, left a
"social cost," even for the permanent families. There were not sufficient farms
for all in the home community; some children had to leave. Gérard Bouchard's
Quebec study has suggested that there most of the parents in such cases left, too,
to preserve family solidarity. Finally, Gordon Darroch has attacked the tran-
siency thesis that characterized Canadian writing on the subject and suggested, on
the basis of a survey of the European and American literature, that movement
took place largely under family auspices. David Gagan and Herbert Mays, "Historical Demography and Canadian Social History: Families and Land in Peel
County, Ontario," *Canadian Historical Review* 54 (1973): 35; Michael Katz,
*The People of Hamilton, Canada West: Family and Class in a Mid-
Nineteenth Century City* (Cambridge, Mass. 1975), 111; Herbert Mays, "'A
Place to Stand': Families, Land and Permanence in Toronto Gore Township,
1820–1890," Canadian Historical Association, *Historical Papers* (1980), 186,
207; Gérard Bouchard, "Family Structures and Geographic Mobility at Later-
riere, 1851–1935," *Journal of Family History* 2 (1977): 366; A. Gordon Darroch, "Migrants in the Nineteenth Century: Fugitives or Families in Motion?"
Journal of Family History 6, no. 3 (Fall 1981): 257–78.

4 The best known of such studies is Peter Knights's ongoing investigation of
native-born outmigrants who left mid-nineteenth-century Boston; see the preliminary conclusions in his *The Plain People of Boston, 1830–1860: A Study in
City Growth* (New York 1971), 103–18, and his "The Role of Genealogy in
Social History," Ontario Genealogical Society, *Seminar Annual* (Toronto 1985),
53–63. Such migration studies in Canada will soon be made much easier by
publication of the Ontario Genealogical Society's Ontario 1871 Census Index,
but the limitations discussed below will still apply to such investigations. The
first six of thirty volumes have already appeared: Bruce S. Elliott, ed., *Index to
the 1871 Census of Ontario* (Toronto 1986–7).

5 John Mannion placed too much emphasis on political boundaries and proximity
in both Canada and Ireland in his denial of the existence of chain migration to
the "Irish parts" of eastern Canada. John J. Mannion, *Irish Settlements in Eastern
Canada: a Study of Cultural Transfer and Adaptation* (Toronto 1974), 13,
16–21.

6 I am aware of only one other study that approaches the question of geographical
mobility by tracing migrants in different areas who came from a common

overseas place of origin. William Lawson's investigation of emigration to various parts of Canada from the Outer Hebrides is still in progress but an introductory article has appeared: "Emigrants to Ontario and Quebec from the Western Isles," Ontario Genealogical Society, *Seminar Annual* (Toronto 1984), 125–34. More commonly, historians have outlined the clustered regional origins of immigrants or inmigrants into a community or region or discussed outmigration in the context of a community analysis. Handcock studied the origins of English migrants into the whole of Newfoundland: W.G. Handcock, "Spatial Patterns in a Trans-Atlantic Migration Field: The British Isles and Newfoundland during the Eighteenth and Nineteenth Centuries," in Brian S. Osborne, ed., *Proceedings of the 1975 British-Canadian Symposium on Historical Geography* (Kingston 1976), 13–45. Bowen examined the regional migration patterns that took people from the eastern United States to the Willamette Valley of Oregon, using aggregate census data: William A. Bowen, *The Willamette Valley: Migration and Settlement on the Oregon Frontier* (Seattle 1978). Marianne McLean has examined the Scottish origins of the settlers of Glengarry County, Ontario: "Peopling Glengarry County: The Scottish Origins of a Canadian Community," Canadian Historical Association, *Historical Papers* (1982): 156–71, and "Achd an Rhigh: A Highland Response to the Assisted Emigration of 1815," in D.H.Akenson, ed., *Canadian Papers in Rural History* 5 (1986): 181–97. An American study of outmigration from a community is Linda A. Bissell, "From One Generation to Another: Mobility in Seventeenth-Century Windsor, Connecticut," *William and Mary Quarterly*, 3rd Series, 31 (January 1974): 79–110, and a Scottish regional example using mostly home sources is Marjory Harper's "Emigration from North East Scotland in the Nineteenth Century," *Northern Scotland* 6, no. 2 (1985), 169–81. Other methods of defining the subject population are illustrated by Thomas Dublin's attempt to trace the fates of New England millworkers in *Women at Work: The Transformation of Work and Community in Lowell, Massachusetts, 1826–1860* (New York 1979), Robert M. Taylor Jr's migration study of 200 members of the Olin family: "Genealogical Sources in American Social History Research: A Reappraisal," *New England Historical and Genealogical Register* 135 (January 1981): 3–15, and Randy Widdis's recent study of 177 families from the Belleville area using an eighty-year-old genealogical compilation, *Pioneer Life on the Bay of Quinte:* "'Pioneer Life on the Bay of Quinte': An Evaluation of Genealogical Source Data in the Study of Migration," *Canadian Geographer* 26, no. 3 (Fall 1982): 273–82. A similar New England study using colonial New England genealogies is John W. Adams and Alice B. Kasakoff, "Migration and the Family in Colonial New England: The View from Genealogies," *Journal of Family History* 9 (Spring 1984): 24–43.

7 Akenson has suggested that this image of the Irish abroad derives from the American literature: "Whatever Happened?" More recently he has expressed doubts about the validity of common perceptions of the American Irish in "An

Agnostic View of the Historiography of the Irish-Americans," *Labour* 14
(Fall 1984): 123–59. Both articles are reprinted in his *Being Had* (Port Credit,
Ontario 1985). It has been noted that Irish Protestants at present "constitute
one of the largest ethnic groups in America – larger for example, than Irish
Catholics." Christopher Jencks, "Discrimination and Thomas Sowell," *New
York Review of Books* 30, no. 3 (3 March 1983): 34.

8 Exceptions to this literature are William Nolan's fine study of northeastern Kilkenny, *Fassadinin: Land, Settlement & Society in South-East Ireland, 1600–
1850* (Dublin 1979), and Donald Akenson's history of Islandmagee, County
Antrim: *Between Two Revolutions: Islandmagee, County Antrim 1798–1920*
(Port Credit 1979).

9 National Library of Ireland, ms 352, Abstract of Information in Answer to
Queries concerning the Parishes in the Dioceses of Killaloe and Kilfenora, 1820.

10 Paul E.W. Roberts, "Caravats and Shanavests: Whiteboyism and Faction Fighting in East Munster, 1802–11," in Samuel Clark and James S. Donnelly Jr,
Irish Peasants: Violence and Political Unrest, 1780–1914 (Madison 1983), 66.

11 Akenson, "Whatever Happened?" 234–5.

12 D.H. Akenson, *The Irish in Ontario: A Study in Rural History* (Kingston and
Montreal 1984).

13 Because the Canadian-born neighbours in Akenson's 1861 data include the children of long-settled Irish farmers, the slight comparative underdevelopment
of the farms of the native-born may actually be a function of the length of time
the farms had been in occupation rather than a result of ethnic differences.
Ibid., 241–63.

14 David P. Gagan, "The Indivisibility of Land: A Microanalysis of the System of
Inheritance in Nineteenth-Century Ontario," *Journal of Economic History* 36
(March 1976): 126–46.

15 The pioneering article on inheritance strategies is James A. Henretta, "Family
and Farms: 'Mentalité' in Pre-Industrial America," *William and Mary Quarterly* 35 (1978): 3–32. In this sense the Irish were not so different from many
other nineteenth-century North American farming families.

16 In this study I will use the terms "emigration" and "immigration" to refer to
the transatlantic movements out of Ireland and into North America, and the
terms "outmigration" and "inmigration" to refer to internal migration within
Ireland or within North America.

17 Genealogical Office, Dublin (GO), ms 641, Latter-day Saints (LDS) microfilm,
reel 011239, "Diocese of Killaloe, Particulars of Catholic Parochial
Registers."

18 Another limitation of this study, of course, is that it focuses on the migration
process itself and, though it establishes the link between migration and the
family economy, does not address the wider issue of cultural transfer and adaptation. Assessing the impact of clustered settlement patterns upon local reli-

gious, political, and social life, and the degree to which the Irish functioned in Canada as an ethnic group, requires another large volume.

19 Nellie McClung, *The Stream Runs Fast* (Toronto 1945), x. Nellie Letitia (Mooney) McClung was the daughter of John Mooney, a native of Moneygall, who emigrated to Canada in 1830. I am grateful to Carole Caldwell of British Columbia for this quotation.

CHAPTER TWO

1 William J. Smyth, "Land Values, Landownership, and Population Patterns in Co. Tipperary for 1641–1660 and 1841–1850: Some Comparisons," in L.M. Cullen and F. Furet, eds., *Ireland and France 17th–20th Centuries: Towards a Comparative Study of Rural History* (Paris 1980), 80.

2 National Library of Ireland, Dublin (NLI), ms 352, Abstract of Information in Answer to Queries concerning the Parishes in the Dioceses of Killaloe and Kilfenora, 1820.

3 Smyth, "Land Values," 59.

4 Samuel Lewis, *A Topographical Dictionary of Ireland* (London 1847), 584.

5 Owing to boundary changes in the 1920s, Mountshannon is now in County Clare.

6 Emigrants from the Kilcooly region of Tipperary are discussed in Appendix D.

7 See Map 2.

8 William Nolan, *Tracing the Past: Sources for Local Studies in the Republic of Ireland* (Dublin 1982), 9.

9 Rev. Philip Dwyer, *The Diocese of Killaloe from the Reformation to the Close of the Eighteenth Century* (Dublin 1878), 8–10.

10 Smyth, "Land Values," 65–9.

11 Dermot F. Gleeson, *The Last Lords of Ormond* (London 1938), 10.

12 Ibid., 34.

13 Ingeborg Leister, *Peasant Openfield Farming and Its Territorial Organisation in County Tipperary* (Marburg 1976), 11.

14 Smyth, "Land Values," 75.

15 Ibid., 61.

16 See Map 3.

17 Calculated from statistics given in British Parliamentary Sessional Papers, HC (1835) XXXIII, First Report of the Commissioners of Public Instruction, Ireland.

18 Robert C. Simington, ed., *The Civil Survey A.D. 1654–1656, County of Tipperary* (Dublin 1931–4), II: 153, 138, 141, 142, 152, 157, 167.

19 Gleeson, *Ormond*, 71–80.

20 Seamus Pendar, ed., *A Census of Ireland circa 1659* (Dublin 1939), which despite the editor's argument to the contrary is now generally regarded as a poll-tax levied in 1660; Thomas Laffan, *Tipperary's Families: Being the Hearth Money Records for 1665–6–7* (Dublin 1911), passim; William J. Smyth,

"Property, Patronage and Population: Reconstructing the Human Geography of Mid-Seventeenth Century County Tipperary," in William Nolan and Thomas G. McGrath, eds., *Tipperary: History and Society* (Dublin 1985), 104–38, especially Fig. 7.7 on 134.

21 Public Record Office (PRO), Dublin, Religious Returns 1766, Diocese of Cashel; HC (1835) XXXIII.

22 Gleeson, *Ormond*, 50.

23 Thomas Lalor Cooke, *The Early History of the Town of Birr, or Parsonstown* (Dublin 1875), 36–47.

24 Ibid., 36, 41–2, 66, 69–71, 383–4.

25 Gleeson, *Ormond*, 53–67.

26 The rumour that the Protestant population was of Cromwellian descent has long-standing foundations, for one finds a local landlord writing to the Colonial Office in 1825 that the residents of his neighbourhood included "a good many Protestant Families ... from 3 or 4 of Cromwells Regiments have got Debentures [of] Lands here, that had been forfeited." PRO, Kew, Colonial Office Records, CO 384/11, f. 263, PAC, microfilm, reel B-883, Richard Falkiner to R.W. Horton, Mountfalcon, Borrisokane, 25 April 1825; Gleeson, *Ormond*, 157.

27 John P. Prendergast, *The Cromwellian Settlement of Ireland* (New York 1868), map opposite 225.

28 Ibid., 70, 74; Prendergast (136–7) quotes an assignment of 1656 whereby thirty-four men sold their scrip to their captain for £136, or £4 per man.

29 Gleeson, *Ormond*, 161–4.

30 Ibid., 244–53; E.H. Sheehan, *Nenagh and Its Neighbourhood* (Nenagh 1976), 37, 54, 70.

31 Smyth, "Property," 137.

32 Gleeson, *Ormond*, 176–87.

33 Ibid., 168, 249.

34 Major F.S. Stoney, *Some Old Annals of the Stoney Family* (1879), 1–5.

35 George Cunningham, *Roscrea and District* (Roscrea 1976), 46–7. The Damers' wealth became legendary. Dáithí Ó hÓgain discusses the folklore in "An tÓr Buí: staidéar ar ghné de sheanchas Thiobraid Árann" (with English summary following), in Nolan and McGrath, eds., *Tipperary*, 139–47.

36 Laffan, *Tipperary's Families*, passim; cf. Gleeson, *Ormond*, 195–201.

37 Lists of the grantees still exist: see Gleeson, *Ormond*, Appendices.

38 Smyth, "Land Values," 64, 80.

39 The southern part of the county appears much more densely populated: Simington, ed., *Civil Survey*, 2 vols., passim; see also Smyth, "Land Values," 75.

40 L.M. Cullen, *Irish Towns and Villages* (Dublin 1979), no page; Gleeson, *Ormond*, 165.

41 Simington, ed., *Civil Survey*, II: 295.

42 John Bradley, "The Medieval Towns of Tipperary," in Nolan and McGrath, eds., *Tipperary*, 50–2; Gleeson, *Ormond*, 164.

43 Simington, ed., *Civil Survey*, I: 29.

44 Gleeson, *Ormond*, 248–9.

45 Cf. NLI, Down Survey map, parish of Boris, and Ordnance Survey maps, 1840; copies of the latter are in the PAC, National Map Collection; Gleeson, *Ormond*, 166–7.

46 Smyth, "Land Values," 84.

47 *Nenagh Guardian*, 25 April 1981.

48 *Association for the Preservation of the Memorials of the Dead, Ireland* (hereafter *Memorials of the Dead*) 8 (1910): 633, 666–7.

49 Gleeson, *Ormond*, 166, quoting Dwyer, *Diocese of Killaloe*.

50 Gleeson, *Ormond*, 165–6.

51 "Extract from Further Report of the Assistant Deputy Keeper of the Records of the Court of Record of the County Palatine of Tipperary," *The Sixth Report of the Deputy Keeper of the Public Records in Ireland* [26 March 1874], c.963, appendix 5, 87, no. 108, Chancery Inrolments, County Palatine of Tipperary.

52 Irish plantation acres were about half again as large as English or statute acres: 1 plantation acre = 1 acre, 2 roods, 19 perches. Thus Harrison's grant was the equivalent of over 1458 acres English measure. A useful conversion table may be found in volume I of Lewis's *Topographical Dictionary*.

53 Gleeson, *Ormond*, 248.

54 Simington, ed., *Civil Survey*, II: 288–9; also NLI, Down Survey map of parish. The Harrisons enlarged their estate by purchasing adjoining properties from the non-resident assignees of military grantees until they owned the eastern half of the parish. The process may be traced in "Extract from Report of the Assistant Deputy Keeper of the Records of the Court of Record of the County Palatine of Tipperary," *Fifth Report of the Deputy Keeper* [26 April 1873], c.760, appendix 3, 32–81 (fines and recoveries); "Extracts from Further Report ..." *Sixth Report of the Deputy Keeper* [26 March 1874], c.963, appendix 5, 44–88 (cause list and rolls of Chancery); and T.U. Sadleir, "Manuscripts at Kilboy, Co. Tipperary, in the Possession of the Lord Dunalley," *Analecta Hibernica* 12 (Jan. 1943): 131–54.

55 Smyth, "Land Values," 76.

56 Prendergast, *Cromwellian Settlement*, 82, 163; Smyth, "Property," 135–6.

57 *Burke's Peerage and Baronetage* (London 1970); Gleeson, *Ormond*, 166. For details of the ownership of the estate see *Memorials of the Dead* 8 (1910): 666–7.

58 Dorothy Boake Panzer, *The Beech Tree* (Downey, CA 1970), 45–6, 50.

59 Bruce S. Elliott, "The Hopper Family," *Irish Ancestor* 1982, no. 2, 59–61. The Hoppers are known to have lived at their former place of residence at Killoughy at least as early as 1709: Raymond Refaussé, "Extracts from the Church

of Ireland Parish Registers of Ballyboy, King's County (Offaly), 1709–48 and 1797–1868," *Irish Ancestor* 1986, no. 1, 11.

60 London Public Library, Seaborn Diaries, "Memoirs of Richard Jones Evans," 755.

61 Such a story from a nineteenth-century family source about the Joneses of Clandeboye, near Lucan, Ontario, led the author of a National Museums publication to describe cabinetmaker Francis Jones as a member of London Township's Welsh settlement rather than as a member of Biddulph and McGillivray's much larger Tipperary group. L.A. Koltun, *The Cabinetmaker's Art in Ontario, c1850–1900,* National Museums of Canada Mercury Series, History Division Paper 26 (Ottawa 1979), 5–7.

62 Maurice Lenihan, *Limerick: Its History and Antiquities* (Cork, nd), 356.

63 NLI, ms 787, County Tipperary freeholders list, 1776.

64 Information from Jean Kelly, Lambeth, Ontario; PRO, Dublin, Killaloe and Castletownnarra parish registers.

65 The earliest ancestor of the Rathnaveoge family, Benjamin Sparling (c1693–1769), would have been among those who came from Germany around 1709 if he was of the Limerick colony, but there is no record of him at Rathkeale. Elliott, "Hopper Family," 62; correspondence with Jean Kelly of Lambeth, Ontario.

66 The Palatines of Kilcooly are discussed in Appendix D.

67 Irish names borne by Protestant emigrants are Beynon, Butler, Carroll, Caughlin, Cavanagh, Collins, Delahunt(y), Doolan, Dooley, Fitzgerald, Flynn, Gallagher, Gleeson, Guilfoyle, Hanley, Hayes, Healey, Heeney, Hogan, Kennedy, Keough, Kilduffe (though some of this emigrating family may have been Catholic), Lynch, Maher, Mooney, Moran, Morris, O'Brien, O'Neil, Ryan, Scully, and Walsh.

68 The vicar of Bourney and Burrisnafarney, south of Roscrea, reported in 1820 that there were several converts in his parochial union before the 1798 Rebellion but none thereafter. NLI, ms 352, Killaloe questionnaire, 1820. Desmond Bowen has suggested that the "age of accommodation" lasted up to the launching of a "Protestant Crusade" by Church of Ireland evangelicals in 1822. Bowen, *The Protestant Crusade in Ireland 1800–70* (Dublin 1978), x–xi.

69 Gleeson, *Ormond,* 35–45. On the Penal Laws see William P. Burke, *The Irish Priests in the Penal Times (1660–1760)* (Waterford 1914).

70 See Smyth, "Land Values," map, 66–7. Burke was a native of Ballyartella in the parish of Dromineer, but his relationship to the Fogarty family indicates his connection with the Burkes who held land near Borrisoleigh in the nineteenth century. Obituary, *Ottawa Citizen,* 4 February 1854; Archives of Ontario (AO), MU 2367, Thomas Radenhurst Papers, George Lyon to Thomas Radenhurst, 31 August 1829; Registry of Deeds, Dublin, 847/286/567286, Marriage Articles of William Burke Fogarty and Catherine Burke; PRO, Dublin, Tithe Applotment Book, parish of Glankeen, Latter-day Saints (LDS) reel 256614.

71 Public Archives of Canada (PAC), RG 31, 1852 census, Bytown, West Ward, 89. Burke was listed as Anglican, the rest of his household Roman Catholic. He was buried in the Catholic Cemetery at Richmond by the rector of the Anglican Church at Bytown: Diocese of Ottawa Archives, burial register of Christ Church, Ottawa, 4 February 1854.

72 Jane converted to Catholicism in Canada. I am grateful to Joan Megie of Sterling Heights, Michigan, for information about this family.

73 Terryglass and Kilbarron Roman Catholic parish register, 1827–80, LDS reel 926102.

74 The investigation of medieval migration patterns by studying surname distributions over time has become a staple of English migration research. The English Surnames Series, edited by Richard McKinley of the University of Leicester, has produced four county volumes. The method is outlined in J. Douglas Porteous, "English Surname Studies: A Methodology," *Genealogists' Magazine* 20, no. 2 (March 1982): 295–7. A similar approach has been taken to Protestant settlement in South Derry: W. Macafee, "The Colonisation of the Maghera Region of South Derry during the Seventeenth and Eighteenth Centuries," *Ulster Folklife* 23 (1977): 70–91. Regrettably, suitable listings do not survive to permit a similar analysis in North Tipperary.

75 For example, the Wall families of Carriganeen, Glenaguile, and Burnwood, all of whom sent emigrants to Canada, buried at Dunkerrin in the nineteenth century, as did Walls from Toomevara, Corville, Ballybritt (Aghancon parish), and Templenure, even though no one of the name was born in Dunkerrin during that period. PRO, Dublin, reel 4, Dunkerrin Church of Ireland registers.

76 J.C. Beckett, *The Making of Modern Ireland, 1603–1923* (London 1966), 167–8.

77 David J. Dickson, "Property and Social Structure in Eighteenth-Century South Munster," in Cullen and Furet, eds., *Ireland and France*, 130–1.

78 Leister, *Peasant Openfield Farming*, 5.

79 As was often the case with powerful landlords, the deeds from the Pritties were not registered: Rosemary ffolliott, "The Registry of Deeds for Genealogical Purposes," in Donal F. Begley, ed., *Irish Genealogy: A Record Finder* (Dublin 1981), 140–1. However, a lease of 1776 to the Protestant Mooney family of Cappakilleen was recited in a later transaction. Prittie leased to James and William Mooney [6?]4 plantation acres in Cappakilleen for the term of three lives at an annual rent of seven shillings stg per acre. Registry of Deeds, Dublin, 560/396/375393, Mooney to Mooney, 1804.

80 NLI, ms 787, County Tipperary freeholders list, 1776.

81 NLI, D.23185–215, Croasdaile deeds (not individually numbered), Henry and John Croasdaile to Thomas Lambert, 3 March 1760; *Burke's Irish Family Records,* (London 1976), 290–2, "Croasdaile."

82 Registry of Deeds, Dublin, 188/372/126044.

83 The island of Innisparren lying just off Clarke's land at Clonolia is still known

locally as Page's Island; information from Miss Marion Logan, Mountshannon.

84 Sheehan, *Nenagh*, 56.

85 PRO, Dublin, Otway Deeds, D.20,368 and 20,370.

86 Michael Hewson, "Eighteenth Century Directions to Servants in Co. Tipperary," in Etienne Rynne, ed., *North Munster Studies: Essays in Commemoration of Monsignor Michael Moloney* (Limerick 1967), 332– 4.

87 NLI, Otway Estate maps, 1655–1840, no. 15.

88 NLI, ms 352, Killaloe questionnaire, 1820.

89 On village forms see L.M. Cullen, *The Emergence of Modern Ireland 1600– 1900* (New York 1981), 61–82. For maps and illustrations one must refer to his *Irish Towns and Villages* (Dublin 1979).

90 Cullen, *Irish Towns and Villages,* no page.

91 See the comments on the establishment of a Protestant colony at Kilcooly in Appendix D.

92 NLI, ms 352, Killaloe questionnaire, 1820.

93 Thomas V. MacNamara, pp, *Guide to Mountshannon* (np, nd [1970s]), 16.

94 HC (1836) XXXIII, First Report of Commissioners for Inquiring into the Condition of the Poorer Classes in Ireland, Supplement to Appendix F, 160.

95 The earliest reference to the village that I have seen myself is in a Holland deed of 1772: Registry of Deeds, Dublin, 313/567/210917, Holland to Holland, 22 April 1772. By 1779 four fairs a year were held there; the church was built in 1785. MacNamara, *Guide to Mountshannon,* 76, 16. The village in fact appears to antedate the Tandys. John Daly is said to have estabished fifty Protestant families from the north here to produce linen in 1735. The village was still sometimes called Mountshannon Daly in the early nineteenth century, to distinguish it from another Mountshannon in County Limerick. It is not certain, however, that this early Protestant population remained there. The Charter School Daly established in the 1740s closed by 1753. Cullen, *Emergence of Modern Ireland,* 74, 124–5, 197.

96 HC (1835) XXXIII, 222c-3c.

97 PRO, Dublin, Religious Returns 1766, Diocese of Cashel.

98 HC (1835) XXXIII, 56c. Even if one accepts that the 1766 census underenumerated Roman Catholics, the increase of population recorded in Templemore between 1766 and 1831 was much greater than in the other Tipperary parishes for which returns survive.

99 *Memorials of the Dead,* 1 (1891): 494.

100 Consulted on microfilm in Dublin and at the Rectory, Templemore; the Latter-day Saints possess a typescript copy.

101 Information from Gwen Bergsma, Penn Valley, California.

102 1840 Ordnance Survey map, Tipperary sheet 29, PAC neg. C-104740, reproduced herewith as Map 7; Griffith's Primary Valuation.

103 Town only; parish total 5965. Figures repeated in 1851 census report.

104 NLI, ms 13794(2), Rolleston Papers: Rentals: A Description and Rent Roll of Part of the Estate of Francis Rolleston Esqr. See also Cunningham, *Roscrea and District,* 53.

105 NLI, ms 352, Killaloe questionnaire, 1820; see also Cullen, *Irish Towns and Villages,* no. 39.

106 L.F. Cullen, "The Social and Cultural Modernisation of Rural Ireland, 1600–1900," in Cullen and Furet, eds., *Ireland and France,* 195.

107 K.H. Connell, *The Population of Ireland, 1750–1845* (Oxford 1950), 25.

108 Cormac O Gráda, "Demographic Adjustment and Seasonal Migration in Nineteenth-Century Ireland," in Cullen and Furet, eds., *Ireland and France,* 181, 183–4.

109 Ibid., 185, and especially the map on 186.

110 HC (1835) XXXIII.

111 PRO, Dublin, 1766 Religious Returns; statistics for the Newport area also appear in Rev. Patrick J. Lee, *History of the Parish of Newport* (Thurles 1934?), 33 and Appendix.

112 NLI, ms 8908, Census Return 1766 for the Parishes of Uskeane and Ballingarry, copied by T.U. Sadleir.

113 PRO, Dublin, Tenison Groves Collection, IA.36.40, file Bard (1), 186.

114 NLI, ms 352, Killaloe questionnaire, 1820. Reliability of the statistics in this document varies from one parish to another.

115 For example, David Gagan, *Hopeful Travellers: Families, Land, and Social Change in Mid-Victorian Peel County, Canada West* (Toronto 1981), 100.

CHAPTER THREE

1 Quoted in *The Parliamentary Gazetteer of Ireland* (Dublin 1846), I: lxiii, lxi.

2 Con-acre, commonly called "quarter-ground" in North Tipperary, referred to the letting of patches of potato ground to labourers at high rents.

3 *Parliamentary Gazetteer,* I: lxiii.

4 Ibid., lxvii.

5 J.H. Johnson, "The Two 'Irelands' at the Beginning of the Nineteenth Century," in N. Stephens and R.E. Glasscock, eds., *Irish Geographical Studies in Honour of E. Estyn Evans* (Belfast 1970), 224–43.

6 William J. Smyth, "Land Values, Landownership, and Population Patterns in Co. Tipperary for 1641–1660 and 1841–1850: Some Comparisons," in L.M. Cullen and F. Furet, eds., *Ireland and France 17th–20th Centuries: Towards a Comparative Study of Rural History* (Paris 1980), 77.

7 British Library, add. ms 31882, Papers of the Consistory Court of Killaloe, 1671–1824, vol. II, ff. 157–60, inventory of William Newstead of Derrynaslin, 1749.

8 Arthur Young, *A Tour in Ireland* (Shannon 1970), I: 428.

9 Ibid., I: 430, 437.
10 Ibid., I: 435.
11 Ibid., I: 442–3.
12 Sir Charles Coote, *General View of the Agriculture and Manufactures of the King's County* (Dublin 1801), 21–2.
13 Ibid., 49–50.
14 Ibid., 44–6, 50.
15 Ibid., 21.
16 Ibid., 52.
17 Ibid., 73.
18 British Parliamentary Sessional Papers, HC (1836) XXXI, Poor Laws, Ireland, App. D, 23.
19 HC (1836) XXXIII, App. F, 92.
20 HC (1836) XXXIII, App. F, 377.
21 PRO, Dublin, Modreeny tithe applotment book, 1826/7; first edition Ordnance Survey six-inch map.
22 Registry of Deeds, Dublin, 147/194/99370, Croasdaile to Long, 1745; Public Record Office (PRO), Dublin, Clonrush tithe applotment book, 1830. See Table 8.
23 The 1831 pew list is printed in H.M. Bourchier, *'Boomagong' and the Bourchier Family* (Tocumwal? 1973).
24 Colonial Office Records, CO 384/9, 346–8, Public Archives of Canada (PAC), microfilm, reel B-882, James Martin to earl of Liverpool, Woodpark, Scarriff, 18 September 1823.
25 Coote, *King's County*, 31.
26 Ibid., 158.
27 Evidence taken before Her Majesty's Commissioners of Inquiry into the state of the law and practice in respect to the Occupation of Land in Ireland [known as the Devon Commission], HC (1845) XX, Pt II, 597, evidence of witness no. 557, Denis Egan, Clonegana, and elsewhere.
28 NLI, ms 13,000(8), 1806 and 1824 Otway rentals.
29 HC (1845) XX, Pt II, 619, testimony of witness no. 565, Arthur French, Esq., Carney Castle.
30 Ibid., 545–642, passim.
31 HC (1845) XXI, Pt III, 257, no. 845, J.A. Braddell, Esq., Mallow.
32 HC (1845) XX, Pt II, 636, testimony of witness no. 569, William Henry Head, Esq., Modreeny House.
33 In 1841–3, 4.7 per cent of dwellings in Tipperary were affected. HC (1852/53) XCI, App. 101, 295–8; App. 102, 299–302; recalculated as percentage of occupied dwellings in 1841. In the wake of the Famine, evictions intensified. In 1847 alone 7.9 per cent of the population was made homeless by ejectments, the highest rate in Ireland. S.H. Cousens, "The Regional Pattern of Emigration

During the Great Irish Famine, 1846–51," *Transactions & Papers of the Institute of British Geographers* 28 (1960): 131.

34 For modern reformulations of the typology see Dennis Mills, "English Villages in the Eighteenth and Nineteenth Centuries: A Sociological Approach," *Amateur Historian* 6, no. 8 (1965): 271–8; B.A. Holderness, "'Open' and 'Close' Parishes in England in the Eighteenth and Nineteenth Centuries," *Agricultural History Review* 20 (1972): Part II, 126–39; and Alan Everitt, *The Pattern of Rural Dissent: The Nineteenth Century* (Leicester 1972).

35 Demesne lands are marked on the first edition six-inch scale Ordnance Survey maps, and are also traceable in tithe applotment books and the records of the Primary (Griffith's) Valuation. A general map of demesne lands in County Tipperary may be found in T.W. Freeman, *Pre-Famine Ireland* (Manchester 1957), 215, and in his *Ireland: A General and Regional Geography* (London 1960), 176.

36 HC (1836) XXXIII, Poor Laws (Ireland), Supp. to App. F, 246.

37 HC (1845) XX, Pt II , Devon Commission, examination of witness no. 569, William Henry Head, Esq., of Modreeny House, 636.

38 Ibid., 637.

39 HC (1836) XXXIII, Poor Laws (Ireland), Supp. to App. F, 246.

40 HC (1845) XX, Pt II, Devon Commission, 574 and 582, witnesses nos. 548 and 550, Rev. Cornelius O'Brien, Lorrha, and John Moylan, Redwood.

41 Ibid., 574, no. 547, George Heenan, Parsonstown.

42 Ibid., 611, no. 562, O'Brien Dillon, Esq., Laurel Lodge, Nenagh.

43 Ibid., 638–9, no. 570, James Jocelyn Poe, Esq., Solsborough.

44 Ibid., 594, no. 555, Edmund Byrne, Lissanure.

45 HC (1824) XXII, 1821 census, 648, and 1841 census, figures reprinted with 1851 returns, HC (1852/53) XCI, 289–90.

46 PRO, Dublin, tithe applotment book, parish of Ballymackey, 1825; Griffiths Primary Valuation, 1850.

47 HC (1845) XX, Pt II, 628, testimony of witness no. 567, John Kennedy, Nenagh; 612–13, no. 562, O'Brien Dillon, Esq., Nenagh; HC (1845) XXI, Pt III, 256–7, testimony of no. 845, John Armistead Braddell, Esq., of Mallow, land agent to Mr Cole Bowen.

48 PRO, Dublin, tithe applotment book, parish of Ballygibbon, 1824; Griffith's Primary Valuation.

49 HC (1845) XX, Pt II, 594–5, evidence of no. 555, Edmund Byrne, Lissanure.

50 Ibid., 597, no. 558, Rev. William Minchin, Green Hills near Moneygall.

51 Smyth, "Land Values," 80.

52 Ibid., 77–8.

53 See Map 9.

54 Smyth, "Land Values," 75.

55 Young, *Tour in Ireland,* I: 442.

56 Smyth, "Land Values," 75.
57 Donnelly has suggested that partnership farming may also have "furnish[ed] a basis" for the organization of agrarian disturbances. James S. Donnelly Jr, "The Whiteboy Movement, 1761–5," *Irish Historical Studies* 21, no. 81 (March 1978): 41.
58 HC (1845) XX, Pt II, 629, no. 567, John Kennedy, Nenagh.
59 J. Morphy, *Recollections of a Visit to Great Britain and Ireland in the Summer of 1862* (Quebec 1863), 20.
60 Clipping in Toomevara Roman Catholic parish register, Latter-day Saints (LDS) reel 926103.
61 The Talbot party of 1818 sailed from the Cove of Cork but expressed willingness to travel to the other ports. The Evans family of Roscrea travelled to Dublin in 1831 by taking a jaunting car to Mountmellick and travelling thence by canal boat. London Public Library, Seaborn Diaries, "Memoirs of Richard Jones Evans," 752. The intertown rivalries in the eastern part of the region, certainly, were between Birr and Roscrea on the one hand and the larger centres of Leix and Offaly further east. The papers of William Hutchinson, Esq., of Roscrea include the ditty:
   Ope ye bogs & wallow down
   That Blackguard hole called Phillipstown
   And if your maw should gape for more
   For godsake swallow Tullamore.
   PRO, Dublin, M.3098, Roscrea Yeomanry Papers (1798–1821), no. 15, scribbled on back of a letter from Dublin dated 1803.
62 The census commissioners actually termed Shinrone and Borrisoleigh "villages." See Map 10.
63 1823 directories for Birr, Roscrea, and Nenagh are reprinted as Appendices 14, 15, and 19 in T.L. Cooke's *The Early History of the Town of Birr, or Parsonstown* (Dublin 1875), 398–404, 410–14.
64 PRO, Dublin, tithe applotment books.
65 An outside source of income, usually labouring, appears to have been necessary for countrymen holding less than two Irish acres. No one termed a farmer in the census held less than two acres, while half of the farmers holding from two to five acres were termed "farmer and labourer." Analysis derived by the author from 1821 census in PRO, Dublin, for parish of Seirkieran, Ballybritt barony, LDS reel 100818. McGuire's study of Clare and Limerick wills indicates that in the latter half of the nineteenth century over 50 per cent of testators who called themselves shopkeepers or publicans were also farmers or owned farm land. Maurice McGuire, "Rural Inheritance in 19th Century Clare & Limerick," *Dal gCais* 7 (1984): 50.
66 On the history of the Silvermines see Dermot F. Gleeson, "The Silver Mines of Ormond," *Journal of the Royal Society of Antiquaries of Ireland,* Series 7, vol. 7 (June 1937); M. Ryan, pp, "Mining and History in Tipperary," *Cois*

Deirge (Summer 1978): 18–19; George O'Brien, *The Economic History of Ireland in the Seventeenth Century* (Dublin 1919), 54–5; notes from several mine leases to individuals dating between 1708 and 1801, which were among the Dunalley papers that perished in the burning of Kilboy in 1922, are in T.U. Sadleir, "Manuscripts at Kilboy, Co. Tipperary, in the Possession of the Lord Dunalley," *Analecta Hibernica* 12 (January 1943): 150; *Dublin Evening Post,* 27 January 1807, 3, col. 3; Robert Kane, *The Industrial Resources of Ireland* (Dublin 1845), 199, 209.

67 Kane, *Industrial Resources,* 242–3; *Nenagh Guardian,* 26 October 1842, 2, cols. 2–3, "Report on the Quarries of the Imperial Slate Company"; Una McLoughlin, "Contributions to a History of Castletownearra Parish," *Cois Deirge* (Winter 1980): 28–30; *Nenagh Guardian,* 3 September 1842, 3.

68 Eileen McCracken, *Irish Woods since Tudor Times: Their Distribution and Exploitation* (Newton Abbot 1971), 43–4; Thomas V. MacNamara, pp, *Guide to Mountshannon* (np, nd), 60; NLI, Croasdaile Deeds, D23185–23215, not individually numbered, Henry and John Croasdaile to Thomas Lambert, 3 March 1760.

69 R.A. Butlin, ed., *The Development of the Irish Town* (London 1977), 124.

70 Rev. Edward Ledwich, "Parish of Aghaboe," in William Shaw Mason, *Parochial Survey of Ireland,* 3 vols. (1814), I: 70–1.

71 L.M. Cullen, "The Social and Cultural Modernisation of Rural Ireland, 1600–1900," in Cullen and Furet, eds., *Ireland and France,* 197–8.

72 Young, *Tour in Ireland,* I: 35.

73 Coote, *King's County,* 49.

74 Cooke, *History of Birr,* 404.

75 Coote, *King's County,* 58.

76 Ibid., 76, 78.

77 Ledwich, "Parish of Aghaboe," I: 71–2.

78 Registry of Deeds, Dublin, 217/175/143158, Towers to Haskett, 1762.

79 PRO, Dublin, Roscrea and Templemore parish registers; Registry of Deeds, Dublin, 343/17/229403, Edward Talbot to James Acres, 1781; NLI, ms 787, County Tipperary freeholders list, 1776; correpondence with Gwen Talbot Bergsma of California.

80 Cooke, *Birr,* 404; Hopper correspondence in possession of Harry Hopper of Ottawa, George Hayes to Arthur Hopper, Roscrea, 29 June 1832.

81 Registry of Deeds, Dublin, 861/425/574425, Hardy to Guest.

82 Ottawa City Archives, Carleton County Land Registry Copy Books, no. 337, Rutherford to Hardy (1830); no. 478, Forsyth to Litle (1832); no. 861, Hardy to Hardy (1835); no. 2173, Johnston to Hardy (1836); and other instruments.

83 PRO, Dublin, Templemore parish register; PAC, RG 31, 1842 census of Hull; Ottawa City Directories, passim; obituary in *Ottawa Journal,* 23 August 1888, 1.

84 The closest was the Killenaule coalfield some twenty miles south of Templemore.

85 PRO, Kew, Home Office Papers, HO 100/222, f. 209, Malcomson to attorney general, 24 May 1828.

86 PRO, Kew, HO 100/222, ff. 219–22, Anglesey to Peel, Phoenix Park, 16 May 1828.

87 PRO, Kew, HO 100/222, ff. 234–5, Samson Carter to attorney general, May 1828. Malcomson, who was also consulted by the Castle, was a Quaker. HO 100/222, ff. 209–12, Malcomson to Henry Joy, Esq., attorney general, Clonmel, 24 5mo. 1828; f. 213, W. Gregory to Malcomson, 17 May 1828. On Malcomson see also R.A. Butlin, ed., *The Development of the Irish Town* (London 1977), 126.

88 PRO, Kew, HO 100/222, ff. 219–22, Anglesey to Peel, Phoenix Park, 16 May 1828.

89 E.H. Sheehan, *Nenagh and Its Neighbourhood* (Nenagh 1976), 71.

90 Samuel Lewis, *A Topographical Dictionary of Ireland,* 2nd edition (London 1847), 584.

91 Ibid., 587.

92 HC (1845) XX, Pt II, 628, evidence of no. 567, John Kennedy of Nenagh.

93 The long, narrow fields reclaimed from bogland in numerous townlands are readily apparent on the 1840 Ordnance Survey map.

94 HC (1836) XXXII, Poor Laws, Ireland, Supp. to App. E, 81.

CHAPTER FOUR

1 Several Protestant families from Borrisokane are noted in early American passenger lists, including Massy Haskett who arrived at New York in 1811 but turned up in Halton County in 1824: Donald M. Schlegel, ed., *Passengers From Ireland: Lists of Passengers Arriving at American Ports Between 1811 and 1817* (Baltimore 1980), 22, 121; Public Archives of Canada (PAC), Upper Canada Land Petitions, RG 1, L 3, H14/95. A group from New York that settled in Toronto and Esquesing Townships in 1819 will be discussed later in this chapter.

2 These military settlers will be discussed in chapter 6.

3 PAC, Lower Canada Land Papers, RG 1, L 3L, vol. 82, 40822, Francis A. Evans to A.W. Cochran, St Francis, Drummondville, 8 August 1816.

4 Great Britain, Colonial Office Records, Original Correspondence, Secretary of State, 1816 Lower Canada Miscellaneous, CO 42/170, f. 225, PAC, microfilm, reel B-137, Francis Evans to Earl Bathurst, Quebec, 14 June 1816. Evans was not a descendant of George Evans, first Lord Carbery, as he claimed, but he may possibly have been descended from one of Lord Carbery's brothers; some of their descendants lived in County Limerick. *British Colonist & St Francis Gazette* (Stanstead, LC), 23 November 1826, 2, cols. 2–3, letter of F.A. Evans; *Burke's Peerage and Baronetage* (London 1970), 471–4.

5 PAC, RG I, L 3L, vol. 82, 40814, Evans to Loring, Quebec, 11 June 1816.

6 Ibid., 40824, George Fowler to W. Gibson, Quebec, 16 March 1818.

7 PAC, CO 42/170, f. 225.

8 Francis A. Evans, *The Emigrants' Directory and Guide to Obtain Lands and Effect a Settlement in the Canadas* (Dublin 1833), 27.

9 Public Record Office (PRO), Dublin, Roscrea parish register.

10 PAC, RG I, L 3L, vol. 82, 40822.

11 CO 42/165, f. 199, PAC, reel B-133, Evans to Peel, Roscrea, 18 April 1815.

12 CO 42/165, f. 205, PAC, reel B-133, Evans to Bathurst, Roscrea, 29 April 1815.

13 PAC, RG I, L 3L, vol. 82, 40805, Bathurst to Evans, Downing Street, 20 May 1815.

14 CO 42/165, f. 216, PAC, reel B-133, Evans to Bathurst, Dublin, 3 June 1815.

15 PAC, RG I, L 3L, vol. 82, 40822.

16 Ibid., 40809–10, Evans to Loring, New Carlisle, Bay Chaleur, 1 January 1816.

17 Ibid., 40813, Evans to Loring, Quebec, 11 June 1816.

18 CO 42/170, f. 225.

19 PAC, RG I, L 3L, vol. 82, 40829, Evans to Ready, Drummondville, 15 January 1820.

20 Ibid., vol. 82, 40850, petition of F.A. Evans, Shipton, 2 November 1828.

21 Marriage notice of son in *Quebec Mercury*, 6 June 1833.

22 PAC, RG I, L 3L, vol. 82, 40874, Prospectus of *The Emigrants Guide,* 1830.

23 RG I, L 3L, vol. 82, 40878, petition of F.A. Evans, Quebec, 1 February 1832.

24 Evans, *The Emigrants' Directory,* i and "Advertisement."

25 British Library (BL), Killaloe Consistory Court records, add. ms 31883, f. 191, marriage licence bond of Edward Talbot of Cloonloghan and Esther Allen of Borrisokane, 1762; printed in R.T.D. FitzGerald, "Killaloe Marriage Licence Bonds 1680–1720 and 1760–1762," *Irish Genealogist* 5, no. 5 (November 1978): 589.

26 Land records show that Richard Talbot's father Edward was the eldest son of Richard Talbot, a farmer who leased Garrane, consisting of 114 Irish plantation acres, from George Percy in 1746 (Registry of Deeds, Dublin, 121/452/83574, Percy to Talbot, 1746; 430/378/279606, Talbot to Armitage, 1787). Although the parentage of the elder Richard has not been established, the descent of all the Talbot families in the King's panhandle from a common ancestor is suggested both by their clustered settlement pattern and by the fact that most branches continued to bury in the ancestral parish of Dunkerrin (PRO, Dublin, Dunkerrin burial registers, 1825–76). The pedigree of the senior line of the family is given in W.A. and C.L. Goodspeed, *History of the County of Middlesex, Canada* (Toronto 1889), 1016–19. The basic facts of the latter lineage have been confirmed as far back as the immigrants to Ireland by searches in the Registry of Deeds: information courtesy Dr Ron Mann, Kingston, Ontario.

27 Registry of Deeds, Dublin, 501/558/326834, deed of marriage settlement between John Baird of Cloncloughane and Richard Talbot of Gurrane, 1795.

28 Edward Allen Talbot, *Five Years' Residence in the Canadas* (London 1824), 1: 5.

29 Ibid., I: 3–4. Registered deeds provide a suggestive though incomplete picture of Richard's financial circumstances. His eldest brother George seems not to have inherited any part of Garrane but became a merchant in Borrisokane. Brothers Thomas and John received the Garrane property between them, but lived in Cloughjordan after their father's death in 1798 or 1799, leasing the eighty-eight acres that then remained of their grandfather's old property in perpetuity to John Shortt in the latter year. John soon afterwards emigrated to America, of which more later. Richard appears to have obtained property for the first time under his marriage settlement. The more common procedure was for the wife to bring a "fortune" in cash, and for the husband's family to put some of its lands into trusteeship as her jointure property to ensure her maintenance after the husband died. In this instance Richard had no land and so paid £500 to his father-in-law (possibly with the assistance of his brother-in-law) in exchange for some of Baird's lands in Moneygall as a jointure for Lydia. He thereafter secured a plot of ground (probably a house lot) in Cloughjordan, but mortgaged it to his wife's relative Joseph Hardy of Killymer in 1815 for £313.9. There is no way of discovering whether or not he paid off this mortgage before emigrating to Canada; nonetheless, the precariousness of his circumstances is clear. Registry of Deeds, Dublin, 494/518/336601, Talbot to Healy, 1797; 533/199/352146, Talbott and Talbott to Shortt, 1799; 729/116/497451, Talbot to Gaynor, 1818; 501/558/326834, marriage settlement, 1795; 690/285/474234, Talbot to Hardy, 1815.

30 Talbot, *Five Years' Residence,* I: 5.

31 CO 42/170, f. 170, Richard Talbot to Earl Bathurst, Cloghjordan, 27 February 1816.

32 PRO, Kew, Original Correspondence, Secretary of State, Emigration, North America, CO 384/1, f. 466, PAC, reel B-876, Talbot to Bathurst, Cloghjordan, 29 December 1817. John Talbot was born c1771 and served in the Upper Ormond Cavalry under Lord Dunalley from 1796 to 1800. He soon after emigrated to the United States where his son John was born c1803. By 1810 he was in Upper Canada, probably at his later residence in West Flamborough near Burlington Heights. He claimed to have served in a flank company of the 1st Oxford Militia in 1812. He moved to London soon after his brother's arrival in Canada. John's share of the parental estate, eighty-eight acres in Garrane already let out in perpetuity, was sold for him by Richard just before the latter left for Canada. Registry of Deeds, Dublin, 729/116/497451, John Talbot of Flambro West, Upper Canada, to John Gaynor, 1818; PAC, RG I, L 3, vol. 505, TI/7, microfilm, reel C-2838, petition of John Talbot, London, 18 March 1841, and enclosures. I am grateful to Hazel Runchey of Winnipeg for a copy of the Irish deed. The relationship is indicated by Lord Dunalley's certificate of John's Irish yeomanry service, which names him as a son of the late Edward Talbot of Garrane: ibid., no. 7e. Censuses of West Nissouri; Baptisms in the London and Gore Districts, Ontario Historical Society, *Papers and Records* 5 (1904): 94.

33 CO 384/1, ff. 398–9, Rosse to Bathurst, Parsonstown, 29 December 1817.

34 CO 384/1, ff. 466–7, PAC, reel B-876, Talbot to Bathurst, Cloghjordan, 29 December 1817.

35 CO 43/56, f. 89, printed circular dated 1 February 1818 enclosed with Bathurst to Rosse, London, 27 January 1818.

36 On the £10 deposit plan see Daniel James Brock, "Richard Talbot, the Tipperary Irish, and the Formative Years of London Township, 1818–1826," MA thesis, University of Western Ontario, 1969, 4–12, 31.

37 CO 384/3, f. 542, PAC, reel B-877, Talbot to Bathurst, Cloghjordan, 7 February 1818.

38 CO 384/3, ff. 546–7, PAC, reel B-877, two letters Talbot to Bathurst, Cloghjordan, 7 March 1818.

39 CO 384/3, f. 548, draft letter to Mr Talbot.

40 CO 384/3, f. 549, Talbot to Bathurst, Cloghjordan, 20 March 1818.

41 CO 43/56, f. 135, Goulbourn to Commissioners of HM Navy, Downing Street, 2 April 1818.

42 CO 384/3, f. 551, PAC, reel B-877, Talbot to Bathurst, Cloghjordan, 27 April 1818.

43 CO 384/3, f. 561, PAC, reel B-877, Talbot's settlers to Bathurst, Cove, 11 June 1818.

44 CO 43/56, f. 188–9, Goulbourn to Naval Commissioners, Downing Street, 11 June 1818.

45 CO 384/3, ff. 45–7, PAC reel B-877, Naval Commissioners to Goulbourn, Navy Office, 13 June 1818.

46 CO 43/57, f. 10, Goulbourn to Talbot, Downing Street, 18 June 1818.

47 CO 384/3, f. 51, PAC, reel B-877, Naval Commissioners to Goulbourn, Navy Office, 16 June 1818.

48 Talbot, *Five Years' Residence,* I: 25.

49 Ibid., I: 25–7, 33; University of Western Ontario, Regional History Collection (UWO), Freeman Talbot Papers, Freeman Talbot's memoirs, 3.

50 Talbot, *Five Years' Residence,* I: 30.

51 *Quebec Gazette,* 30 July 1818, no. 2821; Talbot, *Five Years' Residence,* I: 40.

52 Talbot, *Five Years' Residence,* I: 59–61.

53 Ibid., I: 82–3.

54 UWO, Freeman Talbot's memoirs, 3–4.

55 Talbot, *Five Years' Residence,* I: 83.

56 Ibid., I: 83–95; UWO, Freeman Talbot's memoirs, 4.

57 There seems to have been no relationship between the two Talbot families, Col. Talbot being a brother of Richard Wogan Talbot of Malahide, County Dublin, and Richard Talbot a descendant of a seventeenth-century settler in King's County.

58 Talbot, *Five Years' Residence,* I: 103–6; *Quebec Gazette,* 19 October 1818, no. 2844.

59 CO 42/361, ff. 123–4.

60 CO 42/362, ff. 139–47.

61 UWO, Freeman Talbot's memoirs, 5; Talbot, *Five Years' Residence,* I: 111–14.

62 Talbot, *Five Years' Residence*, I: 115–18.
63 One of Talbot's settlers encountered the same difficulty. Thomas Delahunt, an immigrant who had stayed in Montreal, moved to Niagara after being burned out of his previous home. His request to take up his grant in 1837 met with the response that "the Council are not aware of any Emigrants having come out under the auspices of Mr Talbot so as to entitle them to claim any lands at this date." PAC, RG 1, L 3, D/21/16, reel C-1879, petition of Thomas Delahunt, Niagara, 22 September 1837. Talbot had interpreted his correspondence with the colonial secretary to mean that he would receive 5400 acres free of fees, out of which he would convey fifty acres each to the fifty-four settlers over seventeen years of age who accompanied him, leaving himself with 2700 acres. His settlers were, however, located by Col. Thomas Talbot under the usual terms for 100–acre grants, paying fees. The colonel located Richard for 1000 acres, later increased to 1200 acres, the maximum allowable without reference to the home government. Richard protested the requirement that he pay fees when he had been promised exemption (an argument Francis Evans also made and lost), but the lieutenant-governor insisted that Talbot and his settlers had abandoned the arrangements made with Lord Bathurst and accepted land under the normal regulations. Straightened financial circumstances forced Talbot to accept the lieutenant-governor's terms, and he eventually sold his lands to clear his debts. PAC, RG 7, G 16C, vol. 12, f. 153, Hillier to Edward A. Talbot, 26 February 1823; RG 5, A I, vol. 59, ff. 31182–5, Edward A. Talbot to Hillier, York, 27 February 1823; Daniel J. Brock, "Richard Talbot Sold Lands Granted to Him," *London Free Press*, 8 May 1970.
64 Evans, *The Emigrants' Directory*, 30–1.
65 Ibid., 31.
66 PAC, RG 68, General Index to the Registrar General, f. 465, no. 16. His last such appointment was in June 1835: f. 493, no. 10.
67 PAC, RG 9, IB 8, Adjutant General, Upper Canada, vol. 1, Proceedings of a Court Martial on Captn Edward A. Talbot, 4th Regt Middlesex Militia, February 1830; PAC, RG 5, AI, UC Sundries, vol. 102, 58170–4, reel C-6871, Thomas Talbot to Z. Mudge, Port Talbot, 13 October 1830, and enclosure.
68 This reference by his brother Freeman may be to "A new method of Propelling Vessels and Carriages, designated by the name of Talbot's Atmospheric Propelling Engine," which Edward patented 18 July 1834. *List of Canadian Patents, From the Beginning of the Patent Office, June, 1824, to the 31st of August, 1872* (reprinted Ottawa 1979), 9.
69 UWO, Freeman Talbot's memoirs, 6.
70 *Quebec Gazette*, 18 February 1839, 3, col. 3.
71 Goodspeed, *History of Middlesex*, 512–13; *Dictionary of Canadian Biography* (DCB), X (Toronto 1972), 671.
72 PAC, RG 68, f. 256, no. 29.
73 William Kingsford, *The Early Bibliography of Ontario* (Toronto 1892), 82; Evans, *The Emigrants' Directory*, ii.

74 Evans, *The Emigrants' Directory,* ii.
75 PAC, RG I, L 3L, vol. 82, 40858, reel C-2525, Report of Committee of the Whole Council on Petition of Francis A. Evans, 25 February 1829; advertisement as land agent in *British Colonist & St Francis Gazette,* 15 January 1829, 4.
76 CO 42/183, ff. 129–31, Navy Office to Goulbourn, 16 February 1819.
77 The Talbot family's direct influence in stimulating later emigration was probably minimal. John's temporary return to Ireland was motivated by disillusionment and Edward's two-volume book was probably too expensive to appeal to any but the landed gentry, who may have used it to supply useful information to prospective emigrants. Freeman visited Ireland in 1855 at the request of the emigration authorities to lecture on "agricultural opportunities in Upper Canada," but this trip postdated the period of heavy migration from North Tipperary to the province. UWO, Freeman Talbot memoirs.
78 CO 42/165, ff. 201, 207–13, PAC, reel B-134, certificates of settlers.
79 PRO, Dublin, Templeharry parish register; Goodspeed, *History of Middlesex,* 835–6; *London (CW) Times,* 23 June 1848, 3.
80 PRO, Dublin, Templeharry parish register; the relationship of Charles Goulding and Mrs Howard is stated in Archives of Ontario (AO), Heir and Devisee Commission files, RG 40–2826, claim of James Howard, 1846.
81 A later Whitfield Howard was resident in Bourney and is no doubt related to his earlier namesake. Registrar General's Office, Dublin, register of marriages, 1845, vol. 10, 3, Latter-day Saints (LDS) reel 101271.
82 John Lloyd of Gloster, King's County, signed the missing character certificate in 1815 and also wrote letters later for the wife of the emigrant at Williamsburgh. CO 384/10, f. 195, PAC, reel B-882, John Lloyd to Bathurst, Lowland House, Roscrea, 5 May 1824; CO 384/10, f. 260, Mary Robinson, Ettagh, 3 May 1824; CO 384/11, f. 407, PAC, reel B-883, John Lloyd to Bathurst, Lowland House, Roscrea, 11 April 1825; Andrew F. Hunter, *A History of Simcoe County* (Barrie 1948), Part 2, 28; PAC, RG I, L 3, vol. 431, R/15, reel C-2745, petition of William Robinson of West Gwillimbury, 6 March 1827; Theodore F.M. Newton, *Pioneer Chronicle: The Robinson-Newton-Lawson Saga* (Ottawa 1966), 19–30. Connell converted from Catholicism in 1771 and married Mary Wallace in 1779: Eileen O'Byrne, *The Convert Rolls* (Dublin 1981), 52.
83 CO 42/165, f. 199, Francis Evans to Rt Hon. Robert Peel, 18 April 1815.
84 The final list of settlers is to be found in CO 384/3, f. 549, PAC, reel B-877, Talbot to Bathurst, Cloghjordan, 20 March 1818. See Appendix A for compiled passenger list. Origins were determined using various records in Canada and Ireland, including genealogies, parish registers, obituaries, gravestones, and census and land records.
85 Haskett's son John was born at Cloughjordan in 1810. Obituary, *London Advertiser,* 8 February 1878, 1.
86 Hodgins's gravestone in the old Union Cemetery, Hazeldean, Ontario, states his birthplace as Newtown, parish "Motherinny."

87 London Public Library, Seaborn Diaries, Memoirs of Richard Jones Evans; Registry of Deeds, Dublin, 588/94/398869, Waller to Geary, 1806; PRO, Dublin, Templeharry parish register, marriage; Shinrone parish register, baptisms 1808–9; Brock, "Richard Talbot," 153, note 94; Goodspeed, *History of Middlesex*, 824–6.

88 Registry of Deeds, Dublin, 690/285/474234, Talbot to Hardy, 1815. Hardy had children named Joseph North and Deborah, and was probably a grandson of North Hardy of Rahone, County Tipperary, gent., and Deborah Baird of Ballinlogh, King's County, who married in 1754. PRO, Dublin, IA.36.40, Tenison Groves Abstracts, box B2, bundle Bard (1), 307. This Deborah was of the same generation as Mrs Talbot's father, John Baird.

89 PRO, Dublin, Index to Killaloe Diocesan Marriage Licence Bonds; register of St John's, Newport.

90 Joseph Hardy's son Joseph North was born in Nenagh in 1800, according to his obituary in the *London Free Press*, 19 February 1884, 8, col. 3, and the father was recorded as a sadler in Nenagh in 1790, but the family apparently lived in County Galway in 1815. Registry of Deeds, Dublin, 436/15/281588 and 690/285/474234.

91 PRO, Dublin, Otway Estate Papers, D.20,368, Otway to Shouldice, 1759; D.20,370, Otway to Sifton, 1760; National Library of Ireland (NLI), Otway Estate maps 1655–1840, no. 5, Glantane, part of estate of Cooke Otway, surveyed 1794.

92 The emigrant James Shouldice married Jane Boyd in 1807: Family Bible extract courtesy Mrs Jemima Thompson; PRO, Dublin, Index to Killaloe Diocesan Marriage Bonds. It is thus probable that he is the James Shouldice who transferred his lease of Upper Tiermoyle to John Boyd of Falleen in 1814: Registry of Deeds, Dublin, 672/103/461550, Shouldice to Boyd, 1814, and the James Shouldice who occupied 2 a, 2 r, 31 p of the "Fifteen Acres" on the Rolleston estate at Frankfort near Dunkerrin in 1817 and 1818. NLI, ms 13794(6), Rolleston Papers, Surveys of Frankfort, 26 July 1817 and January 1818.

93 NLI, ms 352, Abstract of Information in Answer to Queries concerning the parishes in the Dioceses of Killaloe and Kilfenora, 1820.

94 CO 384/5, 321–2, Charles Rolleston to Earl Bathurst, Silverhills near Moneygall, 4 May [1819].

95 CO 384/1, 466, PAC, reel B-876, Richard Talbot, Cloghjordan, 29 December 1817.

96 AO, Crown Lands Department, petitions, RG 1, C-I-1, petition of Samuel Long of Huntley, 1832.

97 *Quebec Gazette*, 19 October 1818.

98 UWO, Freeman Talbot memoirs, 18.

99 Talbot, *Five Years' Residence*, I: 18.

100 CO 384/5, 321–2, Charles Rolleston to Earl Bathurst, Silverhills near Moneygall, 4 May [1819].

101 British Parliamentary Sessional Papers, First Report of Commissioners for Inquiring into the Condition of the Poorer Classes in Ireland, House of Commons (HC) (1836) XXXI, Appendix D, 23.

102 Talbot, *Five Years' Residence*, II: 198.

103 Wendy Cameron, "Selecting Peter Robinson's Irish Emigrants," *Histoire sociale/Social History* 9, no. 17 (May 1976): 42–4.

104 CO 384/3, f. 561, Petition of settlers to Bathurst, Cove of Cork, 11 June 1818; CO 42/362, ff. 143–6, signatures for receipt of £10 deposit, Port Talbot, 1818.

105 Cameron, "Selecting Robinson's Emigrants," 44.

106 The Stanleys were from Borrisokane, where their son Samuel was born c1810, but had lived briefly at Red Gate in Shinrone parish, where their son William was baptized in 1817. They were noted as "late from the Parish of Shinrone" at the burial in Quebec City of their son James on 31 July 1818. PAC, RG 31, 1852 census of Fitzroy Twp, 81; PRO, Dublin, reel 4, Shinrone parish register; Archives nationales, Hull, parish register of Anglican Cathedral, Quebec City, reel MF-138-2, 1818, f. 28. Relationships among members of pioneer families have often been forgotten by descendants and it is unsafe to assume a sibling relationship on the basis of surname alone. However, some degree of relationship is often implied in Canadian records. Godparents were usually chosen from among relatives where possible. The godparents of William Hodgins's daughter Mary Ann, for example, were Thomas Stanley's children Samuel and Maria, and Eliza Stanley, either his wife or daughter; Stanley's wife was Elizabeth Hodgins. The Stanleys also had a son named Adam, which was a name used by the Hodginses of Newtown, but not by any other of the many Stanley families that came to Canada. William Hodgins himself had a son Adam, who died young; Adam's godparents were Samuel and Elizabeth Stanley and Robert Birch, an 1819 arrival whose wife was Ellen Hodgins. Archives of Anglican Diocese of Ottawa, register of March parish, baptism of Mary Ann Hodgins, 1826; Richmond parish, baptisms of Adam Stanley, 1828, and Adam Hodgins, 1825; PRO, Kew, WO 13/4137, Muster Rolls of Lower Ormond Infantry Yeomanry, list an Adam Hodgins of Cloughjordan, whose age was reported variously as seventy-two and sixty, between 1823 and 1827; PRO, Dublin, TAB 27 N/14, Modreeny tithe applotment book, 1826.

107 CO 42/183, ff. 129–31, Navy Office to Goulbourn, 16 February 1819.

108 J. Richard Houston, *Numbering the Survivors: A History of the Standish Family of Ireland, Ontario, and Alberta* (Toronto 1979), 42–8.

109 *Montreal Gazette*, 16 May 1821.

110 Registry of Deeds, Dublin, 566/92/380549, Reed to Gardiner, 4 July 1801; Genealogical Office, Dublin, Abstracts of Prerogative Wills, vol. 11 (New Series), 233 F-G, 261, will of Thomas Gardiner, 1797.

111 PAC, RG I, L 3, vol. 271(a), K12/73 and K12/81, reel C-2118, petitions of William Kent, 1819; PRO, Dublin, Castletownarra parish register; PAC, gravestone inscriptions, Zion Cemetery, Whaley's Corners, Chinguacousy.

112 Howard's son, Robert Palmer Howard, became professor of medicine at McGill and president of the Canada Medical Association; his grandson married the daughter of Lord Strathcona. PRO, Dublin, Index to Killaloe Diocesan Marriage Licence Bonds; E.J. McAuliffe, "A List of Entries of Marriage Licence Grants in

Killaloe Court and Register Book," *Irish Genealogist* 5, no. 6 (November 1979):
110, Robert Howard and Elizabeth Palmer, 1781; PRO, Dublin, Shinrone parish
register; PAC, RG 1, L 3, vol. 229, H12/149, reel C-2048, petition of Robert
Howard, 1819; Houston, *Numbering the Survivors*, 47, 54; Rev. J. Douglas
Borthwick, *History and Biographical Gazetteer of Montreal to the Year 1892*
(Montreal 1892), 376; George Maclean Rose, *A Cyclopaedia of Canadian
Biography* (Toronto 1888), 511–12; Archives nationales (Montreal), N-B
Doucet, notaire, no. 18271, will of Robert Howard.

113 PAC, RG 1, L 3, vol. 528, W12/107, reel C-2954, petition of Samuel Watkins,
1819; RG 1, L 3, vol. 530, W14/66, reel C-2955, petition of Samuel Watkins Jr,
1824; AO, Wentworth County Surrogate Court, reel GS 1–596, #305, estate file
of Samuel Watkins the Elder of Hamilton, 1864; *Christian Guardian*, 13 January
1869, 8, obituary of F.W. Watkins; *The Canadian Album: Men of Canada*
(1891), I: 265; Thomas Melville Bailey, ed., *Dictionary of Hamilton Biography*,
I: 208–9; inscriptions on Watkins gravestones and vaults in Hamilton cemetery.

114 Bridge did not remain long in Canada, but returned to Ireland, where he married
Ralph Smith's daughter Jane in 1828; they lie buried at Roscrea. PAC, RG 1, L 3,
B12/149 & 162, reel C-1625, petitions of Thomas Bridge; PRO, Dublin, Shinrone
and Roscrea parish registers; Bridge gravestone at Roscrea; AO, Crown Lands
Department Correspondence, RG 1, A-1-6, microfilm, MS 563, reel 28, vol. 31,
env. no. 5, 27342, Smith to Yeilding, Bytown, 2 May 1856; Nicholas Flood
Davin, *The Irishman in Canada* (London 1877), 315; *Burke's Irish Family
Records* (London 1976), 1026; G.N. Nuttall-Smith, *The Chronicles of a Puritan
Family in Ireland [Smith (formerly) of Glasshouse]* (Oxford 1923), 50–1;
Timothy William Bridge, "Notes on the Family History of the Roscrea Bridges,"
typescript, 1921 and 1953. I am grateful to Richard Birch, late of Birchgrove,
Surrey, BC, and Miss M.E. Bridge of Long Ashton, Bristol, England, for copies
of the Smith book and the Bridge manuscript.

115 For the Kilcooly settlers see Appendix D. On Switzer see DCB, VIII (Toronto
1985), 854–5.

116 Houston, *Numbering the Survivors*, 47–8; B. Wesley Switzer, *Some Descendants of Martin Switzer of Streetsville* (Brantford 1981), 2–3.

117 Houston, *Numbering the Survivors*, 18, 27–31, 48–9, 138–41; PAC, RG 1, L 3,
vol. 460, S12/266, reel C-2813, petition of Joseph Standish, 1819.

118 Among them were several Evanses from Roscrea. It is not known at present
whether they were members of the same family as Francis Armstrong Evans, who
had made the first attempt at Tipperary group emigration in 1815.

CHAPTER FIVE

1 CO 384/3, f. 551, Public Archives of Canada (PAC), reel B-877, Richard Talbot to
Earl Bathurst, Cloghjordan, 27 April 1818.

2 CO 384/5, ff. 321–2, PAC, reel B-879, Charles Rolleston to Earl Bathurst, Silverhills near Moneygall, 4 May [1819].

3 CO 384/4, f. 41, PAC, reel B-877, Robert Birch to Earl Bathurst, Borrisokane, January 1819. See Appendix B.

4 CO 384/4, ff. 106–16, PAC, reel B-877, John Baskerville and Robert Boyd to Earl Bathurst, Cloughjordan, 29 March 1819. See Appendix C.

5 CO 384/4, f. 110, PAC, reel B-877, character certificate of Henry Neale and family, 23 March 1819; genealogical notes on the O'Neil family by W.A. Jones, c1890, copy courtesy Heather Jones, Victoria; F.T. Rosser, *London Township Pioneers* (Belleville 1975), 80–4.

6 Clifford Sifton, *The Sifton Family Record* (np 1956), 7; Rosser, *London Township Pioneers,* 54–5, 64, 72–6.

7 Copy of Robinson's marriage licence bond, courtesy late Mrs W.G. Clothier, London, Ontario.

8 Information from late Mrs W.G. Clothier.

9 Archives nationales, Montreal (ANQ(M)), parish register of Christ Church Anglican.

10 PAC, Baby Collection, MG 24, L 3, vol. 17, 9904, G.H. Monk to George Birch, 11 February 1822; PAC, Upper Canada Land Petitions, RG 1, L 3, vol. 48, B14/201, petition of George Birtch, Caledonia, 1825; Archives of Ontario (AO), Land Records Index; AO, Prescott County deed no. 1976, George Birch to James Cross, 4 October 1834; Carleton County deed no. 636, Robert Birtch to George Birtch, 25 July 1833, and other instruments.

11 CO 384/4, f. 114, PAC, reel B-877, character certificate of Bull family, 24 March 1819.

12 PAC, RG 1, L 3, G12/149, reel C-2031, petition of Thomas Goulding, 1820; the relationship is revealed in the marriage licence bond of Reed's daughter and William Clarke, another 1819 immigrant, PAC, Upper Canada marriage licence bonds, RG 5, B 9, vol. 16, reel C-6778, 840–1.

13 Public Record Office (PRO), Dublin, Roscrea parish register.

14 CO 384/4, f. 109, PAC, reel B-877, certificate of Goulding brothers, Roscrea, 26 March 1819.

15 ANQ(M), registers of Christ Church, Montreal, and Chambly.

16 PAC, RG 1, L 3, vol. 206(a), G12/86, reel C-2030; Ontario Historical Society, *Papers and Records,* IX; University of Western Ontario (UWO), register of St Paul's, London; obituary, *London Free Press,* 22 March 1875, 4, col. 1.

17 CO 384/4, ff. 111–13, reel B-877, certificates of William and Robert Carden, 25 March 1819; J. Richard Houston, *Numbering the Survivors: A History of the Standish Family of Ireland, Ontario, and Alberta* (Toronto 1979), 35–6; ANQ(M), registers of Christ Church, Montreal, and Chambly.

18 Or does it? As I go to press I am in receipt of a letter from Tom Prittie of Palmyra, NY, who questions the identity of Adam Prittie's wife. The only source identifying her as a Caswell is a note on the flyleaf of a Caswell family Bible printed in 1886 which identifies the sisters of the immigrant Caswells as Mrs John Brindley, who remained in Ireland, and Mrs Thomas McCullough and Mrs Adam Prittie, who came to Canada. Mr Prittie reports a strong family

tradition that his great-grandfather Oliver Prittie's sister Kate married her cousin Adam and preceded Oliver to Canada, settling in Perth where Oliver's son John later stayed with him. An Adam Prittie of Mucklin married a Mary (not Kate) Prittie of Silvermines by Killaloe licence in 1816, and an Adam and Mary Rettie [sic], with one daughter, appeared in 1819 in John Baskerville's list of prospective emigrants, printed in Appendix c. The Perth Anglican register records the burial on 24 October 1826 of a Mary Prettie, and Adam had married again by 1831 when a daughter by wife Jane Hewitt was born. Tom's grandfather may have been right about his aunt's marriage but wrong about her name. The Caswell family Bible now appears unreliable in other details for Sarah, Mrs Thomas McCullough of Drummond Township, called a native of Nenagh at her burial, is most likely the Sarah Ardell who married Thomas McCulloch by Killaloe licence in 1819; a Catharine Ardell lived with Sarah in 1861. There remains the question of why the Pritties settled in Drummond rather than in the main Ottawa Valley Tipperary colony a few miles to the east, if they were not drawn there by the Caswells. Shirley Mayse, *Our Caswell Relatives,* 3rd edition (Vancouver 1980), 12–19, 185–9; PAC, Perth Settlement Register, MG 9, D 8–27; CO 384/9, f. 523, PAC, reel B-882, Andrew Young and Samuel Lowes to Earl Bathurst, Ballingrane, County Limerick, 11 April 1823; PRO, Dublin, Index to Killaloe Diocesan Marriage Licence Bonds; *Irish Genealogist* 5, no. 6 (November 1979): 717; Anglican Diocese of Ottawa Archives, registers of Perth and Carleton Place; PAC, RG 31, 1861 census of Drummond Township, 24.

19 CO 384/4, f. 177, PAC, reel B-877, Cantrell to Bathurst, Nenagh, 27 January 1819; PRO, Dublin, Shinrone parish register; Cantrell gravestone at Nenagh.

20 CO 384/5, f. 298, PAC, reel B-879, Rud to Bathurst, Templemore, 17 March 1819.

21 CO 384/5, f. 418, PAC, reel B-879, Sutherland to Bathurst, Templemore, 8 April 1819.

22 CO 384/4, f. 505, PAC, reel B-878, Howard to Bathurst, 1819.

23 CO 384/4, f. 414, PAC, reel B-878, Fitzgerald to Bathurst, Templemore, 12 April 1819.

24 CO 384/5, f. 58, PAC, reel B-878, Martin to Bathurst, Clonrush Glebe, Scarriff, 16 March 1819.

25 CO 384/5, ff. 294–5, PAC, reel B-879, James Read to Bathurst, Moynoe House, Scariff, 17 March 1819.

26 PAC, UC Land Petitions, RG 1, L 3, vol. 102, C12/257, reel C-1723; Land Book K, 333, reel C-103; David P. Acres and Bruce S. Elliott, "The Acres Families of Carleton County, Ontario," *Families* 20, no. 3 (1981): 131–2.

27 CO 384/16, f. 499, reel B-888, memorial of William Owens, Borrisokane, 24 April 1827.

28 UWO, Freeman Talbot memoirs, 18; *Carp Review,* 29 April 1920, 5.

29 *Limerick Advertiser,* 25 June 1819, 2, 3. I am grateful to John D. Blackwell for this reference.

30 PAC, RG I, L 3, "P" leases/44, reel C-2738, petition of George Portt, 14 July 1820; /45, John Portt; /102, William Portt Sr; /103, Robert Portt; P12/113, reel C-2491, William Portt Sr, 5 April 1820.

31 PAC, MG 27, II, D 15, vol. 289, reel C-2178, Sifton Papers, recommendation of Joseph Wallis, 1819; PAC, RG I, L 3, vol. 529(a), W13/100, reel C-2955, petition of Joseph Wallis, Belleville, 5 June 1823; PAC, RG 5, B 3, vol. 6, 393–4, petition of Joseph Wallace, nd; vol. 11, 1492–3, petition of Rebecca Wallis, nd; Anglican Diocesan Archives, Kingston, 7–B-1, register of St Thomas, Belleville, baptism 23 November 1823.

32 PAC, RG I, L 3, vol. 498(a), T12/139, reel C-2835, petition of Benjamin Tydd of Barton, York, 29 March 1820. On the Tydds see also Genealogical Office, Dublin (GO), ms 572, extracts from Modreeny returns by T.U. Sadleir; PRO, Kew, WO 13/4137, rolls of Lower Ormond Infantry Yeomanry; PRO, Dublin, Index to Killaloe Diocesan Marriage Licence Bonds; *Irish Genealogist* 6, no. 5 (November 1978): 590; *Memorials of the Dead* 12, no. 5 (1930): 557; Hamilton Public Library, Special Collections, H.F. Gardiner Scrapbooks, vol. 77, 115.

33 PAC, RG I, L 3, vol. 498(a), T13/42, reel C-2835, petition of Benjamin Tydd of Barton, 18 April 1822.

34 PAC, RG 5, B 9, vol. 17, 1324, marriage bond Duffy-Hayes; Benjamin Tydd, jailor of Hamilton, was a surety. William D. Reid, *Death Notices of Ontario* (Lambertville, NJ 1980), 163.

35 AO, Wentworth County Surrogate Court, will register 1816–34, 216–17, will of Benjamin Tydd of Hamilton, gentleman, 1832.

36 Helen I. Cowan, *British Emigration to British North America: The First Hundred Years* (Toronto 1961), 73.

37 PRO, Kew, CO 384, passim.

38 Bruce S. Elliott, "The Hopper Family," *Irish Ancestor* 1982, no. 2, 71–3.

39 PAC, RG I, L 3L, vol. 201, 94824–6, reel C-2568, Elizabeth Waller to Lord Gosford, Beehive Cottage, 25 September 1833; RG I, L 3, vol. 527(a) W11/117, reel C-2953, petition of Mr Jocelyn Waller, York, 1 October 1818; *Burke's Peerage and Baronetage* (London 1970), 2740; *Quebec Gazette*, 4 December 1828.

40 On Hodgins and his police career and trial see W.A. and C.L. Goodspeed, *History of the County of Middlesex, Canada* (Toronto 1889), 546; H.R. Page and Co., *Illustrated Historical Atlas of the County of Middlesex, Ont.* (Toronto 1878), 19; Lester Hodgins, *Hodgins – Kindred Forever* (Vancouver 1977), 47–51; Ray Fazakas, *The Donnelly Album* (Toronto 1974), 8–10, 13, 28, 61; CO 384/29, 269–70, PAC, reel B-951, James Hodgins to colonial secretary, Roscrea, 18 January 1832; A. Brewster, *A Report of Seven Trials at the Clonmel Summer Assizes of MDCCCXXIX* (Dublin 1830); PRO, Kew, HO 100/228, f. 177, Thomas Waller to Major Carter, Finnoe, 8 August 1829.

41 British Parliamentary Sessional Papers, HC (1836) XXXIII, First Report of Commissioners for Inquiring into the Condition of the Poorer Classes in Ireland, Supplement to Appendix F, 245.

42 Ibid., 249.

43 Ibid., 80.

44 Ibid., 246.

45 Ibid., 81.

46 Ibid., 80.

47 Ibid., 234. Nearly two dozen families of Canadian immigrants have been identified as coming from Templemore.

48 Ibid., 247.

49 National Library of Ireland (NLI), ms 352, Killaloe Diocesan questionnaire,
1820.

50 HC (1836) XXXIII, Supp. to App. F, 78.

51 Ibid., 248.

52 Ibid., 248.

53 Ibid., 249.

54 NLI, Castletownarra Roman Catholic register; PRO, Dublin, Castletownarra
Church of Ireland register; Griffith's Primary Valuation, Parishes of Castletownarra, Youghalarra, and Burgesbeg.

55 The registers of Roscrea at first included substantial rural areas that later acquired
their own clergy and residences were not always specified. Some of the early
emigrants credited to Roscrea may actually have been from Corbally.

56 PRO, Dublin, 1821 census, King's County, Barony of Ballybritt, Latter-day
Saints (LDS) reel 100818.

57 The Mountshannon register is gone, too, but a Vestry Book commencing in
1817, now in the hands of the Rev. Dean Bourke at Killaloe, a list of potential
emigrants sent to the Colonial Office by the Rev. James Martin (CO 384/9, ff.
346–8, PAC, reel B-882, the Rev. James Martin to earl of Liverpool, Woodpark, Scarriff, 18 September 1823), and a pew list from 1831 help to identify
local families. The pew list was torn from the vestry book by a previous
incumbent and given to an Australian visitor; fortunately it was published in
M.H. Bourchier, 'Boomagong' and the Bourchier Family (Tocumwal?
1973).

58 HC (1836) XXXIII, Supp. to App. F, 160.

59 CO 384/5, f. 321, PAC, reel B-879, Rolleston to Bathurst, Silverhills near Moneygall, 4 May 1819.

60 Some few parts of Ireland escaped the devastation of the Famine years almost
completely. Donald Akenson has demonstrated in his Between Two Revolutions (Port Credit 1979) that the Famine was barely felt in Islandmagee, County
Antrim.

61 E.H. Sheehan, Nenagh and Its Neighbourhood (Nenagh 1976), 59–60.

62 HC (1852–3) XCI, Census of Ireland, 1851, 666.

63 Mountshannon Roman Catholic parish register, Minutes of Clonrush Relief
Committee, April 1846.

64 Silvermines RC register, 1840–80, LDS reel 926098.

65 Quoted in W. Steuart Trench, *Realities of Irish Life* (London 1870), 383.

66 Ibid., 107–10, 383–401.

67 S.H. Cousens, "Regional Death Rates in Ireland during the Great Famine, from 1846 to 1851," *Population Studies* 14, no. 1 (July 1960): 70–3.

68 Trench, *Realities of Irish Life*, 103.

69 Cousens, "Regional Death Rates," 70–3.

70 HC (1852–3) XCI. Workhouse populations have been omitted.

71 S.H. Cousens, "The Regional Pattern of Emigration During the Great Irish Famine, 1846–51," *Transactions and Papers of the Institute of British Geographers* 28 (1960): 127–8.

72 Hopper correspondence, Thomas Hayes to Arthur Hopper, Roscrea, 24 September 1849. Courtesy Harry P. Hopper, Nepean.

73 Cousens, "Regional Pattern of Emigration During the Famine," 131.

74 Newspaper clipping inserted at 1849 baptisms in Toomevara Roman Catholic parish register, LDS reel 926103.

75 Hopper correspondence, Thomas Hayes to Arthur Hopper, Roscrea, 2 February 1852.

76 Ibid.

77 PRO, Dublin, Modreeny tithe applotment book, 1826/7 (measures converted from Irish to statute acres by the author); Primary Valuation, 1854.

78 From S.H. Cousens, "Emigration and Demographic Change in Ireland, 1851–1861," *Economic History Review*, 2nd Series, 14 (1961–2): 285.

79 Ibid., 284–5.

80 *The Percy Family 1830–1963* (np 1964), 39. Copy in the Ontario Genealogical Society Library, North York. I am grateful to Marion Keffer for this reference and to Shirley Lancaster for providing me with a copy. The mother's name was Ellen Hunt, not Ralph.

81 UWO, marriage registers of St Paul's Anglican Church, London; parish registers of the Church of the Messiah, Kincardine, consulted in 1982 with the permission of the incumbent, the Rev. J.R. King. Mrs Blackwell was resident in London City when she married. Information on the Blackwells from Lynn G. Clark, Frankenmuth, Michigan.

82 David George Winnett Turvey, *The Winnett Family* (Sydney, NS 1974). I am grateful to Dorothy Luney of London, Ontario for bringing this publication to my attention.

83 Censuses for Hamilton, Bytown, and part of Toronto examined. Parish registers partially remedy the loss of the 1852 census of London City, and the 1861 census of Montreal helps locate permanent residents, but not those passing through who would have appeared in the mostly missing 1852 returns.

84 Cousens, "Emigration and Demographic Change in Ireland, 1851–1861," 275.

85 S.C. O'Mahony, "Emigration from the Workhouse of Nenagh Union, Co. Tipperary," *Irish Ancestor* 1985, no. 1: 12; cf. Sheehan, *Nenagh and Its Neighbourhood*, 60.

86 AO, RG I, C-IV, Township Papers, Ross, Lot 27, Con. 7, "Memoranda: Colonization," written in August or September 1851 and attached to letter of James H.
Burke to Hon. A.N. Morin, Bytown, 5 October 1853.

87 Cousens, "The Regional Pattern of Emigration During the Great Irish Famine,
1846–51," 121–3.

88 S.C. O'Mahony, "Emigration from the Limerick Workhouse, 1848–1860," *Irish
Ancestor* 1982, no. 2: 94.

89 PAC, Neilson Collection, Records of James Allison, emigration agent at Montreal, 1823–45 [sic], MG 24, B I, vol. 21, especially 690–764, 914–24.

90 His father appears to have been John Farmer (c1761–1841) who held 7 acres, 2
roods, 23 perches plantation measure in Cowbawn in 1826. PRO, Dublin,
Modreeny tithe applotment book; Dunkerrin burial register. The Farmers buried
traditionally at Dunkerrin.

91 PRO, Dublin, Modreeny and Birr parish registers, and 1821 census of King's
County, Ballybritt Barony, parish of Kinnity, Cumber townland, LDS reel
100818, family of John Dudley; PAC, RG 31, 1852 census, Huntley Township,
61.

92 AO, Land Record Index; RG I, C-IV, Crown Lands Township Papers, north half
Lot 2, Con. 5, Huntley.

93 William lived at Toura, Shinrone, from 1831 to 1837, apparently moving back to
Cowbawn after brother Samuel went to Birr. PRO, Dublin, Modreeny and
Shinrone registers; AO, Gloucester Township Abstract Index to Deeds and Township Papers; AO, Department of the Provincial Secretary, Office of the Registrar General, 1-6, Sec. B, Ottawa City marriage register, 1858.

94 Primary Valuation of Modreeny, 1854; PRO, Dublin, Dunkerrin burial register.

95 David S. Macmillan, "Commercial and Industrial Society in Great Britain and
Ireland 1814–1824: A Study of Australian Immigrant Applications," *Histoire
sociale/Social History* 7, no. 12 (November 1973): 185, 190.

96 PRO, Kew, CO 201/96, ff. 274–5, Thomas Southerland, Templemore, 1 March
1819; PAC, RG I, L 3, vol. 463(a) S14/193, reel C-2815, petition of Thomas
Southerland, York, 13 September 1825. He emigrated five years before. See also
/192.

97 *Nenagh Guardian,* 13 January 1841, 3, col. 3; 13 October 1841, 3, col. 4; two of
a series of constant examples.

98 Ibid., 13 October 1841, 4, cols. 1–2.

99 Ibid., 28 April 1841, 2, col. 2.

100 Ibid., 27 March 1841, 2, col. 5.

101 Ibid., 13 August 1842, 1, col. 1. The Logan emigration is detailed in Harrold
W. Dart, *Happenings – Historic, Heroic & Hereditary* (1981), 20–1, 25–31.
PRO, Dublin, Stradbally (Castle Connell) parish register and Index to Killaloe
Diocesan Marriage Licence Bonds. I am grateful to Keith Hollier of
Sherwood, Brisbane, for information on the Australian family.

102 Donald Akenson, "Ontario: Whatever Happened to the Irish?" *Canadian Papers in Rural History* 3 (1982): 207.

103 Canada Sessional Papers, 1860, "Report of the Select Committee [on Emigration] to whom was referred the Annual Report of the Chief Emigration Agent."

104 Lois Long of Nepean and Gail (Haskett) Clothier of London, Ontario, have documented this circumstance in the Long families of Mountshannon and the Haskett family of Borrisokane. Dr Phyllis Simons of Melbourne has also provided evidence that members of the Bourchier, Brady, and Holland families as well as the Logans and Longs emigrated to New South Wales from Mountshannon union in the 1850s. See also Bourchier, *'Boomagong' and the Bourchier Family,* and Alan C. Long, *Nothing Without Labor: The Story of James Long and his family in Australia* (Mitcham, Victoria c1982). See Table 8. Another Cox family from Coolereida emigrated to Australia on the same ship as the Logans. New South Wales Archives, Passenger List of the *Lady McNaughton,* arrived Port Jackson, 26 February 1837, copy courtesy Keith Hollier. PRO, Dublin, Stradbally (Castle Connell) parish register. Some interrelated Kents and Sharpleys from Nenagh and Templeharry sailed to Australia in 1853 and settled at Geelong, where James Long late of Mountshannon established a confectionery business in 1856. M.H. Bourchier, *For All the Tullochs* (Cobram, Australia c1976), LDS reel 990293, item 9; Long, *Nothing Without Labor,* 7. Chain migration may also have created North Tipperary "colonies" in Australia, but only further research can reveal how extensive such settlements were. Writing of Irish Catholic bounty emigrants to New South Wales, Brian Maher has noted that "the districts of Tipperary surrounding Cashel, Thurles and Templemore were an especially rich source of emigration to Australia ... This whole region is of primary importance in the history of Irish emigration to N.S.W., and we need to understand more precisely the circumstances which made emigration in those years desirable." "'Ireland Over Here' – Nineteenth Century Irish Immigrants in Southern New South Wales," in Richard Reid and Keith Johnson, eds., *The Irish Australians* (Sydney 1984), 56.

105 The Fullers' emigration to New Zealand is revealed by Ottawa City Archives, Carleton County Land Registry copy books, Torbolton deed no. 25472, James Fuller et al., Queen Charlotte Sound, NZ, to John Boucher, 8 August 1864. On the Fuller and Taylor families see PRO, Dublin, Ogonnelloe parish register; *The Cyclopedia of New Zealand* (Christchurch 1906), 5: 392–3; Ngaire Stace, "Tombstone Inscriptions From Most of the Burial Grounds in the Province of Marlborough," no. 15, Picton, LDS reel 918233. I am grateful to Carole Caldwell of Surrey, BC, for a copy of a letter from William Taylor, Picton, NZ, to his sister Eliza Mooney of North Onslow, CE, 8 May 1861 – "I have never heard that man could go further" – and to Sally Jollans Butler of

Onehunga for obtaining death certificates from the New Zealand registrar
general.
106 Hodgins, *Kindred Forever*, 289–91.

CHAPTER SIX

1 See Map 14, and compare Cecil J. Houston and William J. Smyth, *The Sash
Canada Wore: A Historical Geography of the Orange Order in Canada* (Toronto
1980), 41, Fig. 5. A similar map based on 1852 birthplace data appears in
Edward Mills, *Early Settlement in Ontario*, Parks Canada research paper
(Ottawa 1971/2), 162.

2 A.W. Patrick Buchanan, *The Buchanan Book* (Montreal 1911), 216. On the
Peter Robinson settlers see Edwin C. Guillet, *The Valley of the Trent* (Toronto 1957), 84–130; Alan G. Brunger, "Geographical Propinquity among Pre-
Famine Catholic Irish Settlers in Upper Canada," *Journal of Historical Geography* 8, no. 3 (1982): 265–82; Howard T. Pammett, "The Irish Emigrant Settler
in the Pioneer Kawarthas," *Families* 17, no. 4 (1978): 154–74, which includes references to Pammett's earlier writings on the subject; Wendy Cameron,
"Selecting Peter Robinson's Irish Emigrants," *Histoire sociale/Social History*
9, no. 17 (May 1976): 29–46.

3 Dates of first settlement in each township from *Ontario Agricultural Commission*, Appendix B, II (Toronto 1881), passim. The first settlers to enter a
township sometimes antedated intensive settlement by some years, but mapping
of the dates of first settlement given in the Agricultural Commission Report
effectively indicates the general pattern.

4 Land petitions submitted to the Executive Council by arriving immigrants are
among those to be found in Public Archives of Canada (PAC), RG 1, L 3. Many
in the period of the late 1810s and early 1820s were written on behalf of settlers
by a small number of agents living in York and note that the applicants were
resident in the town at the time. In 1819 immigrants were in York awaiting
completion of surveys in the Mississauga Purchase, now Halton-Peel. PAC, RG
1, L 3, Land Book K, 1819–20, reel C-103, 239.

5 Darrell A. Norris, "Migration, Pioneer Settlement, and the Life Course: The First
Families of an Ontario Township," in Donald Akenson, ed., *Canadian Papers
in Rural History* 4 (1984): 138; Bruce S. Elliott, ed., *1842 & 1851 Census of
Renfrew County*, CW, I: *Horton* (Ottawa 1983): xx-xxii.

6 Bruce S. Elliott, "'The Famous Township of Hull': Image and Aspirations of a
Pioneer Quebec Community," *Histoire sociale/Social History* 12, no. 24
(November 1979): 339–67.

7 PAC, Wright Papers, MG 24, D 8, vol. 84, Journal 1812–15, 168; Anson A. Gard,
Pioneers of the Upper Ottawa and the Humors of the Valley (Ottawa c1906),
Part 4, 71.

8 Loney, Colbert, and Young of the *Brunswick* party had children born in Hull in or before 1820, and George Morgan from Borrisokane worked in Hull as a carpenter for four years before settling with his brothers in March Township. "Hull Births 1800 to 1820," Ottawa Branch, Ontario Genealogical Society, *Ottawa Branch News* 16, no. 1 (January-February 1983), 10; H. Belden, *Illustrated Historical Atlas of the County of Carleton, Ont.* (Toronto 1879), xlvii, col. 2.

9 George F. Playter, "An Account of the Founding of Three Military Settlements in Eastern Ontario – Perth, Lanark and Richmond, 1815–20," Ontario Historical Society, *Papers and Records* 20 (1928): 98–104.

10 PAC, Military "C" Series, RG 8, vol. 624, 24, microfilm, reel C-3158.

11 G.B. Short, *Records and Badges of the British Army* (1895), copy of this information courtesy Donald R. Wilson, Fonthill, Ontario.

12 PAC, RG 8, vol. 624, 80–2, reel C-3158, Cockburn, 13 July 1818.

13 Ibid., 83–4, Cockburn to Addison, Quebec, 17 July 1818.

14 Ibid., vol. 627, 31, Return Shewing the Population in the Townships of this Superintendence, Richmond, 24th September 1820.

15 Ibid., vol. 624, 96, reel C-3158, Burke to Bowles, Richmond, 21 August 1818.

16 On Burke see chapter 2, notes 70 and 71.

17 PAC, RG 1, L 3, vol. 102, C12/257, reel C-1723, petition of Robert, George, John, and William Clarke, 1819; Archives of Ontario (AO), RG 1, C-I-1, petition of Samuel Long, Richmond, 13 March 1832.

18 Nicholas Flood Davin, *The Irishman in Canada* (Toronto 1877), 319–22; manuscript pedigree of the Maxwells of Roscrea, copy courtesy Mrs Douglas Eagles, Sarnia, Ontario.

19 Corporal Arthur Sharpley was born in Modreeny parish around 1784. He worked as a labourer but then enlisted at Dublin in 1804 when the regiment was first raised. He had cleared four acres of his lot in Goulbourn by 1822 and was living there unmarried. He did not remain in the settlement much longer and he may have returned to Ireland as an Arthur Sharpley is recorded holding an acre in the Town Fields of Cloughjordan from Lord Dunalley in 1826–7. Public Record Office (PRO), Kew, WO 25/550, Description Book, 99th (late 100th) Regiment, 1816–17; WO 97/1067, Soldiers' Documents, 99th Regiment, Ray-Sykes, Latter-day Saints (LDS) reel 0861769; AO, RG 21, Johnstown District census and assessment rolls, Goulbourn Township, 17 August 1822; PRO, Dublin, Modreeny tithe apploment book, 1826–7.

20 Hayes enlisted in 1816 at Palmerston. He married in Richmond in 1826, but soon afterwards moved south to Montague Township with his brother(?) Hiram. After several years there they left the area. See same sources as in 19 above; Anglican Diocesan Archives, Ottawa, Richmond parish register.

21 Born in the town of Sligo, Spearman enlisted at Borrisokane, County Tipperary, in 1804. He fought through the War of 1812 with the "Old 100th," mostly on

288 Notes to pages 121–5

the Niagara frontier, and distinguished himself by leading the "forlorn hope" at the storming of Fort Niagara on 19 December 1813. Although I have been unable to verify the relationship absolutely, it appears that he was a son of John Spearman Sr, the oldest member of Richard Talbot's party, who had died at Lachine soon after arriving, for the *Brunswick* Spearmans were also from Borrisokane and some degree of kinship is implied by Andrew's presence at the transfer of a land grant from Old John's widow to her son John Jr in 1833. Regimental records as in note 20; PAC, RG 1, L 3, S16/32, reel C-2816, petition of Andrew Spearman, Richmond, 17 November 1829; S/16/132, petition of Elizabeth Spearman, Richmond, 1 March 1831; Andrew's obituary, *Ottawa Citizen*, 16 August 1867; City of Ottawa Archives, Carleton County Land Registry copy books, deed no. 642, Spearman to Spearman, 12 August 1833. John Talbot wrote a poem on the death of Robert [sic] Spearman in which he stated that Spearman was from Knockshegowna Hill, which is in Ballingarry parish, but this may have suited his aspiring literary purposes – Knockshegowna is the "hill of the fairies" – and John Jr's gravestone at Wesley United Cemetery, Stittsville, records his birthplace as Borrisokane. Freeman Talbot, *A Pioneer's Poems* (Clark, SD 1899), 15–16, courtesy Mrs Allen P. Mann, Robinson, Illinois.

22 PAC, RG 8, vol. 624, 110, reel C-3158, Cockburn to Bowles, Quebec, 11 November 1818.

23 Marjory Whitelaw, ed., *The Dalhousie Journals*, II (1981), 46; Playter, "Three Military Settlements," 98–104.

24 AO, RG 21, Johnstown District census and assessment rolls, 1822, cross-referenced with PAC, RG 1, L 3, Upper Canada Land Papers.

25 PRO, Kew, WO 25/550, Description Book, 99th (late 100th) Regiment, 1816–17.

26 PAC, RG 8, vol. 625, 129, reel C-3159. I found this list late in my research; it was gratifying to note that the individuals included were all members of immigrant groups of which I was already aware.

27 Bruce S. Elliott, "Regional Migration and Settlement Patterns of the Irish in Upper Canada," in Robert O'Driscoll, ed., *The Untold Story: The Irish in Canada* (Toronto 1987).

28 *Bytown Packet*, 8 October 1849, quoted in Michael Newton, *Lower Town Ottawa*, National Capital Commission Manuscript Report 104 (Ottawa 1979), I: 288.

29 The governor noted in 1818 that efforts would be made to locate "emigrants from the same district" as near to one another as possible. *Quebec Gazette*, 28 September 1818.

30 The story of emigration from southeastern Ireland to eastern Upper Canada is developed fully in Bruce S. Elliott, "Emigration from South Leinster to Eastern Upper Canada," in Kevin Whelan, ed., *County Wexford: Economy and Society* (Dublin 1987).

31 CO 384/6, f. 794, PAC, reel B-880; CO 384/8, f. 421, PAC, reel B-882, petition of

James Wilson and John Maguire, 18 December 1822; CO 384/9, f. 357, petition of John & Matthew Maguire, Mullaloghter, Redhills, 5 December 1823; PAC, RG 1, L 3, P14/83, petition of William, Isaac, and Abraham Pratt, John McGuire Sr and Jr, Matthew McGuire, and John Moore, Huntley, read 28 September 1825; CO 384/7, f. 615, PAC, reel B-881, George Argue to Earl Bathurst, Castle Roe, 28 December 1820; CO 384/7, f. 609, PAC, reel B-881, petition of George Argue, Clara, 3 February 1821; CO 384/7, f. 5, PAC, reel B-880, petition of Rebecca Shannon; f. 14, George Argue [a different George from the previous one] and William McDow[el]l, 25 April 1821; f. 15, Sarah Wiggans; f. 18, George Argue on behalf of fifteen families; f. 173, the Rev. Francis Fox to Bathurst, Farnham House, 1 July 1821, for the family of John Armstrong of March Township; f. 238, Thomas Hays, Crosreagh, 12 March 1821. For further detail on this group see Bruce S. Elliott, "Carleton County's Cavan Settlement," *Families,* forthcoming.

32 Correspondence from the Rev. Glenn Lucas, former United Church archivist-historian, Toronto, 22 September 1983.

33 James R. Kennedy, "The Shirreffs and Property Development in Fitzroy Harbour, 1818–1871," unpublished paper, 1980.

34 AO, RG 21, Johnstown District census and assessment rolls.

35 In the Ontario Archives are several censuses and assessment rolls of the townships of Goulbourn, Huntley, March, and Nepean compiled in the early 1820s when these townships were part of the Johnstown District. These documents, combined with Burke's list of locations and the description book of the 99th Regiment, enable us to trace, map, and analyse the pattern of settlement in 1822. Map 15 was compiled from the 1822 censuses and assessments, with the part lot added from location and patent records. Records of locations for the Richmond military settlement, 1820–2, are to be found in AO, RG 1, Rideau military settlements (misleadingly labelled "Scottish Emigration Record"), microfilm MS 154, r. 1, copy at PAC as reel M-5505, item 2, last eighteen pages. Location dates in the "old surveyed townships," 1818–19, are given in PAC, RG 1, L 3, vol. 420 (Perth military settlement), microfilm reel C-2739, 23. No record of the location dates in Goulbourn and Beckwith in 1818–19 seems to survive but comparison of PAC, RG 1, L 3, vol. 421, 48d-k (reel C-2739) with the last list suggests that the dates of completion of settlement duties given therein are three years to the day from the date of location. The latter dates may therefore be easily calculated.

36 AO, Abstract Index to Deeds for relevant townships, passim.

37 Whitelaw, ed., *Dalhousie Journals,* II, 42. This situation explains why Richmond village had been located inland in Goulbourn, despite Cockburn's desire to locate the depot as near to the Ottawa River as possible. The location on the Jock in southeastern Goulbourn was the closest site possible while lands in Nepean were unavailable.

38 PAC, RG 1, IB 9, Upper Canada Militia Nominal Rolls, vol. 29, Carleton County.

The Tipperary names are Burnett, Burns, Hogan, Houlahan, McCarthy, Meara, O'Grady, Sullivan, and Waters. None were recorded in the 1822 census (AO, RG 21).

39 Sara B. Craig, *Hello Nepean* (Ottawa 1974), 115, 123–6, 128–9, 144; Roman Catholic parish registers of Notre-Dame, Ottawa, 1829–47, LDS reel 1301761, and St Patrick's, Fallowfield, 1851–1926, PAC, reel M-1954, and various death certificates, wills, etc.

40 *Ottawa Citizen*, 16 October 1926, 2.

41 A list of old families in the parish of St Michael, Corkery (West Huntley), lists the regional origins as follows: Tipperary 42, Limerick 5, Cork 5, Wexford 2, Carlow 2, Sligo 1, unstated 2, total 59. J.F. Dunn, "Souvenir of the Centennial, St Michael's Church, Huntley" (Almonte 1924), copy courtesy Lois M. Long, Nepean.

42 The surnames of this group included Anderson, Austin, Brown, Donaldson, Finlay, Gabey, Hannah, Hewitt, Jeffery, Little, Lowry, McDowell, Moorhead, Rea, Shields, and Stephenson. Elizabeth M. Gordon, *The Descendants of William Gordon* (Ottawa 1977); Ottawa Branch Library, Ontario Genealogical Society, inscriptions in Lowry Cemetery, Fitzroy Township. The 1852 census of Fitzroy identifies birthplaces of the inhabitants at the county and sometimes the parish level. The ancestral burial ground of many of these families appears to have been at Killinchey. R.S.J. Clarke, *Gravestone Inscriptions: Co. Down*, VI (Belfast 1971).

43 Gourlay, *History of the Ottawa Valley*, 53. The Alexanders who had come from County Tyrone in 1829 and settled in Huntley and Goulbourn were cousins of the Gourlays. Gourlay, *History*, 32; Stittsville Women's Institute, *Farms and Families* [1979], 32–5.

44 Daniel J. Brock, "Richard Talbot, the Tipperary Irish, and the Formative Years of London Township, 1818–1826," MA thesis, University of Western Ontario, 1969, 48–65. Brock provides a detailed account of the early settlement and development of London Township in chapters 4 and 5.

45 Frederick Thomas Rosser, *The Welsh Settlement in Upper Canada* (London, Ont. 1954), 7.

46 Ibid., 9–15. Another account of the Welsh settlement appears in F.T. Rosser, *London Township Pioneers* (Belleville 1975), 105–16.

47 Rosser, *Welsh Settlement*, 17–21 and map at 4.

48 Dan Brock's card file of pre-1826 settlers; Rosser, *London Township Pioneers*, 29, 90–4, 95–9, 122–6; Jennie Raycraft Lewis, *'Llyndinshire' – London Township* (London 1967), 25–7. The surnames borne by this group included Batie, Calvert, Charlton, Headley, Nixon, Ord, Robson, Routledge, Scott?, Shipley, Stilson, Sumner, Taylor, Telfer, Whillans, and White.

49 Brock, "Richard Talbot," 65, 71–2, 138, 139, 144, 148, 163, 165; on the Kinches: Dan Brock's card file of pre-1826 settlers. *Grove Cemetery*, London Branch, Ontario Genealogical Society, publication no. 143 (London 1982). On

Dickenson see also Lewis, *'Llyndinshire,'* 24–5. Biography of George Belton, H.R. Page & Co., *Illustrated Historical Atlas of the County of Middlesex* (Toronto 1878), 20, col. 1.

50 A group consisting of Scythes, Merediths, Bantings, Carters, Goodwins, and others came from the same part of Queen's County to the Bradford-Bondhead area of Simcoe County. A few of these names also turn up in London and Biddulph later. Ersyll and Ivadell Boake, *The Boake Family in Canada 1824–1974* [Islington, Ont. 1974], 174–5. For an account of a journey in 1853 to join an uncle in Biddulph see T.A. Langford's journal in Donal Begley, "The Journal of an Irish Emigrant to Canada," *Irish Ancestor* 1974, no. 1: 43–7.

51 I am grateful to Elizabeth Scheiding of Ancaster and Ralph Gowan for information about these Queen's County families.

52 Clarence Karr, *The Canada Land Company: The Early Years. An Experiment in Colonization 1823–1843* (Ottawa 1974), 5–13.

53 W. Stafford Johnston and Hugh J.M. Johnston, *History of Perth County to 1967* (Stratford 1967), 136–7.

54 H.J. Johnston, "Immigration to the Five Eastern Townships of the Huron Tract," Ontario Historical Society, *Papers and Records* 54 (1962): 208.

55 The loss of the company's internal correspondence prevents us from documenting the process by quoting statements of policy or by recounting the activities of the company's local agents. The function of the latter is not clear, and they are not to be confused with the company's agents in more distant Canadian locations, most of which were terminated in 1835, after which business was "conducted ... through the main office" in Toronto (Karr, *Canada Land Company,* 82–3). The local agents appear to have been local residents who had displayed some initiative in encouraging migration of their friends and relations and were rewarded by being given some degree of supervision over settlement in their respective townships.

56 H. Belden & Co., *Illustrated Historical Atlas of the County of Huron, Ont.* (Toronto 1879), xx, col. 2.

57 James Scott, *The Settlement of Huron County* (Toronto 1966), 167. The Rev. William Bettridge, the rector of Woodstock, came upon this infant settlement sometime in the 1830s while riding through the Huron Tract, and reported that it then had a population of 100 to 150. William Bettridge, *A Brief History of the Church in Upper Canada* (London 1838), 94–6. It subsequently grew to many hundreds.

58 Johnston, "Immigration to the Five Eastern Townships of the Huron Tract," 207–24; locations mapped on 214. Further information about these clusters is provided in chapter 5, "The Racial Blend," in Johnston and Johnston, *History of Perth County to 1967,* 132–53.

59 Stafford Johnston, "Hessian Migration to the Canada Company's Huron Tract," *Families* 15, no. 4 (1976): 160–7.

60 See Darrell Norris's delineation of movement into Euphrasia, Grey County, in

his "Migration, Pioneer Settlement, and the Life Course: The First Families of an Ontario Township," in Akenson, ed., *Canadian Papers in Rural History* 4 (1984): 138. The 1852 census of the nearby township of Bentinck displays a somewhat less dramatic concentration, but the majority of settlers in this township who had children born elsewhere in Upper Canada nonetheless came from York, Peel, and Halton.

61 Walter Allen Knittle, *Early Eighteenth Century Palatine Emigration* (Philadelphia 1937; reprinted Baltimore 1982), 82–91.

62 Appendix D deals with the Kilcooly colony.

63 H. Belden & Co., *Illustrated Historical Atlas of the County of Perth, Ont.* (Toronto 1879), xiii, col. 2.

64 University of Western Ontario (UWO), Huron District census and assessment rolls.

65 Information from Mrs Egon Nielsen, Forest, Ontario; see also PRO, Dublin, Castletownarra and Killaloe parish registers.

66 Howard M. Brown, "The Morphys of Morphy's Falls, Settlers of Carleton Place," (Ottawa 1980). Copy in Library of Ottawa Branch, Ontario Genealogical Society.

67 UWO, 1845 Blanshard assessment roll; Belden, *Perth Atlas,* 44–5.

68 Information on "Tipperary Switzers" courtesy of B. Wesley Switzer, Brantford, Ontario. The founder of the well-known Dublin department store, Switzer's, was the only member of this particular family to remain in Ireland. See *Burke's Irish Family Records* (London 1976).

69 The first settlers were free negroes from the United States, representatives of whom purchased land at the site of Lucan in 1830. However, the cessation of persecution in Ohio, from where many of the blacks had come, and the decision of the Canada Company to bow to pressure from white residents to discourage black settlement, resulted in the failure of the Wilberforce colony to grow beyond thirty-five families; numbers had dwindled to twenty families by 1835. F. Landon, "Wilberforce, an Experiment in the Colonization of Freed Negroes in Upper Canada," *Transactions of the Royal Society of Canada,* Section II (1937): 69–78; Jennie Raycraft Lewis, *Sure An' This is Biddulph* (1964), 15–20; on harassment of the blacks by the Tipperary Irish see William D. Butt, "The Donnellys: History, Legend, Literature," PhD thesis, University of Western Ontario, 1977, 35–8.

70 Norman L. Nicholson, "The Establishment of Settlement Patterns in the Ausable Watershed, Ontario," *Geographical Bulletin* 1, no. 1 (1951): 4–5.

71 PAC, pamphlet collection, 1–1860, "A Statement of the Satisfactory Results which have attended Emigration to Upper Canada from the Establishment of the Canada Company until the Present Period" (London 1842), 52. Robert Hodgins married Anne Maunsell in Ireland in 1831 and lived in Huntley in the early 1830s, as did his brothers, before moving to Huron. He contracted to buy his lot, Lot 19, Con. 1, McGillivray, on 13 January 1836. Anne was burned to death

in a fire in the inn in 1847. PRO, Dublin, Index to Killaloe Diocesan Marriage Licence Bonds; AO, RG I, C-IV, Huntley, Lots 18–19, Con. 6, petition of William Carter, Richmond, 12 March 1832 – Carter mentions Hodgins farming the south half Lot 19, Con. 6 Huntley; Archives of Anglican Diocese of Ottawa, March parish registers, baptisms 1833–4; AO, Land Records Index; *Ontario Register* 5 (1981): 121.

72 Archives nationales, Montreal (ANQ(M)), register of Christ Church Anglican, Montreal; UWO, Spencer Armitage-Stanley Collection, B-4721, "Stanley of Biddulph" file; AO, RG I, C-IV, Lot 25, Con. 16, London Twp., Stanley to Commissioner of Crown Lands, London, 18 May 1850.

73 AO, Land Records Index; all dates of contract and lease in Biddulph come from this source, or from the original contract register, Canada Company, B-3, vol. 19, 1829–68. On the Courseys: PRO, Dublin, Dunkerrin tithe applotment book, 1825, LDS reel 256605; PRO, Dublin, Dunkerrin parish register; UWO, Spencer Armitage-Stanley Collection, B-4716, Coursey file, Armitage-Stanley to Marion –, Toronto, 14 February 1967.

74 PRO, Dublin, Shinrone parish register.

75 AO, RG I, C-IV, Lot 25, Con. 15, London Township.

76 For references to Hodgins's involvement in this affair see chapter 5, note 40. Hodgins is said to have stopped over in the Ottawa Valley but we have no record of him there. Lester Hodgins, *Hodgins – Kindred Forever* (Vancouver 1977), 47–51.

77 Hodgins, *Kindred Forever,* 46, 256.

78 AO, Canada Company, B-3, vol. 19, Register of Contracts: Huron Tract, 1829–68.

79 Poe was shown occupying the east half of Lot 18, Con. 4 on the 1862 Huron County wall map, but he purchased the southeast quarter of the lot in 1879 from Daniel Neil, who bought it from the Canada Company three years before, and apparently leased the northeast quarter from the Canada Company for the first time in 1882, purchasing the next year. AO, Biddulph deeds, no. 4633, Neil to Poe, 25 January 1879; Land Records Index.

80 These figures include only recent immigrants and do not include those coming to the Biddulph area from within Canada; most of the latter came from the Ottawa Valley and settled in McGillivray and, to a lesser extent, Blanshard.

81 Ray Fazakas, Hamilton, Ontario, reports having been told of the two trips; Hodgins, *Kindred Forever,* 48, reports the 1844 expedition, as does Orlo Miller, *The Donnellys Must Die* (Toronto 1967), 34.

82 London *Western Advertiser,* 20 February 1880, 2, col. 4.

83 The 12th to 15th concessions, in the Granton area, were settled in the mid- to late 1840s by Protestant families from various parts of the British Isles and Canada.

84 Karr, *Canada Company,* 26–7.

85 Ibid., 106–7.

86 Ibid., 96–7.

87 Ibid., 105–6.

88 One property was paid for almost immediately, nine were paid off early, and in three cases the final instalment was made in the year required by the contract. AO, Canada Company, B-3, vol. 19, Register of Contracts: Huron Tract, 1829–68.

89 Talbot, *Five Years' Residence*, II, 198.

90 Belden, *Carleton County Atlas*, xlii.

91 This circumstance is reflected in the mixture of Irish dialect elements found in the Carp area, northern Irish elements often coming from a speaker of Tipperary descent and vice versa. Conversations with Ian Pringle and Enoch Padolsky, Linguistic Survey of the Ottawa Valley, Carleton University. See also Pringle and Padolsky, "The Irish Heritage of the English of the Ottawa Valley," *English Studies in Canada* 7, no. 3 (Fall 1981), 338–52.

CHAPTER SEVEN

1 Donald Akenson, "Ontario: Whatever Happened to the Irish?" *Canadian Papers in Rural History* 3 (1982): 231–3.

2 Ibid., 234.

3 Ibid., 240.

4 Mordecai Richler, *The Apprenticeship of Duddy Kravitz* (Harmondsworth, Middlesex 1959), 48.

5 In Woody Allen's film *Love and Death*.

6 D.H. Akenson, *The Irish in Ontario* (Kingston and Montreal 1984), 247–50, 255–6.

7 James Stanley's daughter Ellen was buried at Montreal in 1822. According to family tradition she died on board ship and her body was hidden by the family to avoid her being buried at sea. The family moved on to London Township. University of Western Ontario, Regional Collection (UWO), Armitage-Stanley Collection, B-4721, "Stanley of Biddulph" file, S. Armitage-Stanley to Fred Rosser, Montreal, 21 October 1942; Archives nationales, Montreal (ANQ(M)), parish register of Christ Church Anglican, Montreal, burial of Ellen Stanley, 8 July 1822.

8 George Clarke was "staid at Montreal" by the confinement of his wife; Thomas Acres also had a child born there in the winter of 1819–20, and Clarke and Acres sponsored each other's children. Both moved on to March Township in the spring. Public Archives of Canada (PAC), RG 1, L 3, vol. 102, C12/257, reel C-1723, land petition of Clarke brothers, 1819; ANQ(M), register of Christ Church Anglican.

9 A. Gordon Darroch, "Migrants in the Nineteenth Century: Fugitives or Families in Motion?" *Journal of Family History* 6, no. 3 (Fall 1981): 270–3.

10 On Hopper see Bruce S. Elliott, "The Hopper Family," *Irish Ancestor* 1982, no. 2: 59–73.

11 Nicholas Flood Davin, *The Irishman in Canada* (Toronto 1877), 315.

12 See chapter 4, note 112, for sources on the Howard family.

13 ANQ(M), register of Christ Church Anglican.

14 F.T. Rosser, *London Township Pioneers* (Belleville 1975), 81; notebook of Dr Anson Jones detailing O'Neil genealogy, c1890, courtesy Heather Jones, Victoria; inscriptions in Sandy Hill Cemetery, Bytown, *Ottawa City Council Minutes*, 1911, 628; death notice of Mary (Hardy) Litle, *Ottawa Citizen*, 18 September 1847, 3, col. 2.

15 ANQ(M), register of Christ Church Anglican. The references to these families in the 1825 census of Montreal are as follows: PAC, reel C-718, 2081–2, 2090, 2091, 2099.

16 Davin, *Irishman in Canada*, 324; Leslie H. Saunders, *The Story of Orangeism* (Toronto 1941), 26; ANQ(M), register of Christ Church Anglican, baptism of Henry Samuel Eldon Gowan, 13 December 1829. This was not the first lodge in the city, for a lodge numbered 242 was meeting regularly there as early as 1818. Its membership seems to have been confined to members of polite society. *Montreal Herald*, 11 July 1818, 3, col. 1, and 18 July 1818, 2, col. 5.

17 PAC, 1831 census of Montreal, reel C-5941, 55–6.

18 Ibid., 70.

19 Ibid., 85.

20 Ibid., 78, 83.

21 Hopper correspondence, George Hayes to Arthur Hopper, 1832, courtesy Harry P. Hopper, Nepean; PAC, 1831 census of Montreal, reel C-5941, 91.

22 *Christian Guardian*, 10 July 1830, reprinted in the *Ontario Register* 6, no. 1 (1982): 2; Public Record Office (PRO), Dublin, Index to Killaloe Diocesan Marriage Licence Bonds.

23 ANQ(M), register of Christ Church Anglican; PRO, Dublin, Templemore parish register. The Stanleys soon moved to Bytown. Bruce S. Elliott, "The Stanleys," in *Pioneer Families of Osgoode Township*, XVII (Vernon, Ont. 1987), 9–11.

24 Ersyll and Ivadell Boake, *The Boake Family in Canada 1824–1974* [Islington 1974], 5–7.

25 PRO, Dublin, Modreeny parish register, marriage of John Spearman and Honor Carty, 11 January 1837; ANQ(M), register of Notre-Dame, Montreal, marriage of John Spearman and Mary Linnen, 15 October 1850; PAC, RG 31, 1861 census of Montreal, Ste Anne's Ward, 2145, reel C-1234; see also 2749.

26 R.H. Grant, "Biography of Robert Grant, 1793–1870," typescript courtesy Hon. R.A. Bell; Anglican Diocesan Archives, Ottawa, March parish register, marriage of Edward Lowry and Susan Morris, 17 November 1847; *Christian Guardian*, 27 June 1860, marriage notice Wilson-Morris; PAC, 1861 census of Montreal, Centre Ward, 83, 116, C-1232. See Table 12.

27 Rev. J. Douglas Borthwick, *History and Biographical Gazetteer of Montreal to the Year 1892* (Montreal 1892), 489; death notice of Andrew Holland, *Montreal Gazette*, 30 March 1846; ANQ(M), N-B Doucet, notaire, no. 20063, testa-

ment de Andrew Holland, 7 December 1832; obituary of Robert Holland, *Christian Guardian,* 8 April 1886, 267; obituary of William Lewis Holland, *Ottawa Citizen,* 5 September 1883, 3; information from descendants Howard Dawson, Lachine, and June Usherwood, Kingston. See Table 7.

28 PRO, Dublin, Index to Killaloe Diocesan Marriage Licence Bonds; Templeharry and Shinrone parish registers; Montreal city directories, passim; PAC, RG 31, 1861 census of Montreal, West Ward, 15479, Ste Anne's Ward, 1142; 1861 census of Walpole Township, 11, 13; 1871 census of Ingersoll, FI, 50; clippings and family memoranda courtesy Hon. Irwin Haskett, Ottawa, and extensive research of Gail Clothier, London, Ontario.

29 *Quebec Mercury,* 4 June 1833, marriage notice of Waller-Colclough; *Montreal Gazette,* 20 September 1830, death notice of Sir Charles Waller; *Burke's Peerage and Baronetage* (London 1970), 2740–2. On Jocelyn Waller see chapter 5, note 39.

30 Charlotte Violet Trench, *The Wrays of Donegal, Londonderry, and Antrim* (Oxford 1945), 264–76; Genealogical Office, Dublin (GO), ms 572, extract from 1821 census, Rathbeg, parish of Kilcoleman, King's County; PAC, RG I, L 3, vol. 530(a), WI5/II, reel C-2956, petition of Jackson Wray of Town of York, 1827; vol. 533, WI8/9, reel C-2957, petition of Jackson Wray, Montreal, 1832; ANQ(M), Testaments verifiés, no. 796, testament de Jackson Wray de Montreal; death notice, *Montreal Transcript,* 19 November 1842.

31 Denis H. Crofton, *The Children of Edmondstown Park* (Hythe, England 1980), 21 and Appendix II; correspondence with Mr Crofton, of Tonbridge, Kent; 1861 census of Montreal, St Lawrence Ward, 10864; PAC, Lower Canada Marriage Licence Bonds, RG 4, B 28, vol. 40, f. 2478, reel H-1131.

32 Darroch, "Migrants in the Nineteenth Century," 271.

33 Hull brewer Ralph Smith and Bytown merchant W.H. Thompson were in business for a time in Peterborough and Port Hope, respectively, but both returned to Ottawa. Archives of Ontario (AO), H. Townley Douglas Collection, MU 938, "Geo. Hall & Isaac Smith" file, inventory of letters and papers of Isaac Smith and sons, 1836–74, nos. 76, 80, letters from Ralph Smith, Peterborough, 1853; PAC, RG 31, 1852 census of Peterborough, reel C-978, 21; AO, Crown Lands Department Correspondence, RG I, A-I-6, vol. 31, env. no. 5, microfilm, MS 563, reel 28, Ralph Smith to Agar [Yeilding], Bytown, 2 May 1856. On Thompson in Port Hope see *Ottawa Free Press,* 16 October 1878 (I am grateful to Michael Newton for this reference); AO, H. Townley Douglas Collection, MU 938, "Geo. Hall & Isaac Smith" file, Memoirs of W.H. Thompson; *Bytown Gazette,* 6 February 1838, 3, col. 3.

34 ANQ(M), N-B Doucet, notaire, no. 12923, donation par A. Hopper à B. Sparling; ANQ(M), parish register of Chambly, LC; Hopper correspondence.

35 Registry of Deeds, Dublin, 771/568/523103, Haskett and others to Tisdall, 1822.

36 W.A. and C.L. Goodspeed, *History of the County of Middlesex, Canada* (Toronto 1889), 716–17.

37 PAC, RG 31, London Township census, 1871, C2, 40; 1881, C4, 39.

38 Ibid., 1871, C2, 52.

39 J. Richard Houston, *Numbering the Survivors: A History of the Standish Family of Ireland, Ontario, and Alberta* (Toronto 1979), 32.

40 ANQ(M), parish register of St Stephen's Anglican Church, Chambly 1819–50.

41 PAC, RG 31, 1852 census of St-Césaire, passim.

42 *Montreal Transcript*, 28 November 1843, marriage notice Cousens-Carden; 1852 census of St-Césaire, 147–53; Ottawa City Archives, Carleton County Land Registry copy books, Bytown deed no. 6421, Baker to Cousens and Carden, 18 May 1853; 1852 census of Bytown, West Ward, 65; 1861 census of Ottawa, Victoria Ward, 292; Cousens monument, Sec. 48, Beechwood Cemetery, Ottawa; AO, Carleton County Surrogate Court, will registers, vol. D, 494, administration of William Cousens, 1885.

43 PRO, Dublin, 1821 census of Ballybritt Barony, King's County, parish of Kinnity, Castle Bernard townland, Latter-day Saints (LDS) reel 100818; PAC, 1825 census of St Henri de Mascouche, reel C-718; correspondence with Gail Clothier re Robinsons and Alexanders, and with Constance Catania, Columbia, Maryland, re Edgehills.

44 Robinson correspondence, Thomas Robinson to John Haskett, Maple Lodge, Mascouche, 24 December 1860. I am grateful to Gail Clothier for copies of the Robinson correspondence, which is held by Neva Loft of Ilderton, Ontario.

45 Archives of Anglican Diocese of Ottawa, March Anglican register, 7 February 1866. A year-old son, Armstrong Robinson, was buried at South March in 1868. Gravestone, St John's Cemetery. The degree of relationship is not certain, but William and Mary Jane can have been no closer than second cousins.

46 Correspondence of Ann Jane (Alexander) Robinson, transcriptions by Lorne Robinson of Niagara Falls, courtesy Gail Clothier.

47 Goodspeed, *History of Middlesex*, 715–16.

48 Dr G.C. Armitage et al., *Armitage: A Family Treatise* (Brampton c1977), 8–9, 18; UWO, Spencer Armitage-Stanley Collection, B-4721, file "Armitage of Biddulph"; AO, Abstract Indexes to Tyendinaga and Ernesttown; parish registers, etc.

49 UWO, Armitage-Stanley Collection, B-4716, file "Sadleir of Biddulph"; Public Record Office of Northern Ireland, Belfast, T/857/1, parish register extracts by Sadleir and Woodward, including extracts from Finnoe and Cloughprior parochial returns; UWO, Lucan LOL certificates, X1786, certificate of Francis Sadleir from Frontenac County LOL #291, 15 October 1849. According to the Register of Warrants at the Orange Archives, Toronto, this was a Kingston lodge. Sadleir was master of Harcourt Lodge #662, Lot 33, Con. 3, Biddulph, 1862–4. Monument at St James Cemetery, Clandeboye.

50 Armitage, *Armitage: A Family Treatise*, 8–9, 18.

51 PAC, John C. Clark, Diary of the Wind and Weather, MG 24, I 149, 21 May 1852. I am grateful to June Usherwood of Kingston for this reference.

52 J.H. Meacham & Co., *Illustrated Historical Atlas of Frontenac, Lennox and Addington Counties, Ontario* (1878), 18, 82. John's three half-brothers farmed their father's lands in Tyendinaga, but only one of them married.

53 AO, Tyendinaga Deeds, vol. C (1858–63), 269, no. 192, reel GS 4321, will of Francis Armitage, 1860.

54 Anglican Diocese of Ontario Archives, Kingston, registers of St Thomas, Belleville, 1823–9.

55 Obituary of William Porte, St Marys *Argus*, 21 September 1899; UWO, William Porte Diaries, family record in Daily Journal, 1869; Goodspeed, *History of Middlesex*, 969.

56 PRO, Dublin, 1821 census of Ballybritt barony, parish Kinnity, Town of Kinnity, household #38, LDS film 100818; Goodspeed, *History of Middlesex*, 969–70.

57 J.H. Beers & Co., *Commemorative Biographical Record of the County of Lambton, Ontario* (Toronto 1906), 176.

58 George Maclean Rose, ed., *A Cyclopaedia of Canadian Biography* (Toronto 1886), 328–9, biography of Captain Jonathan A. Porte; obituary of William J. Porte, *Christian Guardian,* 31 January 1900, 75.

59 Local graveyards and census records yield the Palatine names Doupe, Fizzell, Long, Miller, Piper, Shier, Switzer, and Teskey: three Methodist cemeteries near Centreville and Christ Church Anglican Cemetery, Tamworth. Mrs Henry Caswell was born in County Limerick in 1785; her father was a Long and her mother a Switzer. Her obituary in the *Christian Guardian,* 3 September 1873, identifies her husband as Samuel, but her gravestone at the Milligan Cemetery, Lot 26, Con. 6, Camden East, provides the correction. At least some of the Irish Palatine families were in Camden before the Caswells arrived in 1831. A local history notes that Nicholas Shier, the first settler in the Reidville area, arrived in 1825. James E. Hughes, ed., *Camden Township History – 1800 to 1968* (Centreville 1970), np.

60 Obituary of Henry Caswell, *Christian Guardian,* 17 February 1858; PRO, Dublin, Castletownarra parish register.

61 PRO, Dublin, Index to Killaloe Diocesan Marriage Licence Bonds.

62 Shirley Mayse, *Our Caswell Relatives,* 3rd edition (Vancouver 1980).

63 See 114 and Table 7.

64 See chapter 4, note 82, for sources on the Robinson family.

65 William Perkins Bull, *Spadunk or From Paganism to Davenport United* (Toronto 1935), 29, 81–2; George H. Cornish, *Cyclopaedia of Methodism in Canada* (Toronto 1881), 142; John Carroll, *Case and His Cotemporaries* (Toronto 1867–77), II: 212, 410, 459; III: 13, 59, 414, 455; United Church Archives, Toronto, Biographical files: Rev. Edmund Stoney.

66 Boake and Boake, *Boake Family,* 47; Census of London Township, 1871, C1, 7; 1881, C5, 32.

67 Alexander Kent, a labourer in Esquesing in 1842, was an innkeeper in Hamilton ten years later: 1842 census of Esquesing; 1852 census of Hamilton, St Lawrence Ward, 75.

68 Houston, *Numbering the Survivors,* 143–245; 1871 census of Artemesia, G2, 27.

69 Census returns and gravestone inscriptions in the relevant townships and printed and typescript works cited hereafter. The parish registers of the Anglican parish of Georgina were also consulted by kind permission of the rector.

70 The account of the Browns' store is from a 1937 memorandum on the Abbott Lewis family of McGillivray sent to me by Jean Kelly of Lambeth, Ontario, and of the family's relationships from a typescript history of the Woods family by W.H. Woods of Mount Brydges, 1928, sent to me by Gail Clothier. The Browns were sons of Samuel Brown of Modreeny who was married in 1833 to Hannah Proud of Toura, Shinrone, a niece of William Robinson of West Gwillimbury: PRO, Dublin, Shinrone parish register; Woods ms.

71 Inscriptions at St James Anglican Cemetery, Brooke Township; William H. Johnston, *A Brief History of the Descendants of the Late Eliza England of Mountrath, Queen's County, Ireland* (Exeter, Ontario 1940).

72 Andrew F. Hunter, *A History of Simcoe County* (1948), Part II: 28; H. Belden & Co., *Illustrated Historical Atlas of the County of Perth, Ont.* (Toronto 1879), xxii.

73 W. Stewart Wallace, ed., *The Macmillan Dictionary of Canadian Biography* (London 1963), 370; PRO, Dublin, Templemore parish registers; St James Cathedral Vestry, Toronto, St James Cathedral registers; George Walton, *York Commercial Directory, Street Guide, and Register, 1833–34* (York), 90; Francis Lewis, *Toronto Directory and Street Guide 1843–4* (Toronto), 48; and information from M. Netta Brandon of London, Ontario.

74 Rose, ed., *Cyclopaedia of Canadian Biography* (1886), 532; Goodspeed, *History of Middlesex,* 882–3; information from M. Netta Brandon.

75 *Nenagh Guardian,* 3 March 1841, 1; obituaries of Dr Robert Hobbs, *London Advertiser,* 27 December 1886, 8, col. 4 and *London Free Press,* 27 December 1886, 1, col. 1.

76 PRO, Dublin, Terryglass parish register, marriage of Frederick and Diana Falkiner, 1829; 1852 census of York Township, 11; obituary of Diana Jane Bell Kingsley Falkiner, *London Advertiser,* 28 March 1887. I am grateful to Byron McLeod of London for the last item.

77 Lewis's store is pictured in Robert W.S. MacKay, *The Canada Directory* (Montreal 1851), 447, reproduced in this volume. Family gravestone at Nenagh; PRO, Dublin, Birr parish register, marriage of Rice Lewis, 1829; Index to Killaloe Diocesan Marriage Licence Bonds; AO, York County Surrogate Court, no. 1344, will of Rice Lewis, 1871.

78 Nellie McClung, *Clearing in the West: My Own Story* (Toronto 1976), 13–14.

79 J. Lloyd Armstrong, *Clarendon and Shawville* (Shawville 1980), 17–20.

80 Ibid., 25–66. Prendergast's obituary appeared in the *Montreal Gazette,* 14 August 1834.

81 AO, Crown Lands Township Papers, RG 1, C-IV, east half Lot 21, Con. 2, Fitzroy, Hamnett Pinhey to Peter Robinson, 25 July 1833. There was great demand for clergy lots in this period because they could be acquired on fairly easy terms and

permitted new arrivals to settle near relatives who had crowded the older
townships during the free grant period. See Lillian F. Gates, *Land Policies of
Upper Canada* (Toronto 1968), 196–200. On the occupation of clergy reserve
lots by late arrivals see AO, Township Papers for townships in Carleton and
Lanark counties, passim.

82 Chad M. Gaffield, "Canadian Families in Cultural Context: Hypotheses from the
Mid-Nineteenth Century," Canadian Historical Association, *Historical Papers*
(1979), 63–9.

83 H.F. Walling, "Map of the Counties of Stormont, Dundas, Glengarry, Prescott &
Russell, Canada West" (Precott 1862); R.E. Wicklund and N.R. Richards,
Soil Survey of Russell and Prescott Counties, Report no. 33 of the Ontario Soil
Survey (Guelph 1962).

84 Gates, *Land Policies,* 285.

85 John L. Gourlay, *History of the Ottawa Valley* (Ottawa 1896), 197–8.

86 Ibid., 199.

87 Ibid., 202, 204.

88 Jean Kelly et al., *Shouldice/Sholdice 1980 First International Reunion* [1981],
107.

89 Price termed this sort of movement, by which immigrants who have moved
independently are "drawn together into groups by forces of mutual attraction"
such as a common background, "gravitation" group settlement. C.A. Price,
"Immigration and Group Settlement," in W.D. Borrie, ed., *The Cultural
Integration of Immigrants* (Paris 1959), 270–2. On the Powells and Coxes see
Ronald E. Cox, *The Families of Francis and Ann Cox* (Beaconsfield 1972)
and *Commemorative Biographical Record of the County of Lambton, Ontario*
(Toronto 1906), 231–2, 752–3. An account of the Walls appears on page 832
of the latter work. I have corrected these accounts in my files from research in
parish registers in Ireland and Canada and in Ontario land records. See
Table 12.

90 See Table 7. George Clarke was from Cregg near Mountshannon but married a
daughter of Nicholas Shouldice of Glantane near Castle Otway in 1806. John
Mooney's father William may also have come from the Castle Otway neighbourhood originally. He moved around a lot, being in the Newport area at his
marriage and at Moneygall at John's birth in 1812, but thereafter he lived at
Templederry, very near Glantane. John Mooney told his daughter, Nellie
McClung, that his clergyman in Ireland was the Rev. Mr Jordan; Edmund Jordan
was rector and vicar of Templederry for thirty-eight years until his death in
1822. William Mooney is recorded as an Otway tenant at Templederry in 1824,
and in 1834 he held forty-one acres there. McClung stated that the Mooneys
and Shouldices were related; if this was so then it is even more likely that
William Mooney was returning home when he moved to Templederry. The
discovery by Marsha Shouldice that Nicholas Shouldice's wife was a Mooney
accords well, though not perfectly, with McClung's statement that her father

was a first cousin of Robert Clarke who married her aunt Maria; he could have been a first cousin once removed. E. Marjorie Moodie and Bruce S. Elliott, *The Hazeldean Cemeteries* (Ottawa 1980), 32–5; McClung, *Clearing in the West,* 13, 215, 329; PRO, Dublin, Killaloe parish register, marriage of William Mooney and Mary Scott, both of Lansdown, 31 March 1799; PRO, Dublin, Newport parish register, baptisms of children of William and Mary Mooney of Bloomfield Lodge, 1803–4; PRO, Dublin, Templeharry parish register; National Library of Ireland (NLI), Otway Estate Papers, ms 13,000(8), Rental of the Estates of Henry Otway, Esqr in Ireland, 1st May 1806; An Account of Rents … due to Robt Otway Cave Esqr [1824]; *Memorials of the Dead* 6 (1904–6): 406; PRO, Dublin, Templederry tithe applotment book, 1834; register of Notre-Dame de Montréal, marriage Shields-Sholdice, 17 November 1825; letter of Nellie McClung to Fannie Winram, nd, copy from E. Marjorie Moodie.

91 The surnames are Blackwell, Collins, Dagg, Guest, Hodgins, Howard, Lewis, Loney, Morgan, Owens, Rivington, Smithson, Stanley, and Wall.

92 AO, RG I, C-IV, Lot 24, Con. 3, Ramsay, Francis Collins to Peter Robinson, Ramsay, 20 April 1831, and half Lot 3, Con. 7, Torbolton, Leonard Shouldice to R.V. Thornhill, March, 24 October 1839.

93 On the New Zealand families see chapter 5, note 105.

94 AO, Bruce County marriage register, 1858–69, passim.

95 A similar preference for marrying fellow Irish Protestants, if not those from the same part of Ireland, has been demonstrated elsewhere for some Tipperary families resident in Esquesing near Toronto. J.R. Houston, "Ethnic Patterns in Early Ontario Marriages," *Families* 11 (Winter 1972): 3–12.

96 Norman Robertson, *The History of the County of Bruce* (Toronto 1906), 13. An excellent report on early settlement and farming conditions in Bruce County in 1855 by John Lynch of Brampton appeared in the *Journal and Transactions of the Board of Agriculture of Upper Canada* 1 (1856): 615–58.

97 Robertson, *History of the County of Bruce,* 15–16.

98 Ibid., 51, 67.

99 PAC, 1852 census, Huron Township, f. 12, reel C-11715.

100 The relationship is revealed in AO, Heir and Devisee Commission, RG 40–4676, claim of Eliza Dagg. Eliza's first husband, James Dagg, son of William of Pakenham, was a cousin of her second husband, William, son of James of Biddulph. Old William and old James were not necessarily brothers, for William's wife was also a Dagg. See also PRO, Dublin, Modreeny parish register.

101 If one subtracts the number coming directly into London from Ireland.

102 The two-page memoirs of William Harte Thompson make clear the extensive network of partnerships and marriage alliances among Ottawa Valley merchant families of Tipperary origin. AO, Dr H.T. Douglas Collection, MU 938, "George Hall & Isaac Smith" file. For another account see Thompson's biography in the *Ottawa Free Press,* 16 October 1878.

103 The populations of Bytown and London were similar in 1852: 7760 in Bytown and 7035 in London, but in 1871 the respective populations, exclusive of suburbs, were 21,545 and 15,826. *Census of the Canadas, 1851–2* (Quebec 1853); *Census of Canada, 1870–71* (Ottawa 1873).

104 The 1852 census of the Town of London and of most of the township is unfortunately missing and the families resident there in that year were estimated using other records.

105 See Table 16. These figures take no account of the sometimes considerable numbers of residents in outlying parts of the two regions.

106 Or 23.7 per cent. This figure does not include residents of smaller villages and cross-roads hamlets.

107 AO, Biddulph Abstract Index to Deeds, lots 25 & 26, Con. 1. Transcript courtesy John McMahon, London. Michael Ligar registered a subdivision plan for Lot 27 in 1855.

108 In 1889 only two of the original purchasers still held their lots in the town. Goodspeed, *History of Middlesex,* 462.

109 R.W. Hermon, "New Map of the County of Huron, Canada West" (Toronto 1862), inset of Lucan. PAC, National Map Collection.

110 The disturbed state of the Lucan area had reached such a pitch by 1878, two years before the celebrated "Biddulph Tragedy," that the county atlas, normally a promotional publication, noted of Lucan that "the welfare of the place has of late been imperilled by the unfortunate exhibitions of malice, which have lately culminated in incendiary fires, which have created a great deal of distrust, and checked for a time the progress of the village." H.R. Page & Co., *Illustrated Historical Atlas of the County of Middlesex, Ont.* (Toronto 1878), 13. For a list of the incidents of arson see UWO, Wm Porte Diaries.

111 Including descendants through female lines.

112 Goodspeed, *History of Middlesex,* 461–3.

113 Obituary of John Hodgins, *London Free Press,* 8 June 1915, 10, col. 4. The obituary does not mention his years in Lucan, but he was listed there in the 1871 census nonetheless.

114 See Map 17.

115 See Table 16.

116 See Table 18.

117 Jones correspondence, courtesy Heather Jones, Victoria, BC, F.W. Richardson to Francis Jones, South March, 22 October 1860.

118 Ibid.

119 Jones correspondence, Francis Jones to Richard Richardson, McGillivray, 24 May 1882.

120 Information courtesy Lois Long, Nepean, Ontario. See Table 8.

121 "Reminiscences of J. Willoughby Shore" (1936). I am grateful to the Goulbourn Township Historical Society, Richmond, for a copy of this typescript.

122 See Table 7.

123 Moodie and Elliott, *Hazeldean Cemeteries,* 32–5.

124 Bruce S. Elliott, Introduction to David Patrick Acres, "The Acres Families of Carleton County, Ontario: The First Three Generations," *Families* 20, no. 3 (1981): 130; information from Larry Neil, Sarnia.

125 One of the most famous migrants of Tipperary descent to move to Manitoba from western Ontario, the Hon. John Wright Sifton, had little to do with stimulating the movement of his compatriots to the region, which is ironic when one considers his family's later activity in promoting the settlement of the west.

126 In December 1879 Greenway was acclaimed first member of parliament for the Manitoba riding of Mountain. "Hon. Thomas Greenway," *Winnipeg Daily Tribune,* 18 December 1897, 8.

127 J.E. Parr, "Beginning of Crystal City," in T.G McKitrick, ed., *Corner Stones of Empire: The Settlement of Crystal City and District in the Rock Lake Country* (Crystal City 1940), 1-2. Greenway's foundation of Crystal City and promotion of western settlement may also be compared with the Hon. Malcolm Cameron's development of Sarnia and promotion of migration from Lanark County to Lambton forty years earlier. Cameron, too, was successively a member of parliament for the districts at both ends of the migration route. Jean McGill, *A Pioneer History of the County of Lanark* (Toronto 1968), 158-61; Evelyn Griffiths, "Some Additions to Source Material in Lambton," *Families* 16, no. 2 (1977): 50-2; Eleanor Nielsen, "An Index of Lanark Families Who Migrated to Lambton," Ontario Genealogical Society, *Ottawa Branch News* 15, no. 5 (September-October 1982): 59-61.

128 Prittie was advertising Manitoba excursions in 1879 from his "Manitoba Land Office" in Toronto. *Christian Guardian,* 24 September 1879, 311. I have not discovered whether Prittie was of one of the Tipperary families of the name. Some of the Toronto Pritties were from Tullamore, more likely the town in Offaly than the townland in Monsea parish, County Tipperary. Gravestone at Necropolis Cemetery.

129 Articles on the emigrant trains, including lists of names of many of the passengers, appeared in the *London Advertiser:* "Ho! for the West," 17 March 1880, 1, cols. 8-9; "Ontario's Life Blood," 1 April 1880, 4, cols. 3-4; "Go West," 7 April 1880, 2, col. 5.

130 *London Advertiser,* 17 March 1880, 1, cols. 8-9; Aileen Garland, *Trails and Crossroads to Killarney* (Altona, Manitoba 1967), 31.

131 *London Advertiser,* 30 March 1880, letter from Harry Hambly to the editor, dated Emerson, Manitoba, 22 March 1880: "There are parties leaving every hour for Rock Lake and Turtle Mountain which appear to be the chief places of attraction."

132 *London Advertiser,* 1 April 1880, 4, cols. 3-4.

133 Quoted in McKitrick, ed., *Corner Stones of Empire,* 30.

134 Frederick Fairhall of Stephen was convinced to migrate to Manitoba by one such exhibit. Garland, *Killarney,* 31.

135 Ibid., 33.

136 Ibid., 33–6.
137 Monument, Exeter Cemetery.
138 Garland, *Killarney*, 300–2; Mrs Clifford Gosnell, ed., *Echoes of the Past: A History of the Rural Municipality of Louise and Its People* (1968), 281–2. Only Joseph and his family have been located in the 1881 census: Mountain, Manitoba, CI, 42. The remaining brothers must have been in transit between provinces. Robert, with his wife and one child, were on the emigrant train that left London on 16 March 1880. *London Advertiser*, 17 March 1880, 1, col. 8.
139 Manitoba census 1881, Mountain, CI, 36; *Crocus Country: A History of Mather & Surrounding Districts* (Mather 1981), 171–7; Gosnell, ed., *Echoes of the Past*, 244–6.
140 Garland, *Killarney*, 235.
141 Ibid., 244–5; the 1881 census, South-West Extension [Turtle Mountain], Manitoba, F2, includes the Foxes and Armitages, 21–2.
142 Garland, *Killarney*, 53; Jennie Raycraft Lewis, *Sure An' This is Biddulph* (1964), 31.
143 Garland, *Killarney*, 258–9.
144 Obituary of Joseph Rogers, *Christian Guardian*, 18 August 1897; McKitrick, ed., *Corner Stones of Empire*, 14, and information from Lois Long.
145 *London Advertiser*, 1 April 1880, 4, col. 3.
146 Garland, *Killarney*, 31.
147 Ibid., 34–5; *Exeter Times*, 4 November 1874, and *London Free Press*, 13 March 1876, cited in UWO, Armitage-Stanley Collection, B-4717, "Blackwell of Biddulph" file, Ray Fazakas to Sam Blackwell, 3 November 1970; ibid., Blackwell to Fazakas, Killarney, Manitoba, 28 October 1970.
148 Garland, *Killarney*, 230–1.
149 1881 census, Mountain, Manitoba, CI, 8.
150 McKitrick, *Corner Stones of Empire*, 24–7.
151 Ibid., 75–9; *Crocus Country*, 198–200.
152 Garland, *Killarney*, 34.
153 Ibid., 34; census and baptismal data about the respective families from my compiled family files.
154 McClung, *Clearing in the West*, 40–73.
155 Ibid., 29–32.
156 Ibid., 7.
157 Ibid., 38–40, 48.
158 Ibid., 47.
159 1881 census, Emerson, C, 41–2.
160 1881 census, Dufferin North, G2, 43.
161 Charles R. Baskerville, *Baskerville Family History* (Killarney, Manitoba 1971), 11–13.
162 Advertisement of railway company, *Shawville Equity*, 19 September 1889, 5; article about excursions for the 1890 season, ibid., 27 February 1890, 1, col.

3. As the number of available homesteads in the west declined and demand for seasonal labour increased, the colonists' specials evolved into the harvest excursion trains of the 1890–1929 period. John Herd Thompson, "Bringing in the Sheaves: The Harvest Excursionists, 1890–1929," *Canadian Historical Review* 59, no. 4 (December 1978): 467–89. The role of family and friends in influencing the choice of destination of harvest excursionists is discussed by Gordon Hak, "The Harvest Excursion Adventure: Excursionists from Rural North Huron-South Bruce, 1919–28," *Ontario History* 77, no. 4 (December 1985): 247–65.

163 *Shawville Equity*, 25 April 1889, 1, col. 3.

164 Ibid., 11 July 1889, 1, col. 4. Mrs Ingram visited the Pontiac herself at Christmas 1892, staying about a month before returning to her home at Pine Creek near Calgary, ibid., 1 December 1892, 1, col. 2.

165 Ibid., 18 January 1894, 1, col. 4.

166 Ibid., 8 February 1894, 1, col. 4.

167 Ibid., 1 March 1894, 1, col. 2.

168 1881 census, Prince Albert, NWT, J2, 4.

169 McKitrick, ed., *Corner Stones of Empire*, 43–4.

170 Gosnell, ed., *Echoes of the Past*, 62–3, 102; Mervyn Avery Collins, *From the Shamrock to the Maple* (Simcoe, Ontario 1982), 171–5.

171 Correspondence with Marie Smibert of Etobicoke, Norval Gray of Claremore, Oklahoma, and Stephen Guest of Osgoode, Ontario.

172 Richard J. Hathaway, "From Ontario to Michigan: The Migration and Settlement of Canadians in the Great Lakes State," *Families* 18, no. 4 (1979): 169–83; Marion C. Keffer, "Migrations to and from Ontario/Michigan," *Families* 17, no. 4 (1978): 185–97; Gregory S. Rose, "The Origins of Canadian Settlers in Southern Michigan, 1820–1850," *Ontario History* 79, no. 1 (March 1987), 31–52.

173 *London Advertiser*, 1 April 1880, 4, cols. 3–4. Though examples of individual migrants to these states from the London area have turned up, I have made no attempt to search census records in Michigan, Illinois, Iowa, the Dakotas, or Nebraska to locate any families of North Tipperary origin that may have gone there.

174 Sister Margaret McGinn, "Carleton County Families in Iowa," Ontario Genealogical Society, *Ottawa Branch News* 16, no. 4 (July-August, 1983): 48. The surnames of the Petersville group included Brady, Costello, Dunn, Fitzgerald, Goodall, Hanrahan, Hickey, McGinn, Mears, Monaghan, O'Meara, Shea, Spain, Tierney, and Waters.

175 See 51.

176 Darroch, "Migrants in the Nineteenth Century," 257–78.

177 Goodspeed, *History of Middlesex*, 461.

178 C.A. Price, "Immigration and Group Settlement," in W.D. Borrie, ed., *The Cultural Integration of Immigrants* (Paris 1959), 270–2.

CHAPTER EIGHT

1 Jack Goody, *The Development of the Family and Marriage in Europe* (Cambridge 1983), 112, note 6.
2 See 141.
3 Daniel J. Brock, "Richard Talbot, the Tipperary Irish, and the Formative Years of London Township," MA thesis, University of Western Ontario, 1969, 170; CO 384/3, f. 547, Public Archives of Canada (PAC) reel B-877, Talbot to Bathurst, Cloghjordan, 7 March 1818; memorandum of F.W. Richardson's family by A.A. Richardson, 1908–9, copy provided by Mrs G.O. Skuce, Ottawa; Public Record Office (PRO), Dublin, IA.4.17, Killaloe Court and Register Book, 1707–1868, marriage licence bond of Frederick William Richardson and Anne Haskett, 1816; PAC, RG 17, vol. 2325, no. 30, completed questionnaires by emigrant farmers, 1853: Richard Richardson.
4 Obituary, *Ottawa Citizen*, 5 December 1879, 2.
5 City of Ottawa Archives, Carleton County Land Registry copy books, March, nos. 18689–94, 1862.
6 Bernard Burns et al., *March Past* (Kanata 1972), 58.
7 Jones correspondence, F.W. Richardson to Francis Jones, South March, 22 November 1858. I am grateful to Heather Jones of Victoria for copies of the Jones correspondence.
8 Burns et al., *March Past*, photo opposite 59.
9 Jones correspondence, Richardson to Jones, South March, 22 October 1860.
10 PAC, RG 31, 1861 census of March Township, agricultural, 96, PAC reel C-1014.
11 David Gagan produced no evidence for his initial assertion that the inheriting son was usually the eldest ("The Indivisibility of Land: A Microanalysis of the System of Inheritance in Nineteenth-Century Ontario," *Journal of Economic History* 36, no. 1 (March 1976): 136) and seems since to have withdrawn the assertion, but without comment: *Hopeful Travellers: Families, Land and Social Change in Mid-Victorian Peel County, Canada West* (Toronto 1981), 54. Ontario genealogists have noted for some years that the inheritance of the homestead by the youngest son was the general pattern: Marion Keffer and Robert F. and Audrey L. Kirk, *Some Ontario References and Sources for the Family Historian* (Toronto 1976), 14, and again, Marion C. Keffer, "Migrations to and from Ontario/Michigan," *Families* 17, no. 4 (1978): 187–8. Similar circumstances pertained in the northern United States in the same period: Richard A. Easterlin, "Population Change and Farm Settlement in the Northern United States," *Journal of Economic History* 36, no. 1 (March 1976): 45, 67. While the internal logic of this system determined its practice, other systems were equally logical in other situations. In sixteenth- and seventeenth-century Cambridgeshire, for example, where holdings were smaller than in Canada and life expectancies much lower, yeomen attempted to provide smallholdings or cash for younger sons but left the bulk of the holding to the eldest, who was often only

just of age at the time and in any case seldom married till he had received the holding after his father's death. Margaret Spufford, *Contrasting Communities: English Villagers in the Sixteenth and Seventeenth Centuries* (Cambridge 1974), 85–7, 104–6, 159–60.

12 Gagan, "Indivisibility of Land," 126–46.

13 See my "Sources of Bias in Nineteenth-Century Ontario Wills," *Histoire sociale/Social History* 18, no. 35 (May 1985): 125–32.

14 Goody, *Development of the Family and Marriage*, 238, 257.

15 The latitude given Canadian women is especially evident when contrasted with practices prevailing in other societies. In two of three parishes Spufford examined in Tudor and Stewart Cambridgeshire, for example, widows normally controlled holdings only until the eldest son was of age and then received room and board with him. In the third village most widows held a life interest in the farm, as in Canada. Spufford, *Contrasting Communities*, 88–90, 112–17, 162–4. Friedberger's study of inheritance in the American Corn Belt states revealed that the most common practice was for widows to inherit the entire estate for life, as in the Canadian example. Mark Friedberger, "The Farm Family and the Inheritance Process: Evidence from the Corn Belt, 1870–1950," *Agricultural History* 57 (January 1983): 9. However, because *inter vivos* transfer was far more common among the Canadian group than it was among the American families, a much higher proportion of the widows in Ontario found themselves dependent upon some form of maintenance agreement in later life than did widows in Friedberger's communities. These Canadian widows had, of course, lately shared their dependent status with their husbands.

16 Carleton County Land Registry, Goulbourn, no. 20467, will of John Colbert, Goulbourn, 1863.

17 Gagan, "Indivisibility of Land," 134–5. Such testamentary provisions were characterized as "Patriarchy from the Grave" by Nanciellen Davis in *Acadiensis* 13, no. 7 (Spring 1984): 91–100.

18 Archives of Ontario (AO), Carleton County Surrogate Court, will register D, 138–42, will of William Hodgins, Huntley, 1881.

19 AO, Crown Lands Township Papers, RG 1, C-IV, Huntley, Lot 9, Con. 1, Pinhey to Crown Lands, 10 March 1848; Fitzroy, northwest half Lot 10, Con. 4, Pinhey to Bouthillier, 31 May 1844.

20 AO, Land Record Index, sale 20 May 1850; Huntley Abstract Index, northwest half Lot 10, Con. 2, patent 9 July 1850.

21 David P. Acres and Bruce S. Elliott, "The Acres Families of Carleton County, Ontario: The First Three Generations," *Families* 20, no. 3 (1981): 133–4; Carleton County Land Registry, Torbolton, instrument no. 18818, will of Thomas Acres, 1862; conversation with the late Helen Wimberley of Nepean.

22 Account book of Arthur Hopper's store, Huntley, 1836–9, account no. 77, courtesy Mrs Garrett O'Neill, Ottawa.

23 John Hodgins of Goulbourn died c1830 leaving two sons and several daughters.

The eldest, George, was apprenticed a cabinet-maker in Bytown and practised his trade in Hawkesbury, but was evidently raised by a probable uncle in Fitzroy; he used the name Lewis in his family, the maiden name of his aunt. Michael was living with his uncle (?) Michael in Fitzroy in 1852, but soon after bought his paternal estate from George, the heir-at-law. Their mother had remarried very soon after their father died and had a large family by her second husband, Edward Rollins, in Renfrew County. Goulbourn deeds, nos. 15282, 24136, 24137; census returns.

24 City of Ottawa Archives, Land Registry copy books, Fitzroy, deed no. 18747, Duggan [sic] to Cavanagh, 1862.

25 Goody has pointed out that poor families often did not practise dowry: Goody, *Development of the Family and Marriage*, 241. Easterlin seems to have had no justification for feeling that all children received an equal share in the American case: Easterlin, "Population Change and Farm Settlement," 65. Dowries among the Tipperary Irish of the Ottawa Valley were clearly of less value than 100 acres of improved land, the most common landed provision for boys.

26 Thomas Birtch sold four-and-a-half acres to his daughter Mrs Wilton, wife of a pumpmaker, in 1870, and a farm to his son-in-law Baskerville in 1871, and by his will in 1877 left five acres and a barn to his daughter Jane; will courtesy Gail Clothier, London. Patrick Corbett helped his shoemaker son-in-law, Robert Crowe, buy a lot in Bells Corners in 1859.

27 Carleton County Land Registry, Goulbourn, no. 20467, will of John Colbert, 1863.

28 It was not uncommon for even married daughters to receive a small cash bequest, which may have been an additional payment in consideration of the improvement of the family's circumstances in the years since their marriages.

29 Land Registry, Torbolton, no. 18818, will of Thomas Acres Jr, Huntley, 1862.

30 Land Registry, Fitzroy, no. 925, will of Hugh Carry, 1876, in this case a bequest to a granddaughter.

31 AO, Carleton County Surrogate Court, will register G, 435, will of Thomas Delahunt, 1892.

32 Land Registry, Fitzroy, no. 7210, will of John Barber, 1854. Pinkey was actually a heifer.

33 Land Registry, March, no. 411, will of John Clarke, 1877.

34 Land Registry, Huntley, no. 14307 RO, will of Denis Cavanagh, 1859.

35 George Morgan raised his Scott granddaughters and left them cash bequests.

36 Land Registry, Huntley, no. 2323, will of William Acres, 1884.

37 Jones correspondence, Francis Jones to Richard Richardson, McGillivray, 29 December 1879.

38 Ibid., Glenney to Jones, Brockway, Michigan, 22 July 1861.

39 Ibid., Mary Glenney to Francis Jones, Brockway, Michigan, 15 May 1862.

40 Ibid., Glenney to Jones, Lexington, Kentucky, nd; same to same, Camp Eell, Bishop, Kentucky, 22 January 1863.

309   Notes to pages 204–7

41 National Archives, Washington, military service and pension records of Pte Jos. Glenney, 22nd Mich. Inf.

42 Jones Correspondence, Mary Glenney to Francis Jones, Alpena, 10 February, 6 and 29 March 1890.

43 Ibid., Thomas Jones to William Jones, Victoria, Vancouver's Island, 6 December 1862; Joseph Glenney to Francis Jones, Camp Eell, Bishop, Lexington, 23 December 1862.

44 PAC, RG 31, 1852 census, Goulbourn Township, 101.

45 See Table 12, genealogy of the Grant family.

46 PAC, RG 31, 1852 census, Goulbourn Township, 5.

47 Ibid., 1861 census, Goulbourn Township, 54.

48 Ronald E. Cox, *The Families of Francis and Ann Cox* (Beaconsfield, PQ 1972), B2.

49 Carleton County Land Registry, Huntley Abstract Index A, east half Lot 23, Con. 6; 1861 Huntley Twp agricultural census.

50 R.H. Grant, "Biography of Robert Grant, 1793–1870."

51 Archives of Anglican Diocese of Ottawa, March parish register, marriage 17 November 1847; City of Ottawa Archives, Land Registry copy books, Huntley, no. 3488, Lowry to Grant, 1847.

52 Michael S. Cross, "The Age of Gentility: The Formation of an Aristocracy in the Ottawa Valley," Canadian Historical Association, *Historical Papers*, (1967), 103. On Burke see also chapter 2, notes 70 and 71.

53 Bytown census, 1852, West Ward, 89.

54 Ottawa, St George's Ward, 1861, 21; 1871, 26.

55 George T. Burke's wife by coincidence was named Lydia Grant (gravestone, St Philip's Roman Catholic Cemetery, Richmond); I have no idea whether or not she was related to Robert Grant, but the name Lydia, borne also by the latter's niece Lydia Morris, is said to have been traditional in his family.

56 Land Registry, Goulbourn, no. 8298, memorial of will of Joseph Maxwell of Richmond, Esq., 1855.

57 See 43.

58 E.H. Sheehan, *Nenagh and Its Neighbourhood* (Nenagh 1976), 79.

59 Genealogical Office, Dublin (GO), ms 573, T.U. Sadleir Pedigree Notebooks, 7, pedigree of Cambie, Latter-day Saints (LDS) reel 100153.

60 AO, Carleton County Surrogate Court, will register B, 277–8. The son A.J. Cambie had, however, been educated in England and became, like his father, a Canadian civil servant, dying in 1887 as acting deputy commissioner of patents. Obituary of Alexander Jeffrey Cambie, *Ottawa Journal*, 19 February 1887, 1.

61 Carleton County Land Registry, no. 563 GR, will of R.Y. Greene, 1882.

62 On the Greenes see Naomi Slater Heydon, *Looking Back ... Pioneers of Bytown and March* (Ottawa 1980), 415–38, and on GB, *A History of the Ottawa Collegiate Institute, 1843–1903* (Ottawa 1904), 37–9.

63 Land Registry, March, no. 13902, will and codicil of J.B. Monk, 1859.

64 Cf. Goody, *Development of the Family and Marriage*, 258.

65 Examples of Irish marriage settlements involving emigrants or their ancestors include those of William Burton and Elizabeth Maria Harte, 1811, 642/327/443750; Thomas Thompson and Margaret Harte, 1798, 515/494/335717; Richard Talbot and Lydia Baird, 1795, 501/558/326834; Arthur Hopper and Sarah Maxwell, 1780, 341/143/227907; Joshua Smith and Margaret Kilduffe, 1818, 727/118/496254; and two generations of marriage settlements in a family of merchants in Borrisokane, with the same land used for jointure in two of the settlements: Samuel Haskett and Jane Turner, 1762, 463/498/298638; Samuel Haskett Jr and Mary Gardiner, 1796, 491/556/321087; and Samuel Haskett and Sarah Armitage, 1818, 596/474/408793, all in Registry of Deeds, Dublin.

66 Goody, *Development of the Family and Marriage*, 241.

67 Land Registry, Bytown, no. 522, McDonnell and Burke, marriage settlement, 1852.

68 Goody, *Development of the Family and Marriage*, 258.

69 Public Record Office (PRO), Dublin, T.11803, Dublin, copy of prerogative will of Edward Hart of Cowlowly, 1789; PRO, Dublin, Papers of Hayes & Sons, Solicitors, M.3864(1–18), Harte vs Harte, in Chancery, 1867; in re Charles Harte, 1909; Registry of Deeds, Dublin, 1841 9/71, Swinburn to Dudley.

70 Land Registry, no. 1139 RO, will of Michael Rivington, Huntley, 1837.

71 AO, Carleton County Surrogate Court, will register A, 69–70, will of John Robert Stanley of Bytown, innkeeper, 1850.

72 An Act Respecting Real Property, 22 Vic., c82, sec. 23, 46, *The Consolidated Statutes for Upper Canada* (Toronto 1859).

73 The widow's life interest ceased only upon her death in 1861, but the family arrangements were completed ten years earlier, before the abolition of primogeniture. Carleton County Land Registry, no. 1475, memorial of will of George Clarke, 1839.

74 Mary Morgan, for example, sold to her son George for love and five shillings the family farm rather unusually bequeathed to her absolutely by her husband, with George undertaking to pay her £10 per annum for life in quarterly instalments or £1 per year if she chose to reside with him.

75 Land Registry, March, no. 585, "will" of Patrick Moran (an Irish Catholic), 1882.

76 Carleton County Land Registry, County General Register, no. 1, 48, no. 27612, Hopper maintenance agreement, registered 1867.

77 The Registry Act (1865), *RSO* (1877), c111, sec. 25.

78 Cf. *RSO* (1970), c409, sec. 18 (6).

79 Land Registry, Huntley, no. 444, Vesting Order 1872 re Richard Hodgins vs Francis and Henry Hodgins.

80 Land Registry, March, no. 277, Lis Pendens 1875; no. 297, Dismissal, 1876; nos. 432 and 433, Sale and Mortgage, 1878; no. 438, Lease, 1878.

81 Herbert Mays has indicated that successful permanent residents in Toronto Gore also tended to be early settlers. Mays, "'A Place to Stand': Families, Land and Permanence in Toronto Gore Township, 1820–1890," Canadian Historical Association, *Historical Papers,* 1980, 189–90, 198. Comparative information is scarce, but Mark Friedberger found that in seven townships in Iowa and Illinois only a quarter of the farms transferred from father to son were assigned during the father's lifetime. Friedberger's evidence is drawn from a generally later period than mine, 1870–1950. Friedberger, "Farm Family and Inheritance," 7.

82 See 196–7.

83 See 196.

84 See 211.

85 H. Belden & Co., *Illustrated Historical Atlas of the County of Carleton, Ont.* (Toronto 1879), liv, 20, 43.

86 George Maclean Rose, ed., *A Cyclopaedia of Canadian Biography* (Toronto 1886), 308–9; Rev. William Cochrane, ed., *The Canadian Album: Men of Canada; or, Success by Example* (Brantford 1895), IV: 341.

87 Obituary, *Ottawa Journal,* 21 October 1891. Will, AO, Carleton County Surrogate Court, will register G, 342.

88 Acres and Elliott, "Acres Family," 139–41.

89 A. Bower Lyon, *Westboro, Ottawa's Westmount* (Ottawa 1913); Nepean Abstract Index to Deeds, west half Lot 31, Cons. 1 and A (Ottawa Front).

90 Jones correspondence, Richardson to Jones, South March, 22 November 1858.

91 Rev. John L. Gourlay, *History of the Ottawa Valley* (Ottawa 1896), 61.

92 We have the complaint in 1828 of Pat Lahy, an Irish Roman Catholic immigrant who "stoped in the Township of March and paid Frederick W. Richardson ten dollars for his good will" in certain property, the latter promising to make good to him a forthcoming lease. Richardson "having cut away all the oak he was in a hurry to part [with] it." AO, Crown Lands Township Papers, RG 1, C-IV, Lot 8, Con. 2, March, Patt Lahy to Crown Lands Department, 10 July 1828. We do not hear of Lahy again; no doubt he became a migrant.

93 PRO, Kew, CO 384/5, ff. 294–5, Sir James Read to Earl Bathurst, 17 March 1819. On Boucher see also *Ottawa Citizen,* 18 March 1869, 5, and Nicholas Flood Davin, *The Irishman in Canada* (Toronto 1877), 314.

94 He was called a "lumber dealer" in 1841 when he purchased his first extra lot. Newspaper notice of creditors' meeting, *Ottawa Advocate,* 23 April 1844, 3. Hodgins unfortunately neglected to leave a will and a nasty Chancery suit proved necessary, in 1883, to sort out the disposition of his remaining properties.

95 William Hodgins was called "trader" and "merchant" in a number of deeds between 1840 and 1843, but "yeoman" before and after, shifting to "Gentle-

man" by 1854 as his wealth increased and "Esquire" by 1857. On Hodgins see also Davin, *Irishman in Canada*, 323; *Ottawa Times*, 12 July 1867.

96 City of Ottawa Archives, Land Registry copy books, timber agreement between Hodgins and John Mooney, glued into County Memorial Book at deed no. 2160, Mooney to Pownall, 1844.

97 PAC, Hill Collection, MG 24, I 9, vol. 11, 3230. See also J. Lloyd Armstrong, *Clarendon and Shawville* (Shawville 1980), 174–8.

98 PAC, RG 31, 1861 census of Goulbourn, agricultural, 86.

99 H.F. Walling, *Map of the County of Carleton, Canada West* (Prescott 1863). PAC, National Map Collection.

100 Gourlay, *History of the Ottawa Valley*, 55, 83–4.

101 R.H. Grant, "Biography of Robert Grant, 1793–1870," typescript.

102 *Ottawa Times*, 22 August 1870.

103 University of Western Ontario (UWO), Freeman Talbot memoirs.

104 AO, RG 20, F-27, vol. 19, Ottawa Jail Blotter, 1874–7, 29 May 1876.

105 Gourlay, *History of the Ottawa Valley*, 75–6.

106 A manuscript notation scribbled in a copy of the R.G. Dun & Co. reference book for 1864 states that Birch "absconded." *The Mercantile Agency Reference Book for the British Provinces* (Montreal and Toronto 1864), 306.

107 AO, RG 1, C-IV, Lot 2, Con. 6 (OF), Nepean, Elizabeth Stanley to commissioner of Crown Lands, Richmond, 11 July 1842.

108 AO, Heir and Devisee Commission, RG 40–3072 and 3987.

109 Apart from Adam, who died young.

110 Linda A. Bissell, "From One Generation to Another: Mobility in Seventeenth-Century Windsor, Connecticut," *William and Mary Quarterly*, 3rd Series, 31 (January 1974): 79–110.

111 AO, RG 1, C-IV, Lot 27, Con. B (RF), Nepean, Arthur Hopper to John A. Macdonald, Bytown, 24 February 1848.

112 Obituary, *Christian Guardian*, 11 July 1883, 223. See also Table 8.

113 Archives of Anglican Diocese of Ottawa, registers of March parish, baptisms 1847; PAC, RG 31, 1852 census of Westminster Township, 79.

114 See 162–3.

115 PRO, Dublin, Modreeny parish register; PAC, A.D.P. Heeney Papers, MG 30, E 144, vol. 2, Memoirs, chapter 1, files 2 and 3; PAC, RG 31, 1842 census of Fitzroy; PAC, RG 31, 1861 census of Dundas, 22; 1871 census, 3; Archives of Anglican Diocese of Ottawa, register of parish of Pakenham and Fitzroy, baptisms 1842–4; Archives of Anglican Diocese of Ontario, register of parish of Kemptville, baptisms 1846; correspondence with Karen E. Rebey, Tiverton, Ontario.

116 Archives nationales, Montreal (ANQ(M)), register of Christ Church Anglican; Arthur Hopper's account book in hands of descendant Mrs Garrett O'Neill, Ottawa, account no. 124; PAC, RG 31, 1871 census of Biddulph, F2, 9; 1881 census of McGillivray, D1, 14; UWO, Armitage-Stanley Collection, transcript

of register of St James, Clandeboye, marriage 1873 of George, son of Moses Coates, aged 28, born County Galway.

117 PRO, Dublin, Terryglass parish register; PAC, Governor General's Office, RG 7, G 18, vol. 46, Montreal Emigrant Society Passage Book for 1832, microfilm reel H-962, no. 763; Archives of Anglican Diocese of Ottawa, registers of March parish, baptisms 1833–5; PAC, registers of St James, Hull, baptisms 1849–52; Gourlay, *History of the Ottawa Valley,* 48; Beechwood Cemetery, Ottawa, burial register entry no. 3889, burial of Luke Hogan, 1887.

118 The number of elementary or nuclear families involved in this multi-generation migration was actually half again as large as the number of families cited (forty-five) because of the numbers of children already married and with children of their own who acquiesced in their parents' decision to move the clan to a new location and accompanied them. Fifteen of the forty-five instances took this multi-generational form.

119 Cf. A. Gordon Darroch, "Migrants in the Nineteenth Century: Fugitives or Families in Motion?" *Journal of Family History* 6, no. 3 (Fall 1981): 257–77. Friedberger, in his study of American inheritance strategies, is bound by the community focus of his investigation and implies that migrant families had no "planning mechanism." Friedberger, "Farm Family and Inheritance," 6–7. A community focus also prevents Kathleen Neils Conzen from coming to grips with migrants in her study of family and inheritance in a largely Prussian farming community in Minnesota. Conzen rejects Easterlin's findings as based upon insufficient evidence of actual land transmission patterns and cites new evidence to support older views of the weak family ties and wandering habits of the native-born "Yankee" farmers. She instead credits the attempts of German farmers to provide land for their children near the parental homestead to an imported desire to preserve the familial attachments engendered in the peasant agricultural systems of Europe. In this context she stresses the importance of both ethnic concentration and availability of land in permitting such family economic strategies to operate in rural America. K.N. Conzen, "Peasant Pioneers: Generational Succession among German Farmers in Frontier Minnesota," in Steven Hahn and Jonathan Prude, eds., *The Countryside in the Age of Capitalist Transformation* (Chapel Hill, NC 1985), 259–92.

120 AO, RG I, C-IV, Lot 9, Con. 5, Fitzroy, Francis Neil Sr to Peter Robinson, Fitzroy, 12 December 1831.

121 Mervyn A. Collins, *From the Shamrock to the Maple: A Collins Family Story, 1775–1982* (Simcoe 1982), 9–14; correspondence with Mr Collins; PRO, Dublin, Templeharry, Shinrone, and Modreeny parish registers; Modreeny tithe applotment book, 1826/7; Canadian land records.

122 AO, RG I, C-IV, Lot 24, Con. 3, Ramsay, Francis Collins to Peter Robinson, Ramsay, 20 April 1831.

123 Gravestone at Boyd's Cemetery, Lanark.

124 Bruce S. Elliott, "The George Blackwell Family of Renfrew Co., Ontario," *Blackwell Newsletter* 4, no. 2 (December 1982): 27.

125 Mrs Collins was living with her daughter Mrs Thomas Foster in Ramsay in 1861 but died in 1867 and was buried at Bervie. PAC, RG 31, 1861 census of Ramsay, 13; inscription in old cemetery south of the Durham Road, Bervie.

126 William Haskett to Thomas Haskett, Goldross, March 1834; I am grateful to Mrs Neva Loft, Ilderton, Ontario, for transcripts of the Haskett letters.

127 National Library of Ireland (NLI), ms 787, County Tipperary freeholders list, 1776; PRO, Dublin, Borrisokane tithe applotment book, February 1826, TAB27 N/8; Griffith's Valuation. At the time of this correspondence Joseph's brothers John and Thomas were already in Canada. His brother William was a prosperous merchant in the neighbouring parish of Ardcrony, leaving £100 per annum to his widow and his house and stock to his only daughter at his death soon after.

128 Joseph Haskett to Thomas Haskett, Goldross, 22 September 1835.

129 Rebecca Haskett to Thomas Haskett, Golross, 15 May 1849.

130 NLI, Otway rentals, 1806, 1824; tithe applotment book, 1831.

131 PRO, Dublin, Index to Killaloe Diocesan Marriage Licence Bonds, 1821, George Carter and Mary Read.

132 PRO, Dublin, Otway Deeds, D.20,370, Otway to Sifton, 1760.

133 NLI, ms 13,000(8), Otway rental, 1824.

134 Obituary, *Christian Guardian*, 19 December 1877.

135 PAC, Sifton Papers, MG 27, II, D 15, vol. 288, 5–6, reel C-2178, Rebecca Sifton to Harry Sifton, London, 20 August 1927. Miss Sifton credits this bit of family lore to Robert's only daughter, Rebecca Sifton Pearce (1849–1923).

136 NLI, ms 13,000(8), Otway rental, 1824.

137 Goody, *Development of the Family and Marriage*, 209, referring specifically to age at marriage.

138 The few Irish studies of kinship and inheritance have all traced very different patterns but most have, unfortunately, dealt with the post-Famine period: Conrad Arensberg, *The Irish Countryman* (New York 1937), 76–104; Conrad Arensberg and Solon T. Kimball, *Family and Community in Ireland* (Cambridge, Mass. 1968), 65, 105, 111; Robin Fox, *The Tory Islanders: A People of the Celtic Fringe* (London 1978), 82–126; Elliott Leyton, *The One Blood: Kinship and Class in an Irish Village* (St John's 1975). Cormac O Gráda has noted that literary evidence suggests that ultimogeniture may have prevailed in rural Ireland for the same practical reasons it did in Canada, though Arensberg and Kimball in their twentieth-century study of Clare detected no pattern and O Gráda's own manipulation of the 1911 census suggests a preference for primogeniture that only the larger farmers could realize, because they alone had sufficient land to induce the eldest son to remain at home. Cormac O Gráda, "Primogeniture and Ultimogeniture in Rural Ireland," *Journal of Interdisciplinary History* 10, no. 3 (Winter 1980): 491–7. Maurice McGuire's

interesting study of the surviving late nineteenth-century wills of Limerick and Clare farmers confirms a shift to impartible inheritance after·the Famine and a marked preference for primogeniture, but suggests also that subdivision may have been practised more by larger than by smaller farmers until the 1870s: "Rural Inheritance in 19th Century Clare & Limerick," *Dal gCais* (1984): 49–55. A paucity of adequate source material prevented Akenson from examining the question in his study of a community of substantial farmers in County Antrim who managed to avoid subdivision. Akenson, *Between Two Revolutions*, 43, 188. Kerby Miller sums up recent scholarship on the pre-Famine era by noting that "traders, graziers, and strong farmers in market-oriented eastern Ireland had practiced impartible inheritance for generations," and that after 1814 it became increasingly common among middling and small farmers, except in the west. He notes, however, that "there seemed to be no fixed rule of succession," farmers designating their heirs upon retirement: Miller, *Emigrants and Exiles* (New York 1985), 216–18, 57. Subdivision itself is easy to document, but the extent of the practice is more difficult to determine. I have suggested that among Tipperary Protestants the adoption of emigration as a strategy of heirship in the early nineteenth century facilitated the preservation of the integrity of holdings, notably in freeholders' communities like Modreeny. It is likely that the formation of new Protestant colonies within Tipperary, outlined in chapter 2, to some extent performed a similar function in the eighteenth century. There is little reason to believe that Irish systems of inheritance were any less varied before the Famine than after it.

139 AO, RG I, C-IV, Lot 16, Con. 1, Torbolton, Thomas Acres Jr and William Acres to Crown Lands Department, March, 28 April 1832.

140 Adam Acres married Mary Ann Didsbury, whose father was the second husband of Jane (Hopper) Sproule, widow of the artist Robert A. Sproule and sister of Albert S. Hopper, a merchant who had himself obtained the South March farm by marrying a childless widow. Bruce S. Elliott, "The Hopper Family," *Irish Ancestor* 1982, no. 2: 65–7; on Didsbury: "Mr and Mrs G.B. Acres Give Portrait," *Horaceville Herald* 8 (March 1987): 7. By the time Acres rented this land (1861 census) the Hoppers had lost it to William Hodgins, though Albert Hopper's widow was allowed to remain on the property to the end of her life, despite two later changes of ownership.

141 Most of the six sons of George Blackwell of Ramsay, for example, were able to purchase near their father's new farm in Horton thanks to this recent policy.

142 Land Registry, Huntley, no. 7413 RO, will of Thomas Hodgins, 1854.

143 AO, Charles Shirreff Family Papers, MU 3289, rent rolls of Fitzroy Harbour, nd, 1835, 1836, 1838.

144 Ibid.; AO, Carleton County Surrogate Court, will register M, 54, will of John Nicholson of Fitzroy, 1900.

145 PAC, Wright Papers, MG 24, D 8, vol. 26, 10252–5, Ralph Smith to Philemon Wright & Sons, Shinrone, 17 October 1838.

146 PRO, Dublin, Modreeny parish register; ANQ(M), register of Christ Church, Montreal; Archives of Anglican Diocese of Ottawa, registers of Christ Church, Bytown; *Bytown Gazette,* 29 September 1836, 3, col. 2; 23 February 1837, 3, col. 3; 18 October 1837, 3, col. 4; *Ottawa Advocate,* 15 November 1842; gravestone of brother Leonard Stanley, Greely Anglican Cemetery; Bruce S. Elliott, "The Stanleys," in *Pioneer Families of Osgoode Township,* XVII (Vernon, Ont. 1987), 9–11.

147 Ottawa Public Library, Ottawa Room, Ottawa History Scrapbook no. 5, 60, "Bridge Keeper Mossop"; Archives of Anglican Diocese of Ottawa, registers of Christ Church, Bytown, and Osgoode parish; PAC, RG 31, 1852 census of Bytown, West Ward, 164; 1861 census of Ottawa, Victoria Ward, 82.

148 PAC, RG 31, 1861 agricultural census of Goulbourn.

149 Belden, *Atlas of Carleton County,* liv; obituary, *Ottawa Journal,* 21 January 1908, 9, col. 3.

150 Obituary of Thomas Butler, *Ottawa Journal,* 15 March 1904, 1, col. 1.

151 Obituary printed in E. Marjorie Moodie and Bruce S. Elliott, *The Hazeldean Cemeteries* (Ottawa 1980), 83.

152 *Ottawa Citizen,* 15 January 1864, 2, col. 2; 19 January, 2, cols 2–7, and 3, col. 1; 22 January, 2, col 4; 26 January, 2, col. 3; 2 February, 2, col. 4; Archives of Anglican Diocese of Ottawa, Huntley Anglican baptismal register, 7 June 1864.

153 Death notice, *Ottawa Journal,* 4 December 1891, 1.

154 E.J. McAuliffe, "A List of Entries of Marriage Licence Grants in Killaloe Court and Register Book," *Irish Genealogist* 5, no. 6 (November 1979): 710; ANQ(M), register of Christ Church Anglican.

155 Obituary, *Ottawa Journal,* 4 June 1897, 7.

156 Davin, *Irishman in Canada,* 324.

157 Obituary, *Ottawa Journal,* 3 July 1890, 1.

158 Two obituaries courtesy Gwen Brouse, Riverside, California. See also "Re Francis Abbott and His 7 Sons," *Ottawa Citizen,* 28 October 1933, 2.

159 Obituaries in the Methodist *Christian Guardian:* Richard, 15 January 1896, 43; John, 6 February 1895, 91; John's wife Ellen, 12 April 1893, 235.

160 Cochrane, ed., *Men of Canada,* IV: 276.

161 *Prominent People of the Province of Ontario* (Ottawa 1925), 91.

CHAPTER NINE

1 Jones correspondence, R.H. Jones to E.O. Jones, Crescent City, California, 16 November 1879.

2 Many of the Stafford families are buried at St Stephen's Anglican Church in Micksburg, where gravestones bear the following Wexford names, most of which families are traceable to Beckwith: Burgess, Hawkins, Hill, James, Kenny, Kidd, Leach, Libby, Lumax, Rath, Tomlinson, Wallace, and Warren.

Other cemeteries in the neighbourhood yield the relevant names Code, Edwards, Jackson, Lett, May, Sutton, and Tennant. Inscriptions in Micksburg United (Methodist) Cemetery; Micksburg Presbyterian Cemetery; abandoned Methodist Cemetery, Wilberforce Township; Greenwood Cemetery, Westmeath. Cf. Anglican Diocesan Archives, registers of Perth, Richmond, and Franktown; H.M. Brown, ed., "Nominal Rolls and State Papers: North Lanark Data," vol. 1 (ms 1973), a collection of Beckwith and Ramsay census, assessment, and militia records given to me by the compiler.

3 The censuses of Adelaide, Brooke, and Warwick in 1852 and 1861 include the relevant names Bolton, Edwards, Evoy, Holbrooke, Keyes, Lett, Lucas, Rothwell, Saunders, Shirley, Sutton, and Willoughby. Inscriptions in St James Anglican Cemetery, Brooke, yield the additional names: Kerfoot, Kidd, Leach, Lewis, and Taylor. Also correspondence with Elizabeth Cahill of Montreal. As stated in chapter 6, the "Wexford group" was composed predominantly of people from that county, but also included families from neighbouring parishes of Kilkenny, Carlow, and Wicklow.

4 The movements of the Kilcooly people are discussed further in Appendix D.

5 Kerby A. Miller, *Emigrants and Exiles: Ireland and the Irish Exodus to North America* (New York 1985), 271–3.

6 Ibid., 236.

7 Ibid., 235.

8 Ibid., 59.

9 Ibid., 272–3.

10 Ibid., 216.

11 Ibid., 57.

12 Ibid., 273.

13 Ibid., 133.

14 Ibid., 134–5.

15 Bruce S. Elliott, "'The Famous Township of Hull': Image and Aspirations of a Pioneer Quebec Community," *Histoire sociale/Social History* 12, no. 24 (November 1979): 339–67; Robert Leslie Jones, *History of Agriculture in Ontario 1613–1880* (Toronto 1946), 112; Philip Gabriel et al., *Architectural Heritage of the Pontiac* (Quebec 1981), 57. Wright's farms also supported a wide range of commercial enterprises.

16 Jones, *History of Agriculture,* 109–21.

17 There were, of course, exceptions. Catharine Wilson of Queen's University, Kingston, is studying the Canadian estates of Lord Mountcashell, notably on Amherst Island in the St Lawrence. Most farmers on the island were initially tenants of an absentee landlord resident in Ireland (an interesting reversal of the pattern one comes to expect). Demesne agriculture as such was non-existent on Mountcashell's Canadian estate, though the earl did retain a local agent. Catharine Anne Wilson, "Family Emigration from the Ards, Co. Down, Ireland to Amherst Island, Canada, in the 19th Century: A Project in Progress,"

Ulster Genealogical and Historical Guild, *Subscribers' Interest List* 9 (1986): 77–80.

18 Jones, *History of Agriculture*, 250–65; Robert E. Ankli and Wendy Miller, "Ontario Agriculture in Transition: The Switch from Wheat to Cheese," *Journal of Economic History* 42, no. 1 (March 1982): 207–15.

19 D.H. Akenson, "An Agnostic View of the Historiography of the Irish-Americans," *Labour/Le Travail* 14 (Autumn 1982): 123–59.

20 Exchanges between John S. Atkinson and Leonard D. Stanley in the *Lucan Enterprise*, May-September 1883. No copies of the *Enterprise* are known to exist in public repositories, but cuttings of the poems are preserved in John Atkinson's scrapbook, now in the possession of his descendant, Charles P. Corbett of Ailsa Craig, Ontario.

APPENDIX D

1 Deed from Sir William Barker, 20 October 1773: Marjorie Smeltzer, *The Smeltzers of Kilcooly* (Baltimore 1981), 32–3; complete transcript of deed courtesy Mrs Egon Nielsen, Forest, Ontario. The 1776 freeholders list names also four Palatine Millers at Bawnleigh. W.G. Neely, *Kilcooley: Land & People in Tipperary* (Belfast 1983), 57.

2 Copy courtesy Eleanor Nielsen; cf. also Public Record Office (PRO), Dublin, Kilcooly tithe applotment book; Neely, *Kilcooley*, 54–7, 94–5.

3 The name Cantelon is prominent among Protestant families in Kilcooly. Family traditions trace the family to Williamite, Huguenot, or even Viking origins. The family were probably converts of Anglo-Irish origin. Harold R. and Leon C. Cantelon, "Romantic Cantelon History" (typescript, 1960, Baldwin Room, Metropolitan Toronto Library), 2: 730, 751, 3: opening pages.

4 The surnames found in this colony included Bowles, Caesar, Cantelon, Colclough, Cole, Cook, Cowen, Dolmage, Douglas, Hickey, Lawrence, Miller, Orr, Perdue, Shepherd, Shier, Smeltzer, Sparling, Sparrow, Switzer, Vanston, Webster, and Young. Public Archives of Canada (PAC), Halton and Peel County maps; Archives of Ontario (AO), MS 360, r 1, parish register of St Peter's Anglican Church, Erindale, commencing 1827; *Brown's Toronto City and Home District Directory 1846–7* (Toronto 1846). On Switzer see *Dictionary of Canadian Biography* VIII (Toronto 1985), 854–5.

5 University of Western Ontario (UWO), M-770–771, parish registers of St George's Anglican Church, Goderich, commencing 1835; Huron District Census and Assessment Rolls, 1842 and 1845. Surnames included Cantelon, Colclough, Cole, Cook, Douglas, Dulmage, Miller, Perdue, Shepherd, Smeltzer, Sparling, Sperin, Switzer, Vanston, Webster (in Ashfield Township), and Young. See also Neely, *Kilcooley*, 93. In later years many emigrants from Kilcooly found employment at Eaton's department store in Toronto; its vice-president, Harry McGee, was from the parish. Neely, *Kilcooley*, 130–1.

6 In 1841 forty-one freeholders travelling from Kilcooly to Clonmel to cast their votes for their landlord Mr Barker were attacked by a mob lying in wait for them near New Birmingham. Despite being protected by eight constables, several of the freeholders were seriously injured and the party was forced to return to Kilcooly and await reinforcements. *Nenagh Guardian*, 17 July 1841, 1, col. 5.

7 Nicholas Flood Davin, *The Irishman in Canada* (Toronto 1877), 301.

8 Streetsville anniversary newspaper, 1942. Transcripts of the newspaper articles mentioned were sent to me by Eleanor Nielsen of Forest, Ontario.

9 *Streetsville Review and Port Credit Herald,* 16 September 1937.

10 Ibid., 29 May 1913.

11 Manuscript biography of Henry Cole, sent to me by the author, Mrs T.N. Parr, Rexdale, Ontario; Upper Canada Sessional Papers, 4–5 Vic., 1841, App. M, Convicts discharged from Provincial Penitentiary in the year ending 1 October 1840.

12 Obituary in the *Christian Guardian,* 18 February 1880, 55.

13 Obituaries in *Christian Guardian,* 22 February 1882, 63; 13 September 1882, 295; 4 May 1881; 5 January 1887, 11; 5 September 1855; and 11 April 1877.

14 Streetsville anniversary newspaper, 1942.

15 PRO, Dublin, Templemore parish register.

16 PRO, Dublin, Templeharry parish register.

17 Cantelon and Cantelon, "Romantic Cantelon History," 3: 245–6.

A Note on Sources

Identification of the families upon which this study is based has been a time-consuming and involved process. Very few lists of emigrants or immigrants survive. The researcher must therefore build up his own list of immigrants from a region from detailed genealogical study and constant comparison of Irish and Canadian sources. The most valuable of these are the Church of Ireland parish registers and marriage licence bond indexes in Ireland, and parish registers, census returns, land records, and gravestone inscriptions in Canada. After a time the limited pool of surnames found in the Irish region becomes apparent and facilitates identification: a Hodgins married to an Ardell or a Haskett to a Goulding could scarcely be from anywhere outside North Tipperary. Cross-checking with other sources is nonetheless essential, and inevitably one must follow for a time lines that are eventually eliminated once non-Tipperary origins are discovered, especially in the case of common names such as Thompson or Smith that can be found in any part of Ireland. Though this bibliographical note includes the most useful sources, important details were also discovered in other specific documents of less general relevance; many of these are noted in appropriate places in the references to the text.

IRELAND

Irish genealogists and demographically inclined historians are understandably discouraged by the knowledge that most of the primary records useful for this kind of research (census, wills, and Church of Ireland parish registers) were centralized in Dublin's Four Courts in the late nineteenth century and were subsequently destroyed by shelling and an ensuing explosion and fire during the Irish Civil War in 1922. Though the losses were disastrous one cannot help but be impressed by the amount of transcription and abstracting of wills, in particular, which had been done before the fire and the extent to which these copies help to remedy the loss of the originals, at least for basic genealogical purposes. When one compares the lists of Church of Ireland parish registers that were in the Four Courts in 1922 (in the early *Reports* of the deputy keeper of the records) with the list of current survivals and copies, however, what impresses is not how much was lost but rather the recent vintage of most of the destroyed material, a consequence of lax record-keeping by the clergy. Few of the North Tipperary registers lost in the conflagration predated 1800 and a fair number from the early nineteenth century still survive, either because they were returned to the parishes under retention orders when the clergy demonstrated that they could provide safe storage, or because the books were still 'in use in parishes with small Protestant populations when the registers were called in.

The North American historian is aided in Irish research by the fact that the Church of Jesus Christ of Latter-day Saints (LDS or Mormons) have microfilmed massive quantities of the Irish records mentioned below, including the Deeds Registers and indexes, the Genealogical Office (GO) manuscripts, the tithe applotment books, the records of the Valuation Office, the civil registration indexes, and the early registrations themselves, many will indexes and copies, and the indexes to marriage licence bonds. The Mormon filming has generally not extended to Church of Ireland parish registers, estate records, maps, and newspapers. Microfilms may be viewed in the Mormon Genealogical Library in Salt Lake City or in numerous branch libraries around the world.

Handbooks

When I began work on this study there were no published guides to sources for Irish local studies apart from a few articles, notably Kenneth Darwin's "Sources for Townland History" in *Ulster Folklife* 3 (1957): 55–63. There were a number of genealogical handbooks, which were especially relevant because of the genealogical nature of much of my research. The best of these remains Margaret Dickson Falley, *Irish and Scotch-Irish Ancestral Research,* 2 vols. (Baltimore 1981), originally written in 1962 and because of its thoroughness unlikely to be superseded for some time yet, though it is now woefully out of date. On a number of specialized subjects, such as the Registry of Deeds, newspapers, and the records of the Inns of Court, however, the articles in Donal F. Begley, ed., *Irish Genealogy: A Record Finder* (Dublin 1981), are essential reading. Also useful because of its fairly recent vintage is Breandan Mac Giolla Choille, "Sources for Family History in the Public Record Office of Ireland," in *World Conference on Records: Preserving Our Heritage,* vol. 5, part 1, series 402 (Salt Lake City 1980). A parallel article for the north is Brian Trainor, "Sources for Genealogical Research in Ireland with Particular Reference to Ulster," *Canadian Genealogist* 1, no. 3 (1979): 132–54. A local guide to genealogical materials has recently appeared: Nancy Murphy, *Tracing Roots in North West Tipperary: Genealogical Sources for the Baronies of Upper Ormond, Lower Ormond, Owney and Arra* (Nenagh 1982). It deals mostly with national sources but does list the dates of local Roman Catholic registers and the locations of burial grounds and provides a handy alphabetical list of the townlands in the three baronies.

Since my work began, geographer William Nolan has published *Sources for Local*

Studies (Dublin 1977) and an enlarged version entitled *Tracing the Past: Sources for Local Studies in the Republic of Ireland* (Dublin 1982) which fill a very great need. The Public Record Office (PRO), Dublin, has provided S.J. Connolly, *The Public Record: Sources for Local Studies in the Public Record Office of Ireland* (Dublin 1982). A few regional guides are now available, Michael Byrne's *Sources for Offaly History* (Tullamore 1978) being the most relevant to my purposes. A guide for Westmeath has recently been published: Marian Keaney, *Westmeath Local Studies: A Guide to Sources* (Mullingar 1982). As a guide to source materials in numerous repositories the indispensable reference is Richard Hayes's multi-volume series *Manuscript Sources for the History of Irish Civilization* (Boston 1966 and supplements). At the National Library of Ireland the NLI reports on collections in private hands, some of which have since come to the library, are also valuable and informative tools.

Vital Statistics

The most important sources for identifying North Tipperary emigrants were the indexes to marriage licence bonds and the Church of Ireland parish registers. The marriage licence bonds for Killaloe Diocese (1719–1845) and for Cashel and Emly (1664–1857) perished in the Four Courts, but the indexes survive and name both parties and state the year. For Killaloe, original notations from 188 bonds dating between 1777 and 1845 survive in the Killaloe Court and Register Book (1707–1868), now in PRO (IA.4.17), and since printed in *The Irish Genealogist* 5, no. 6 (November 1979): 710–19. The British Library also has miscellaneous records of the Consistory Court of Killaloe, 1671–1824, add. mss 31,882–3 of which ms 31,883 consists of original marriage licence bonds (1680–1720 and 1760–2), since printed in *The Irish Genealogist* 5, no. 5 (November 1978): 580–90. Neither of these series is covered by the surviving PRO index. Both of these latter collections give the townlands of residence of the parties, the groom's occupation, and the names, addresses, and occupations of the bondsmen. For a few families the indexes to the Ossory, Ferns, and Leighlin bonds provided needed references, as did the Dublin consistorial index for several mercantile and gentry families, some of whose members married in the city.

Most of the surviving Church of Ireland parish registers in the dioceses of Killaloe, Cashel, and Limerick have been microfilmed by the Public Record Office (which has recently resumed filming in other parts of the Republic after a hiatus of several years), though a couple which they missed are in private hands. I know of several registers in other parts of Ireland which have disappeared within the last ten years, in part due to the disruptions caused by the amalgamation of parishes with dwindling Protestant populations, but in large part to plain carelessness. These sources are irreplaceable and it is shocking to realize that the disaster of 1922 has not impressed upon all of the clergy the importance of preserving these records. I must stress that the clergy with whom I had personal contact in the course of my research were unfailingly courteous and helpful and some devote considerable attention to the records in their charge. The Rev. Canon F.StG.H. Johnston at Templemore, for example, has indexed the registers of his union. I attempted to consult all registers from their commencement to 1850. The dates listed below are the dates seen, not the dates the registers cover; most continue after 1850. Where I located extracts from destroyed registers, these have been noted. c = Christenings, M = Marriages, B = Burials.

Aghnameadle	CM 1834–50, B 1834–1980. Held by Mrs Albert Shortt, Garraun, Cloughjordan.
Aglishcloghane or Eglish	C 1828–1903, M 1845–77. Photocopies in PRO, M.5218 and M.5216.
Ballingarry	CMB 1790–1925. Extracts for surname Robinson, PRO, Thrift Abstracts, vol. 3, bundle 20, 256.
	M 1845–50. Register at rectory, Cloughjordan.
Birr	CM 1760–1803, B 1786–1803. PRO, reel 2.
Birr and Lockeen	C 1802–58, M 1803–44, B 1801–38. PRO, reel 2.
Borrisnafarney	C 1827–54, M 1827–51, B 1828–60. PRO, reel 4.
Castle Connell	See Stradbally.
Castletownarra	C 1802–53, M 1803–46, B 1802–40. PRO, reel 5.
Cloughjordan	C 1846–52. PRO, reel 4.
	M 1845–54. Register at rectory, Cloughjordan.
	See also Modreeny.
Corbally	C 1834–49. PRO, reel 4.
Dunkerrin	CMB 1790–2, 1799–1825. Extracts for name Sparling, PRO, T. Groves Abstracts, box S, Sparling file.
	CMB 1790–1815. Extracts for names Hayes and Sparling, courtesy D.H. Crofton, Tonbridge, Kent.
	C 1825–52, M 1826–45, B 1825–76. PRO, reel 4.
Ettagh	C 1825–9, 31, 41, 46–52, M 1826–31, 37, 44, B 1826–31, 48–56. PRO, reel 4.
Inniscaltra	CMB 1803–26. Extracts for name Callaghan, PRO, Thrift Abstracts, vol. 3, bundle 20, 263.
	C 1851–76. PRO, reel 4.
	M 1845– . Register at the Deanery, Killaloe.
	B 1851–74. Transcript, PRO, M.5234.
Kilbarron	M 1851–67. Register at the rectory, Nenagh.
Kilcolman	C 1839–51. PRO, reel 4.
	B 1839–72. PRO, M.5235.
Killaloe	CMB 1679–1845. PRO, reel 5.
	C 1845–72, B 1846–73. PRO, reel 5.
Killeigh	C 1808–23, M 1808–32, B 1808–34. Transcript, PRO, M.5115.
Kilmastulla	C 1755–8, 1780–2. PRO, reel 2. See also St John's, Newport.
Kilmore	CMB 1781–1827. Extracts for name Armitage, University of Western Ontario (UWO), Armitage-Stanley Collection, B-4721.
	M 1847–50. Register at the rectory, Nenagh.

Kilruane	M 1845–50. Register at the rectory, Nenagh.
Modreeny	CMB 1786–1826. Extracts. GO, ms 572.
	CMB 1787–1827. Extracts for name Armitage, UWO, Armitage-Stanley Collection, B-4721.
	C 1827–40, M 1827–48. Transcripts, PRO, M.5238–39.
	M 1845–50, B 1878–1958. Registers at the rectory, Cloughjordan. See also Cloughjordan.
Monsea	C 1808–14. Extracts for names Beard and Poe, PRO, T. Groves Abstracts, IA.36.40, box B3, Bard (2).
Nenagh	CMB 1740–92. Extracts for several names, PRO, T. Groves Abstracts, IA.36.40, box B3, Bard (2).
Ogonnelloe	C 1807–65, M 1807–77, B 1836–75. PRO, reel 5.
Roscrea	C 1784–1859, M 1792–1836, 1845–57, B 1792–1896. PRO, reel 3, and at the rectory, Roscrea.
Shinrone	C 1741–1856, M 1741–1844, B 1741–1827. PRO, reel 4.
St John's,	C 1782–1852, M 1789–1849, B 1783–1853. PRO, reel 2.
Newport	See also Kilmastulla.
Stradbally	
(Castle Connell)	C 1824–51, M 1824–44, B 1824–53. PRO, reel 3.
Templederry	M 1845–50. Register at the rectory, Nenagh.
Templeharry	CMB 1800–34. Mrs Albert Shortt, Garraun, Cloughjordan.
	C 1835–53, M 1835–45, B 1830–77. PRO, reel 4.
Templemore	CMB 1791–1811. Typescript, LDS reel 990092.
	C 1811–53, M 1812–45, B 1813–54. PRO, reel 7, and at the rectory, Templemore.
Templetuohy	C 1787–1834, M 1794–1834, B 1793–1835. PRO, reel 7.
Terryglass	C 1809–55, M 1809–53, B 1809–57. PRO, reel 3.
Toem	C 1802–65, M 1802–45, B 1802–77. Typescript, LDS reel 924692.

The Latter-day Saints have only a few transcripts of registers for this area. The entries in these registers are, however, included in the Irish section of the International Genealogical Index (IGI), a massive microfiche index to parish register copies in the Salt Lake library. The IGI would have been a tremendously useful tool had my research centred upon England or Scotland, for its coverage there is impressive and increasingly comprehensive. The Mormons have filmed a number of the Tipperary Roman Catholic registers and have prepared a typescript guide entitled "Roman Catholic Parish Registers for the Diocese of Killaloe" (1982). Genealogical Office ms 641 (LDS reel 100239), "Diocese of Killaloe: Particulars of Catholic Parochial Registers," provides an excellent description of the contents and condition of the records, but of course does not give the LDS microfilm numbers. Because access restrictions were only recently lifted by the bishop of Killaloe, none of the Catholic entries are yet in the IGI. The LDS collection of Catholic registers is not as complete as that in the National Library, Dublin, which undertook its own microfilming program some years ago.

Since my research was completed, a number of local heritage organizations have begun indexing both Protestant and Catholic registers. In the area with which this study is concerned the active groups have been the Offaly Historical Society in Tullamore, the Nenagh and Roscrea Heritage Centres, and a group based at the Ursuline Convent in Thurles. Lists of parishes covered by the Tullamore, Roscrea, and Thurles groups may be found in "Reports by County on Research Activities in Ireland," *Irish Family History* 1 (1985): 7–8. The northern Tipperary parishes indexed at Nenagh are listed in an insert to *Irish Family History* 2 (1986). A general article which explains the origins of the indexing projects and long-term prospects for co-operative efforts among the various organizations involved is Michael Byrne, "Irish Parish Register Indexing Projects," *Irish Family History* 1 (1985): 19–26.

Methodists comprised only a small proportion of the Protestants of the North Tipperary region in the period covered by this study. The Killaloe Diocesan questionnaire of 1820 (NLI, ms 352) notes that most had not yet separated from the Church of Ireland. Methodist registers for Borrisokane (marriages from 1870), Cloughjordan (baptisms from 1834 and marriages from 1877), and Nenagh (marriages from 1873) have been indexed by the Nenagh District Heritage Society. The Roscrea Heritage Centre in Damer House has indexed the Roscrea Methodist registers (baptisms 1830–1900, marriages 1870–98). The Public Record Office of Northern Ireland has a "Register of Baptisms for the Various Methodist Circuits, 1815–58," Mic 429. Returns for most circuits begin later than the date indicated and most end in the early to mid-1840s. This is a largely unused source very important for research into Methodist families. The returns relevant to this study are for the Cloughjordan circuit, 1834–44, 89–91; Roscrea circuit, 1830–42, 83–6; Limerick circuit, 1824–46, 59–79; Tullamore circuit, 1831–45, 97–105; Maryborough and Mountrath circuit, 1834–46, 124–8; Killaloe mission, Kilrush, and Ennis, 1844 and 1857, 540; and Kilkenny and Tipperary mission, 1837–41, 542, the first two being by far the most important. An article on "Methodism in Cloughjordan" by the Rev. D.A. Levistone Cooney appeared in Daniel Grace and Rev. Edward Whyte, eds., *Cloughjordan Heritage* (Cloughjordan 1985), 16–19.

Civil registration of births and deaths in Ireland began only in 1864, so these records were of no use in the present research. However, civil registration of Protestant marriages commenced in 1845, and these records, the earliest extant for some parishes, were very useful in tracing later emigrants. The indexes only may be searched at the General Register Office, 8–11 Lombard Street East, Dublin 2 (formerly in the Customs House), and certificates ordered for a reasonable fee or, better still, the indexes and original registers for the first few decades may be viewed on LDS microfilm. The register volumes are organized by registration district within each year, so a search of a region using the LDS films may be made expeditiously by a researcher engaged in local studies.

I searched numerous graveyards in the region, but Protestant gravestones tend to be of the higher classes and, despite a few finds that were of major importance in establishing individual pedigrees, the attempt generally did not repay the effort devoted to it. The Ormond Historical Society in Nenagh has recently published the inscriptions for many of the parishes in the three northern baronies, but one must be aware that many monuments lie buried at a considerable depth beneath the surface of wild, abandoned graveyards, or are hidden in impenetrable bush in corners of still-operative churchyards. Selected "interesting" inscriptions for a number of graveyards may be found in the *Journal of the Association for the Preservation of the Memorials of the Dead, Ireland* 1–13 (1888–1933/4) and inscriptions at Uskane and Kilmore were published in *The Irish Genealogist* 3, no. 2 (July 1957): 74–5, and 2, no. 10 (July 1953): 317–21, respectively.

Census Records

Early census records in Ireland were superior in content to those in England and so their loss is particularly to be deplored. The 1821 returns, for example, provided the names and ages of every member of the household, their relationships to the head, their occupations, including multiple occupations, identification of children in school, and, for the head, the number of acres of land held and the number of storeys in the house. The destruction of most of these records in the 1922 conflagration has been called the greatest single loss of that day (Rosemary ffolliott in Begley, *Record Finder,* 58) and certainly its destruction removed any chance of this book including a quantitative socio-economic analysis of emigrants compiled from individual data. Fortunately the returns for Ballybritt Barony in King's County, including the town of Birr, have survived (LDS film 100818), but I was able to identify barely two dozen emigrant families in it. A notebook of abstracts that the North Tipperary-born herald Thomas Ulick Sadleir made from the destroyed returns for the more relevant Clonlisk and the North Tipperary baronies includes a couple of hundred, mostly gentry, families (GO, ms 572). These notes, while highly valuable for reconstructing the individual families concerned, were of course far too selective to permit any statistical analysis of the type that would be possible using the Ballybritt returns.

Parts of some earlier enumerations also survive. For the earliest period Thomas Laffan's shoddy transcript of the hearth tax returns for 1665–7 (*Tipperary's Families,* Dublin 1911) permitted some analysis of the beginnings of Protestant settlement. On its deficiencies see Edward MacLysaght, "Moloneys and the Tipperary Hearth Money Rolls" in Etienne Rynne, ed., *North Munster Studies: Essays in Commemoration of Monsignor Michael Moloney* (Limerick 1967), 533–5. The 1766 religious census for the diocese of Cashel exists (PRO) and for numerous parishes on the southern fringe of North Tipperary it provides the names of Protestant and Catholic heads of families, generally with the numbers in each household of each faith. Statistics derived from the returns were useful for comparing the distribution of religious persuasions with later records and determining differential rates of population growth, and the individual returns for the Newport and Templemore areas were helpful for those regions. Unfortunately, the original returns from the Glankeen area, location of the Otway estate, were merely statistical. Sadleir copied the nominal returns for Ballingarry and

Uskane and his transcripts, now in the National Library (ms 8908), hint at the valuable information on the distribution of surnames which was once available for all of Lower Ormond, as indeed for the whole of Ireland. A census of Protestants in Mountshannon union in 1855 is written into the cover of the parish register and was useful for reconstructing the families of some very late emigrants to Huron County. However, most of the Protestants were gone from the union by then and some once-numerous names were only sparsely represented. On census material of this sort see Steve Royle, "Irish Manuscript Census Records: A Neglected Source of Information," *Irish Geography* 11 (1978): 110–25, and "Irish Manuscript Ecclesiatical Census Returns: A Survey with an Example from Clogherny Parish, Co. Tyrone 1851–1852," *Local Population Studies* 29 (Autumn 1982): 35–49. The Public Record Office at Kew, Surrey, has quarterly muster returns of the various yeomanry companies beginning in 1823 (WO 13) which, of course, are not comprehensive censuses, but they do help to link individual emigrants with particular localities.

Wills: Indexes and Abstracts

The proportion of even the Protestant population of Ireland who left wills before the nineteenth century was pitifully small, if the surviving indexes are any indication, though there is evidence that many wills were not preserved in the Killaloe consistory files. The best guide to indexes and transcripts of Irish wills is probably the typescript finding aid "Irish Probates Register" (1979) compiled by the Reference Staff of the Latter-day Saints Genealogical Library in Salt Lake City. Though coverage is limited to the collections microfilmed by the Mormons, it does include all the major ones. The finding aid also includes useful county maps showing parish and diocesan boundaries. Betham's abstracts (PRO) of the wills of some wealthier families, proved in the Prerogative Court of Armagh and indexed in Arthur Vicars, *Index to the Prerogative Wills of Ireland, 1536–1810* (Dublin 1897), were helpful. Of the diocesan probates only the index to Killaloe wills (1653–1800) edited by Gertrude Thrift and printed by Phillimore (*Indexes to Irish Wills,* vol. 3 (London 1913)) and the manuscript index to administration bonds c1706–1857 (PRO) survive, though abstracts of dozens of the wills fortunately were made by Sadleir and are now in the Genealogical Office (GO, mss 424–7, LDS reel 100177).

Though the Killaloe wills do not survive, many of the corresponding estate inventories do, scattered in add. ms 31,882 in the British Library (Records of the Consistory Court of Killaloe, 1671–1824). This is a very valuable collection, though little apart from the marriage licence bonds is of use for migration studies. Extensive extracts from the collection, excluding the inventories and bonds, were published in Rev. Philip Dwyer, *The Diocese of Killaloe from the Reformation to the Close of the Eighteenth Century* (Dublin 1878). Several of the inventories have been printed in Rosemary ffolliott, "Household Stuff," *Irish Ancestor* 1, no. 1 (1969): 43–51. The inventories are too few to be the basis for statistical analysis, but ffolliott points out what they can tell us about the material circumstances of the various social classes in North Tipperary.

Land Records

Several types of records give information about landholding. At the very least these records connect individuals with particular properties; the best give full details of tenurial arrangements and some indications of family relationships. The best known are the tithe applotment books of 1823–37, in the PRO (or LDS film), and the printed volumes of the Primary (or Griffith's) Valuation of the early 1850s in the National Library and republished on microfiche by Irish Microforms of Dublin. The applotment books record by townland the names of all inhabitants holding titheable lands (at the very least a garden) at the date a parish commuted tithes in kind for a money payment and state the quantity of land held and sometimes the landlord's name. These can exclude half the population in an area where labourers were plentiful, and identification based on name alone is hazardous. The Primary Valuation, compiled after the Famine, names all householders by parish and townland, names the immediate lessor, and provides details of buildings and lands, if any. The National Library of Ireland compiled an index to surnames in these two sources. Arranged by county, the Householder's Index lists surnames alphabetically and notes the number of times the name appears in the Primary Valuation in each barony and whether it is listed in the tithe applotment books. PRO also has original field, town, house, and rent books describing holdings at various dates intermediate to the tithe applotments and the Primary Valuation. They were prepared as a preliminary to the latter, and provide similar, though often more detailed, information. They have never been microfilmed and have been largely ignored. The lack of microfilming, indeed, prevented me from making much use of them, but I did find the Modreeny and Cloughjordan volumes very useful. For further details see *Analecta Hibernica* 17 (1949): 349–50. The Primary Valuation has been updated annually in manuscript volumes keyed to six inch to the mile Ordnance Survey maps, retained in the Valuation Office, Ely Place. It is possible to trace a property from the early 1850s to the present using these records.

Before the 1820s the major sources on landholding are freeholders lists (the only surviving one for Tipperary in this period being that of 1776 in GO, ms 787), deeds, and estate records. In Ireland a lease of longer than thirty-one years duration conveyed a freehold and one may find such holdings referred to in the Registry of Deeds as well as in the freeholders lists. The Deeds Registry was established in Dublin in 1708 and is still located in the King's Inn at the end of Henrietta Street. Registration was not compulsory and leases from great landlords (such as Lord Dunalley) were seldom registered as the chances of challenging them successfully in court were limited. Nevertheless, the Registry of Deeds is an indispensable source for tracing eighteenth- and nineteenth-century freeholders, though it is long, difficult work because of the voluminous nature of the index books and the absence of any index to grantees. Numerous estate records are now in the National Library and that repository and the PRO both have many land records in private and solicitors' collections. Estate records may consist of rentals, leases and deeds, accounts, and maps. Of particular use in the current project were the Cole Bowen rentals for Ballymackey, 1788–1854 (NLI, reel P.5553) and associated maps (ms 2043), Croasdaile deeds for the Mountshannon area

(D.23185–215), Otway rentals of 1806 and 1824 (ms 13,000(8)), maps (21.F.129), deeds (D.20344–87), and accounts, Rolleston Papers for Dunkerrin (mss 13794–5) and maps (16.M.11), and a 1769 rent roll of Roscrea (reel P.5553). Sadleir inventoried the surviving papers of Lord Dunalley (now in NLI) in *Analecta Hibernica* 12 (January 1943): 131–54, but the collection contains no rentals. In some cases the present owners of properties which were freeholds in past centuries still retain boxes of deeds. For example, Dorothy Worrall of Knockbrack and Frank Holland of Nutgrove, both near Mountshannon, hold deeds to these two Holland properties which recite transactions back to the 1770s when the two holdings were one. Deeds, rentals, and wills are also found in the extensive records of the late nineteenth- and twentieth-century landed estates courts held by the Irish Land Commission, a detailed card index to which is available at the National Library.

Local Histories

We have no scholarly study of North Tipperary to match William Nolan's *Fassadinin* (Dublin 1979), or Don Akenson's *Between Two Revolutions* (Port Credit 1979), but Ingeborg Leister's *Peasant Openfield Farming and Its Territorial Organisation in County Tipperary* (Marburg 1976) and an article by William J. Smyth, "Land Values, Landownership, and Population Patterns in Co. Tipperary for 1641–1660 and 1841–1850: Some Comparisons," in L.M. Cullen and F. Furet, eds., *Ireland and France* (Paris 1980), 59–84, represent the first academic scholarship on the region. These first efforts have been supplemented recently by a major collection of nineteen articles edited by William Nolan and Thomas G. McGrath, *Tipperary: History and Society* (Dublin 1985). There are numerous amateur local histories, the best of which is Dermot F. Gleeson's fine study *The Last Lords of Ormond: A History of the "Countrie of the Three O'Kennedys" during the Seventeenth Century* (London 1938). Rev. John Gleeson's *History of the Ely O'Carroll Territory or Ancient Ormond* is clearly antiquarian but the new edition edited by George Cunningham (Kilkenny 1982) contains a large bibliography for the entire region. It is unfortunate that the older generation of Irish antiquarians confined their researches largely to the Cromwellian and earlier periods in the years when the PRO collections were intact. E.H. Sheehan's *Nenagh and Its Neighbourhood* (reprinted Nenagh 1976), which covers a large area of the Ormond baronies, is a work lacking both narrative and analysis but replete with detail, much of it secured by a ransacking of the Registry of Deeds. Valuable more for its author's nineteenth-century recollections than for its older historical material is Thomas Lalor Cooke's *The Early History of the Town of Birr, or Parsonstown* (Dublin 1875). North Tipperary was blessed in the late 1970s with an excellent amateur local history quarterly entitled *Cois Deirge*, edited by Paddy O'Brien of Ashley Park, Ardcroney. Though many of the parish monographs recently published are the derivative antiquarianism found in so many countries, many of the articles in *Cois Deirge* are quite useful.

There are two local historical societies in the region which have become increasingly active since the late 1970s. The Ormond Historical Society is based in

Nenagh, and the Roscrea Heritage Society, centred in Damer House, Roscrea, has published some excellent archaeological work: Geraldine T. Stout, *Archaeological Survey of the Barony of Ikerrin* (Roscrea 1984).

CANADA

Handbooks

The best guides to the sources useful for tracing migrants are Eric Jonasson, *The Canadian Genealogical Handbook* (Winnipeg 1978), Brenda Dougall Merriman, *Genealogy in Ontario: Searching the Records* (Toronto 1985), and Bruce S. Elliott, *Tracing Your Ottawa Family*, 2nd edition (Ottawa 1984). The two primary archival repositories in Ontario, the Public Archives of Canada in Ottawa (PAC) and Archives of Ontario in Toronto (AO), have each published booklets outlining their major collections: Patricia Kennedy and Janine Roy, *Tracing Your Ancestors in Canada* (Ottawa 1983) and *Genealogical Sources: Archives of Ontario* (Toronto 1981).

Census Records

Sources concerned directly with immigration have been noted in the introduction and their limitations explained there. The most important sources for tracing migrants once they arrived in Canada were the censuses of 1842, 1852, 1861, 1871, and 1881 (PAC, RG 31). The 1891 returns were not then available but have since been released. Only a few of these censuses have been indexed, the most relevant being the microfiched typescript and index of the 1852 census of Middlesex County prepared by London Branch, Ontario Genealogical Society (OGS), the card index to the 1852 Carleton County returns by Ottawa Branch, OGS, at Public Archives of Canada, and George Smith's printed *Index to 1861 Census of Lambton County*, 12 vols. (Wyoming, Ont. 1974). A listing of such census indexes is now available: Norman Crowder, *Indexes to Ontario Census Records* (Toronto 1987). The author is at present co-ordinating a joint project of the Ontario Genealogical Society and Machine Readable Archives, Public Archives of Canada, to index the heads of families and strays in the 1871 census of Ontario. Publication of a 30–volume series of county indexes began in the spring of 1986. Annual censuses and assessment rolls listing, among other things, the name of the head of family, the existence of a wife and the numbers of male and female children, and the lot and concession number, were returned to the district clerks of the peace in Upper Canada before 1850 and, where these survive, they are now mostly in the Archives of Ontario (AO) Municipal Records Series, RG 21. Survival is unfortunately very spotty, but among the best returns are those for the old Johnstown District, which included Carleton County before 1823. Some excellent returns are therefore available covering the earliest years of settlement in the Ottawa area. No early returns for London Township survive, but returns for the Huron District, 1842–50, are in the Regional Collection, University of Western Ontario, London (UWO), as are an 1835 return for Biddulph and an 1836 roll for McGillivray. A partial substitute is the Upper Canada Militia Nominal Rolls (PAC, RG 9, IB 2) which list, often with ages, males in the requisite age group, which varied as the Militia Act was amended. The most comprehensive lists are those of 1828, which include males between nineteen and thirty-nine years of age, soon to be published by OGS.

Vital Statistics

The other invaluable source was parish registers, particularly those of the Church of England. A record of baptism is often the first and sometimes the only evidence that a family was in a given community, particularly if assessment rolls are missing and the family never owned land there or waited a time before acquiring it. The Dioceses of Ontario (centred upon Kingston) and Ottawa require their clergy to deposit completed registers in the Diocesan Archives and have done so since the 1870s. Most of the hundreds of registers in Ottawa Diocese have been indexed. Diocese of Huron Archives has hundreds of registers but there is no compulsory deposit rule. Fortunately, the Diocesan Archives at Huron College and the Regional Collection at UWO have between them originals, microfilms, or transcripts of most of the early Anglican registers of the London area. The collection becomes less compehensive as distance from London increases. Research in the Toronto area was hampered by the lack of a compulsory deposit rule in that diocese and the consequent necessity of tracking down registers in church offices. Because parishes subdivided into smaller ones as the population grew, one must consult on average the registers of four separate parishes to obtain the records of a couple's marriage and of the baptisms of all their children, even if the family remained on one farm throughout the period. The centralization of registers in a diocesan archives certainly makes family reconstitution much easier. On registers in PAC see Patricia Birkett et al., *Checklist of Parish Registers, 1981*. The Archives of Ontario unfortunately no longer maintains a single list of registers in its custody. Barbara L. Craig and Richard W. Ramsey's recent *Guide to the Holdings of the Archives of Ontario*, 2 vols. (Toronto 1985), provides a summary listing, but the researcher must laboriously search out more recent accessions under placenames in the institution's general card catalogue.

Only a minority of the North Tipperary Protestants were Methodists, but the denomination grew in the nineteenth century and Canadian Methodist registers become increasingly important. The United Church Archives in Toronto has made no attempt to locate and preserve the earliest registers of its antecedent denominations but accepts them for custody when local congregations offer them. However, the Church Archives does have the central baptismal registers of the Wesleyan body beginning in 1843. At that date, ministers were required to submit returns to church headquarters annually. Copied into large ledgers by township, the entries are fairly comprehensive until the 1860s and then become increasingly spotty before ending completely in the 1890s. On the nature of Methodist registers see Bruce S. Elliott, OGS, *Ottawa Branch News* 17, no. 1 (January-February 1984): 10, and on Ontario church records generally, Bruce S. Elliott, "Utility and Variety of Early Church Records," *Families* 16, no. 4 (1977): 207–24.

The right to perform marriages in Upper Canada was extended to dissenting denominations in 1831 on condition that such marriages be registered with the district clerk of the peace. These district registers are mostly in the Archives of Ontario and have been partially printed and indexed in recent volumes of the periodical *The Ontario Register*. In 1858 all marriages had to be registered with the clerks of the peace, and the amount of information recorded was increased to include birthplace (often just country) and names of parents. The 1858–69 registers are also at the Archives of Ontario, and are being indexed in a continuing series of publications by William Britnell and Elizabeth Hancocks published by Generation Press of Agincourt, Ontario. The Public Archives of Canada holds large collections of early nineteenth-century marriage licence bonds for both Upper and Lower Canada (RG 5, B 9 and RG 4, B 28), but they appear to be far from complete. Local returns of baptisms, marriages, and burials to the clerk of the peace for the Huron District, 1841–69, under the provisions of a law more honoured in the breach than in the observance, provide an unusual source for that area (LDS reel 0886646). Full civil registration of births, marriages, and deaths began in Ontario in 1869, but records are closed to researchers. Individual extracts are issued to descendants upon payment of $15, but requests to open at least the indexes have so far been refused, for reasons which are understandable, if frustrating to the historian. Sometimes death certificates state an immigrant's county of birth, making civil registration a potentially valuable source for migration studies but a largely untapped one under present conditions.

Civil registration in Quebec province in the period with which this study is concerned involved the annual transmission of duplicate copies of parish registers to the district prothonotaries. These judicial transcripts for western Quebec were destroyed in the Hull Court House fire in 1900, but the Archives nationales, Hull, has since microfilmed the original church registers. The *état civil* copies for the Montreal judicial district are at Archives nationales, Montreal, and appear to be reasonably complete for mainstream Protestant denominations, but submission was sporadic for some of the smaller Methodist sects. The Archives nationales, Montreal, has comprehensive nominal indexes for all such records in its keeping.

Birth, marriage, and death notices and obituaries in newspapers were also an important source of biographical and genealogical information. Canadian newspapers have always published notices from much further down the social ladder than did the nineteenth-century Irish press, and by the early twentieth century the coverage of obituaries was fairly comprehensive, until the 1960s when most urban papers eliminated them, the paid notices only remaining. Special mention must be made of the obituaries of Methodists published in the Wesleyan weekly *The Christian Guardian* from 1829 up to church union in 1925. The thousands of obituaries of church members in Ontario, Quebec, and the Canadian west provide much biographical information on ordinary, largely rural, people, and are fairly consistent in supplying details of moves made during the deceased's lifetime. Though only a minority of the Tipperary families were Methodists, the obituary information was so useful that an issue by issue search of nearly eighty years of the paper was time well invested. The last decade has seen considerable indexing of newspapers, particularly the vital statistics notices. Obituaries in the *Christian Guardian* to 1860 have recently been abstracted by Donald Mackenzie in *Death Notices from the Christian Guardian,* 2 vols. (Lambertville, NJ 1982–4). Also useful for notices before the mid-1850s are W.D. Reid, *Death Notices of Ontario* and *Marriage Notices of Ontario,* and Thomas B. Wilson, *Ontario Marriage Notices* (Lambertville 1980–2). Numbers of Wilson's journal *The Ontario Register* also include many marriage notices from various papers, including a good run from the *Christian Guardian.* All of these volumes have place as well as name indexes. Also useful to the current project were the Ottawa Public Library's index to notices and obituaries in the *Ottawa Journal,* 1886–1918, the National Capital Commission's abstracts of the *Ottawa Citizen* notices, 1860–79, Louise Hope's abstracts from the *Perth Courier* (1834–1902) on microfilm at National Library and AO, Kingston Public Library's newspaper card index, and an index to early issues of the *London Free Press* notices by London Branch, OGS.

In Canada, gravestones proved to be a much more important source than they were in Ireland; their proliferation says something of the improved economic circumstances of many emigrants. Inscriptions in 2238 of Ontario's 4249 known cemeteries have been recorded by members of the Ontario Genealogical Society and transcripts deposited in the Public Archives of Canada, the Archives of Ontario, and the OGS library in North York. Consult Kenneth F. Collins, *Inventory of Recorded Cemeteries in Ontario 1983* (Toronto 1983) for further details. I visited hundreds of graveyards all over Ontario and in western Quebec in the course of my research; many which I visited personally have since been recorded, and many of the twenty-six branches of OGS publish the inscriptions in their areas. The interment registers of Beechwood Cemetery in Ottawa, at the Cemetery Office (since microfilmed by the City of Ottawa Archives), and of St Marys Cemetery, St Marys, Ontario (AO microfilm), and of Woodland Cemetery, London (UWO film), were useful.

Land Records

Land records were the essential source, in conjunction with my pedigree files, in working out family strategies, but they were also useful in determining family relationships and approximating dates of arrival and departure. Up to 1826, ordinary settlers in Upper Canada could obtain land from the crown by free grant upon payment of fees and fulfilment of certain obligations to occupy and improve, or by purchase thereafter. One-seventh of the lands of the province were set aside for the profit of the Protestant clergy, and these clergy reserves could be leased before 1832 or purchased from 1827 onward. Another seventh of the lands were set aside as crown reserves. The few leased before 1827 were turned over in that year to King's College, and could thereafter be purchased from University of Toronto, and the remainder were sold in 1827 to the Canada Company along with the entire million-acre Huron Tract, which resold them to settlers at a profit. The clergy reserve and Canada Company lands were especially sought after by settlers arriving after 1827 as these lots were interspersed amongst those taken up by relatives who arrived in the free-grant era. For a detailed study see L.F. Gates, *Land Policies of Upper Canada* (Toronto 1968).

Patricia Kennedy, "Records of the Land Settlement Process in Pre-Confederation Canada," *Families* 16, no. 4 (1977): 193–8, and "Deciphering the Upper Canada Land Books and Land Petitions," in D. Wilson, ed., *Readings in Ontario Genealogical Sources* (1979), and John Mezaks, "Records of the Land Settlement Process in the Home District: the System and the Existing Records," *Families* 16, no. 4 (1977): 193–8, provide the best guides to the myriad records of the land granting process, but the essential sources on those who arrived in the free-grant period are the Upper and Lower Canada land petitions (RG 1, L 3 and L 3L) and the Upper Canada Land Books (minute books of the Executive Council land committee, RG 1, L 1) at PAC, all indexed on cards there. Many petitions note place of origin, date of arrival in Canada, and details of occupation and family. However, the earliest settlers in the Ottawa area dealt with local military administrators rather than directly with the colonial administration, and London residents applied for land through Col. Thomas Talbot. The records generated by these processes are described in the notes to chapter 6.

Frequent changes in regulations and laxity of administration allowed squatting to proliferate virtually unchecked, but squatting did not always imply merely occupying a property. The slowness of the land granting process very early gave rise to recognition by the general public and grudging toleration by the administration of the sale of "good will" or rights to occupation, as occurred also in Ireland. Many transactions which took place before patenting (alienation of land by the crown) are recorded in the "Township Papers" series at AO (RG 1, C-IV), arranged by lot within township, and pre-patent transfers occasioned by the death of an official locatee were submitted for adjudication to the Heir and Devisee Commission (AO, RG 40; see John Mezaks, "Records of the Heir and Devisee Commissions," *Families* 16, no. 4 (1977): 199–206). However, the annual assessment rolls, where they exist, are the most comprehensive source on occupation, as opposed to ownership, of land.

The most useful sources on the purchase of crown lands after 1826 and on the purchase of clergy reserves are the Township Papers (RG 1, C-IV), petitions (RG 1, C-I-1), and the computerized Land Records Index at AO. Biddulph, McGillivray, and Blanshard were Huron Tract townships owned by the Canada Company; the company's sale and lease registers are also at AO and are indexed in the Land Records Index. A handy compilation of early Canada Company sale records may also be found in Thelma Coleman's book *The Canada Company* (Stratford 1978).

One may trace transactions after patenting in the Abstract Indexes to Deeds (AID) in the County Land Registry Offices, arranged by township, concession, and lot number; the AID provides the numbers of the deeds themselves. The LDS have filmed most nineteenth-century AID books and deposited copies in the Archives of Ontario, and the copy-books of deeds have been placed in various archives around the province; the Carleton County volumes are at Ottawa City Archives. For further details see A. David McFall and Jean McFall, "Land Records in Ontario Registry Offices: A Genealogical Guide" (Toronto: OGS 1982), R.W. Widdis, "Tracing Property Ownership in

Nineteenth-Century Ontario: A Guide to the Archival Sources," in D.H. Akenson, ed., *Canadian Papers in Rural History* 2 (1980), 83–102, and John Clarke, "Land and Law in Essex County: Malden Township and the Abstract Index to Deeds," *Histoire sociale/Social History* 11, no. 22 (1978): 475–93.

Many land records of western Quebec were destroyed when the Court House at Hull burned at the turn of the century. The Archives nationales, Hull, is attempting to reconstruct as much land-ownership information as possible from surviving notarial records. Patent dates of Quebec lands may be located in the book *List of Lands Granted in the Province of Quebec* (Quebec 1891).

A series of county wall maps bearing the names of landowners, generally published in 1862–3, and a series of county atlases including similar information published in 1878–80 are probably the most commonly consulted land records. The Public Archives in Ottawa has published catalogues to both series: Heather Maddick, *County Maps: Land Ownership Maps of Canada in the 19th Century* (Ottawa 1976), and Betty May, *County Atlases of Canada: A Descriptive Catalogue* (Ottawa 1970).

Wills and Administrations

Wills and intestate administrations were probated in Ontario in County Surrogate Courts. The records of these are on LDS films at the Archives of Ontario, which has recently prepared a nominal index to the pre-1858 estate files. From 1859 the Surrogate Clerk's Index serves as a province-wide finding aid. A provincial Court of Probate, a court of superior jurisdiction similar to the Prerogative Courts of Canterbury and Armagh in England and Ireland, also sat at Toronto from 1793 to 1859 (AO, RG 22, 6–1-A). In many parts of the province, however, the majority of wills appear never to have been probated, but were registered as deeds to record the transfer of real property. Those specifying lot and concession numbers may be located in the Abstract Index to Deeds; those not so specifying were recorded in county general registers, indexed by name. For further details on wills, see Bruce S. Elliott, "Sources of Bias in Nineteenth-Century Ontario Wills," *Histoire sociale/Social History* 18, no. 35 (May 1985): 125–32, and Catherine Shepard, *Surrogate Court Records at the Archives of Ontario: A Genealogical Research Guide* (Toronto 1984). In Lower Canada (Quebec), wills were filed with notaries, but some were also probated by the district superior courts. Registered wills for the Montreal District and some of those filed with notaries there have been indexed at Archives nationales (Montreal).

Biographical and Genealogical Material

Pocket biographies of many nineteenth-century residents of Canada are available in numerous biographical dictionaries. The most useful are *The Canadian Biographical Dictionary*, 3 vols. (1880), George Maclean Rose, *A Cyclopaedia of Canadian Biography*, 2 vols. (1886–8), William Cochrane, *The Canadian Album: Men of Canada, or Success by Example*, 5 vols. (Brantford 1891–6), and H.J. Morgan,

Canadian Men and Women of the Time (1898 and 1912 editions). The Public Archives library in Ottawa has a card index to several hundred such books, but the index does not include all the works cited above. Such biographies may also be found in general histories such as Alexander Fraser, *A History of Ontario: Its Resources and Development,* 2 vols. (1907), and J.E. Middleton and F. Landon, *The Province of Ontario: A History,* vols. 3 and 4 (1927), in Nicholas Flood Davin's *The Irishman in Canada* (London 1877), in the biographical sections of the county atlases of the late 1870s, and in local histories such as W.A. and C.L. Goodspeed, *History of the County of Middlesex, Canada* (Toronto 1889) and scattered through J.L. Gourlay, *History of the Ottawa Valley* (Ottawa 1896).

Some collections of relevant family papers have been placed in public repositories. Especially useful were the W. Bertal Heeney (MG 30, D 164) and A.D.P. Heeney Papers (MG 30, E 144) and the Sifton Papers (MG 27, II, D 15) in PAC, and the Freeman Talbot Papers and the extensive Spencer Armitage-Stanley genealogical collection at UWO. The latter must be used with caution, as Armitage-Stanley's genealogical interpretations include much guess-work, and his method of record-keeping does not always permit one to separate his guess-work from his research and oral evidence. I made use of about a hundred manuscript and printed genealogies, many of the latter published for limited circulation and not in any libraries. I am grateful to the authors for providing me with copies. Nonetheless, the quality of these works varies, and I did not rely upon undocumented assertions that I was unable to confirm by my own research. For a list of these works, and a detailed listing of local histories and parish registers consulted, see Bruce S. Elliott, "The North Tipperary Protestants in the Canadas: A Study of Migration, 1815–1880," PhD thesis, Carleton University, 1984.

Correspondence with Genealogists and Descendants

During the course of my research I exchanged information with numerous descendants of the families who formed the subject of this study. It is a pleasure to record their names here, and I do so with gratitude:

Mrs G. Benning Acres, Nepean. (Thomas Acres)
David Patrick Acres, Vanier. (Thomas Acres; Geo. Dagg of Clarendon)
Dorothy Adams, Campbell River, BC. (William Morgan)
William D. Amell, Peterborough. (Haskett of Newmarket)
Isabel Arkley, Ottawa. (Robert Delahay)
Dr G.C. Armitage, Brampton. (John Armitage of Biddulph)
J. Lloyd Armstrong, Ottawa. (Eades)
Susan Armstrong, Bracebridge. (Armstrong of Muskoka; Piper)
David G. Arntfield, London. (John Morgan)
Mrs C.R. Bardon, London. (John Hodgins and Mary Casey)
[Charles R. Baskerville, Killarney, Man. (John Baskerville)]
David Baskerville, Thorndale. (Baskerville, W. Nissouri)

Barbara Belding, Woodlawn. (Prittie)
Gwen Talbot Bergsma, Penn Valley, California. (Talbot of Templemore)
Mrs Ralph Bidgood, South March. (F.W. Richardson)
Dick and Muriel Birch, White Rock, BC. (Birch of Roscrea)
Lorelee Birch, Navan. (Thos. Birch)
Douglas Bisson, Hull. (Thomas Acres)
John D. Blackwell, Hensall and Kingston. (John Blackwell)
Pam Blincoe, Hamilton, New Zealand. (Fuller)
late Mrs V. Ersyll Boake, Islington. (Boake)
Mrs Markley A. Bond, Hickson. (Shoebottom)
Josephine Beynon Boos, Barrie. (John Beynon)
Iola E. Boyce, Maple Ridge, BC. (Robert Grant)
Eleanor Boyd, Durham. (Rivington of Huntley)
Cheryl D. Boyle, Kyle, Sask. (Leonard and Mary Shouldice)
M. Netta Brandon, London. (Kingsmill)
Amelia Bretzloff, Aylmer, PQ. (Eades)
M.E. Bridge, Long Ashton, Bristol, England. (Bridge of Roscrea)
Gwen Brouse, Riverside, California. (Francis Abbott)
W. Douglas Brown, Mississauga. (Freeman Blackwell)
John Leslie Bulger, Guelph. (Bulger)
Carole Caldwell, Surrey, BC. (John Mooney of Onslow)
Arthur M. Campbell, Ottawa. (Gleason)
Constance Catania, Columbia, Maryland. (Edgehill, Alexander)
Laverne Christianson, Carroll, Man. (James Armitage, Torbolton)
Lynn G. Clark, Frankenmuth, Michigan. (Richard Blackwell of McGillivray and
    Kinloss)
Mrs Austin Clipperton, Walford. (John Mooney)
Gail and Bill Clothier, London. (Birch, Haskett)
Mervyn A. Collins, Simcoe. (Collins, Stringer, Keough)
Charles P. Corbett, Ailsa Craig. (Patrick Corbett)
Ralph B. Cowan, Toronto. (Ralph)
Denis Hayes Crofton, Tonbridge, Kent. (Hayes of Dunkerrin and Dublin)
late Yvonne Crouch, Kingston. ("Red John" Hodgins)
Michael A. Dagg, Ottawa. (Daggs of Pakenham and Bruce Co.)
late Dr Richard E. Dagg, Montreal. (John Dagg of Clarendon)
Sandra Davey, Thessalon. (Henry Caswell, Drummond and St Vincent)
A. William Davidson, West Vancouver. (Thomas Blackwell of London City)
Howard J. Dawson, Lachine, PQ. (Geo. A. Holland)
late Judge John A. Dawson, Nepean. (George Clarke)
Mr and Mrs Douglas Eagles, Sarnia. (Arthur Hopper)
Joan Colbert Ellerbusch, Rochester, Michigan. (Colbert of Wakefield)
Fred Elliott, Dollard des Ormeaux, PQ. (Eades)
Gerald L. Elliott, London. (Francis Guest)

John A. English, Etobicoke. (Mary (Saney) Davis)
Helen Fairbairn, Richmond, BC. (Ralph Smith)
Heather Fawcett, Pierrefonds, PQ. (William Corbett)
Russel E. Foster, St Thomas. (George Foster)
Mary Garbutt, Toronto. (Baskerville of Oro)
Marjorie Gosling, North Ryde, NSW, Australia. (Armitage of Templeharry)
Ralph Gowan. (Gowan)
Norval Gray, Claremore, Okla. (John Gray)
Stephen C. Guest, Osgoode. (Thomas Guest of Oxford)
Norah Hanson, Cumberland. (Colbert of Wakefield)
late George Flannan Haskett, Parteen, Co. Limerick. (Haskett)
Hon. Irwin Haskett, Ottawa. (Samuel Goulding Haskett)
Barbara and the late Reg Haslam, Birr, Co. Offaly. (Oakley and Eades)
Marion Headrick, Ottawa. (Wilson descendants of John Boucher)
Pat Hewitt, Edmonton. (Leonard Stanley of Biddulph)
Lady Naomi Slater Heydon, Forrest, ACT, Australia. (Greene)
Judy Hodgins, London. (George Carter; Flynn and Clarke of Stephen)
Lester Hodgins, Vancouver. (Hodgins)
Frank Holland, Nutgrove, Whitegate, Co. Clare. (Holland)
Keith T. Hollier, Sherwood, Queensland, Australia. (Dyas, Logan)
J. Alan Hopper, Barrie. (Arthur Hopper)
Harry P. Hopper and the late Mrs Hopper, Nepean. (Arthur Hopper)
Mrs Fred Horner, Sudbury. (Richardson)
Opal L. Howey, Brantford. (Thomas Blackwell of Brantford)
Heather Ibbotson, Delhi. (Rivington)
Gloria Jackson, Ridgetown. (Shoebottom)
Louise Jeffries, Reed City, Mich. (Edw. A. Talbot)
Julie Ann Johnson, Seattle, Wash. (Holland)
Alvin B. Jones, Victoria. (Jones of March and McGillivray)
Heather Jones, Victoria. (Jones of March and McGillivray)
James Howard Jones, Sidney, BC. (Jones of March and McGillivray)
Mrs H.M. Kelcher, Edmonton, Alta. (Taylor)
Mrs E.R. Kelly, Lambeth. (Leonard and Mary Shouldice)
Bill Kern, Norton, Ohio. (Atkinson)
Kae Kirk, Ottawa. (Colbert, Dagg, and Farmer of Huntley)
Robert C. Kittle, Syracuse, NY. (William Hayes of Huntley)
Henry Law, Guelph. (Bulger)
Noel S.A. Layton, Sydney, NSW, Australia. (Harte)
E. Douglas Lince, Bremerton, Wash. (Ardell)
Mrs Beryl Loft, Ilderton. (Haskett, Hodgins)
Lois M. Long, Nepean. (Michael Long, Oakley)
Dorothy Luney, London. (Winnett and Winder)
Wallace MacAlpine, Agincourt. (John Harding of London)

Jean MacDougall, Sault Ste Marie. (William Hayes of Huntley)
Lynne MacKenzie, Ottawa. (Robert Keays)
Mrs Allen P. Mann, Robinson, Ill. (Richard Talbot)
Dr Ronald F. Mann, Kingston. (William Healy of Goulbourn)
M. Gail Heney Martin, Ottawa. (Greene)
Ann Maxwell, Ottawa. (Matthew Hodgins)
Shirley I. Mayse, Vancouver. (Caswell of Drummond Twp.)
Mark McClung, Ottawa. (Mooney of Chatsworth)
Dorothy McKendry, Nepean. (Edward Owens)
Ruth McLaughlin, South Porcupine. (Young)
Bea McMillan, Burnaby, BC. (John Mooney of Onslow)
Joan Megie, Sterling Heights, Mich. (Giles)
Lorna Meredith, Ottawa. (Geo. Clarke)
late Mrs Walter Moffatt, Lucerne, PQ. (Nicholas Shouldice)
Maj.-Gen. Lloyd C. Morrison, Smiths Falls. (Francis Abbott)
Dorothy Munro, Richmond. (Abbott)
Dr James Neelin, Ottawa. (Michael Hodgins)
Alton Neil, Toronto. (Neil of Fitzroy)
Bob Neil, Halifax, NS. (Neil of Fitzroy)
Larry Neil, Sarnia. (Neil of Fitzroy)
R.P. Neil, Plattsburgh, NY. (Francis Neil of Fitzroy)
Mrs Egon Nielsen, Forest. (Sparling)
Ben Oakley, Williamstadt House, Whitegate, Co. Clare. (Oakley of Birr, Co. Offaly)
Kenneth Reid Olive, Ottawa. (John Olive, John Reid)
Mrs Garrett O'Neill, Ottawa. (Arthur Hopper)
Barbara Owens, Nepean. (Edward Owens, John Olive, John Reid)
Douglas R. Parker, Gloucester. (Benjamin Sparling)
Ruth Parr, Rexdale. (Henry Cole of Streetsville)
Calvin Patrick, Renfrew. (Patrick)
Arthur Pattison, Ottawa. (John Spearman)
Blanche R. Piper, Baysville. (Charles Piper)
Edward Powell, Ottawa. (Powell of St Thomas)
Dick Prette, Victoria, BC. (Pritt[i]e)
Thomas J. Prittie, Palmyra, NY. (Pritt[i]e)
Doris Purdy, Oakville. (Howard of Fitzroy, Thos. Reid)
Mrs C.W. Pybus, Winnipeg. (Samuel Blackwell of Biddulph, Sheppard of Goderich)
Cathy Raven, Ottawa. (Edmund Roche, St Thomas)
Shirley P. Rawlinson, Corvallis, Ore. (William E. Roche)
Karen E. Rebey, Tiverton. (Moses Wall)
Alan B. Reed, Ottawa. (Thos. Hodgins and Stanleys of Clarendon)
Leonard Reeve, Grenfell, Sask. (Blackwell and Ashton/Austin)
Cora L. Reid, Enterprise. (Joseph Morgan)

341   A Note on Sources

Susan Richardson, Ottawa. (Richardson of Clarendon)
Mr and Mrs Wm. J. Richardson, Kanata. (Richardson)
Beryl Robbins, Winnipeg. (Loney)
late Madaline Roddick, London. (Howard)
J.A.E. Rollins, Vancouver. (Rollins)
Hazel J. Runchey, Winnipeg. (Philip P. Harding of Howick)
Elaine Sanderson, Red Deer, Alta. (Atkinson)
Olive Sawyer, Tisdale, Sask. (Hobbs)
Elizabeth Scheiding, Ancaster. (Langford, Westman, Garrett)
Drew F. Shouldice, Ottawa. (Nicholas Shouldice)
Julie Shouldice, Ottawa. (Nicholas Shouldice)
Marsha Shouldice, Gloucester. (Nicholas Shouldice)
Wayne Shouldice, Kitchener. (Nicholas Shouldice)
Phyllis Simons, Carleton North, Victoria, Australia. (Longs of Clonrush)
Mrs G. Simpson, Ottawa. (Geo. Blackwell of Renfrew Co.)
Vera Simpson, Thunder Bay. (Davis, Portis, Ryan)
Mrs G.O. Skuce, Ottawa. (Richardson)
H. Marie Smibert, Etobicoke. (William Carry and Edward Fitzgerald of London Twp.)
Mrs Ralph Smith, Torbolton. (James Armitage)
Wilma Smith, Calgary. (O'Neil)
Tom Stanley, Moncton, NB. (Thomas Stanley of London City)
Charles E. Stearns, Billerica, Mass. (Talbot of Templemore and United States)
Thomas S. Sterling, Ottawa. (John Boucher)
Percy C. Stoney, Delta, BC. (Rev. Edmund Stoney)
Anne Storey, Etobicoke. (Thos Morgan; Loney of Nepean and Torbolton)
Laurena Storey, London. (Francis Guest, Portis)
B. Wesley Switzer, Brantford. (Switzer)
Mary Tasker, Weston. (Neil)
Mrs G.S. Thompson, Port Coquitlam, BC. (Nicholas Shouldice)
Everett L. Truax, Hamilton. (Thomas Rolleston Ashbury, Bentinck)
Mildred Turner, Courtenay, BC. (Prittie)
Jeanette Tyson, Toronto. (Henry Davis of Templemore and St Thomas)
June Usherwood, Kingston. (William L. Holland)
Dan Walker, Delhi. (Haskett of Newmarket)
Betty Warrilow, Owen Sound. (George Foster)
Betty Wasserfall, Willowdale. (Lynham)
Erva Watkins, Orleans. (John Spearman)
Erlene Way, Ottawa. (Michael Rivington)
Carol P. White, Gresham, Ore. (Robinson of Mascouche)
Blanche E. Wilson, Cambridge. (Larrett)
Dorothy Wilson, Winnipeg. (Quinton Berryhill)
Marilyn Wilson, Ottawa. (T. Acres)

late Helen Wimberley, Nepean. (George Clarke)
Margaret Wimberley, Nepean. (George Clarke)
Helen Woolsey, Edmonton. (John Mooney of Onslow)
Dorothy Worrall, Knockbrack, Whitegate, Co. Clare. (Holland)
Nellie Young, Erinsville. (Geo. Young of Hungerford)
Rev. Roger A. Young, Fitzroy Harbour. (Robert Young of Goulbourn)
Terry Young, Ottawa. (Matthew Serson, Michael Young)

Index

Placenames in Ireland are grouped by parish, in Ontario and Quebec by mid-nineteenth-century county, and in the rest of Canada by province. Isolated references to places as the residences of individuals are indicated "res. of" and grouped at the end of the entry.

35. *See also* Population trends

Dempsey, James 188

Derham, William 21

Derry, Co. 122, 263n.74

Derry Castle (on Lough Derg) 17

Destinations: of Ottawa Valley migrants 160 table 13; of Tipperary Protestants, major 83–4, 98 Fig. 1

Devon Commission 42–3, 46

Devonshire settlement (near London, Ont) 133–4; 131 map 17; res. of 185, 186

Dickenson 131, 291n.49

Didsbury, Mary Ann (Mrs Acres) 315n.140

Dobbs, James 155

Dobbs, Joseph 154

Dobbs, Mary (wife of James) 155

Dobbs, Mary (Mrs Alexander) 155

Dolla (Tip): Traverston, res. of 83, 249

Dolmage 251, 253, 318n.4. *See also* Delmage; Dulmage

Dolmage, John 30

Dolmage, William 30

Dolphin (ship) 127

Donaldson 290n.42

Donnelly murders (in Biddulph, 1880) 140, 188, 292n.69, 302n.110

Doolan 39, 262n.67

Dooley 262n.67

Dorrington 201

Douglas 318nn.4, 5

Douglass 252

Doupe 135, 298n.59

Down, Co.: emigrant groups from 127, 317n.17; res. of 88 table 7, 169

Ards 317n.17

Comber 127

Killinchey 127, 290n.42

Killyleagh 127

Saintfield 127

Dowry 199, 201–3, 207–9, 308n.25

Doyle 131

Draper 136

Dromineer (Tip): Protestants in 15

Ballyartella, res. of 121, 262n.70

Drummond Co. (PQ): Wendover, res. of 63

Drummondville military settlement 63

Dublin 10, 122; exports through 39; res. of 338

Malahide, res. of 273n.57

Dudley 30

Dudley, John 284n.91

Dudley, Joshua 229

Dudley, Samuel 209

Dugas, André (Andrew Deugo) 201

Dulmage 318n.5. *See also* Delmage; Dolmage

Dunalley, Baron 19. *See also* Prittie

Dunalley estate. *See* Modreeny

Dundas Co. (Ont): Williamsburg, res. of 72

Dunkerrin (Kgs): burial place of Wall family 263n.75; emigration from 100, 101, 102 table 9, 103; town planning at 30–1; res. of 74, 246, 338

Clonbrennan, res. of 137

Cooraclevin, res. of 188

Mountheaton, res. of 157

Dunn 305n.174

Durham Co. (Ont): Cartwright, Irish in 117

Cavan, Irish in 117

Manvers, Irish in 117

Port Hope, res. of 296n.33

Durham Road 172; 168 map 25c

Dyas 339

Dyas, Alice (Clarke) 91 table 7, 157

Dyas, Alice (Mrs Armstrong) 91 table 7

Dyas, Ann (Mrs Young) 91 table 7

Dyas, Elizabeth (Mrs Logan) 91 table 7, 114, 158

Dyas, Lucy (Mrs Cox) 91 table 7, 157–8

Dyas, Thomas 91 table 7, 157

Eades 337, 338, 339

Eades, Emma (Mrs Richardson) 191

Easterlin, Richard 308n.25, 313n.119

Eaton's department store (Toronto) 318n.5

Economic policy, for North Tipperary 55–60

Economic strategies. *See* Inheritance

Edgehill 155, 338

Education, as inheritance strategy 228–31. *See also* Teachers

Edwards 19, 317nn.2, 3

Egan, John & Co. 241

Ejectment. *See* Evictions

Elgin Co. (Ont) 70: St Thomas, res. of 340, 341

Southwold, res. of 130

Ely O'Carroll 16

Emigrants: geographical origins in North Tipperary 101–6

Emigrants, socio-economic status of: in Biddulph 140–1; 1830s 100–1, 103–6; in Famine 111–13; Francis Evans on 68–71; landlords' opinion 60; of Robinson emigrants 75–6. *See also* Success

Emigrants' guides 63, 69–70, 275n.77

Emigration, assisted 62, 64–5, 93; applications for 75, 82–93, 123, 125, 247–51; New South Wales 114; from workhouses 112. *See also* Robinson, Peter, emigrants

Emigration, to Australasia 113–14, 285n.104

Emigration, causes of 36–7, 52, 58–60, 62, 99, 110–11, 115, 187–8, 224–6

Emigration, chronology of: beginnings 61–81, 98 Fig. 1;

358   Index

DATE DUE

FEB 2 4 1982			
MAR 3 1 1982			
DEC 3 1991			
MR 14 '98			
		PRINTED IN U.S.A.	
GAYLORD			